Reading Readings

Reading Readings

Essays on Shakespeare Editing in the Eighteenth Century

Edited by
Joanna Gondris

Madison • Teaneck
Fairleigh Dickinson University Press
London: Associated University Presses

Associated University Presses
440 Forsgate Drive
Cranbury, NJ 08512

Associated University Presses
16 Barter Street
London WC1A 2AH, England

Associated University Presses
P.O. Box 338, Port Credit
Mississauga, Ontario
Canada L5G 4L8

The paper used in this publication meets the requirements
of the American National Standard for Permanence of Paper
for Printed Library Materials Z39.48–1984.

Library of Congress Cataloging-in-Publication Data

Reading readings : essays on Shakespeare editing in the eighteenth century / edited by Joanna Gondris.
    p. cm.
  Includes index.
  ISBN 0-8386-3712-4 (alk. paper)
  1. Shakespeare, William, 1564–1616—Criticism, Textual.
2. Shakespeare, William, 1564–1616—Criticism and interpretation—History—18th century. 3. Shakespeare, William, 1564–1616—Editors. 4. Editing—History—18th century. I. Gondris, Joanna, 1959– .
PR3071.R43   1998
822.3'3—dc21   97-9794
                                                                   CIP

PRINTED IN THE UNITED STATES OF AMERICA

Contents

Acknowledgments

Tʜɪs collection of essays began life in a seminar entitled "Editing Shakespeare in the Eighteenth Century: Territoriality, Anonymity and Erasure" at the Shakespeare Association of America meeting held in Albuquerque in April 1994. Fourteen of the essays in this book were written for that seminar. Bernice W. Kliman, the seminar leader, has provided a different essay from the one she wrote for the seminar. Almost all the essays have benefited from written and oral responses from the other participants, including those of William Slights and Evelyn Tribble, the only members of the seminar whose papers are not represented here. To Catherine Alexander, Irene Fizer, and Laurie Osborne, who did not have the benefit of participating in the seminar, and nonetheless produced highly polished essays in the curtailed time allowed them, special thanks are due. But the most important acknowledgement is to Bernice W. Kliman, who guided the group interactions before, during, and after the seminar with unerring skill and unending enthusiasm, whose idea this collection was, and who remains the shaping force behind the whole book. Her role as progenitor, of course, does not implicate her in the inadequacies or errors of the editing and introducing of the collection, which remain entirely my own.

Introduction

Joanna Gondris

I<small>N</small> the last few years, Shakespeare's afterlife has been expertly chronicled. The extraordinary phenomenon of Shakespeare's status—what Gary Taylor, in *Reinventing Shakespeare,* calls the "blunt fact of his cultural dominance"—has been analyzed and interrogated, and the process by which this dominance has come about has been put to special scrutiny.[1] In *The Making of the National Poet,* Michael Dobson provides a usefully compact narrative of recent studies of Shakespeare's afterlife, and maps out the crucial areas of interpretive difference.[2] Isolating three differing models of "appropriation," Dobson infers three major schools:

> For some [recent critics], Shakespeare's texts appropriate their readers. . . . For others, individual readers either misappropriate Shakespeare's texts (if they are bad readers), or both appropriate them and are appropriated by them (if they are good readers). . . . For others still, the hegemonic discourse of the ruling oligarchy appropriates both Shakespeare's texts and his readers. (11–12)

Dobson's analysis of interpretive difference is purposely simplified and invites complication.[3] *Reading Readings* focuses on the phenomenon of the emergence and development in the eighteenth century of a critical genre that changes the possibilities of appropriation. This genre—the Shakespeare edition—complicates Dobson's model because the formal procedures, constraints and purposes of an edition themselves reposition reader and text.

This repositioning is especially clear in the Shakespeare editions of the eighteenth century because it upsets the preexistent structures of neoclassical criticism. For example, the orthodox (Aristotelian) hierarchy of rhetorical analysis in which language—as afterthought to fable, characters and sentiments—is always accorded the last place is entirely reversed by the intensity and priority of the editor's engagement with the wording of a text. The related eighteenth-century prescription of attending to the literary "whole" rather than the fractured and negligible "part" is similarly overturned by the editor's responsibility to scrutinize each tiny unit of the text. The burden of collation, moreover, brought with it a knowledge of the varying text, which must have been disturbingly at odds with the eighteenth-century determination to monumentalize and canonize Shakespeare. Together, these editorial exigencies—engagement with the language, detailed explication, collation of the variant texts—subvert or put pressure on established eighteenth-century critical procedures, and intimate alternative ways of reading Shakespeare.

This collection of essays, therefore, augments and modifies Dobson's account of appropriation dynamics by charting appropriations of Shakespeare that are empowered by editorial rules of procedure and the particular uses of an edition. It also—to make use of Dobson's identification of three recently deployed models of appropriation—details ways in which Shakespeare's early folio and quarto texts provoked and were susceptive to eighteenth-century editing; the ways in which individual editors ("good readers" and "bad") reacted to editorial responsibilities and Shakespearean texts; and the ways in which a whole network of pressures outside the editorial function and form were brought to bear on the edition.

The history of Shakespeare editing in the eighteenth century has been well documented.[4] In recent years, it has been seen as partaking in the whole cultural industry that formed itself around Shakespeare. In *Reinventing Shakespeare,* Gary Taylor deftly weaves a history of eighteenth-century Shakespeare editing into his narrative, granting it an integral part in his "Shakesperotics" (the "history of Shakespeare's evolving reputation") (6) . Brian Vickers, in his capacious six-volume *Critical Heritage,* includes a wealth of passages from the prolegomena and from the notes of eighteenth-century editions, and carefully tracks, in the Introductions to each of his volumes, the part that eighteenth-century editing plays in the development of Shakespeare reception.[5] This melding—in studies of Shakespeare reception—of editorial matter with other kinds of Shakespeare criticism does allow us to investigate the part that eighteenth-century editing in general played in the massive investment of energy that set up Shakespeare's hegemony. But it blurs the significance of the particularity of the response to Shakespeare registered in an edition.

The difference between editions and noneditorial criticism as forms of Shakespeare reception in the eighteenth century has been perhaps most obscured by the accessible critical anthology of David Nichol Smith, *Eighteenth-Century Essays on Shakespeare* (printed in 1903 and then reprinted sixty years later).[6] Smith isolates the prefaces of eighteenth-century editions from the text and the commentary that they usher forth, and, interweaving them with noneditorial Shakespeare criticism, he effectively obliterates their source by renaming them "Essays."

Eighty-eight years later, Margreta de Grazia, whose critical starting point is very different from Smith's, nevertheless perpetuates, in her book, *Shakespeare Verbatim: The Reproduction of Authenticity and the 1790 Apparatus,* Smith's severance of editorial prefatory matter from text and commentary.[7] De Grazia, scrutinizing Malone's 1790 Apparatus (the voluminous introductory material that prefaced his edition), provides a cogent analysis of it as a catalyst of the Enlightenment reconstitution of the subject. De Grazia's attention is fixed so intently on the Apparatus that, in *Shakespeare Verbatim,* the main body of Malone's edition (Shakespeare text and commentary) has only the shadowiest of presences. Finding in the Apparatus strong evidence of the ideological impress she is tracking, she assumes that the editorial material that follows simply bears out the abstract prescriptions of the Apparatus:

> [A]n apparatus is not simply curatorial. It is preparatory: it prepares the text for the reader by submitting it to certain procedures, and it prepares the reader for the text by equipping him or her with certain kinds of information. (12)

De Grazia's invocation of Enlightenment "procedures" systematically determining an unresisting "textual object to be delivered" (10) makes necessary a counterbalancing assertion of the shaping force of editorial procedures quite differently generated and governed from the ones she so skillfully exposes in Malone's Apparatus. *Reading Readings* redirects attention to procedures demanded by an eighteenth-century edition's primary purpose. My title insists on the essentially editorial act of choosing among variants, of attending to the possibilities of meaning in small lexical and syntactic units configured differently in the various printed versions of a text.[8] This fundamental editorial task charges the act of interpretation inscribed in eighteenth-century editions, for, in these editions, the interpretive possibilities of a text are inextricably bound up with its minute variants.

The editorial compacting of interpretation with variable textual configuration is mirrored in a semantic shift recorded in the *OED.* "Reading," which, from at least 1557, meant (among the complex network of senses that the *OED* maps out), "The form in which a given passage appears in any copy or edition of a text; the actual word or words used in a particular passage," suddenly enlarges its reference at the end of the century to mean, as well, "The interpretation or meaning one attaches to anything, or the view one takes of it. . . ."[9] The *OED* dates this extension of meaning—from "reading" as specific graphic formulation to "reading" as interpretive analysis—from 1792, a year that falls between the two most important variorum editions of the eighteenth century: Malone's ten-volume 1790 edition and Steevens's fifteen-volume 1793 edition.[10] The plethora of critical analyses recorded in the commentaries of these editions, and provoked by the different printed forms and the possible emendations of tiny parts of Shakespeare's texts, was notorious. The concurrence of the voluminous expansion of editorial commentary with the semantic development in the possible senses of "reading" signals a crucial way in which the eighteenth-century edition changes the possibilities of appropriating Shakespeare: in an edition, the variable graphic formulation of a text becomes the locus of interpretation and of interpretive difference.

Reading Readings begins with an essay written by a critic who has insisted on a radical—and, indeed, detrimental—change in the possibilities of reading Shakespeare wrought by eighteenth-century editions. In a panoply of essays, written under a panoply of near-homophonic names, Random Cloud has held eighteenth-century Shakespeare editions up as a foil to the subtle and delicate compositorial transmissions of manuscript that he locates in the earliest printed Shakespeare texts.[11] Cloud systematically asserts the quarto or folio readings and brands the eighteenth-century Shakespeare editions as contrastively obtuse misrepresentations and traductions of the evidence. The usefulness to him of eighteenth-century editions is clear. The very specificity of the editorial response, allowing a precise measurement of divergence from the preferred quarto or folio, enables him to cast the acuity of the seventeenth-century compositors into the sharpest relief through differential reading. The acuity of Cloud's own reading, his extraordinary responsiveness to the graphic medium of Shakespeare's printed texts, serves to qualify his decrial of eighteenth-century editions. For he is not so irreparably divided from the eighteenth-century editors (who authorize emendation-filled conflated texts rather than quarto or folio) that he does not also resemble them in his focus on the semantic difference of the minutest variants in a text.

The positioning of the first essay in this volume (an essay written by the most eloquent discreditor of eighteenth-century editing) is therefore complicatedly polemic. Its placement at the front of the volume acknowledges the substance of his criticism and the provocativeness of his writing. Its inclusion within the volume also makes possible a questioning of Cloud's emphatic devaluation of eighteenth-century editions, for the essays which his ushers forth assert—as Cloud's writing itself does in the very energy of his reaction—the power of eighteenth-century editions to engage and inform the late twentieth-century reader.

Reading Readings is divided into four sections. These sections do not reflect the chronological emergence of the editions analyzed but, rather, suggest four separable but related sets of readings of eighteenth-century editions.[12] These four sets lend themselves to arrangement on an axis whose poles are the edition as self-determining, as empowered and constrained by its own function and form, and the edition as social construct, determined by pressures and constraints that lie quite outside itself. While the sections have been organized around this shifting stress from formal exigency to social construct, it is of course recognized that the two kinds of pressure are inextricable in effect (they operate simultaneously) and in genesis (the form has been socially adopted by the age that deploys it). This simultaneous assertion of the edition as self- and as socially-determined is most explicit in the third section (which lies on a midpoint of the axis), but it of course underlies all the essays in this book, essays whose individual particularities resist any overarching organization.

I

The first section, "Attending to the Words," focuses on the radical foregrounding, in eighteenth-century editions, of the graphic, lexical, and syntactic properties of a text. An editor's responsibility to establish the precise wording (or wordings) of a text and to make sense of each word or phrase that does not easily yield up its meaning brings into his vision aspects of Shakespeare's printed texts that eighteenth-century criticism outside the editions never had to contend with or accommodate. In the first essay, "Shakespeare Babel," Random Cloud holds up two passages from *All's Well that Ends Well,* that make this compulsory redirection of focus most exacting. The passages whose various editorial transmissions Cloud scrutinizes contain the nonsense language improvized to terrorize Parolles into exposure of his own cowardice. The passage itself has a clear dramatic meaning; examined analytically, the precise syntactic and lexical workings of each word or line are altogether more elusive. For "Chough's language"—a term coined by one of Parolles's tormentors for the improvized tongue—"is pure linguistic *form*. It is pure linguistic form as pure *graphic* form.

And purity is a bugger for editors."

Indeed, Cloud has put his finger on a Shakespearean passage scrutiny of which forces editors to the lowest imaginable depths of the Aristotelian hierarchy, for "Chough's language" is language entirely severed from the redeeming categories of sentiment, character, and plot.

Isolating a passage that puts eighteenth-century editors at the furthest remove from methods of analysis that their age sanctioned, Cloud charts their unstable transmission of the nonsense words in order to show by contrast the Folio compositor's inventiveness or his responsiveness to the literary cues in the graphic medium of his copytext. Cloud presents a Tall Tower of Chough variants as ironic testimony to the failure of eighteenth-century editors (and their descendants in all English and foreign-language editions) to heed the subtleties of Chough, whose graces and whose phonetic, morphological, grammatical, and metrical possibilities Cloud expounds. Cloud's irony cuts many ways. When Cloud accords eighteenth-century editors the title, "the Fathers of Shakespeare editing," the distancing in the mock-honorific capitalization does not shut out a recognition of these editors as powerful and influential. Indeed, Cloud's tracing of culpability to the eighteenth-century "Fathers" for the traduction of the subtle construct of the Folio text marks out eighteenth-century editions as crucial objects of investigation.[13]

In the final pages of his essay, Cloud examines versions of Chough in twentieth-century promptbooks. Here, the difference is clear in Cloud's perception of the obligations of an editor (who lays himself open to the charge of incompetently misrepresenting the earliest text) and the license of an actor or director (who can make free with Chough). The essay that follows Cloud's, Ann Thompson's "'Making Him Speak True English': Grammatical Emendation in Some Eighteenth-Century Editions of Shakespeare, with Particular Reference to Cymbeline," focuses on another aspect of the text (in another Shakespeare play) that makes much severer demands on editors (or their readers) than on actors (or their audience). Thompson examines eighteenth-century editorial response to the notoriously convoluted syntax in Cymbeline. Like Cloud, she presents the lines on which she focuses as a special test case for the editor: "[the] language [of Cymbeline] has always baffled and exasperated editors."[14] Unlike Cloud, she traces a developing sensitivity in eighteenth-century editors to the demands of the passages she isolates. Offering examples of eighteenth-century editors' emendation and annotation of the more grammatically deviant lines and passages in Cymbeline, Thompson observes a growing responsiveness to the deviation. This responsiveness runs counter to any expectations of eighteenth-century practice that are founded on a reading of Dryden's prescriptive neoclassical criticism. Thompson ends by placing the eighteenth-century editors' adjustment from grammatical prescription to description in the context of late twentieth-century destabilization, in textual and critical studies, of notions of meaning and interpretation.

The final essay in this section, Linda McJannet's "'The Scene Changes'?: Stage Directions in Eighteenth-Century Acting Editions of Shakespeare," analyzes those parts of an edition where the graphic medium of a printed text most conspicuously codifies performance. Taking her examples from five eighteenth-century editions of Henry VIII, McJannet examines the form of stage directions and compares them to the verbal and visual conventions that governed Elizabethan and Jacobean stage directions. Like Cloud, she uses the eighteenth-century editions to uncover a systematic graphic encoding in the Folio text that would otherwise be much less visible. This encoding of stage direction is so potent (McJannet summarizes its merits as its "self-effacing voice and efficient visual design") that eighteenth-century editions largely preserve the whole formal system. McJannet offers evidence that this preservation peculiarly marks eighteenth-century editing of Shakespeare: the unique uninflected "enter" is used uniformly in Shakespeare editions, but the grammar is naturalized in an edition of Fletcher and in an eighteenth-century adaptation of *As You Like It*. The essence of Shakespeare is perceived as locked into the syntactic, lexical, and graphic properties of the printed text.

II

Just as the editor's attention was directed inexorably away from the most highly valued neoclassical category of fable and towards the negligible matter of a text's wording, editorial procedure demanded another radical change of focus: the editorial exigency of line-by-line analysis broke up the text into tiny units which, even when taken in the aggregate, were very far from the "whole," that idealized and selective essence held up as the true object of critical attention. Indeed, in the Preface to his *Shakespeare,* Johnson warned his readers of a damaging relocation of the implied repositories of meaning in an annotated text and prescribed a corrective approach to Shakespeare that could counteract the ruinous effects of editorial notes:

> Parts are not to be examined until the whole has been surveyed; there is a kind of intellectual remoteness necessary for the comprehension of any great work in its full design and its true proportions; a close approach shews the smaller niceties, but the beauty of the whole is discerned no longer.[15]

Johnson's warning is emphatic: it asserts an irremediable conflict of vision between a commentator (or his readers) and any critic properly responsive to the true significance of a great work. Drawing its title from Johnson's warning, the second section in this volume, "Examining the Parts: Line-by-line Analysis and the Redistribution of Meaning," scrutinizes eighteenth-century editors as they engage in an act in which, as Johnson's pronouncement shows, a deeply valued structure of thought was ineluctably inverted.

The first essay, Peter Seary's "Lewis Theobald, Edmond Malone, and Others," makes clear that which in Johnson's warning is left implicit: the uncomfortable position of an eighteenth-century editor committed to minute textual analysis. Lewis Theobald, the editor who pioneered editorial rigor (of collation and analysis) provokes in subsequent editors an equivocal response: an implicit acknowledgment of the efficacy of his methods (later editors adopt his procedures or steal his readings) and a pronounced detachment from him. Attributing this reluctance to acknowledge Theobald as their progenitor to his successors' desire to distance themselves from the low social status that adhered to textual scrutiny, Seary sees Johnson's reaction as symptomatic of the discomfort Theobald aroused: "A horrified sense of recognition, followed by repression or complete rejection." Johnson's denigration of Theobald sets the pattern for subsequent editors. Malone, in his bias against Theobald, was "fully complicit with Johnson." This bias is so strong that Seary is able to track it through to the twentieth century where scholars and critics persist in distancing themselves from Theobald, and aligning themselves instead to Pope, Johnson, and Malone.

However much minute textual analysis (in the shape of Theobald, its first practitioner) was theoretically decried or resisted, the method itself was adopted by subsequent editors. The consequent fracturing of the idealized "whole" (the fracturing that Johnson warns against) reaches its zenith in the variorum editions of the late eighteenth century. In these many-volumed editions where the Shakespearean text is shadowed by an ever-growing array of interpretive notes, the breakdown of the interpreted text into tiny parts is compounded by a fracturing of the editorial response itself: each small unit of text provokes a welter of contradictory readings. My own essay, "'All This Farrago': The Eighteenth-Century Shakespeare Variorum Page as a Critical Structure," presents examples of the variorum response to single words (embodying textual and interpretive cruxes) in Shakespeare's plays to show how the very capaciousness of the variorum page, its evenhanded registering of interpretive opposites, constitutes a particular hermeneutic. Indeed, the variorum edition, by its comprehensive detailing of minute textual variant and interpretive difference, generates an alternative "whole" to the one invoked by Johnson—a "whole" made up, in the long variorum entries, of structured narratives accommodating the most radical of textual and interpretive differences.

The eighteenth-century reviewer whose denunciation of the variorum endeavor—"all this farrago"—begins the title of my paper, endorses Johnson's warning of the disruptive powers of annotation on a reading of a text, but confesses himself unable to resist the allure of editorial notes. In "Chedworth and the Territoriality of the Reader," Paul Nelsen examines the response of "a solitary, recondite reader and avid note writer—John Howe, Baron Chedworth" who exulted in his own participation in the "veritable conference of alternative perspectives" provided by the late eighteenth-century Shakespeare variorum editions. Chedworth, a gentleman scholar, recorded in manuscript notes (published posthumously in 1805) his reactions to the variorum commentary. Nelsen ably interprets Chedworth's truncated and cryptic "meta-notational comments" and sets them in the context of the variorum responses to which Chedworth is reacting and in the larger context of a shifting emphasis in the late eighteenth century to the "validation of individual response."[16] "Chedworth," Nelsen writes, "is attracted to the variorum apparatus precisely because it allows him to participate in the hermeneutic process: not just passively receiving an understanding, but actively authorizing his own."

Nelsen's stress on Chedworth's keen participation in the "delectable enterprise of studious investigation" signals an unabashed acceptance, in Chedworth at least, of just the kind of reading—minutely analytical—that Johnson condemns as essentially disruptive. Frank N. Clary Jr.'s "Hamlet's Mousetrap and the Play-within-the-Anecdote of Plutarch" presents as its epigraph a quotation from Malone that confirms this disregard of Johnson's qualms about annotation by emphatically validating the minutest and intensest genealogical probings of Shakespeare's plays:

> When our poet's entire library shall have been discovered, and the fables of all his plays traced to their original source, when every temporary allusion shall have been pointed out, and every obscurity elucidated, then and not till then, let the accumulation of notes be complained of.[17]

The narrative that Clary tells, however, is quite at odds with Malone's declaration. The epigraph becomes ironic, for, as Clary clearly shows, "eighteenth-century editors progressively compromised the analogical reference" of an allusion, in one of Hamlet's soliloquies, to a Plutarch anecdote, "until it was effectively excluded from consideration as a confirming historical instance." Indeed, Malone himself, reversing his endorsement of the most detailed and comprehensive genealogical annotation, summarily dismisses the relevance of this anecdote. The epigraph reattaches itself to Clary who, by scanning the whole series of eighteenth-century editorial responses to the *Hamlet* lines (responses whose interpretive possibilities Malone emphatically shuts out), exposes an extraordinarily rich web of allusion radiating out from the Plutarch anecdote. By following through the cues in the earlier genealogical investigations and reversing their erasure, Clary reengages Shakespeare text to classical antecedent.

Clary's opening up of the allusive underpinnings of the *Hamlet* lines demonstrates the interpretive consequences of such intricate tracking of sources: those genealogical complexities offer themselves for projection into Hamlet's—and Shakespeare's—capacities of discourse, and change the way both character and author are defined. Recovery of the allusive possibilities of the Plutarch anecdote increases the reader's "appreciation for Shakespeare's conservative originality and for the recesses of Hamlet's memory."

Where Clary shows Shakespeare redefined by the editorial act of genealogical investigation, Caroline Roberts, in "Lewis Theobald and Theories of Editing," shows the concept of Shakespeare's authorship transmuted by Theobald's concern, in the explanatory notes, with the genesis, the stage history, the transmission, and publication of Shakespeare's texts. Theobald's recognition of the importance of consumption in determining textual content, and his sensitivity to the interactions of texts with stage management, for example, carry with them a set of assumptions about the author quite at odds with the view held simultaneously by Theobald, of the artist as an autonomous figure. Roberts relates these two distinct conceptions of the author to two schools of textual criticism in both of which Theobald can be seen to participate. "Theobald adumbrates a Greg-Bowers school of eclectic editing by collating and conflating different states of Shakespeare's texts [in order to] . . . reproduce as much of 'what Shakespeare wrote' as possible." At the same time, Theobald's explanatory notes "may be thought to anticipate a social theory of textual criticism" such as that proposed by Jerome McGann or the "sociology of texts," elaborated by Donald McKenzie, that "directs us to consider the human motives and interactions which texts involve at every stage of their production, transmission and consumption."

Roberts ends her analysis with an image, "the broken phial," McKenzie's reworking of Milton's characterization of books as preserving "as in a violl the purest efficacie and extraction of that living intellect which bred them." Theobald's edition presents itself both as a phial, "closed, stable and determinate," and as a broken phial, "open, unstable and multiform." Roberts's recognition of the part of Theobald's edition which presents itself as a "broken phial" lends itself to comparison with Johnson's account of the irrevocable fracturing of "the beauty of the whole" consequent to editorial analysis. They both describe the breakdown of idealized textual entities made untenable by certain kinds of editorial analysis. Indeed, all the essays in this section show Johnson's warning to be precise and prescient. Line-by-line analysis wrought a redistribution of the implied repository—and the source—of a text's meaning: from whole to part, from text to the massive accretion of commentary, from magisterial editor to enfranchised reader, and from Shakespeare as an autonomous writer to Shakespeare's texts collaboratively produced and disseminated.

III

The emphasis in the first two sections has been on the ways in which the formal and functional exigencies of eighteenth-century editing subvert contemporary habits of reading and structures of rhetorical analysis. This is not to say that eighteenth-century ideologies are not in operation in eighteenth-century Shakespeare editions. Indeed, the minuteness of the editor's focus on single words of the text (even a play's speech prefixes and its staged exits, as two of the papers in the next section show), together with the choices offered him by the textual variants and the possibilities of emendation, make editorial response an extraordinarily detailed and sustained record of how ideologies shape a reading of a text.

The five essays in the third section, "Codifying Gender: the Disturbing Presence of Women," show eighteenth-century editors contending with passages from Shakespeare that resist strongly held eighteenth-century orderings—textual, linguistic, and social. In particular, these essays all focus, in differing degrees, on passages that put pressure on eighteenth-century expectations of how female characters should be textually represented. The editorial acts that these passages provoke (emendation, explication, regulation, deletion) are proof of the editors' recognition that the passages disturb dearly held notions of decorum. Scrutiny of the editorial responses thus locates the parts of the Shakespeare text that eighteenth-century editors found most discomforting and reveals the workings of their preferred discursive and social models as the editors strive to rework those parts into forms that are less disturbing.

The first essay, Laurie Osborne's "Editing Frailty in *Twelfth Night*: 'Where lies your Text?',", examines the editorial response to lines in a soliloquy in which Viola confronts the problems of her male disguise. Tracing the different forms of two crucial lines from the Folios, through the eighteenth-century emendations, to the version adopted in present-day editions, Osborne makes use of the radical differences between the eighteenth-century versions of the lines to "disrupt . . . the comforting unanimity represented in the modern texts." The "Frailty" of Osborne's title is a crucial term in the lines, a term ushered in differently in First Folio and Second—the F2 version "anchor[ing] that weakness as only female in a speech which generally entertains far more gender ambiguity." Osborne scans the versions of the lines in eighteenth-century scholarly and performance editions. A pattern of reaction emerges that signals the uneasiness that the lines provoke. Editors explicate or emend the lines to obfuscate Viola's troubling exposition of the boy-actress within the role and to reduce the double meanings of the words in the speech and the possibilities of gender implied within it. "Frailty," thus, in Osborne's title, invokes both the word itself (and the array of different characters—and variously constructed genders—that it can be seen to implicate) and the eighteenth-century editors themselves, who must contend with parts of the text that subvert their ideologies of gender construction.

In the next essay, Hardin Aasand's "'The young, the beautiful, the harmless, and the pious': Contending with Ophelia in the Eighteenth Century," the provocation of Shakespeare's textual representation of a female character is intensified by the provocation of the representation of her madness, "indecorous and appalling." Noting that eighteenth-century performance history signals a sensed threat of Ophelia's repressed sexuality, Aasand examines the response of eighteenth-century editors to the disturbing presence of the mad Ophelia. To Aasand, entrances and exits are critical to the eighteenth-century sense of Ophelia: thus, the disparity in the staging formulations of quarto and folio compounds textually eighteenth-century unease at Hamlet's (and Shakespeare's) disposal of her: Ophelia "resurfaces in eighteenth-century editions and treatises as a spectral presence to be mourned and eulogized over." In a careful collation of eighteenth-century editions of the play, Aasand provides a compelling narrative of eighteenth-century struggles to "render madness dramatically lucid and rational" and evoke an Ophelia whose textual and dramatic representation violated less deeply eighteenth-century desires for clarity and fixity.

In "The Rowe Editions of 1709/1714 and 3.1 of *The Taming of The Shrew*," Margaret Maurer examines the role of Bianca as it evolves in the versions of a single scene from the First Folio to Theobald's edition in 1733. As in Hardin Aasand's essay, a textual difficulty (here, an uncertainty of speech assignment suggested by a doubled speech prefix) intensifies and particularizes the more general problem of how a text should represent a female character.[18] Maurer analyzes Rowe's disposition of the lines to show how his version of the scene projects a witty and willful Bianca. The capacity of this playful Bianca to dominate the scene is epitomized in an erudite play on words in a line that all earlier versions attributed to her, but that Theobald, in a spirit of "true Regulation," takes from her and assigns instead to a male speaker: Lucentio, her suitor.

Maurer sets the early eighteenth-century editing of the *Shrew* scene in the context of a popular Restoration stage version of the play by John Lacey. Lacey, intent on the play's central business of Kate's taming, "streamline[s] the Biancha intrigue" as part of a systematic reduction of the role Biancha is allowed to play. Irene Dash, in "When the Culture Obtrudes: Hanmer's *Winter's Tale*," sets Hanmer's editing of that play in a related context of its stage history. She finds evidence, in the very ordering of the cast list of a 1741 production, of a radical limitation of

Hermione's part in the play: Hermione, who in the traditional hierarchy of cast lists should top—at least—the female characters, is accorded the very last place. If—as Maurer suggests—it is the evidence of Bianca's capacity to play on a line in Ovid that provokes editorial (and stage) taming of her speeches, Dash shows that the eighteenth-century curbing of Hermione's role is reactive to the insufficiently veiled references, in the play, to her pregnancy and motherhood.

Dash's comparison of Garrick's and Morgann's adaptations to Hanmer's editing of *The Winter's Tale* is instructive. Garrick's and Morgann's reworkings of the play (involving immense cuts) suggest strong ties between eighteenth-century expectations of a play's sexual propriety and their desires for its structural decorum (*The Winter's Tale* being the play in which Shakespeare most flamboyantly violates the Aristotelian unities). Hanmer, whose editorial constraints cannot allow him Garrick's drastic reorganization of the play (Garrick cuts the entire first half) has to content himself with altogether more localized changes, restoring geographic credibility by emending "Bohemia" to "Bithynia" (a country conveniently supplied with a sea coast) and demoting sexually indecorous textual matter to small type at the bottom of the page. On the other hand, Hanmer's engagement with the words of Shakespeare's play pushes him beyond prescription (or deletion) to careful explication (very seldom credited by subsequent editors) of some of the more obtuse archaisms of Autolycus and the rustics in the pastoral scenes.

Dash insists that Hanmer's Oxford edition is directed at a particular audience: "a culture-hungry, increasingly affluent, Puritan-oriented, merchant class . . . that had participated in the clamor leading to the passage of the *Licensing Act* in 1737." Hanmer's edition is thus shaped by the expectations and needs of that audience, even as it is reactive to the constraints and possibilities of editing itself. The next essay in the collection, Irene Fizer's "Emballing, Empalling, Embalming, and Embailing Anne Bullen: The Annotation of Shakespeare's Bawdy Tongue After Samuel Johnson," is similarly alert to the part that eighteenth-century editions play in ratifying eighteenth-century cultural values. Fizer places Samuel Johnson's Shakespeare edition in the context of his *Dictionary:* "both massive projects participate in the eighteenth-century move toward linguistic standardization as the vehicle for the institutionalization of cultural standards." Fizer's essay shows clearly how eighteenth-century editorial annotation perpetuates the lexicographical taxonomy of proper versus vulgar usage (a taxonomy deployed ruthlessly, as Dash shows, by Sir Thomas Hanmer in his edition). Characterizing eighteenth-century editorial reaction to vulgar slang as "active indifference or . . . abundant and overdetermined annotation," Fizer provides a revealing test case of this editorial reflex. She scrutinizes eighteenth-century editorial versions of some lines in *Henry VIII*—a servant's lessons to Anne Bullen in sexual economy—"In faith, for little England / You'ld venture an emballing." The last, crucial word (whose sound-alike, more decorous editorial versions are spelled out in Fizer's title) is annotated first by Johnson, who thus "sets into place its position as a problematic term." Following through the annotations of the subsequent eighteenth-century editors, Fizer provides telling examples of the commentators' collusion to "keep the vulgar meaning of 'emballing' from erupting within their proper frame [and] . . . prevent the alignment of Shakespeare, the reigning cultural deity and 'master of the language,' with the scurrilous and bawdy tongue of a female servant." The paradoxical result of this collective resistance of eighteenth-century editors to the vulgar, Fizer shows, is a subversion of their purpose: "Rather than working as strict standardizers, they begin to engage in an elaborate textual punning. Their lexical distortions, although censorious, also inadvertently open up a play of signification— a slippage of meaning from emballing to empalling to embalming and back again."

IV

In their insistence on an eighteenth-century edition's ratification of the expectations and desires of the audience at which it was directed, Dash's and Fizer's essays—the last two sketched out—anticipate the fourth, the final, section of this collection: "Editing and the Market-Place." Dash's and Fizer's exposure of the reciprocity of eighteenth-century editing and eighteenth-century market forces signals a counterbalancing shift of emphasis in this volume from the formal exigencies of editing (attention to the words of a text, in the first section, and the procedure of line-by-line analysis, in the second) to the social constructs of the age in which the editing is practiced. The essays in the fourth section, continuing and underscoring this shift, chart ways in which eighteenth-century editions are most clearly determined by constraints that lie quite outside pressures of form and generic function: the constraints of printing house practices, the complexities of copyright law, and all the pressures of consumer demand.

The first essay in this section, Bernice W. Kliman's "Samuel Johnson and Tonson's 1745 Shakespeare: Warburton, Anonymity, and the Shakespeare Wars," provides an instructively complex narrative of the eighteenth-century "struggle for territorial rights to Shakespeare." The edition on which the narrative turns is a reprisal edition, Jacob Tonson's republication in 1745—with the addition of notes that attached names to previously unaccredited emendations—of Sir Thomas Hanmer's 1744

Oxford edition. Tonson used the 1745 edition to assert his claim (because of his copyright ownership) to all published Shakespeare. His ploy was successful. The name of Tonson is associated with all major eighteenth-century editions. "Thus," Kliman writes, "the textually insignificant 1745 edition is pivotal in eighteenth-century copyright claims."

Booksellers are not the only agents in the "Shakespeare Wars." Kliman also tracks the "complex moves of competition and collaboration" involving Pope, Theobald, Hanmer, Warburton, and Johnson. Her narrative is directed by her challenge to the repeated assumption that Warburton provided the attributive notes for the 1745 edition. Arguing for the implausibility of Warburton's involvement, Kliman offers Johnson, instead, as a much more viable candidate. She traces Johnson's connection with the edition to a warning letter sent by Tonson to Johnson's publisher, Edward Cave, after Cave appended to Johnson's *Miscellaneous Observations on the tragedy of Macbeth* a proposal for a new Shakespeare edition. Suggesting that Tonson, "to soften the disappointment of the failed project," asked Johnson to edit the reprisal edition, Kliman fills up a gap in Johnson's biography and indicates a prelude to Johnson's later work both in the *Dictionary* and in his Shakespeare edition.

Kliman's essay ends on a call for further examination of anonymity in editing Shakespeare. She contrasts the easily breached "coy anonymity" of Hanmer's edition with the 1745 note-writer's anonymity which "was not meant to be breached and resists exposure." The anonymity of both is noteworthy. For, as Eric Rasmussen points out at the beginning of his essay, "Anonymity and the Erasure of Shakespeare's First Eighteenth-Century Editor," "anonymity" is strongly associated not with the eighteenth century, that era of multiple volume octavos blazoned with the individual editor's names, but with the seventeenth century, "an age of monolithic folios and unnamed compositors." Rasmussen challenges the "elegant simplicity" of that division by pointing out the existence of a folio very possibly of the early eighteenth century, "an edition without an editor, a text literally without rules."

The history of this anomalous text is as follows. In 1951, Giles Dawson discovered that seventy scattered pages of the Shakespeare Fourth Folio had been reset and reprinted. Arguing that this reprinting occurred substantially later (circa 1700) than the original 1685 printing, Dawson termed these pages F5. Rasmussen, deploring later scholars' disregard of Dawson's revelation, suggests that the cause of this resistance is a deeply ingrained "prejudice against anonymous editors in favour of those with names." Redressing this resistance, Rasmussen scrutinizes the text of F5. His findings challenge the assumption that anonymous folio compositors make different alterations to the text than named eighteenth-century editors. Indeed, F5 anticipates Rowe, Pope, and Theobald in an array of emendations. Rasmussen calls for the inclusion of F5 alterations into the category of significant textual change.

Rasmussen argues eloquently for a rethinking of what constitutes editing. Indeed, all the essays in this section raise the question of what should count as an edition. Thus, in "Johnson's Shakespeare of 1765: a Comparison of the Two Editions of *A Midsummer Night's Dream*," Richard Kennedy examines the versions of that play in the two distinct editions of Johnson's *Shakespeare* (the later version published one month after the first) to establish whether the differences between the two are compositorial or editorial. In a meticulous demonstration of the hard task of textual collation, Kennedy shows that Johnson probably did not revise the second edition. The causes he suggests for the differences between the two editions intimate the complexity of the transmission of any text, the liability of a text to change at any stage of that transmission, and the difficulty of separating purposeful editorial change from compositorial slip.

Both Rasmussen and Kennedy make clear that the reprintings that they are chronicling offer evidence of a large market demand for the reprinted product. In "Visual Images of *Hamlet*, 1709–1800," Alan Young stresses the crucial role market forces play in determining the editorial product. Indeed, Young endorses Michael Dobson's determination to redress the commonly assumed "equat[ion of] commercial success with historical insignificance." Like Dobson, Young declares that versions of Shakespeare that are "designed to capitalize on popular taste" are "more useful indicators of the contemporary reception of Shakespeare's works 'than some of the self-consciously "higher" literary forms criticism has traditionally privileged.'"[19] Young, who is preparing a computer-generated database recording information about eighteenth-century and nineteenth-century illustrations of *Hamlet*, pays special attention to illustrations within printed texts "designed to access a less affluent market." Young, who provides sample entries from his database, suggests ways in which examination of the illustrations in an edition can augment and broaden the study of eighteenth-century editing. Illustrations reveal stage and editorial privileging of scenes and characters and suggest evidence about the intended readership of the editions. Noting the complicating factor of the possible independence of editor and his edition's illustrations (perhaps chosen, instead, by publisher or printer), Young nonetheless asserts the irrefutable part an illustration plays within the edition, "its existence as part of the final editorial artifact."

The last essay of the section—and the last in the collection—tells the story of the marginalization, in the editions, of a part of Shakespeare's writing that remained outside the canon until late in the eighteenth century. In "Province of Pirates: The Editing and Publication of Shakespeare's Poems in the Eighteenth Century," Catherine Alexander chronicles the disassociation of Shakespeare's poems from plays, a disassociation that springs from the poems' exclusion from the folio collections and that was reenforced by subsequent exclusions from all the major eighteenth-century editions until Malone's 1790 *Poems and Plays of William Shakspeare.* This exclusion projected the poems into the hands of the more disreputable eighteenth-century publishers anxious to take advantage of the commercial opportunity Tonson's apparent disregard of his rights to the poems allowed them. Curll, whose nefarious activities Pope immortalized in *The Dunciad,* for example, capitalizes on Rowe's six-volume edition of the plays by publishing a boldly named "Volume the Seventh" containing Shakespeare's poems. Alexander contrasts the reputations of the editors and publishers of Shakespeare's poems in the early eighteenth century with the establishment figures of Rowe and Pope. The contrast explains the prolonged status of the poems as an "adjunct or a dubious additional volume . . ." and their abandonment—in striking contrast to the plays—to a critical vacuum.

Alexander's analysis of the editing and publishing of Shakespeare's poems serves as a useful ending for this collection by setting in strong relief the very magnitude of editorial energy that was directed at Shakespeare's plays. While the poems' long exclusion from the principal editions left them "relatively free from prejudice and received opinion," the whole, cumulative mass of the eighteenth-century editorial endeavor had irrevocably reshaped the reading of Shakespeare's plays.

V

This collection of essays examines the acts inscribed in eighteenth-century Shakespeare editions and demonstrates the forms of interpretation that those acts elicit from twentieth-century readers of those editions. The title of the collection is purposely equivocal for it invokes both the eighteenth-century editorial acts and the twentieth-century forms of interpretation. Thus, "Reading Readings" defines both the eighteenth-century editor's task of collating and choosing between the variant readings of the Shakespeare text, and emending and explicating them; and it describes the interpretive act, registered in the essays collected here, of the late-twentieth-century critic or scholar shaping out distinctive strategies of analysis most responsive to the particularity of those texts—the eighteenth-century editions (in which the act of reading is so rigorously inscribed)—and to the most cogent concerns of late-twentieth-century criticism. The echo in the title, moreover, is a reminder of the doubleness of the interpretive acts recorded in this book. Our reading of the eighteenth-century editions is always preceded by the eighteenth-century editor's reading of Shakespeare.

The eighteenth-century Shakespeare editions provide readings of Shakespeare and offer themselves up for readings of the eighteenth century. Between the first printed quartos of Shakespeare's plays and us lie four hundred years. Malone's and Steevens's variorum editions of Shakespeare (in which the vast accreted commentary of the whole eighteenth century is represented) are poised equidistant from those two points. To scan one age's editorial adjustment of and response to the texts of another age is to be told (in the most extraordinary detail) of the complex network of pressures—formal, functional, discursive, social, economic—that affect how we appropriate and how we are appropriated by a text.

NOTES

I am grateful to all of the contributors who gave me their comments, and most of all to Bernice W. Kliman and Randall McLeod.

1. Gary Taylor, *Reinventing Shakespeare: A Cultural History from the Restoration to the Present* (New York: Weidenfield and Nicholson, 1989), 5.

2. Michael Dobson, *The Making of the National Poet: Shakespeare, Adaptation and Authorship, 1660–1769* (Oxford: Clarendon Press, 1992).

3. Dobson prefaces his account, "To simplify and exaggerate the debate. . ." (11). He himself insists on the viability of all three models: their differentiation allows him to place his own book in exact relationship with each one.

4. See, besides works mentioned elsewhere in these notes, Ronald B. McKerrow, "The Treatment of Shakespeare's Text by his Earlier Editors, 1709–1768," in *Library of Shakespearean Biography and Criticism* (Freeport, NY, 1970; first publ. 1933); Arthur Sherbo, *Samuel Johnson, Editor of Shakespeare* (Urbana, IL: Univ. of Illinois Press, 1956); Richard Foster Jones, *Lewis Theobald: His Contribution to English Scholarship* (New York: Columbia Univ. Press, 1966; first publ. 1919); Thomas R. Lounsbury, *The Text of Shakespeare* (New York: Charles Scribner's Sons, 1970; first publ. 1906); Peter Seary, *Lewis Theobald and the Editing of Shakespeare* (Oxford: Clarendon Press, 1990). See also Grace Ioppolo, *Revising Shakespeare* (Cambridge: Harvard University Press, 1991), 19–31 and Barbara Mowat, *Renaissance Drama* 19 (1988): 97–126.

5. Brian Vickers, ed., *Shakespeare: The Critical Heritage,* 6 vols. (London: Routledge Kegan Paul, 1974–81).

6. David Nichol Smith, ed., *Eighteenth-Century Essays on Shakespeare,* 1903, 2d ed. (Oxford: Clarendon Press, 1963).

7. Margreta de Grazia, *Shakespeare Verbatim: The Reproduction of Authenticity and the 1790 Apparatus* (Oxford: Clarendon Press, 1991). The references to the Prefaces of Rowe, Pope, Theobald, Warburton, Hanmer, and Johnson follow Smith's *Essays* and suggest that de Grazia relied on Smith's volume for representation of the practices of the editors whose prefaces he includes.

8. Editors performed this act with varying degrees of diligence, and varying assumptions of the permissibility of inserting their own emendations, but all

eighteenth-century editors acknowledge the necessity of collation however rigorously they practice it.

9. The *OED* definitions quoted are the sixth and the ninth, respectively.

10. Edmond Malone, ed., *The Plays and Poems of William Shakespeare,* 10 vols., 1790; George Steevens, ed., *The Plays of William Shakespeare,* 4th ed., 15 vols., 1793.

11. See Randall McLeod, "UN *Editing* Shak-speare," *Sub-stance,* 33/34 (1982): 26–55; Random Cloud, "The Psychopathology of Everyday Art," *Elizabethan Theatre,* 9 (1986): 100–168; "The Marriage of the Good and Bad Quartos," *Shakespeare Quarterly,* 33 (1982): 421–31; "'The very names of the Persons': Editing and the Invention of Dramatick Character" in *Staging the Renaissance: Reinterpretations of Elizabethan and Jacobean Drama,* David Scott Kastan and Peter Stallybrass, eds. (New York and London: Routledge, 1991): 88–96; and Random Clod, "Information on Information," *TEXT,* 5 (1991): 241–81.

12. For a contrastingly chronological survey of eighteenth-century editing, see Arthur Sherbo, *The Birth of Shakespeare Studies: Commentators from Rowe (1709) to Boswell-Malone (1821)* (East Lansing, MI: Colleagues Press, 1986).

13. A graph in Cloud's essay shows that fifty percent of Chough was transformed in the folio tradition alone. The culpability of the eighteenth-century editors, therefore, lies in their failure to use the tools that they had at their disposal to resist the drift of Chough.

14. Thompson's quotation from John Porter Houston should make obvious the parallels between the nonsense language that Random Cloud analyses in *All's Well that Ends Well* and the syntax in *Cymbeline.* Houston writes that the "disintegration of normal sentence movement" has gone so far in this text that "A certain ideal of coherent discourse has been abandoned" (*Shakespearean Sentences: A Study in Style and Syntax,* Baton Rouge: Louisiana State Press, 1988, 208).

15. Arthur Sherbo, ed., *Johnson on Shakespeare,* Vols. 7 and 8 of The Yale Edition of the Works of Samuel Johnson, General Ed. John H. Middendorf, 16 vols. to date (New Haven: Yale University Press, 1958-), 111.

16. Nelsen here quotes from Jean Marsden, "The Individual Reader and the Canonized Text: Shakespeare Criticism After Johnson," in *Eighteenth-Century Life* 17 (February 1993).

17. James Boswell, ed., *The Plays and Poems of William Shakespeare* (London: F. C. and J. Rivington, 1821), 1:236.

18. It is not clear whether any of the eighteenth-century editors Maurer discusses in the essay was reacting to the doubled speech prefix since no early eighteenth-century editor seems to have worked from F1 (the only folio text to contain the anomaly). Maurer, however, lists other anomalies in the passage that could have prompted the change in speech attribution that Rowe, for example, introduced.

19. Dobson, 5–6.

Reading Readings

Part I
Attending to the Words

Alarum within.

Lo E. Throca movousus, cargo,cargo,cargo.   1978

All. Cargo,cargo,cargo, villianda par corbo, cargo.   1979

Par. O ransome, ransome,

Do not hide mine eyes.

Inter. Boskos thromuldo boskos.   1982

Par. I know you are the *Muskos* Regiment,

And I shall loose my life for want of language.

If there be heere German or Dane, Low Dutch,

Italian, or French, let him speake to me,

Ile discouer that, which shal vndo the Florentine.

Int. Boskos vauvado, I vnderstand thee, & can speake   1988

thy tongue : *Kerelybonto* sir, betake thee to thy faith, for 1989

seuenteene ponyards are at thy bosome.

Par. Oh.

Inter. Oh pray, pray, pray,

Manka reuania dulche.   1993

Lo.E. Oscorbidulchos voliuorco.   1994

Int. The Generall is content to spare thee yet,

And hoodwinkt as thou art, will leade thee on

To gather from thee. Haply thou mayst informe

Something to saue thy life.

Par. O let me liue,

And all the secrets of our campe Ile shew,

Their force, their purposes : Nay, Ile speake that,

Which you will wonder at.

Inter. But wilt thou faithfully?

Par. If I do not, damne me.

Inter. Acordo linta.   2005

Come on, thou are granted space.   *Exit*

A short Alarum within.

X 3   *Lo. E*

Enter Parolles with his Interpreter.

Ber. A plague vpon him, muffeld; he can say nothing

of me : hush, hush.

Cap.G. Hoodman comes : *Portotartarossa.*   2227

Inter. He calles for the tortures, what will you say

without em?

Par. I will confesse what I know without constraint,

If ye pinch me like a Pasty, I can say no more.

Int. Bosko Chimurcho.   2232

Cap. Boblibindo chicurmurco.   2233

Int. You are a mercifull Generall : Our Generall

bids you answer to what I shall aske you out of a Note.

Shakspear Babel

Random Cloud

for George Walton Williams

READ[1] the parts of Act Four of *All's Well that Ends Well*, shown opposite, from the first folio, 1623, and you'll discover, along with his English, Shakesper's "terrible", "linsie-wolsy", mixed yarn of a tongue — "Choughs language".[2] Literally 'for the birds', Chough is extemporized before our eyes. This language has no past. No mother ever intoned it to her lisping babe. And what of its future? Never will it take flight, never prove capable of mimesis. It is a language in which (fashionably) writing and reading may have preceded speech; for there need never have been anterior or exterior sounds which these written words evoked.[3] Nor were there necessarily objects or ideas to which they referred. Although in performance, players will arbitrarily match Chough's letters with sounds ("euery one ... a man of his owne fancie"), their vocalizations are simply *after* the fact — after the *litteral* fact. And so, it may be best to define Chough as *manuage* rather than language — as *hand* rather than tongue.

    Most curious is the question of meaning. To be sure, the mere babbling of Chough does have a meaning in the play — an ironic one; for Chough is improvised by the group to hoodwink a lone auditor, Parolles (that manifold linguist), into thinking that it is a *semantic* language, like all the neighbouring ones of which he has a smack — German, Danish, Low Dutch, French and Italian. But, however much the communal thunder of the soldiers' line 1979

> *All. Cargo, cargo, cargo, villianda par corbo, cargo.*

may terrorize their victim, the core of each of these Chough paroles is semantically empty. Hence, their critical value for this essay: Chough is pure linguistic *form*. It is pure linguistic form as pure *graphic* form.

And purity is a bugger for editors.

Pyrrho-
corax
pyrrho-
corax

1

These two Chough forms occur in lines 1978 and 1988.

movouſus *vauvado*

At first glance, the pronunciations of them may seem to present no challenge. Indeed, if we ascribe typical English sounds to the letters, don't the words fall comfortably within our phonotaxis? Pronounce them, then, will you?[4]

Yes, yes, of course, one hesitates, realizing it is not always correct (or 'correct') to ascribe *English* values, variable as they can certainly be, to *foreign* tongues. But let's set that obvious truth aside, and explore more subtle grounds for uncertainty.

In 1623, when the first folio was published, English readers would have been even less confident of the pronunciations than we. You see, print then did not generally use the lower-case *shapes* v and u to distinguish consonant from vowel (as we do), but merely to distinguish the beginning of words from later positions. In fact, v and u, were merely positional variants of the *same* letter — which was consonant or vowel, as occasion demanded.[5]

| Consonant: | very | ouer | proud | vuula |
| Vowel: | vp | out | proud | vuula |

Got that? Well then, a set of the potential 17th-century sounds of our two folio words can be suggested by the following — where I mean the shapes v and u to have their modern *phonetic* values. Pronounce them now, will you, please?

movousus	vauvado
mouousus	uauvado
movovsus	vavvado
mouovsus	uavvado
movousvs	vauuado
mouousvs	uauuado
movovsvs	vavuado
mouovsvs	uavuado

So, to each first-folio form of *movouſus* and *vauvado* a contemporary reader could easily have attributed eight different pronunciations! To be sure, some of them feel awkword in an English-speaking mouth. But isn't that to be expected of a foreign language I mean *manuage*?

To reiterate: the single letter v/u in the first-folio setting of each of these outlandish words did not then, and does not now, *specify* the pronunciation; rather, it *generalized* it. Look, I'm really sorry about it, but that's just how the graphic medium worked in 1623. And graphics — why, that's all we've got.

Now, when contemporary readers saw a printed word like "vp", they had a choice of pronouncing it as two consonants, or a vowel and a consonant. Since only the latter is an English word, they would not have taken long in practice to make a choice. (Not as long as you did for *vuula*!) But as *movousus* and *vauvado* are not English words (or words, perhaps, in *any* language), there was no resolution by conventional means to the question of phonetic ambiguity occasioned by the shapes *v* and *u* — that is, by recourse to usage, or to a dictionary. On the one hand, you can lament that the graphic resources of Shakespear's day did not deliver his contemporaries (or us) from ambiguity. But, on the other, if you — if you actually *like* jokes, you can just enjoy the ridiculous effusion of possibilities.

(I forget whether I told you that *All's Well* is a comœdy?)

❦

V, Has two powers, expreſſed in modern Engliſh by two charaĉters, *V* conſonant and *U* vowel, which ought to be conſidered as two letters ; but as they were long confounded while the two uſes were annexed to one form, the old cuſtom ſtill continues to be followed.

Sam. Johnson, *Dictionary*

In 1632, when the second folio was printed (nine years after the first), the graphic medium had undergone a revolution. The difference of shapes had come to differentiate sounds: v was exclusively a consonant now, u a vowel. This new usage will strike us as modern, of course. But be careful — for many decades after 1630 (in Dr. Johnson's *Dictionary* of 1755, for example) V and U were still merely different shapes of the *same* letter, V. Thus, Johnson sorted *Voyager* directly before *Up*, because — get this — *o* precedes *p*.

If graphics is all we are considering, we might conclude that the second folio rendered the words in question conservatively.

movouſus   *vauvado*

So, where's my revolution? Well, in 1632 the same graphics did not symbolize the same phonetic values; the second folio radically limited the first folio's scope for pronunciation, reducing the eight suggested options for each word to one. And isn't it interesting that the pronunciation stipulated by the second-folio setting of each of these words is the very pronunciation *you* chose at the top of page 2 — am I right? — when you didn't even *know* you had a choice?

Shakspeare's

ALL'S WELL THAT ENDS WELL,

A COMEDY;

ADAPTED TO THE STAGE BY

J. P. KEMBLE;

AND NOW PUBLISHED AS IT IS PERFORMED AT

THE THEATRES ROYAL.

LONDON:

PRINTED FOR JOHN MILLER, 25, BOW-STREET, COVENT-
GARDEN; AND SOLD IN THE THEATRES.

1815.

[*Price One Shilling.*]

This loss of *phonetic* play was not the only consequence of the graphic reforms in the second folio. There was also loss of *morphological* play. In the first folio, each of these words is graphically anomalous. Here is the old rule: *v is the form of this letter at the start of words; and u is its form everywhere else.* Thus the use of medial *v* in these two words in the first folio requires that we see each word as beginning twice, as it were — once at the left (of course), but then again (startlingly) several letters to the right:

$$movoufus = mo + voufus$$
$$vauvado = vau + vado$$

Now, one might suppose that these two uses of medial v in 1623 were errors. But precedents for the occasional medial use of v exist. In *Shake-speares Sonnets*, 1609, for example, there appear three forms of the word "unused".[6]

vnuſ'd   vn-vſ'd   vnvſdє

The first example plays by the rules; it appears as a unified word. The hyphen in the next one asserts a compound, as does the (redundant) v that follows it. And the last example shows that medial v, without a hyphen, can evoke the sense of a compound all by itself.

(Test yourself with this line from G3v in *Romeo and Iuliet*, 1597.)

Hunting thee hence with Huntſvp to the day.

It would have occurred to some of Shakespeare's contemporary readers, therefore, that *mo* and *vau* and *voufus* and *vado* are separate Chough words or affixes. I expect that for us, by contrast, the first folio's non-differentiation of vowel v/u from consonant v/u may well make its graphic medium seem quaint to us — seem literally and phonetically inept. But the present examples show that the graphic variants of this letter could evoke a morphological subtlety our own alphabet doesn't even know to *dream* of.

(A hyphen is as close as we can get — *Hunt's-up*[7].)

Take note of these other first-folio Chough forms (in lines 1993 and 1994).

    reuania   *voliuorco*

Here are typical applications of the rule: v is initial; u is medial. (No evocations of compounding here.) Seeing that some first-folio words obey the v/u rule while others don't, we may suspect, more than before, that Chough's graphic anomalies deliberately encode linguistic subtleties.

In the new graphic regime of the second folio, these two words are represented differently than in the first.

    revanta   *volivorco*

The t for i in the first word seems an easy misreading. But the v's for medial u's in both words do not. The re-settings have merely resolved the first-folio's ambiguous v/u's — as consonants. For in 1632, the compositor had to specify — consonant v or vowel u. It was no longer possible to equivocate. True, his choices of shape were arbitrary; but he did chose among the actual options of pronunciation that single letter v/u offered in the first folio. Again using the phonetic values of our two modern letters u and v, let me evoke the options that faced this compositor, when he responded to the one *v* and the two *u*'s of *reuania* and *voliuorco* in his first-folio copy.

reuania   voliuorco
revania   uoliuorco
                    uolivorco
                    volivorco

The second-folio's arbitrary distribution of *v*- and *u*-shapes in the four Chough words considered so far echoes throughout all modernizing[8] English editions, *none* of which informs readers of the second-folio bias. In them, these four graphic forms elicit only four pronunciations out of the total of twenty-two suggested here and on page 2. And *this* is how editorial culture sleeps Shakespeare's text. And who's the wiser for it?

But all these letters have made me *hungry*. How about you?

❦

Despite its distortions of *letters*, 18th-century editorial scholarship tended to conceive of Shakspeare's plays as essentially *litterary* documents. One defense of this bias is that contemporary performance sophisticated Shakspear. You can smell what was wrong in a titlepage like that reproduced in the previous opening. It was this same actor-manager, John Philip Kemble, who, in his 1793 edition of this play[9], ADAPTED TO THE STAGE the first folio's

Boskos thromuldo boskos

as

Muskos thromuldo muskos.

In those days, a *litterary* text could thus have been defended as more conservative than a *theatrical* one. This alienation of scholarly editing from the stage in general, and from Renaissance staging in particular, has been much redressed in our own century. Modern scholarship holds that Shakespear wrote 'for performance'. We still must *read*, of course; but we now know to read his scripts teleologically — with *performance* in mind. And who would ever take exception to such an enlightened view?

But what happens to the graphic play we have been considering, when we read a script for production values? Purely litterary, the graphic can have no projection on the stage. In a teleology of dramatic production, one must assign graphic play to limbo.[10] Before we chuck it, though, shouldn't we ask who might be responsible for the graphic in this play? Suppose it was the folio compositor. Suppose his copy read (according to the rules)

mououfus   *vauuado*

— and that the medial *v* shapes in the first folio

movoufus   *vauvado*

originated with him. Whether we like private morphologizing, the possibility that a compositor could make so free with a text (and make free with it so whimsically and wittily) would mean that our ability to separate the author's from the compositor's share may sometimes be nil: Shakspeare's play may already have been played with before we receive it. Shakespear-beyond-collaboration may simply not be recoverable.

If it was not the compositor who was guilty, was it the scribe? Well, as *All's Well* is held to have been set into type directly from the author's foul-papers, this line of enquiry points to Shakspere as the culprit! A corrupting compositor diverts us from the author's to his own genius. But a corrupting author diverts us from the theatrical to the litterary.

The litterary. Although it makes good sense to say that Shakespeare's scripts were written for performance, it is simply not possible to *perform* a script. Rather, one *reads* the script and performs the reading. And so we might as well go 18th-century and say that Shakesper's plays were written to be *read*. And, of course, among the more famous readers of *All's Well* was — ready? — the playwrite himself! **Shakspere.** And he must have been *mightily* chuffed to see his work appear before him, letter by letter where it was subject to? to? to to? to to

65.5°

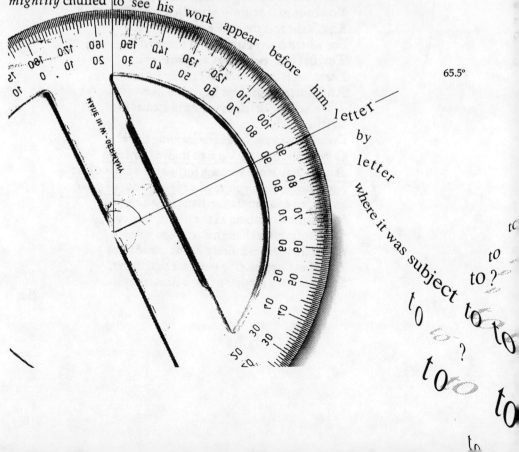

A pleasant conceited Comedie:

Confider what you firft did fweare vnto:
To faft, to ftudy, and to fee no woman:
Flat treafon gainft the kingly ftate of youth.
Say, Can you faft? your ftomacks are too young:
And abftinence ingenders maladies.
And where that you haue vowd to ftudie (Lordes)
In that each of you haue forfworne his Booke.
Can you ftill dreame and poare and thereon looke.
For when would you my Lord, or you, or you,
Haue found the ground of Studies excellence,
Without the beautie of a womans face?
From womens eyes this doctrine I deriue,
They are the Ground, the Bookes, the Achadems,
From whence doth fpring the true *Promethean* fire.
Why vniuerfall plodding poyfons vp
The nimble fpirites in the arteries,
As motion and long during action tyres
The finnowy vigour of the trauayler.
Now for not looking on a womans face,
You haue in that forfworne the vfe of eyes:
And ftudie too, the caufer of your vow.
For where is any Authour in the worlde,
Teaches fuch beautie as a womas eye:
Learning is but an adiunct to our felfe,
And where we are, our Learning likewife is.
Then when our felues we fee in Ladies eyes,
With our felues,
Do we not likewife fee our learning there?
O we haue made a Vow to ftudie, Lordes,
And in that Vow we haue forfworne our Bookes:
For when would you (my Leedge) or you, or you?
In leaden contemplation haue found out
Such fierie Numbers as the prompting eyes,
Of beautis tutors haue inritcht you with:
Other flow Artes intirely keepe the braine:
And therefore finding barraine practizers,
Scarce fhew a harueft of their heauie toyle.

But

called Loues Labor's lost.

But Loue first learned in a Ladies eyes,
Liues not alone emured in the braine:
But with the motion of all clamentes,
Courles as swift as thought in euery power,
And giues to euery power a double power,
Aboue their tunctions and their offices.
It addes a precious feeing to the eye:
A Louers eyes will gaze an Eagle blinde.
A Louers eare will heare the lowest found.
When the suspitious head of theft is stopt.
Loues feeling is more soft and sensible,
Then are the tender hornes of Cockled Snayles.
Loues tongue proues daintie, *Bachus* grosse in taste,
For Valoure, is not Loue a *Hercules*?
Still clyming trees in the *Hesperides*.
Subtit as *Sphinx*, as sweete and musicall,
As bright *Appolos* Lute, strung with his haire.
And when Loue speakes, the voyce of all the Goddes,
Make heauen drowsie with the harmonie.
Neuer durst Poet touch a pen to write,
Vntill his Incke were tempred with Loues sighes:
O then his lines would rauish sauage eares,
And plant in Tyrants milde humilitie.
From womens eyes this doctrine I deriue.
They sparcle still the right promethean fier,
They are the Bookes, the Artes, the Achademes,
That shew, containe, and nourish all the worlde.
Els none at all in ought proues excellent.
Then fooles you were, these women to forsweare:
Or keeping what is sworne, you will proue fooles,
For Wisedomes sake, a worde that all men loue:
Or for Loues fake, a worde that loues all men.
Or for Mens fake, the authour of these Women:
Or Womens fake, by whom we Men are Men.
Lets vs once loose our othes to finde our felues,
Or els we loose our felues, to keepe our othes:
It is Religion to be thus forsworne.

F 3   For

Yes, to *revision*. In the previous opening, you can see revisional strata on F2v-3r of the first quarto of *Loues Labours Lost* (1598). Here the variant versions occur in a speech of a single character, Berowne. But variants can cross from one speaker to another. As we read down D4v of *Romeo and Iuliet* (1599), for example, a four-line speech is assigned first to green Romeo and then again immediately, with several changes of diction, to grey Friar Lawrence.[11] As it may seem absurdly redundant to deliver both strata in a single performance, we might say (with an eye to paradox) that at least one stratum was written to be chosen *not* to be performed.[12]

If we want to be *very* naughty, we can dress this realization as a full-blown teleological statement:

𝕾𝖍𝖆𝖐𝖊𝖘𝖕𝖊𝖗𝖊'𝖘 𝖘𝖈𝖗𝖎𝖕𝖙𝖘 𝖆𝖗𝖊 𝖓𝖔𝖙 𝖋𝖔𝖗 𝖕𝖊𝖗𝖋𝖔𝖗𝖒𝖆𝖓𝖈𝖊.

As you can imagine, the making of teleological statements leads to *no end* of mischief. This one is partly true, just as its opposite without the **not** is partly true. (I like my bad teleological edict better, though, because it doesn't misrepresent how a playtext is *created*.)[13]

In any case, whoever it was cooked up the litterary effects of the folio *All's Well* — author or compositor, they are an *inalienable* part of the text.

(Unless, of course, you *edit* it.)

❦

Another delectable litterary concoction? Consider lines 2232-3:

> *Int.* *Bosko Chimurcho.*
> *Cap.* *Boblibindo chicurmurco.*

Isn't that capital at the start of *Chimurcho* an interesting texture, especially in contrast to the lower-case initial in the look-alike *chicurmurco* in the next line? Except for first words in sentences, *Chimurcho* is the only Chough word in the first folio to start with a capital. Ten compositors kept its *C* for 150 years, until Capell's edition, in 1767. I suppose they must have seen some kind of significance in this capital — and what kind of significance if not *litterary*?

Now, in Shakespeare's time, the appearance in print of an initial capital on a word that is not at the beginning of a sentence or of a line of verse suggested a proper adjective or a proper noun, as in "*Muskos* Regiment" (l. 1983)[14], but occasionally also a common noun, like "Pasty" (l. 2231). Earlier, the various use of v/u in words like *movoufus* and *reuania* made us query the *phonetics* of Chough, and speculate about its *morphology*. Now this upper-case *C* in *Chimurcho* pushes us to guess at its *grammar*.

It was also Capell who first changed *Chimurcho* to *chimurco*. (Was he eye-rhyming it with *chicurmurco* in the line below, one wonders?) But a decade later in Strassburg, *C* was given a new lease on life as 𝕮, in Johann Joachim Eschenburg's translation of *All's Well*, the first into any language.[15]

246   Ende gut, alles gut.

Dollmetſcher. Er läßt die Tortur kommen. Wollt Ihr nicht noch vorher bekennen?

Parolles. Ich will ohne Zwang bekennen, was ich weiß; wenn ihr mich auch zwicktet, wie eine Paſtete, ſo kann ich nicht mehr ſagen.

Dollmetſcher. Bosko Chimurcho.

2. Edelmann. Boblibindo chicumurko.

In this 18th-Century German Environment, the Function of the initial Capital to indicate a Noun is shtronger than in any English Environment, even that of the First Folio. By conserving the distinctions between upper- and lower-case, this translation played up Chough's litterary effect — altering it though, for it made *Chimurcho* seem less equivocally a noun or proper adjective. And, of course, subtle new interpretations *rush* upon us with Johann Joachim's *neue ganz umgearbeitete Ausgabe* (Zürich, 1799), where the 𝕮 — or the 𝕰, rather — multiplied (as *C* had in the fourth folio[16]):

Dolmetſcher. Bosko Chimurcho.

2. Edelmann. Boblibindo Chicumurko.

— to which we can compare the multiplied *C* of Diego Angeli's *Tutto è bene quel che finische bene* (Milano-Roma, 1932):

IL PRIMO SOLDATO.

Bosco Chimurcho.

IL PRIMO SIGNORE.

Boblibindo Chicomurcho.

— both of which babel so *very* differently (each deeply in its own German or Italian way, of course) than when the *C* and *c* merely *swap*, as they do in the French Chough of George Duval's *Tout est bien qui finit bien* (Paris, 1908).

PREMIER SOLDAT.

Bosko chimurcho.

DEUXIÈME SEIGNEUR.

Boblitindo Chicurmurco.

TLN	F1 (1623)	F2 (1632)	F3 (1664)	F4 (1685)
1978	Throca	→	Throco	→
	movousus	→	→	→
1979	cargo, cargo, cargo	→	→	cargo, cargo, oargo
	Cargo, cargo, cargo	Cargo, cargo	→	→
	villianda	→	villiando	→
	par	→	→	→
	corbo	→	→	→
	cargo	→	→	→
1982	Boskos	Baskos	→	→
	thromuldo	→	→	→
1988	boskos	beskos	→	→
	Boskos	→	→	Baskos
1989	vauvado	→	→	→
	Kerelybonto	→	→	→
1993	Manka	Mancha	→	→
	reuania	revanta	revancha	→
1994	dulche	→	→	→
	Oscorbidulchos	Osceorbidulchos	→	→
2005	voliuorco	volivorco	→	→
	Acordo	→	→	→
2227	linta	→	→	→
	Portotartarossa	→	→	→
2232	Bosko	→	→	→
	Chimurcho	→	→	→
2233	Boblibindo	→	Biblibindo	→
	chicurmurco	→	→	Chicurmurco

Rowe (1709)	Pope (1725)	Theobald (1733)	Hanmer (1743-4)	TLN
→	→	→	→	1978
→	→	→	→	
cargo, cargo, cargo	→	→	→	1979
→	→	→	→	
→	→	→	→	
→	→	→	→	
→	→	→	→	
→	→	→	→	
→	→	Boskos	Baskos	1982
thromaldo	→	thromuldo	thromaldo	
→	→	boskos	beskos	
→	→	Boskos	Baskos	1988
→	→	→	→	
→	→	→	→	1989
→	→	→	→	1993
ravancha	→	→	→	
→	→	→	→	
Osceoribi dulchos	→	→	→	1994
→	→	→	→	
→	→	→	→	2005
→	→	→	→	
→	→	→	→	2227
→	→	→	→	2232
→	→	→	→	
→	→	→	→	2233
→	chicurmurco	→	→	

TLN	Warburton (1747)	Johnson (1765, 1769)	Capell (1767-8)	Johnson, Steevens, Reed (1785)
1978	→	→	Throca	→
	→	→	→	→
1979	→	→	→	→
	→	→	→	→
	→	→	villianda	→
	→	→	→	→
	→	→	→	cobo
	→	→	→	→
1982	Boskos	→	Boskos	→
	thromuldo	→	→	→
	boskos	→	→	→
1988	Boskos	→	→	→
	→	→	→	→
1989	→	→	→	→
1993	→	→	Manca	Manka
	→	→	revanta	revania
	→	→	→	→
1994	→	→	Osceorbi dulcos	Oscorbi dulchos
	→	→	→	→
2005	→	→	→	Acorda
	→	→	→	→
2227	→	Portotarossa	Porto tartarossa	→
2232	→	→	→	→
	→	→	chimurco	chicurmurcho
2233	→	→	Boblibindo	→
	→	→	→	→

Malone (1790)	Bell (1812) [Johnson, Steevens]	Boswell (1821)	Johnson, Steevens, Reed (1829)	TLN
→ →	} Throcamovousus	Throca movousus	→ →	1978
→ →	→ Crago, crago	→ Cargo, cargo	→ →	1979
→ →	→ →	→ →	→ →	
corbo →	→ →	→ →	→ →	
→ →	→ →	→ →	→ →	1982
→ →	→ →	→ →	→ →	1988
→ →	→ Kerylybonto	→ Kerelybonto	vanvado →	1989
→ →	Mane a →	Manka →	} Mankarevania	1993
→ →	→ Osceoribi du chos	→ Oscorbidulchos	→ →	1994
→ Acordo	volivorcho →	volivorca →	→ →	2005
→ →	→ Pariotartarossa	→ Porto tartarossa	→ →	2227
→ chimurcho	→ Chimurcho	→ chimurcho	→ →	2232
→ →	→ →	→ →	→ →	2233

One of the very soberest features of editorial scholarshit — *The Band of T* error — collates variant readings in and between editions. Why is it that Chough almost *never* figures there, when *every* Chough word goes variant in one edition or another? John Munro's 1958 *London Shakespeare*[17] provides the fullest collations to be found in the dozens of 20th-century editions I have consulted.[18] But his commentary is on merely a single line, 1993:

73 Manka] F²⁻⁴ Mancha   revania] F² revanta F³˒⁴ revancha

Do you see the problem with his second lemma? — "reyania" is his reading of the first folio's *reyania*. The modern editor cannot disentangle Chough from the second folio's alphabetagraphical reforms — its *modern* reforms.

One may wonder why Munro bothered to spell out even this much nonsensical history of nonsense. If he was going to do it at all, why not really *go* for it? why not record that his own reading was arbitrary nonsense? that, though the first-folio reading can support his phonetics, its graphics suggests another possibility? And why cite only these two variants, when (as I count them) there are altogether *fourteen* Chough words that go variant in the first four folios alone (which are this editor's range of collation)? That rate of mutation is *very* high, don't you think? In fact, since the appearance of Chough in the first folio, its litterary half-life was only six decades — the time between the first and the fourth folios.

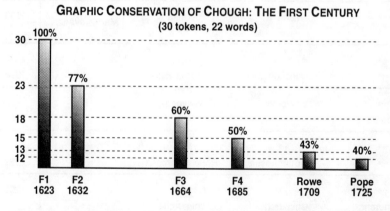

GRAPHIC CONSERVATION OF CHOUGH: THE FIRST CENTURY
(30 tokens, 22 words)

In other words, half the vocabulary changed in three re-printings over 62 years. The preceding tables (on pages 12-15)[19] may suggest the rate slowed somewhat in the 18th century; but, as many editors kept alive the errors of the recent editions they marked up as copy,[20] all of them — by Rowe, Pope, Theobald, Hanmer, Warburton, Johnson —were still prone to error. Even in the stringent regimes of Capell, Johnson-Steevens-Reed, Malone and Boswell, errors continued — as they do to this very day. For example, Capell's splitting of *Portotartarossa* (the longest of Chough words) into *Porto tartarossa*[21] springs eternal in Gary Taylor's Ox ford original-spelling and modernized editions — with something unprecedented: a*justifiction*.

                                                    ^

> F prints as one word, but division makes the 'meaning'
> (= bring the tortures of hell) clearer

Now, Oxford cites no precedent for this emendation. So, who knows whether (a) it simply follows the Modern Library edition? or Halliwell? or Dyce? or Boswell? or Malone? who followed Johnson-Steevens-Reed, who followed Capell? Or (b) unwittingly re-originates it? Or (c) is inspired by Gundolf's or von Schlegel und Tieck's Teutonic — *more* meaningful — *Porto Tartarossa*? In any case, Taylor is the first (likely the only) editor ever to *argue* for emendation of Cough. His criterion?

the 'meaning'

Doesn't the editor's semantic defense — 'defensiveness', even — imply that Chough has Indo-European roots?[22]

    In 1897 David Charles Bell also divided the word at *just* this place, in *The Reader's Shakespeare: His Dramatic Works Condensed, Connected, and Emphasized, for School, College, Parlour, and Platform*.[23] But his footnotes for each Chough word or phrase brand them "nonsense words". Where should we place our trust, then, in Taylor's *meaning* or in Bell's *nonsense*?

    Doesn't their common division of *Portotartarossa* into *Porto tartarossa* reflect a preoccupation with the *graphics*, with the *word-division* of Chough? How reminiscent this division is of the conventions (are they Shakspeare's? the compositor's?) — of the conventions at play in some *other* Chough settings in the first folio. That such diverse editors deem the text is *for production*, but nevertheless both style their print *for reading* (whether on platform or in parlour) shows there's just *no end* to subtleties when you go tele-illogical.

    Now, Gary Taylor and David Bevington do not always see I to I. I don't know whether the latter is keen on Indo-European derivations. But even if he is, would he countenance *both* etyma of *tartarossa* — L *Tartarus* and LL *tortura* — as the Ox ford editor seems to? For Bevington's editions read

Portotartarosa

— with a single, not a double s. Why, *rosa* may be the emphasis of the word now, or *arosa* — whatever *that* nonsense means? Or perhaps emphasis falls on *-osa*?[24] We know that Taylor did consider his alteration. But, as Bevington's reading is not defended, it is hard to know whether the more senior editor *thought* his Chough straight through. Maybe he merely recycled Hardin Craig's? Wasn't it his 1951 edition that Bevington revised? And did Craig in his turn really *weigh* his Chough? — or just take it uncritically from the nonsense of the 1876 Howard Shakespeare? or the 1875 White edition?

or the 1863-66 Clark & Wright, Cambridge edition?[25] — where this tradition
originated, well over a century ago (without comment, without defense),
and whence it came home (via the Heinemann *Favorite Classics* edition) —
home to the stage in Stratford-upon-Avon, of all places?[26]

A 1963 *Sve je dobro što se dobro svrši* offers something of a Serbo-Croatian
compromise between Taylor and Bevington:

> Por-/totar tarosa!

Bell editions of 1773 and 1774 sometimes divide the folio's *Portotartarossa*
where Taylor does, and sometimes not:

> Parta torturossa   Partatorturossa.

But changes in the first four vowels here lead to different etymological
evocations of 'meaning': of *parting*, for the first time (< L *partire*); and,
though again of *torture*, not again of *Tartarus*, as in the Ox ford portmeantau.

Others style Shakspeare's Chough diversely. A 1766 Pope edition reads

> Portotartaressa.

Kemble's edition of 1793 offers

> Partotartarossa

— which lends itself to one half of Tay lor's allegory, while Kemble's 1815
edition lends itself to the other:

> Porto torturossa.

From 1765 and 1792 Johnson editions come these, a syllable *down*,

> Portotarossa   Partotarossa

— and this, a syllable *up*, from an 1812 Johnson-Steevens edition:

> Pariotartarossa.

And just *wait* till you see the French, Catalan, Polish, German and Czech:[27]

> Porto tartarona
> Porto artarona
> Portotastarrosa
> Parto tartarassa
> Porto mučidlosso *and* Porto mučidloso.

— and so on, &c, usw, ecc, atd, stb, rrm.

All this variety! I bet you're *starving*?

You think I've been talking nonsense all this while, but look – today *I'm* the sane one. It's those editors are crazy. Haven't done their homework. But I'd be choughed to buttocks to do it for them *just this once*, because — because, ever since I was a kid, I had this Towering Ambition to edit. *Collating?* Don't you talk to *me* about collating. Why, I ate and slept collation for years. *For years* my Mom and my Dad scrimped for this certain editing career plan. Which was *entirely* my idea. Yes, it was my idea and they believed in me. *Years* of toil. A choice between study and shoes? I went *barefoot*. No sacrifice was too great for *my* Mom and Dad. We marched as one, a family, rain or shine. Family was family then. She'd of been happy for me — if editing had "panned out" for us. I mean it, a protective woman, my Mom. A team player. What happened? Well, one day there was this certain career change of plan: "If you cannot edit," she said, "do theory. Why, you could *teach*." I can hear her voice, dark and rough like it was yesterday. *There*'s my Mother for you in a nut case. *She* was not a woman to hold back what you thought.

So, now I teach. Yes, I teach some. And I do a bit of theory. Theory's OK. So, no, to answer your question, I'm — I'm not bitter, really. I am *not* a bitter man. Do I *sound* bitter? Just because I didn't become some fucking big-bucks editor?

衆
人
卡
哥
，
卡
哥
，
維
利
安
達
・
拍
・
考
薄
，
卡
哥
。

Now, my Mom — my Mother had this knack for consolation. Why, she could cheer up a *saint*. She'd always say — get his — "Look, Jack, life's a comœdy." (I didn't tell you this already, did I? — because who wants to repeat themself?) You see what I mean, though? A *card*, my old lady. But *she* was one to repeat herself. "Life is a comœdy. So why be bitter?" Positively singing, a voice of gold. Always bright, always smooth. A card, my Mom. Always. "Anyway," she'd say, "it's soon over. It's just a comœdy, after all. Ask for a lovely daughter, and you get a son. But you take what you get in this life. It's not a *tragedy*, for Christ's sake. It is *not* a tragedy." So, in my family, we always figured, Why should *anybody* kick against the pricksI suppose *you* do, do you, Miss Goody Two Shoes? Well, a word to the wise, girl: Don't try it in those BirkensLook, I apologize for blurting out about "my past" and "how the shoe fits." But you think I have no empathy, don't you. *Don't* you? Well excuse *me*. Do you know how long I've *waited*? I've been empathizing for *years*. For years I've empathized *this* person. For years I've empathized *that* person. Well, I'm *sick* of it, do you understand? It's *my* turn now. Emphasize *me* for a change. Before this day is over, you're damn well going to *know* what it would of meant to my Mother, after all the tragic years of her stinking life, for her son the teacher to tower forth — 'Variorum Editor for a Day'! Over soon or not, she'd of been dead chuffed.

❧

Starting on page 24, and going for page after page after page after page, you'll find my modest **Tower of Variants**. The beginning of each paragraph registers in bold the F1 form; thereafter follows what editors and translators have made of it *over the years* and *around the world*. Should F2 conserve the graphics of any occurrence of v/u, that form is also given, and tagged "F2". (Remember, though it *looks* the same, it *reads* differently, less variously.) A caret registers an omission in at least one edition. Occasionally I've collated unexpected punctuation. Variants in English editions are quoted first. After the asterisks come novel Babel from whatever foreign tongues came to hand — their names are heaped in the previous opening — during the *years* of my research, in archives *all over Europe* and *around the world*.

It's too bad, really, but since I have to limit myself to the Latin alphabet, I won't be gleaning Chough from editions of old What's-his-typeface

ШЕКСПІР or 莎士比亞

in Cyrillic, for example[28]. Take the phrase "*Cargo, cargo, cargo, villianda par corbo, cargo*". Bulgarian (see 1, opposite) is close, isn't it? Like, in punctuation? (And doesn't punctuation open *volumes* about Chough *syntax* and *phrasing*?) Just one *l* in *vilianda*, though. Ukrainian (2) is also close, but two sentences now. With no vertical serif on its *g* (which Ukrainian reserves for foreign words), *cargo* sounds [karho] (for Slav |g| > Ukr [h]). So, the translator lost an opportunity to register the *otherness* of Chough! Pity, eh?

1.   ВОЙНИЦИТЕ
           Карго, карго, карго, вилианда пар корбо, карго!

2.   *Уеі разом*   Карго, карго, карго! Вільянда пар
                    корбо, карго!

3.   **Солдаты**

      Карго, карго! Вилианда пар корбо! Карго!

4.   Всѣ. Карго, карго! Виліанда паръ корбо, карго!

5.   **Всѣ. Карго, карго, вилліанда паръ карбо, карго.**

6.   **Солдаты**

      Карго, карго. Вилиада пар карго, карго.

7.   **солдаты. Карго, карго, карго, вилліанда паркорбо каръ!**

The rest are Russian. (3) has three sentences (!!!). But only two initial *cargo*s — and so with (4). *паръ* may seem to have four letters, but the last is merely a terminal 'hard sign'. (5) is back to one sentence. Two *l*'s in *villianda* again, but *carbo* for *corbo*. (6) pioneers *Viliada*, and *cargo* for *corbo*. In 7, *corbo* returns, but it's linked up before: *parcorbo* — and, after it, there's mere *caръ* for *cargo*. See that terminal 'hard sign' again? Since it's not in *parcorbo*, we know the fusion of *par* and *corbo* isn't the result merely of an accidental loss of space, which would have made that terminal *medial*, **if** a *ъ* had been used (which it wasn't). But mom's the word *on stage*. Because this is all *litterary*!!!

Now the Chinese. For McLuhan, alphabets link meaningless signs to meaningless sounds. But logographs can evoke objects or concepts directly, without phonetic mediation. In the moments of indecision, when Chinese readers (whatever their language) start into logographic Chough and find it indecipherable, they must deal with exactly the same absurd *semantic* combinations before they catch on: that the logographs are being used "merely for their *sounds*". (In this case, it is Mandarin sounds, not Cantonese, that evoke Chough more or less as English speakers would utter it.)

Two logographs render the word *car-go*. The first sounds [ka]; it is the only logograph for this sound. I presume it's echoic (as it means "chough").[29] But *eleven* logographs can sound [go]. That in the 1960 translation (on page 20) means "elder brother" — a standard ABEL-BAKER-CHARLIE way to evoke [go]. But the 1933 translation (on this page) offers an unconventional and vulgar *go*, for among its meanings is the apt "military latrine"! There is, after all, therefore, a teasing potential for *semantic* functioning in these logographs. (Didn't I tell you Cough was a comœdy?) Nevertheless, neither translator's crafting of *go* conditions auditory response *in the theatre* — for the logographs are purely *litterary*, right? *Go* is just a sound, [go]. Not your *brother*. Not your *latrine*.[30] So, it's too bad, really, that I have had to limit myself to the Latin alphabet. You see, I have — well, I have these limits

衆

卡溝

，卡溝

，維利安達

、怕敲波

，卡溝

ℐ

。

אויסגעװעהלטע װערק

Throca
throco
Throcamovousus
*****
Trokamofusus
Troka
Troca
Trocca
Throca,
Thraca
Throka
Thvoca
Vantroky troky

movousus
movousus (F2)
movo-/usus
movousus,
movousus∧
*****
Movousus
movausus
movusus
movusos
movousu
movounsos
movon-/sus
mowosus
mowousus
morousus
moronsus

morovousus
movo vousus
mavousus
mavusus —
novusus
novousus
novuozus

cargo, cargo, cargo
cargo, cargo, cargo,
cargo, cargo, oargo
*****
^
cargo! Cargo! Cargo!
cargo! Cargo, cargo!
Cargo! Cargo! Cargo!
Kargo, kargo, kargo
kargo, kargo, kargo

Cargo, cargo, cargo
Cargo, cargo
Cargo, Cargo!
Crago, crago
*****
^
Cargo, cargo, cargo —
Cargo, cargo, cargo!
Cargo, Cargo
Kargo, kargo

villianda
villianda (F2)
villiando
valliando
*****
^
villiana,
villanda
villianda —
Villianda
villiande
villiand
vilianda
viljanda
willjanda
willianda

par
*****
∧
por
per
pat

corbo
cobo
*****
∧
corbo!
corbo —
carbo
karbo
korbo
Cargo! cargo!
cargo!

cargo
*****
∧
Cargo
carbo
kargo
Cargo, cargo

Boskos
Baskos
Boskus
Bosko
Muskos
*****
Boskos,
Boskos —
Barcos
Boscos
Boscos,
Boszkosz
Bosckos
Bos-/kos

thromuldo
thromuldo (F2)
thromaldo

thromuldoboskos
*****
thromuldos
thromu
tromuldo
thromuldo,
tromuldo;
tromuado
thromu ! do
Hsvomuldo
kastro muldo

boskos
beskos
b skos
bascos
muskos
*****
bos-/kos
boskos —
Boskos
bosckos
boscos
boskes
boskas
boszkosz
bosbos

Boskos
Baskos
*****
Boscos
Bosko
Boskas
Baskas
Bosckos

vauvado
vauvado (F2)
vauvado?
vouvado
vanvado
vauvad
*****
vau vado

vaufado
vuvados
vovado
vouvada
Vauvado
wauwado ...
cauvado
ravanvado
Vau vej ado

Kerelybonto
Kerely-/bonto
Kerely-bonto
Kerylybonto
*****
kerelybonto
Ke-/relybonto
Kere-/lybonto
Kerelybonto!
Kerelibonto
Kerely bonto
Kerely bouto
Korelybonto
Kerdybonto!
Kerelydonto
Kereligbonto
Kergtibonto
Krelybonto
kesclibonto
kve relaj bonto

Manka
Mancka
Mancha
Manca
Mane a
Mankarevania
*****
^
Men kere vaniae
Man-/kanvevania
Manza
Manche
Man-/che
Man-/cha
Mank
Mank,
Mauka

reuania
revanta
revancha
ravancha
revania
revanie
*****
^

rivania
rewania
rewanja
revanja
revancia
revanca
revanda

dulche
dulche (F2)
dulce
dulche?
dul-/che?
*****
dulche!
dultsche
Dulche
dulče
dulsze
dulchi
dultschos
dulke
fulke

Oscorbidulchos
Osceorbidulchos
Osceorbi dulchos
Osceoribi dulchos
O eoribi dulchos
Osceorbi dulcos
Oscorbi dulchos
Ofceoribi dulchos
Osceoribi du chos
*****
Oscorchi dulchos
Oscor bilduchos
Oschorbi dulchos
Oskeoribi dulchos
Oscoribi dulcos

Oskorbi dulszos
Oskorbi dultschos
Oskorbi dulkos
Oscorbidulkos
Oscorbidulhos
Oskorbi dulčos
Oscorbi, dulchos
O, scorbi dulchos
O scorbidulchos
Os corbi dulchos
Oscorbidulcios
Oscobidulčos
Oscorbidulches
Oscorbindulches
Oscorbis
Osegorbi dulchos

voliuorco
volivorco (F2)
volivorca
volivorcho
*****
Volivorco
volivorco ...
voli vorco
voliforco
volivorio
volivoreo
volivorea
volivorriere
volivorko
volworko
woliworka
voli tolko

Acordo
Acorda
Accordo
*****
^
Akordo
Acordolinta
Akordolinta

linta
linia
linta?

*****
linta!
linto
linte
liuta
linda

Portotartarossa
Portotartaressa
Portotarossa
Partotartarossa
Partatorturossa
Parta torturossa
Porto tartarossa
Porto tartarosso
Porto torturossa
Porto torturosa
Pariotartarossa
Portotartarosa
Porto tar-/tarossa
Portotar-/tarosa
*****
Por-/totartarossa
Porto-/tartarossa
Portotarta-/rossa
Porto tarta-/rossa
Por-/totar tarosa
Porto Tarta-/rossa
Porto Tartarossa
Porto tartarossa!
Porto tartarossa ...
Porto tartarossa. ... Porto tartarossa!
Portotastarrosa
Parto tartarossa
Parto tartarassa
Porto mučidlosso
Porto artarona
Porto tartarona
Porta tartarossa
Porto tartaros

Bosko
Bosko,
Bosco
Basko
*****
ᴧ

Bosto
Boskochimurko

Chimurcho
Chimurcho (F2)
chimurcho
chimurcho?
Chimurco
chimurco
chimurko
chimarcho
Chirmurcho
chicurmurcho
cimurcio
*****
^

chicurmurco
chicumurko
chicumurro
chicurmuro
chicururcho
chimurchurco!
ohimurcho
ckimurcho
čimurčo
cimurco
szimurszo
chimurrcho
kimurko
kimurka
himurco!

Boblibindo
Boblebindo
Biblibindo
biblibindo
*****
^

Boblibindo,
Boblitindo
Boblinbindo
Roblibindo
Bobliblindo
Bablibindo   ☜   (This just in from
                         *Sve je dobro što
                         se dobro svrši*,
                         Beograd, 1963)

chicurmurco
chicurmurco (F2)
Chicurmurco
chicarmurcho
chicurmurcho

*****

^

chichurmurko
chicururcho
cimurmurco
chicuurcho
čimurčo
chimurchurco
chimurmurcho
chicumuro
chicumurro
chicumurco
Chicumurko
cicurmurco
chicur-/murco
chicurmurko
chicur murcho
chicurmuro
szikurmurko
Chicormurcho
chicurmurrcho
kikurmurko
kirurmurko
chirurmurco
chircurmurco
hikurmurko

Eₓcᴜsᴇ me. I'm very sorry. Please excuse my Tall Tower — well, my tower
has a few limitations. For, to understand how variations arose in transmission, doesn't one have to see *actual settings* of type? You'll look in vain for
ſ in my little tower. But isn't it necessary to explain the ƒ in the 1795

Oſceoribi dulchos

as a response to the ſ of the first folio's

Oſcoribidulchos

via this setting in Rowe's edition, 1709?

Oſceoribi dulchos

And Capell. Can't do justice to *him* in my tiny tower. That man had a *big*
quirk. Except for the ambiguous *s* found always at the ends of words in his
edition, he used ſ exclusively for [s] and *s* exclusively for [z]. So we really
don't need to guess how *he* pronounced medial sibilants in *movouſus, boſkus,*
Oſceorbi, tartaroſſa and *Boſko.* That's right — all unvoiced.[31] But would you
know his [s] from his [z] in my inadequate tower? Would you? So, I apollo-
gize. I'm sorry.

And isn't it important to know into what language *All's Well* has been
translated? Encountering *woliworka* in *Wszystko dobre, co kończy się dobrze*
poses no big problem, right?[32] But there is a *very* big problem when *O*
scorbidulchos volworko shows up in *Tutto è bene quel che finisce bene.*[33] Because
Polish has w, but Italian does not. Neither does Old Chough. (Nor does it
have f, q, x or z — though you'll see more than one of those letters in my
dinky tower.) But I simply cannot detail *all* this information in a first daft.
I just *can't* take the space to say — well, for example, I can't take the space
to say that *szikurmurko* is from Poland; *chicurmurko* and *chimurchurco* from
Denmark; *chicumurro, chicur murcho* and *kirurmurko* from Germany; and
hikurmurko from God knows where. (It's from Riga, actually: *Gals labs, viss*
labs, 1964.) Let it be enough that they are *all* Chough. Chough is international. (Besides, I've got this page limitation.)

But, with the very *smallest* of examples, let me just *suggest* the richness of
speculation that attends our knowing the fate of the first folio's *Chimurcho*
— I'll take just this one word to save time. We'll be done in a trice, you'll see.
—in two Italian translations, one very early, one very recent. They are

ckimurcho

in Rusconi's 1852-3 *Tutto è bene quello che a bien riesce,* and

cimurco

in Melchiori's 1976 *Tutto è bene quel che finisce bene.* Let me focus this very *briefest* of sketches on the letter c. (A mere *outline*, that's all.) Of course, a great problem for English speakers confronted by an unfamiliar word with this letter — the word "Chough", for example — is to decide whether (alone, or with its mates) the c sounds like

[k] in *character*
[č] in *charter*
[š] in *chandelier*
[s] in *city*

— or

[ts] in *czar*
[z] in *czardas*

— or not at all

[ ] in *cnemical*.

And then there's the poor Scots — and don't forget the Jews!

[x] in *loch* — and *Chanukah*.

In the folio, the problem is brought sharply to our attention by the slight variation between the end of this word and that of its look-alike in the next line:

Chimurcho ... chicurmurco.

As this pair of lines of Chough dialogue seems to function as challenge and response, these words may well strike one as cognate, but differentiated through the Chough equivalent of conjugation or declension. (It's like that — that *Ablaut* feeling you get, when the second folio changes the first folio's

Boskos thromuldo boskos

to

Baskos thromuldo beskos.)

The first word, *Chimurcho*, has one medial *ur* (a morpheme?), the second, *chicurmurco*, has two. That fact, and the presence or absence of *h* after the latter *c* may provoke more questions on Chough grammar and morphology.

But let's ask, instead, how an Italian would react to the letters alone? In Rusconi's example, *ckimurcho*, ck and ch would provoke a native speaker to say [k ... k ...], just as if the word had appeared as *kimurko* in an English edition. (This form is actually found in Körner's German translation, 1836.) But the two usual ways Italian provokes this pronunciation would be *chimurco*. Although *k* is indeed found occasionally in Italian words like

il weekend   *il rock*

(and Italians do, therefore, know how to pronounce it), it is not *really* part of their alphabet. There is thus an outlandish effect, not only in its mere appearance in *ckimurcho*, but also in its generating the same [k] sound as the conventional *ch* does.

Furthermore, although the *ch* digraph provokes an Italian to pronounce [k], this spelling is found only before the high front vowels, spelled *e* and *i* (as in the words *che*, *chi* — or *Melchiori*), which would sound [č] without it (as in *ce* and *ci*). It is not found before the other vowels (including the one in question, spelled *o*), which require merely a *c*, not a *ch*, to evoke the [k] sound (as in the words *calo*, *col* — or *Carlo Rusconi* — and *culo*). Therefore, *ciechi* (meaning "blind") is pronounced ['čeki]; and *chierici* (meaning, and cognate with, "clerics") is pronounced ['kjeriči].

This will all seem less arbitrary, if you compare the different values of *c* before the same vowels in English words. Before the high front vowels in *city*, *census* and *cyst*, *c* sounds [s]. Before the low-front and back vowels in *cab*, *cost*, and *cut*, *c* sounds [k]. Obviously, Italians use *h* after *c* to "harden" it (to keep it velar), whereas English often uses an *h* after *c* to "soften" it (to palatalize it).[34] Therefore, the *h* in the first folio's *-cho* looks redundant to an Italian, for there is no conceivable difference to the pronunciation of the regular *-co* and the bizarre *-cho*; but to an English speaker the *h* can signal a pronunciation of the *c* as [č] — which it can scarcely do without the *h*.)

Thus, it is hard to know whether Rusconi's *ckimurcho* employs *ch* before *o* to conserve the first-folio evidence, or to provoke a ludicrous *litterary* effect in the eyes of its Italian readers (an effect unknown to English readers of the folio) — as if the news hadn't reached Italy that Shakspeare is *for production*. It is also hard to know whether his *k* is an error, or is part of some calculated outlandish effect. Was he making a joke? Or was Ruschoni the joke?

That he rendered the folio's *Boskos* as *Bosckos*, and *Manka* as *Mancka*, suggests that he may indeed have calculated the ludicrous *k* — or even more ludicrous, *ck* —before such vowels as *o* and *a*. For, if he had changed the spelling of the former word to Italian-looking *Boscos*, he would have provoked the [k] sound from Italian readers, just as readily as the form *Boskos* provokes it from English readers; and he would have naturalized the form graphically. (How mischievous, then, are those Italian and Portuguese translations that offer "*Boscos thromuldo boskos*"!) In any case, these diverse English and Italian slants on Chough make a protractor a *must* for those who study Comp. Lit. (See page 7.)

Now, how about Melchiori? By not conserving either *h*, his *cimurco* will provoke Italians to pronounce the initial *ci-* as [či-]. Melchiori's spelling of the end of the word removes the *h*, which would look redundant to Italians, coming as it does after *c* and before a non-high-front vowel. His much revised spelling — it looks strangely truncated to us — seems conceived to deliver to Italians a word that is graphically and phonotactically unexceptional. Italians would surely pronounce it [č ... k ...] — whereas, if anglophones saw this editor's *cimurco*, they might well respond [s ... k ...], which in turn is a most unlikely response to the first folio's *Chimurcho*. (But who really knows? Chough is neither Italian nor English, is it?)

Some obscure light may be thrown on Melchiori's and Rusconi's behaviour by their treatment of the look-alike *chicurmurco* in the next line. (It's alright. I'm *sure* we have time.) Melchiori offers

cicurmurco

— again dropping the folio's *h* before *i*. His seeming concern to naturalize into Italian orthography a typical English pronunciation ([č]) at the start of this Chough word is certainly not weakened by this new example; nor is it weakened by his rendering of *dulche* as *dulce*, or of *Oscorbidulchos* as *Oscorbidulcios*. The thought creeps in, though, that, in the previously discussed Chough word, he may have dropped the *h* before the final *o* (*Chimurcho* → *cimurco*) in order to eye- rhyme it with *cicurmurco*. Eye-rhyme? Isn't that what Capell was up to?   See p. 11.

As for Rusconi, he added a second *h*,

chicurmurcho

— perhaps to eye-rhyme this word with his *ckimurcho* — or even to have it echo the front end of itself (where, strangely, there is no editorial *k* this time).

Compare these with the translations by Carcano, Angeli, and Lodovici, spread through the intervening century:

Rusconi	Carcano	Angeli	Lodovici	Melchiori
1852-3	1882	1932	1960	1976
ckimurcho	chimurcho	Chimurcho	chimurco	cimurco
chicurmurcho	chicurmurcho	Chicomurcho	chicumurco	cicurmurco

All five of these editors increase graphic resemblance at the ends of these look-alike words[35] — by adding or dropping *h*. Thus, they too force a rhyme, of *both* consonant and vowel, on [-ko] — *euery one a man of his own assimilation.* (Of course, for many anglophone readers of the first folio's *Chimurcho* ... *chicurmurco*, only the vowels rhyme, not the consonants.) And all but Melchiori ask Italians to say [k] at *both* ends of the words.

Now, it may be that it was *not* Rusconi the Italian who originated the re-styling of the end of *chicurmurco* as *chicurmurcho*; for this wacky spelling first appeared in England, in the Johnson-Steevens-Reed edition of 1785!

Inter. Boſka chicurmurcho.
2 Lord. Boblibindo chicurmurco.

Perhaps the ridiculous Carlo was just conserving the reading of ridiculous Sam, George and Isaac? But note: their *chicurmurcho* cannot be a spelling mistake for the folio's *chicurmurco*; for it appears in the line *above*! — as a mistake for *Chimurcho*. Johnson-Steevens-Reed's *chicurmurcho* thus seems to blend the terminal spelling appropriate for this line, *-cho*, with the wrong number of syllables — the number appropriate to the line below.

In my nifty tower, you'll surmise that other continental editions may have been seduced by Johnson-Steevens-Reed's transformation of *Chimurcho* into *chicurmurcho*, for they read *chicurmurco, chicumurko, chicumurro, chicurmuro,* and *chimurchurco*. But who knows? Such inspirations may have arisen spontaneously to the fancies of editors *all over Europe*! Nonsense is everywhere, after all. (It's not just the English are stupid.)

Had Rusconi been influenced by this 1785 English edition, therefore, he would have had to compensate for its eye-skip in *one* direction with eye-skip of his own in the *other*. Plus he would have had to go to some other edition to find the copy for the word he represented as *ckimurcho* for the first of these look-alikes. Perhaps Rusconi *collated* his nonsense? But no — it could not really be that easy: in his 1858-59 edition — to give the merest *hint* of the complicating evidence one would have to consider — his *chicurmurcho* appears merely as

chicuurcho

— and in a 1838 edition, it appears as

chicururcho.

To estimate how truly conservative or unconservative Rusconi was in this instance, wouldn't one have to know what his copy was, and how he handled *each* and *every* Chough word, in *all* his editions, even these posthumerous ones, and — and this is my point — this is *much* too complicated a task for such a *short* paper as this. I'm *not*, after all, an editor. I'm — well, I'm just an *amateur*. And besides, I've got this page limit.

In fine, you can't know quite *everything* about Chough by climbing to the top of my little tower. At least it's little as constituted *at present*. (But know that I have *big* plans.) In any case, rest assured that behind each and every nonsensical derviation lie a *thousnd* such nice disintctions.

ꙮ

While we're in Italy . . . The editing of character names in *The Naming of the Shrew* shows Italians and English misunderstanding each other's c. It's a funny story, and it won't take a moment. (There's *lots* of time yet.)

Ariosto's *I suppositi* (1509) was adapted for English by George Gascoigne as *Supposes* (1566). The Englishman invented a mute servant, *Petrucio* whose name appears only in the *dramatis-personae* list and in one stage direction.

Shakespere seems to have drawn part of his *Shrew* plot from Gascoigne's play. And some suppose he also found there the name of his protagonist, *Petruchio*. But how does one prove the idea — that Shakespear saw *Petrucio* and wrote *Petruchio*? And how, in any case, did Shakspeare pronounce this *Petruchio*? More to the point, how do *you* pronounce it don't read the next sentence until you have answered the question in this one. OK?
                    OK?   Did you? Well **do** it, then!
                        Thank you. Now, how did you sound that *-chio*? One syllable? Two? And the consonant? [č]? Or [k]?
    Introducing Brian Morris. (The *Arden* editor should know.)[36]

> The name Petruchio must be pronounced with the 'ch' as in
> English 'much'; never as 'Petrukkio'.

But why? And how many syllables must we always count? And how many must we never count?
    Speaking of their Editorial Principles, Wells and Taylor, in their Compete Oxford edition, say that

> Foreign-language ... names are normally presented in their
> modern equivalents (e.g. Anthonio, Petruchio, and Iachimo
> become Antonio, Petruccio, and Giacomo).

Note that *-chi-* occurs in two of these old forms, *Petruchio* and *Iachimo*. Its modernization in one case (to *-cci-*) sounds [č ...] in Italian, and in the other (to *-co-*) sounds [k ...]. It is not easy, therefore, to say how *-chi-* in a folio spelling was or is to be pronounced. How does Arden know?[37]
    To say that *Petruccio* is the modern equivalent of *Petruchio* is a dubious statement. Who's to say that Shakespear could pronounce or spell contemporary Italian names? How smart was he? If he simply "got it wrong", the editor is not modernizing, but correcting — and surely that's not equivalent.[38]
    And who's to say that Shakespere did not merely invent an Italian *sort* of name? Like *Borachio*. Not exactly a familiar name — not a name, in fact, and therefore hard to find its modern equivalent in [č] or [k]. It seems to be cooked up out of a late Romance word for a military-style canteen: French *bourache*, Italian *borraccia*, Spanish *borracha* — and there is also the cognate Spanish word for a "drunk", *borracho*. If we see the spelling of *Borachio* as Spanish, we say [č]; if we see it as Italian, we say [k]. Is it Italian? *Much Ado* is set in Messina, after all. But, as *this* Messina is populated with the likes of *Don Pedro*, whose *Peter* is clearly not the Italian *Petruccio* (or *Petruchio*), how does one know? The editorial *Petruccio* may merely substitute the reflex of a *real* name for a Shakspearean neologism, and so smudge the line between

those olde equivalents, reality and fancie. Then how would we separate editors from artists, who are always smudging this very line? *There's* a question for you: How *would* you separate editors from artists?

Certainly, the Oxford notion of equivalency is not applied systematically. In today's Rome, one hears not that old name *Iulius Caesar*, but *Giulio Cesare*. The Oxford editor does not normally present these modern equivalents, although ancient Rome has grown to be a modern city — or even *Jules*, although the play is mostly in English, a modern language. Nor does he antique Shakespere's *Marc Antony* to M A R C V S · A N T O N I V S, to make it consistently ancient Roman. In other words, he allows Latin and English naming to coexist in Shakespear's Renaissance idiom, although such a mixture was anachronistic in the author's time, and is anachronistic in ours. Anachronism is Shakespearian. Got it? So, why do the Oxford editors normalize in one instance and retain the abnormal in another, when both normality and abnormality are Shakspearian and artistic?

Stanley Wells' notes to *Shrew* state that Shakespere's

'Petruchio' clearly represents the Italian name[39]

— and thus he offers *Petruccio* in modern-spelling (though he does retain *Petruchio* in the original-spelling edition,[40] because it's   well, because it's original. (Maybe it's even Shaksperian!) No doubt Carlo Rusconi knew an original Italian name when he saw one. (Carlo was Italian.) His 1838 translation of *Shrew* offers *Petrucchio* — with an extra *c*, but still with the *h* that keeps a preceding *c* hard. Baskervill, Heltzel and Nethercot's 1934 edition of *Supposes* reconfigures Gascoigne's *Petrucio* as *Petruchio* — in deference, one supposes, to a Shakespearean standard (the very one Oxford is dismantling). In other words, editors set up various standards in other authors, other eras and other countries, and busy themselves like money changers. *Much* work to be done. Much *good* work. But what does it all have to do with art? What does it have to do with historical understanding? And what does it *not* have to do with packaging?

Consider Beaumont and Fletcher's response to *The Taming of the Shrew* — *The Womans Prize, or the Tamer Tamed*, as it appears in their first folio (1647). One of Shakspeare's names, *Bianca*, is repeated there, but with a remarkable change of spelling: *Byancha*. Another of Shakespere's names, *Petruchio*, is repeated with a remarkable conservation of spelling: *Petruchio*. If the wacky *-ch-* spelling in *Byancha* can be pronounced [k] — or do you *really* suppose Beaumont and Fletcher pronounced it [č]? — why can't the *-ch-* in *Petruchio* be pronounced [k]?

And what about Middleton's rather Portuguese-looking *Brancha* in *Women Beware Women* (1657), which is based on the life of Bianca Capello?[41]

And what about John Lacey's adaptation, *Sauny the Scot, or The Taming of the Shrew*, first performed in 1667? *Biancha* again![42]

And what about the name Zan*ch*e in Webster's *The White Deuil*, printed
in 1612? Should we Arden? —

> The name Zanche must be pronounced with the 'ch' as in
> English 'much'; never as 'Zankke'.

Well, if you insist — but the text also spells it *Zanke*.[43]

Compare the editorial treatment of the various folio forms of another
character's name in *Shrew*: *Katerina, Katherina, Katerine, Katherine*. Here the
editor *standardizes* to the 2- or 3-syllable *Katherine*; but when a 4-syllable
Katerina or *Katherina* is needed to fill out a folio pentameter, he standardizes
to *Katherina*. There are standards, and there are standards.

Now, that vowel on the end of Katherina Minola's first name is not very
English-looking, is it? Perhaps

> 'Katherina' clearly represents the Italian name, 'Caterina'.

— except Italians don't really have a k, or an h in the middle of the name, or
that English soft th [θ]). So, there you have it. What seems to the editor to
be an unItalian spelling of the male protagonist's name is clearly to be
altered to an Italian spelling; but the unItalian spelling of the female protagonist's first name clearly is not. (Did they tell you it's a sexist play?)

In altering the name to *Petruccio*, is the editor appealing to *mimesis*? —
the play is set in Italy, so everything should look Italian? Well, what about
the servants, Nathaniel, Joseph, Philip and — and especially Peter? Try to
make *his* name look Italian, and it'll interfere with the protagonist's? No,

> 'Peter' clearly represents the English name, 'Peter'.

Mimesis isn't everything in editorial theory. Or unity of place. Some of
these Italian servants just have to be left English. Besides if everybody
spoke Italian, who would understand? Only wops would come. The play
is in *English*; for this we have Shakspear's authority. You see, you must
remember that the play is also a *construct*. Not *just* mimesis, but a construct
as well. Just as we can have two forms of *Katherina*'s name for reasons of
metrics (and, well,   'not-metrics'), we can have two forms of *Peter*'s name
to differentiate characters on the stage (*differance*). And this creates *subtlety*
— and subtlety, why that's the name of our editorial game. Once the text is
normalized — look, four names for one character is ridiculous, two is all you
need in this world, for prose and verse — *then* you can have a free fight of
signifiers. Four to two ... then *infinite* subtlety. Economically. Believe me,
it'll sell.

Let me show you what I mean in my Ox ford edition of *Shrew*. Take this
line, 2.1.71. You see I've altered it to the Italian name it clearly represents.

Saving your tail, Petruccio, I pray.

Now (and this is subtle) — How many English readers do you think realize (I mean *consciously* realize) that the Italian name *Petruccio* has only 3 syllables — [pɛ-**tru**-čo]? Go ahead, try it. Don't be afraid of the International Phonetic Alphabet: [pɛ-**tru**-čo]. (Was it Byron called it that smooth bastard Latin?) Good. But say it that way and the line is *crippled*. Voilà. *These* are the very things that we editors have to know to do our job right. Most English people are *naturally* going to get it right. It is comnon sense to us English. We don't *know* that the Italians don't pronounce the i, nor do we need to know. (Listen to the actors in the BBC TV production. Four syllables to a man. Well *that*'s the indomitable English for you, ethneccentric to a man.) But editors do, you see. I have to *know* this shit. In Italian the i just says that the c before it is soft. (I hope you won't think I'm "patronizing" you to tell you this *simplest* fact about Italian.) [pɛ-**tru**-či-o] — why that's not Italian for *Peter*, is it? The modern Italian name is only *three* syllables. Are you clear on this now, because I've explained it fully? But the average uniⁱ-formed Englishman, why, they'll drag in 4 syllables every time, won't they? — one, two, three, four — either because they don't know Italian well, or they are remembering Shakspeare's *Petruchio* (however you say it), which does have 4 syllables in our long and venerable tradition in EngliWell, we've been saying it long enough, it's English now — a good reason to **change** it, then, *because the play is set in Italy!!*) So, do you see how subtle the editorial understanding ofEditors have to know to project the Italian *look* on the page. A kind of mimetic verislimiitude: *Petruccio*. But when it comes to *saying* it (and plays are *for performance*, not for reading, you know), you have to utter as many syllables as Shakespear's *Petruchio* does — 1 - 2 - 3 - 4. *Four*, right? Pe-tru-chi-o. The man could *count*, after all. He was a *poet*.

Sa-ving your tale, Pe-tru-cci-o, I pray = 10 syllables

This is what editors have to be on top of. It clearly represents Italian, but it *isn't* Italian. (That's the beauty of fiction.) Not everyone rises to this Editorial Level. It's a lonely life. Many are called, but few are chosen. Dropped by the wayside, the lot of them. Laced up their boots in the grey of morning. Marched the whole day, through all kinds of weather, steadily worsening, straight up Parnassus. Endured endless privation and sacrifice. No toil and sacrifice too great for them. Idealist lads to the core. Every one a man of his own ideals. Individuals. Why, they'd have climbed the last mile *barefoot*, with nary a thought for themselves, so great was their dedication. Oxford. Cambridge. But when it came to the final assault, could they take textual matters in their own bare hands? could they face the exercise of cold power? could they take charge, like men, each alone, far from base camp? could they create? Could they? No, they couldn't. They could not. Failures, the lot of them. And where are they now, palely loitering, sucking the dummy tits of their own refined sensibilities? If you're going to edit, I say, *edit*. You can't be an editor just by leaving the text as it "is". *I* certainly don't. *That*'s not editing. That's not the future of our textual endeavour. That's not the future of Shakespeare scholarship. You have to grow up *some* day. So, grow up.

Anyway, the average English reader, not fully conscious, maybe, but that's where we editors come in, we taylor it to their prejudices, and everything comes out right. Four syllables. Some readers, especially Italians are going to see an Italian name and *pesto* — they'll think they know where they are — home — and they'll just plug in three syllables, the dumb arseholesClearly the play is *crippled* with just nine syllables. I'm not saying anything against Italians. You need ten. Some of my best friends come from *questa bella paese*. (And some of my best friends don't edit.) But what do they know about *English* metrics? No, this is what I've done. Editorially. You've got to *see* three Italian syllables (Pe-tru-ccio), but *pronounce* four, the *English* way (Pe-tru-cci-o). Because the verse is Pentameter (Greek for 5). Just be sure to pronounce it [č], though, because clearly it represents the *Italian* name — but with an extra syllable, the *English* way of saying it, pentameter, because it'sExcuse me for interrupting. Did you know that Doctor Stanley Wells also edits *Shakespeare Survey*? The *Survey* is England's premier Shakspeare journal. Did you also know that if you want to submit to submit an essay for publication in *Shakespeare Survey*, it should be keyed to his modern-spelling Compete Oxford Shakespeare (1986)? "Unless otherwise indicated". *That's right*. Just read the instructions at the front of eachNo, no, it's just a little Random Survey I'm conducting. Just wanted to know how many of you good people — *before* you otherwise indicSorry toI'm *very* sorry to interrupt, I   Excuse me. Please carry on.

And you thought Cough was hard?
^

Hi, it's me again, Randalino? Is the coast clear? My tower — remember my little Cloud-capped Tower? — well, it dealt purely with changes *internal* to Chough. We are also able to characterize this nonsense in its *external* relations. You know — with *English*. To do this, we'll need to consider meter. So, we'll have to break for lunch a little later than I said, OK? This won't take long, though. I *know* you're hungry. I am too. (Besides — my page limit, remember?)

Shakspear's speeches are highly rhythmic, right? Their graphic representations in quartos and folios, however, can often mislead. The speeches can most aptly be characterized in potential: as *metricable* (in reading) rather than actually *measured out* graphically (in print). In the early texts, verse can parade as prose, and prose as verse. When the 18th-century editors took upon themselves the simple task of relineating the early quartos and folios to specify metrical values, they offered us a pretty Kessel of Fisch. For they didn't allow that the written forms of Chough might sometimes merely be promptings for nonsensical *ad libido* utterances by the actors — as unmetrical as, say, stage directions, with which they might be close cousins.

Here are several lines from the first folio.

> *Par.* O ranſome, ranſome,
> Do not hide mine eyes.
> *Inter. Boskos thromuldo boskos.*
> *Par.* I know you are the *Muskos* Regiment,
> And I ſhall looſe my life for want of language.
> If there be heere German or Dane, Low Dutch,
> Italian, or French, let him ſpeake to me,
> Ile diſcouer that, which ſhal vndo the Florentine.

(We'll begin with the complexities of our own metrics, before we head into those of Chough, and, crucially, of their combination.)

However short, the first two lines appear as verse. For they are not justified right, and they each begin with a capital letter (the second being the first letter of a verb in the middle of a sentence). As each line has five syllables, it is not surprising, really, that they have been ranged as one line since Pope's 1723 edition. And rightly so, you might think. But Hunter, the Arden editor (who also unifies them) suggests that the
shortness
of the folio lines may have allowed time for stage business![44]

?

(Did you know that? Did you know that the graphic medium of playscripts was *sensitive* that way? (*We* sure didn't). In his view, lineation is not purely a litterary concern. *That's* what's was going down in New Haven in 1959.)

For the moment, let me pass over the following (Chough) line, to turn to Parolles' next speech. Each of his lines is decasyllabic, except the last, which has 12 syllables, if we pronounce "Florentine" with 2 syllables, or 13, if we pronounce it with 3. Both readings are too long to allow this iambic line to be pentameter. Perhaps it's prose? (A prose line would also begin with a capital — and "I" always begins with a capital, right? It might be prose.)

The line did not change until 1767, when Capell tucked the first word back onto the previous line. As that line was 10 syllables before, it would have stretched to 11, had he not deleted the word "or". Good. *That* kept things even. Odd, rather. (11 is odd.) Very good, then. (Look, it was only one word. Just a monosyllable. So, why make a fuss?) At the beginning of the next (altered) line, Capell changed "discouer" to "Discover", signaling, with the D, a definitely verse line. It pushes 12 syllables; but pronouncing "Florentine" as 2, you can reign it back to a not too exceptional 11. Subtle?

> *Italian, French,* let him ſpeak to me, I'll
> Diſcover that which ſhall undo the *Florentine.*

The next two editions, by Johnson and by Johnson-Steevens-Reed, sided one with the folio, one with Capell. (Maybe Johnson got over-ruled.) It was Malone who broke new ground — not by putting the front end of the line, "Ile" above, as Capell had done, but expanding it where he found it in the folio, to "I will", and by turning the other end of the line under (I'll photo-quote his later, 1790, edition, which is to hand.)

> I will diſcover that which ſhall undo
> The Florentine.

— leaving a sure pentameter verse, followed by what — a verse fragment?

My point in detailing editorial exercises in *English* metrics is that the immediately following speech begins in *Chough.* The big question is, "Will Shakespeare's English metrics, so deftly quarried by the 18th-century editorial tradition from the unpromising rock of the folio, dovetail (don't mind my metaphor) with the metrics, yet unexplored — or better still — yet *unfledged,* of Chough?" If it will, then we can *read* how the Fathers of Shakespeare editing actually *measured* Shakspeare's nonsense. (If anyone's an expert on that topic, it'll be these Fathers.) Look at the ground we've covered already: phonetic ambiguity (a), morphology (b), grammar (c), syntax and phrasing (d) ... and now (e) *metrics!* Once deemed closed, the Book of Chough may well prove more open than one would ever of thought.

Here, then, is the following speech in the folio.

> *Int. Boſkos vaⱷvado,* I ⱴnderſtand thee, & can ſpeake
> thy tongue : *Kerelybonto* ſir, betake thee to thy faith, for
> ſeuenteene ponyards are at thy boſome.

No editor took exception to its seemingly prosy nature till Capell,

> 1. S. *Boſkos vauvado :* —
> I underſtand thee, and can ſpeak thy tongue : —
> *Kerelybonto :* — Sir,
> Betake thee to thy faith, for ſeventeen poniards
> Are at thy bosom.

who forged — is it a 5-syllable line in "*Boskos vauvado :* —" ? and a 6-syllable one in the fusion of Chough and English: *Kerelybonto :* — Sir,"? One might think at first that the dashes indicated broken verses, but as they occur only where Chough and English interface ('meet') in a speech, they seem merely to be a buffer between tongues. (Otherwise you might be halfway into a Chough word, before you realized it wasn't one of ours.) He was followed by both Johnson and Johnson-Steevens-Reed this time, and the same line- ation and dashes can be seen in modern editions (like the recent Compete Oxford). Malone reverted to prose. But Boswell's Malone followed Capell. To be sure, this 18th-century struggle between verse and prose animates editing to this very day. 18th-century editing, therefore, is *scarcely* irrelevant to us. (Someone should do a book on this.)

Now, here's where it gets interesting. Boswell also took over a part line in Malone, "The Florentine" (which looks like prose there), and Capell's part line (also seemingly prose), "*Boskos vauvado :* —." But evidently both constitute *verse* now,

The Florentine.
1 SOLD. *Boskos vauvado :*——

— because the latter phrase is indented! (Do you see that?) This empty space signals that the two part-lines are in the *same* metrical scheme. Subtle?

What are we to do with this unity, this sudden *éclaircissement*? If, for a change, we give "Florentine" its maximum of 3 syllables, and stretch *vauvado* to 4, *va-u-va-do* or *ua-vu-a-do* or *va-u-ua-do* &c, we can fill out a pentameter. (Such rhythms in this Chough word may come as a surprise, for I imagine that most of you have been pronouncing it to yourselves with just 3 syllables, *vau-va-do*. But you see how you can correct ignorant first impressions, if you read really closely in the editorial tradition.) There are some who might be unwilling to go this route, always *someone* in a crowd who is content to leave a 9-syllable line of verse, or an 8-syllable one (if we pronounce "Florentine" with 2 syllables). But what do they know? Verses that short do start to look like prose. And what is Shakespeare, if not the eternal *poet*? a true *pentameter* poet. And *nine* syllables isn't *penta*meter.

In Capell and Boswell there follows in the next line a full, masculine, English iambic pentameter — but let me quote the whole context in both editors, so you don't have to take my analysis all piece-meal, and so you can make up your own mind on these complex questions, OK? Capell first.

> *Italian, French,* let him ſpeak to me, I'll
> Diſcover that which ſhall undo the *Florentine.*
>   1. *S. Boſkos vauvado :* __
> I underſtand thee, and can ſpeak thy tongue : __
> *Kerelybonto :* __ Sir,
> Betake thee to thy faith, for ſeventeen poniards
> Are at thy boſom,
>   *PAR.* Oh, oh!
>   1. *S.* Pray, pray, pray. __
> *Manca revanta dulche.*
>   1. *L. Oſceorbi dulcos volivorco.*

Italian, or French, let him speak to me,
I will discover that which shall undo
The Florentine.
 1 *Sold.*   *Boskos vauvado :*——
I understand thee, and can speak thy tongue :——
Kerelybonto :——Sir,
Betake thee to thy faith, for seventeen poniards
Are at thy bosom.
 Par.   Oh !

sc. i.   THAT ENDS WELL.   429

 1 *Sold.*   O, pray, pray, pray.——
Manka revania dulche.
 1 *Lord.*   *Oscorbi dulchos volivorca.*

In Boswell, what follows is another mixture of Chough and English:

 Kerelybonto : — — Sir,

which, at 6 syllables, seems light verse indeed — even with the weighty double dash. (Perhaps it's prose?) It is followed by another, all-English line, that compensates with heaviness, for it has as many as 13 syllables or, more satisfactorily, as few as 11 (if "seventeen" and "poniards" have only 2 syllables each). (Maybe it's verse? It *does* begin with a capital letter.)

 Anyway, in what happens next, a Boswell leaves a Capell behind, fusing three prose speeches (you'd guess they were prose in the folio or in Capell) into one line of *verse.* Check out the indents.

 Are at thy bosom.
  PAR.   Oh !
  1 *SOLD.*   O, pray, pray, pray.— —

And isn't that *grand?* Now, while one is attending a performance, it can be difficult (I know) to conceive of these lines as constituting a pentameter, especially if the actors are violently shouting out their lines simultaneously, instead of waiting their turns. (I mean, you know actors? They'll take Chough as a cue to *ad lib* or something.) So, it's nice really to have a script that gives the correct Shakesperean form of dramatic speech (scripts are *for production* after all) to fall back on when you get home late from the theatre (say), and after you've had something from the fridge, left-over ricotta cheese-cake, a diet-coke, maybe, chips, beer, a cinnamon muffin — and you need to get clear on the little things that — well the little things on that Teleological World of the Boards, that just went by you too fast because maybe you're not smart enough out there in the stalls to get all the details of this *big* picture. Besides, it was late in the show, & you probably needed to pee. It's OK, though, because I didn't understand Shakspear first time round either. I wasn't *born* an editor. Editors aren't *born*, you know, they're *made*. Also try not drinking so much just before curtain. Or suppose you are an actor, and don't know the play yet and don't want to blurt out, like some jerk, "Oh! —", the wrong way in rehearsals like a jerk, it's very helpful (and this is where actors should thank editors — and readers too, readers should thank editors, because they'll do something *just as wrong* as the actors, any day), it's very helpful to know that Shakspear didn't mean your "Oh! —" as some kind of Existential SOLO for Christ's sake, but as integrated into the Community of Human Speech. Look, in one and the same measure, your "Oh! —" is surrounded on the one side by "Are at thy bosom." and surrounded in the same pentameter measure on the other hand by "O, pray, pray, pray. — —". I mean, *look*, Are you alone? No, you're not alone. You are not alone. And all that can be shown so subtly by lineation, and by what's indented. And by what's not indented. And by poetry. It's not just prose. (It's poetry after all.) And it's the *graphics* that tells you all this, so you really have to pay attention to the graphics. *Just* what I've been saying all along. *Pay attention to the damned graphics!*

Now, and this is my point, understanding the principles of Shake-spearian verse here in English (Step A, "The First Step") prepares us for one of the crowning editorial breaktroughs in the interpretation of Chough (Step B, "The Final Step"). Boswell's next two lines, as the indentation of the second shows, constitute merely *one* line of verse.

> *Manka revania dulche.*
> 1 LORD.   *Oscorbi dulchos volivorca.*

Now, because the paper's almost over, I don't have time to point out the really subtle differentiations — graphic, phonetic — of Boswell's *revania* from the folio's *reuania*, or his *Oʃcorbi dulchos* from the folio's *Oʃcorbidulchos*, or even his *volivorca* from the folio's *voliuorco* (any more than I can pause to comment on Capell's *revanta* or his *Oʃceorbi dulcos*, with it sextra syllable and Italianate dropped-h, and all, to make 10 syllables in that line, or on his giving the "Oh!" by "*Inter*" (Capell and Boswell calls him "1. *S.*" or "1 *SOLD*", of course) to "*PAR.*" (that man of words), thus leaving only 3 syllables of English ("Pray, pray, pray. —" followed by only 7 in Chough (Capell follows the second folio's *revanta*) in the "*Lo.E.*" line (which, of course Capell gives to "1. *L.*" and Boswell to "1 *LORD.*") and — and **BINGO!**

$$3 + 7 = 10.$$

Because the main point's the *meter*. If there were more time I could really spell this out — But listen, you can hear the caterers getting ready in the hallway (so I'll hurry now) — but Boswell's *revania* could easily be 3 or 4 syllables, and so deliver a line of 16 or 17 syllables in all. You get the picture, don't you? (Don't mind that racket in the hall. It's just the caterers setting up for the buffet.) If we remember that any *v* could really be a *u* in disguise in *revania* and *volivorca* (remember that's how the paper started?), we could squeeze as many as 5 syllables from *re-u-an-i-a* and 6 from *u-o-li-u-or-co*, and so could drive that number as high as 21, with 9 syllables in the first part, and 11 in the second. Sounds like a double-decker to me. A double-decker with a feminine ending. More is feminine, like chromosomes. What a din. I don't know about you, but, God, it makes me hungry.

I suppose Conservatives might feel that that would be going beyond the warrant of Boswell's *v*. But the Liberals, they might go even farther; if you interpret this line through the *continental* reflexes. Just check the Tower — because Shakspeare isn't *just* for the English. So, *Manka* could have 1 syllable (*Mank*) or 2; *reuania* 3 or 4; *dulche* 1 (*dulce*, for example — think of it as seaweed — with a silent *e*) or 2 (*dultschos*); *Oſcorbidulchos* 3 (*Oscorbis*) to 7 (*Oskeoribi dulchos*); and *voliuorco* 3 (*volworko*) to 5 (*volivorea*). Depending on one's Procrustean style, the edited line could yield, *on authority*, not only the upper limit of 20, but a lower limit of 11 — which is coming close to the traditional length of a Shaksperean feminine line! — more traditional than "Ile discouer that which shall vndo the Florentine", which was a verse line, wasn't it? — an alexandrine, wasn't it?, though with the potential to be a pentameter if you put part of the line up (Capell) or down (Malone) and/or explore the option of pronouncing "Florentine" or "Ile" with two syllables each. (And keeping
stage business to a mini-
mum.)

Yes, here we behold the extension of numbers into nonsense — an epiphany, really. Intellect of a very high order. Very high. I'm sure it can *like the* be successfully argued with a little more research, not only of advanced *Timaeus* Chough scholarship, in particular, but also of Shakspere's nonsense, in general. You'll see Boswell's long metrical unit surviving in the Arden edition or Dover Wilson's Cambridge edition. But Taylor's recent Compete Oxford edition accepts Capell's earlier relineation, not that he *says* that's where he got it, because it's commo nsense, really, which gives mutlicultural *tr* Chough-English lines of only 5 or 6 syllables. Depending. Clearly, editors don't *totally* agree on this matter yet. More editions will be necessary. (It's OK, though. I'm leaving extra room at the bottom of our Tower on page 31.)

Food's coming. So I'll really hurry through the next section. But without sacrificing intelligibility! You'll see.

❦

Shakespere's nonsense is — it's funny, don't you think? I mean, in and of itself? Funny. And the nonsensical, mistaken editorial versions of his nonsense are also funny? Though they can amount, of course, to the dumbest scholarship (for which the angels weep), they do sit well as comic

> Int: He calls for the tortures. What will you say without 'em
> Par. I will confess what I know, without constraint; If you pinch me like a pasty, I can say no more.
> Int. Bosko Chimurcho.
> 2 Lord. Biblibindo chicurmurco!
> Int: You are a merciful General! — Our General bids you answer to what I shall ask you out of a note.
> Par. And truly, be ~

invention (if only one can get as high as the gods, who must look down and laugh at this latter-day instability of Shakespear's text). And comic invention — isn't that the name of the game? (Did I forget to tell you that *All's Well* is a comœdy?) It may be exactly where we fail as individual scholars that we are collectively true to the spirit of nonsense in this play.

NONSENSE

The play's the thing. What *is* the Spirit of Nonsense? What might the text of this play look like if we stopped aping scholarship and just *played* straight for it?

Displayed across the top of this opening are facing pages from the earliest extant prompt-book of *All's Well*, a 1773 Bell edition, perhaps used in Covent Garden in the 1780's.[45] The cancelled letterpress atop the recto must reflect an even earlier staging. It reports a phrase you won't find in the folio: "*Damabous news*". Apparently, earlier actors had taken Shakspeare's Chough as a license to invent their own. Doesn't his new diction offers food for thought to those scholars who regard Chough as Indo-European: for it translates into the sound-alike (and therefore cognate?) English that follows.

Dam	-a	-bous	news.
Down	on	your	knees.

(This seems to be the first edition (and one of the very few) ever, to offer *critical* commentary on Chough. The footnote to the elided phrase

Bosko, chimarcho biblibindo chicurmurco

— or to

Basko, chimarcho biblibindo chicurmurco

ALL's WELL, THAT ENDS WELL. 28ɪ

Ber. Releaſe him, and bring him forward.

Int. *Damabous news*---you muſt down on your knees.

Par. O dear !

Int. *Partatorturoſſa*---he calls for the torture.

Par. I will confeſs what I know, without it; if you pinch me like a paſty, I can ſay no more.

Int. *Boſko, chimurcho biblibindo chicurmurco,** a merciful general---you muſt anſwer to what I ſhall aſk you of note.

(as it appeared in 1778) reads, "The sonorous jargon uttered in this scene, to rouse the timidity of *Parolles,* is well introduced and extremely laughable.")

Other things to observe: Restoration of the folio version of the dialogue can be seen in pen and ink atop the verso, an interleaf. Capital *C* in *Chimurcho* looks very conservative, doesn't it? And so do the endings *-cho* and *-co,* though *biblibindo* can't be earlier than, and may just come from, F3.

Here is a preparation copy said to have been made by William Winter for Augustin Daly c1882.[46]

39

Enter Soldiers, *with* PAROLLES,

Bertram. A plague upon him! muffled! he can say nothing of me; hush, hush !

ɪ *Lord.* Hoodman comes ! Portotartarosa.

ɪ *Soldier.* He calls for the tortures; what will you say without 'em ?   ɪɪɪ

Parolles. I will confess what I know without constraint; if ye pinch me like a pasty, I can say no more.

ɪ *Soldier.* Bosko chimurcho.

ɪ *Lord.* Boblibindo chicurmurco.

ɪ *Soldier.* You are a merciful general.—Our general bids you answer to what I shall ask you out of a note.

Compared to the foregoing edition, the Chough of this one is only a bit off the folio; *Portotartarosa,* for example, *is* one word, though it does lack an s. (That *Cambridge* problem again.) And *chimurcho* does not begin with a capital. (That's Capell's fault; he was a Cambridge man too.) The annotator's Chough, by contrast, is very inventive. *Incho Chincho* comes after *Portotartarosa;* after *Bosko chimurcho* comes *Smoko Loko.* Isn't this in the spirit?

The most outrageously erotic of all the nonsensical prompt annotations

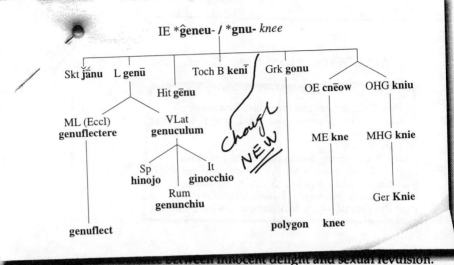

Recent prompt-books and videos offer vivid evidence of nonsensical creation. The shooting script of the BBC production first broadcast on 4 January 1981 transcribes the Alexander text literally, except that *Boblibindo* appears over an erasure. Unfortunately, since the BBC Written Archives Centre retains only a microfilm, it is impossible to resurrect what was erased here.[47] The video, however, reveals unscripted utterances elsewhere: something like *akaravan moo-jay*, *most-woo*, and *fungo mingo*.

The two promptbooks for B. Iden Payne's 1935 Stratford-upon-Avon production show many antiphonal repetitions of Chough dialogue.[48] Look how a speech, ① (opposite), is transformed in one of the books (6065).

> *All.* Cargo, cargo, cargo, villianda par corbo,
>   cargo.
>   2nd
>   Sold
> 1st Sold. *All.* Cargo, cargo, cargo, villianda par corbo,
>   AL.L   cargo. **cargo. cargo** .

Besides investing old Chough sounds with new fury, this production transforms grammatical constructions and creates new vocabulary. The period in *First Sold*'s "Manka revania dulche.", ②, changes to a question mark. Without any change of diction or punctuation, *Sec. Lord*'s assertion, "Oscorbidulchos volivorco", thus becomes an *answer*.[49] In dialogue added in two lines of ink in the margin, this answer is queried by 1st Sold, then modified by 1st Lord, whose "Volicorco" proves the final word on the matter — for, in a third, pencilled, line, All repeat the 1st Lord's answer.[50]

> 1st Sold: Volivorco?
> 1st Lord. Volicorco.
>   All: "

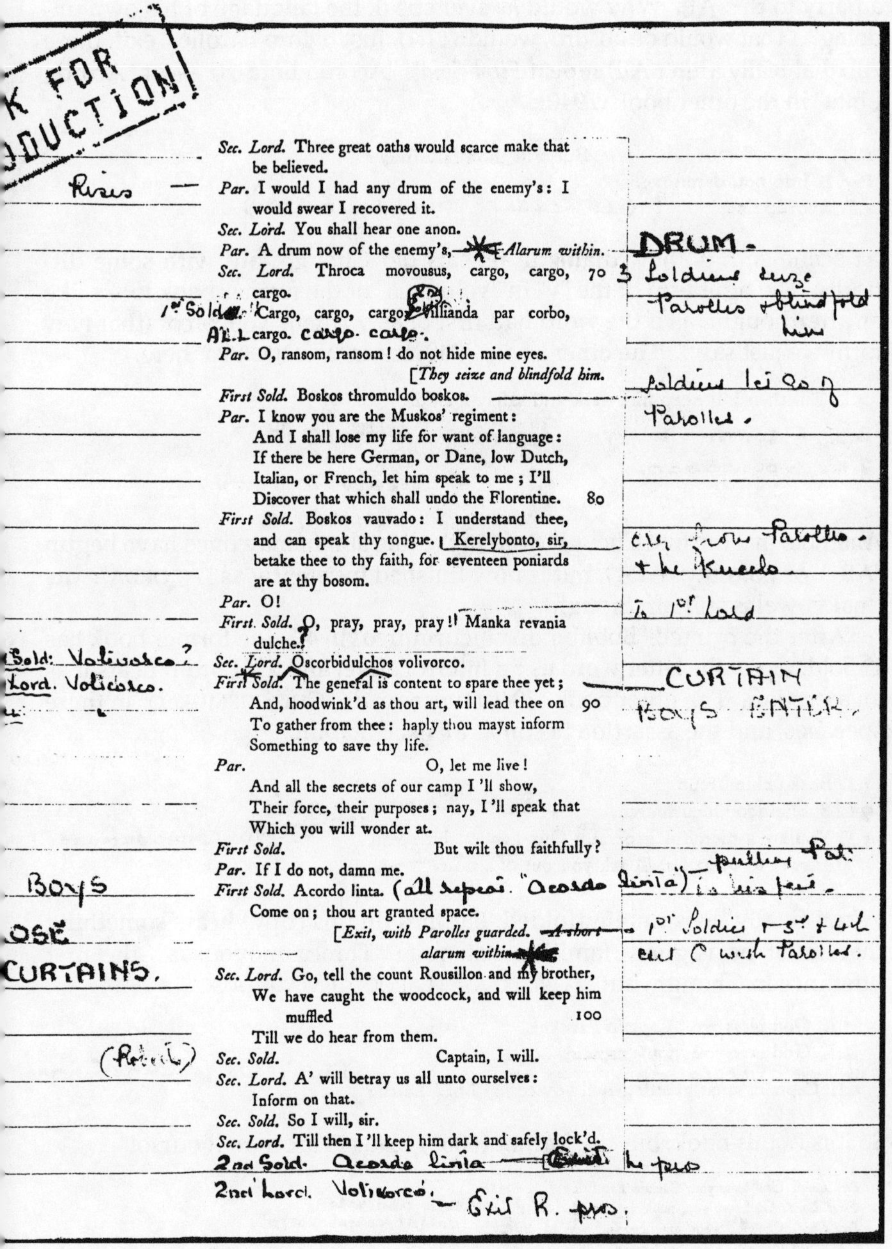

Rises

Sec. Lord. Three great oaths would scarce make that
be believed.
Par. I would I had any drum of the enemy's: I
would swear I recovered it.
Sec. Lord. You shall hear one anon.
Par. A drum now of the enemy's, — *Alarum within.*
Sec. Lord. Throca movousus, cargo, cargo, 70
cargo.
1ˢᵗ Sold. Cargo, cargo, cargo, villianda par corbo,
All. cargo. cargo. cargo.
Par. O, ransom, ransom! do not hide mine eyes.
[*They seize and blindfold him.*
First Sold. Boskos thromuldo boskos.
Par. I know you are the Muskos' regiment:
And I shall lose my life for want of language:
If there be here German, or Dane, low Dutch,
Italian, or French, let him speak to me; I'll
Discover that which shall undo the Florentine. 80
First Sold. Boskos vauvado: I understand thee,
and can speak thy tongue. Kerelybonto, sir,
betake thee to thy faith, for seventeen poniards
are at thy bosom.
Par. O!
First Sold. O, pray, pray, pray! Manka revania
dulche.
Sec. Lord. Oscorbidulchos volivorco.
First Sold. The general is content to spare thee yet;
And, hoodwink'd as thou art, will lead thee on 90
To gather from thee: haply thou mayst inform
Something to save thy life.
Par. O, let me live!
And all the secrets of our camp I'll show,
Their force, their purposes; nay, I'll speak that
Which you will wonder at.
First Sold. But wilt thou faithfully?
Par. If I do not, damn me.
First Sold. Acordo linta. (*all repeat* "Acordo linta")
Come on; thou art granted space.
[*Exit, with Parolles guarded.* *A short*
alarum within.
Sec. Lord. Go, tell the count Rousillon and my brother,
We have caught the woodcock, and will keep him
muffled 100
Till we do hear from them.
Sec. Sold. Captain, I will.
Sec. Lord. A' will betray us all unto ourselves:
Inform on that.
Sec. Sold. So I will, sir.
Sec. Lord. Till then I'll keep him dark and safely lock'd.
2nd Sold. Acordo linta —
2nd Lord. Volivorco. — Exit R.

Handwritten margin notes left:
Bold: Volivorco?
Lord. Volivorco.

BOYS
OSE
CURTAINS.

(Robert)

Handwritten margin notes right:
DRUM
3 Soldiers seize
Parolles + blindfold him ①
Soldiers let go of
Parolles.
cry from Parolles
+ he kneels.
To 1ˢᵗ Lord ②
CURTAIN
BOYS ENTER
pulling Par is his feet ③
1ˢᵗ Soldier + 3ʳᵈ + 4th exit C with Parolles.
④

All? It would be absurd, though, to suppose that Parolles himself would be a party to this All. Why would *he* ever speak the language of his own un-doing? (That would be absurd, wouldn't it?) Just before Parolles' exit, these All (that really aren't All) repeat *First Sold*'s "Acordo linta", ③,— or "Acorda Linta" in the other book (7940):

> 1.*S.*   But wilt thou faithfully ?
> *Par.* If I do not, damn me.
> 1.*S.* Acordo linta.   (all repeat "Acorda Linta)

At scene-end, ④, new dialogue repeats old Chough, but with some dif-ficulty. The right arm of the "v" in "Volivorco" of the former book looks like an afterthought, as if the word had first been written "Volicorco" (that new form we just saw). The other book, 7940, reads "VOLIUORCO" here.

> 2.*L.* Till then I 'll keep him dark and safely lock'd.
> 2 S. Acordia Linta   Extant L pros
> 2 L. Volivorco.   ariv R pros

And note that the first Chough word in the line above may once have begun "AR-" (or possibly "AP-"), but is now finished insistently as "ACORDA". (Its final vowel is still off, though).

After the printed "Boblibindo chicurmurco" in 4.3, the former book has 1st Sold. repeat the latter word as an interrogative, and 2nd Lord repeats it as an assertion. The other book (7940) twice reads "CHIRCURMURCO" in these speeches, and the assertion becomes an exclamation.

> 1.*S.* Bosko chimurcho.
> 2.*L.* Boblibindo chicurmurco.   1st Sold "Chircurmurco"?
> 1.*S.* You are a merciful general. \ Our general bids you   2nd Lord "Chircurmurco"!
>   answer to what I shall ask you out of a note.

When finally he is unblindfolded, Parolles (in this copy) hears something that must be vaguely familiar: not quite "Throca movousus", the first utterance in Chough, but "THROCO [or "TAROCO"] MAUVOUSO"

> 2.*L.* God bless you, Captain Parolles.
> 1.*L.* God save you, noble captain.
> 1 Sold "Troco Mauvouso   — --- -   Fill: "Carjo. Carjo. Carjo"
> 2.*L.* Captain, what greeting will you to my Lord Lafeu?

So it is in this book; but the former (6065) reads "Throco mavourso!"

> *Sec. Lord.* God bless you, Captain Parolles.
> *First Lord.* God save you, noble captain. ✳ 1st fold: 350 Throco mavourso!   ·up.
> *Sec. Lord.* Captain, what greeting will you to my All. carjo! carjo! carjo!
>   Lord Lafeu? I am for France.

In Tyrone Guthrie's 1959 Stratford-upon-Avon production, the prompt-book attests to hilarious stage business beginning just before Parolles' entrance in 4.1.[51]

The annotated prompt-book text (left column):

2.L..He must think us some band of strangers i' the adversary's entertainment. Now he hath a smack of all neighbouring languages ; therefore we must every one be a man of his own fancy, not to know what we speak one to another ; so we seem to know, is to know straight our purpose : choughs' language, gabble enough, and good enough. As for you, interpreter, you must seem very politic. But couch, ho ! here he comes, ~~to beguile two hours in a sleep, and then to return and sweat the lies he forges~~

Enter Parolles

Par. Ten o'clock. within these three hours 'twill be time enough to go home. What shall I say I have done ? It must be a very plausive invention that carries it : they begin to smoke me ; and disgraces have of late knock'd too often at my door. I find my tongue is

Handwritten margin notes (left): Exts (visual) / ps perch on — / on hardwick.

Handwritten/typed margin notes (right):
X
Woodthorpe replies.
Buck "
Russell replies.
Hawtrey cotinues
Hardwick No.
Hawtrey still continues
then as the others
gather round him
slowly fades, salutes and sits.

In their dialogue, 2. *L.* (Longaville, played by Paul Hardwick) and I. *S.* (the First Soldier, played by Peter Woodthorpe) establish the linguistic aspect of the ambush. At the moment the officer invokes Chough language, the subordinate is prompted to reply — presumably in Chough. He is followed in unscripted speech by two more soldiers, played by David Buck and Robert Russell, who seem to figure out the game fast, but then by another, played by Nicholas Hawtrey, who must be clueless: for he "cotinues" and "still continues" even in the face of his officer's "No", until finally he is quelled by all his mates, acting together.

O, to have heard Hawtrey speak Chough *outlandishly*. But alas, his, like the others' speeches, is not recorded. Though a prompt-book may be for production, a production need not be for a prompt-book. Neither by the book, nor for it, theatre goes its own way — and so does Chough, it seems. (Was I hasty to constrain it as manuage, Joanna? Sorry. Maybe this tongue belongs in the mouth after all? I'll have to rethink it for the final version.)

Before Parolles' entrance, the soldiers scramble for cover.[52]

Hardwick, Woodthorpe, Buck hide in truck ...
Russell in tent vs ps. Hawtrey hides under sacking on truck
Parolles enters ps pit whistling   X to truck goes to sit on Hawtrey changes his
mind — then sits on Hawtrey.

When Parolles eventually moves off, the unfortunate

Hawtrey stands starts long high pitched coughs.

His mates brow-beat him into silence again:

All stands and
slowly circle him, slowly he stops salutes. Hardwick returns salute, he sits again.

Parolles has neither seen nor heard Hawtrey's hacking exit from the sack.
When he goes to sit down on it again, Parolles "does a double-take" — and
sits elsewhere.

Now, Hawtrey's coughing after his ordeal seems involuntary? But there
are other newly-scripted coughs which are played as intentional. For
example, when Parolles enters hooded in 4.3, the prompt-books shows
coughing for Hardwick — cheek by jowl with Shakspearian Choughing.

> Hard: Hoodman comes. *Enter Parolles guarded, and First Soldier* (5).
> Ber. A plague upon him ! muffled ! he can say nothing of
>   me : hush, hush !
> 1.L. Hoodman comes. Portotartarossa.
> 1.S.. He calls for the tortures : what will you say without
>   'em ?
> Par. I will confess what I know without constraint, if
>   ye pinch me like a pasty, I can say no more.
> 1.S. Bosko chimurcho.
> 1.L. Boblibindo chicurmurco. *Hardwick: Coughs.*
> 1.S. You are a merciful general. Our general bids you
>   answer to what I shall ask you out of a note.

And we see more prompted coughing soon thereafter.

> Ber. What shall be done to him ?   X
> 1.L. Nothing, but let him have thanks. Demand of him   Wood: Well, thats set down.
>   my condition, and what credit I have with the Duke.   More Coughs.
> 1.S. Well, thats set down. You shall demand of
>   him, whether one Captain Dumain be i' the camp,
>   a Frenchman ; what his reputation is with the Duke,

One wonders whether *cough* and *Chough* are confused in this book. How
did Guthrie — or how did Maurice Daniels, his stage director — pronounce
these two words? (How do *you* pronounce them?)

The last line of Chough in 4.1, "Acordo linta", is excised, and instead
Wood[thorpe] is directed to cough. (See "84" in the left margin.) Coughing
could *very well* be Choughing here.

> Something to save thy life.
> Par.   O, let me live !
> And all the secrets of our camp I'll show,
> Their force, their purposes ; nay, I'll speak that
> Which you will wonder at.
> 1.S.   But wilt thou faithfully ?
> Par. If I do not, damn me.

> 84 WOOD — COUGHS
> Hardwick Long talk.
> Wood: The general says, come on.

69/ O P Rohh (Trucks)

69 ELXS Q 21 (B·O)
  ORCH Q 14

The next line, "Hardwick Long talk.", is ambiguous. "Long talk.", may seem at first glance to be a stage direction to the actor, Hardwick, that his character, *Long*aville, should talk. But perhaps it calls for a pro*Long*ed talk from Hardwick. Certainly, if he spoke in aside, out of the hearing of both Parolles and the audience, no dialogue would have been required. But it is hard to imagine that such a long *silence* could have added vividly to Parolles' terror; would it not have been more theatrical effective that the (unscripted) "Long talk" should be audible? But, if Hardwick's speech were in English, Woodthorpe's explanation of it to Parolles would not have been necessary. Mustn't the talk have been Long in the *Chough*, then?

In any event, if "Long" means plain "long", the fact that such a lengthy speech should boil down to a mere "come on", as Woodthorpe finally translates it to Parolles (who, one imagines, must have hung fearfully on its every syllable), is simply ludicrous. Parolles would think that Chough is mighty windy.

Somewhat earlier in the scene, prompter's notes actually do specify "More choughs" (*not* coughs, this time) from Woodthorpe, Buck and Russell.

Somewhat apart from these are "more choughs" from Hawtrey. (Is he successful this time?) And finally a "Short Russian prayer". As it is not written down, we cannot know whether "Russian" means the real thing or some Slavic-sounding mumbo jumbo.

Prompter's notes call for general noise and singing here. Parolles is already on his knees, submissive, at this point. But with the prayer, the others kneel too, except Hardwick and Woodthorpe. The latter holds a pencil, of all things, (in place of "seventeen poniards") against Parolles' bosom. Finally even this soldier kneels, leaving only his superior standing. Staging like this evokes liturgy more than ambush — or perhaps liturgy as ambush. (Doesn't each genre have its sacrificial victim?) Parolles, of course, is blind to all of this staginess. But it is plain to us. The metatheatrical staging opens out the metalingustical in Chough.

John Barton's 1967 Stratford-upon-Avon *All's Well* may have taken notes from Guthrie, for it calls for "Russian" half a dozen times in 4.1 and 4.3.[53]

(And the last word of the folio's line, "He must think us some band of strangers", is not struck out, but above it in ink is "Muscovite".)

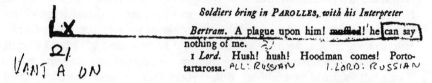

In this next photoquote, Chough loses a *Throca movousus*, but gains an *ONIET* (l. 70) — as if the tormentors respond "OH NO!" to Parolles' assertion, "I know you are of the Muskos' regiment". The termination "-niet" conjures up the Russian for "No" (нет), though the prefix "O-" is not recognizably Russian, and sounds, in fact, raaather English.

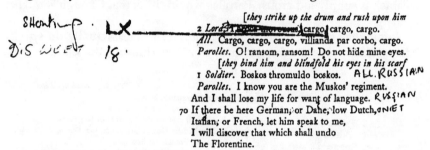

A glance at the prompt-book for Richard Cottrell's 1982 Stratford, Ontario production is useful here. It invokes no Russian, but a video of the production shows soldiers shouting нет in turns, when Parolles asks if they know this language or that. (Guthrie had a major role in the creation of the Canadian Stratford Festival, and his own stagings may well be echoed in Cottrell's.) An unscripted *Fandango, fandango* follows, as the Interpreter silences his mates' reaction to Parolles' promise to undo the Florentine. After "O, pray, pray, pray", the soldiers intone *Manka revania dulche* ritualistically. Such staging may help to explain Guthrie's "Russian prayer".

In the next scene of Cottrell's production, the prompt-book scripts new dialogue for Lord 2,[54]

> *Enter Parolles [guarded,] with [First Soldier as] his*
> *Interpreter.*   BOSLINDO, BOSLINDO
> ¹¹O⁷ BERTRAM A plague upon him! muffled! He can say
> ₗₒₐₒ ₂ ₜᵥ nothing of me.

— but instead of this scripted "BOBLINDO, BOBLINDO", the video offers something like *Skiletto*. After the Interpreter tells Parolles that tortures are called for, there is murmuring of *Torture, tort...* in the background, but *Porto tartalou* resounds in the foreground. It is followed by what seems to be *Porto chimercho* ([č ... č ...]), instead of the expected *Bosko chimurcho*.

Back to Barton's production. The phrase *Acordo linta* is repeated correctly by 2 LORD in a typewritten addition, but then, with a familiar typo in the first word (o over a) by ALL

1 *Soldier.*   But wilt thou faithfully?
Parolles. If I do not, damn me.
1 *Soldier.*   Acordo linta.
2 LCRD: Acordo linta
ALL: Acorda linta

— which, again, can't really mean "All", because why would Parolles ever be party to all this? And I see it on the next page too, where, in the pencilled additions — in the pencilled a

Come on, thou art granted space.
PAROL: Acocoo [*the interpreter and other soldiers carry off*
              linta   *Parolles, the drum beating*
2 *Lord.* Go, tell the Count Rousillon, and
          my brother,
We have caught the woodcock, and will keep
him muffled   90

— O God, help us all! Parolles has parroted this very lingo *himself!*[55] Oh, Joanna, I **am** sorry. I can't believe it. What a godawful mess. I'm really, really sorry. I'll have to eat my words (once I get my food out of it). *Parolles'* Chough offers to undermine my thesis — (I knew it, I should *never* have started.) — my thesis that Chough's destiny was forever to be a *non-semantic manuage*. I've already given up on the idea of *manuage*. Now I have to give up on the *non-semantic* too. No, I really do. Look, even though the meanings Parolles must attribute to the words of Chough he mimics are utterly undermined by irony, his wrong meanings *are* meanings, nevertheless, aren't they? Hasn't sense — however stupid — seeped into nonsense? *Semantic* Chough? *Nonce* sense? I'll have to eat my words. And damn it all, anyway — what difference will they see between me and Gary now?

And there's *another* problem. Remember I said in the "*All: Throca movousus ...*" speech — remember I said that "*All*" had to mean "All but Parolles"? But I just thought of a *new* wrinkle: a *choral* speech is a flat contradiction of the fundamental *ad-lib* terms of Chough: "euery one ... a man of his *own* fancy". So, even leaving Parolles aside, *All* can't really mean *All*. It's euery one a man of *one* fancy. How could I, of all people, have forgotten that *one* and *own* were homophones in Shake-speare's time? (Can't you still hear the old pronunciation in cognates of *one*: like al*one*, l*one*, l*one*ly, at*one*?) Joke's on me, as usual. *And to have come so far.*

But, what the hell, it's not a tragœdy. (There you are, Mom. Just like you said.) And what thesis doesn't fall apart in the end? What *ever* ends well? Never you mind, though, for I see the caterers have now brought in the Great Feast of Language — I *told* you we'd finish on time — and there's an end. (We certainly won't perish for want of language.) So, why don't we just take care of hunger and thirst now, and clean up all this intellectual #@%$ tomorrow? See if there's anything left to scrape together for a paper tomorrow? I'm really, really *sorry*, Joanna. *Really* sorry.

[*He approaches the spread.*]

Why don't we lift our spirits with this dainty 1844 French confection, *Paroles,* translated by Paul Meurice and Auguste Vacquerie? Not only new nonsense —

Foscorbin
Chamodovania?

— but also extensive rearrangements and refined adaptations of the folio Chough. *Very* tasty. Don't you think? You've got to hand it to those French — at least in cooking. Feeling better already. Eating well can sure make a difference. Look, there's more.

a morovousus par corbo villiande !
Boskos thromu boscos !
Boskos ravanvado.
Dulche volivorriere.

Very ravanvado. *Very* volivorriere. And here's more recent Franco-Chough, Eric Westphal's 1982 *Tout est bien.* The plan here is to use *un charabia de votre invention,* so that Paroles will think they speak a Siennese dialect.

Aboujakamikikikoda ! Ah ! Ah !
Troca macousu ! Aissa ! Aissa !
È pericoloso sporgersi !
Nicht hinauslenen !
Don't lean out of the window !

(To which Paroles replies: « Mon Dieu, les Siennois ! »)

Cargo ! Cargo ! Boskos tolmuda sipara !
Muerta la vacca ! Rauous ! Schnell !
Banda los miros ! Banda los miros !
Mota morte la salopar !
Espioune, espioune ! La morte, la morte !

(To which Paroles choughs: « Non, non, pas espioune, ami, amigos ! »)

Quoiqu'ce ?
Alumodi samofa tetraf okibu.

(At this point « *l'autre tient à Paroles un discours* ad libitum ... »!)

Sibouma jata kel pora pur ...
Kamara soutra. Epouqua mesi jipu koda.
Silencio !
Let's go, my dear.
Let's go.
Avanti, avanti, grosse couillounous ...
Porto tartarossa torturo chemuki espioune.   ☞ See pp. 17 - 18
Boblinbido comatica.
Puta las sassi cogna les tresmendures.
Puta puta puta !
La vacca permuta sporgerso, chianti !
Puta puta puta !
Crima zouro peto le cgarias.
Hombre, hombre.
Cavala, cavali, cavalo.
Pica la morte, Coupa la teta. Presto, presto.
Barca, la morte ! Ameni espioune deve le muros. Prepar las espadounes.

Espadounes, indeed! And check out what's on this table: Hans Rothe's robust 1960's *Ende gut*. Look at this 4.3. (There is no 4.1 in this *Übersetzung*.)

Babschdána klapskutzi.
Furtissima maxamarante.
Rapappél murx colombambino.
Camelio affaríno.
Quanti soldatereski in heerhaufénowitsch fiorentino?
Excrementíssima, sapristipíssilimíssili!
Murko boblindo.
Finischlussus. O mistissimo schnauzokoffki!
Lausana wánzikus.
Samkalatscháli!

All Europe has gone into the making of these French and German Choughs — and they *really* schmeck! And what's next? What a splendid *Koniec všetko napraví* is this. Bratislava, 1975. That *was* a good year, a *very* good year. These Slavs can sure cook up a storm. I'm half agglombadated already.[56]

Bohatieros, pif-paf-puf do bohatiera!
Do boha, tiera, do boha, tiera, pif-paf-puf, šiky-miky-fuk,
Držando papulos!
An tan, tataran.
Cimbul, škarvaran.
Eden beden, štetka, hrebeň!
Enci menci, cinci minci.
An tan, tataran.

Čin čan mučidlan.
Cinci minci.
Enci menci.

Not bad, eh? And now that we won't have actually to write this paper, why don't we bust out of this claustrophobic ABC and go for something really erotic? ΑΒΓ? Break out the retina! ΤΕΛΟΣ ΚΑΛΟ ΟΛΑ ΚΑΛΑ.[57]

Τράκα μοβόζα, κάργα, κάργα, κάργα
Κάργα, κάργα, κάργα, βιλιάντα παρ κόρμπο, κάργα
Μπόσκος τρομούλντο, μπόσκος
Μπόσκος βαουβάντο
Κερελυμπόντο
Μάνκα ρεβάνια ντούλτσε
Οσκορμπιντούλκος βολιβόρκο
Ακόρντο λίντα
Πόρτο ταρταρόσα
Μπόσκο κιμούρκο
Μπομπλιπίντο κικουρμούρκο

Wine helps a little, eh? (It usually does.) Can— can you tolerate a philil-logical observation? Well, in Ancient Greek δ sounded [d]. But in Modern Greek it sounds [ð] (as in "this"). To represent the [d] in Modern Greek, a digraph is now used, ντ. That's why *Acordo* is rendered *Ακόρντο* (fourth-to-last line). (You're not supposed to say [Akornto], stupid! That would be misapplied knowledge.) But what does this "ντ = [d]" convention do to the word after it, *λίντα*? Wouldn't you have to say it [lida]? If you said it [linta], you'd be speaking Ancient Greek, not Chough. Is this super-subtle, or what? (Or is something just lots in translation?)

Anyway, look at those accents: *ά ί ό ύ*. We've had insights into *pronunciation*, into *syllabification*, into *semantics*, and into God knows what else. Into *metrics* too. And now *stress*! (If only we'd had this Greek on hand when we were doing metrics. *Nothing* is right since they dropped classics).

Or how about some Deonagari? Poona, 1912. I'll translitterate, just in case you've not been to Maharashtra recently. (Or are too buzzed with the retsina?[58])

(भेवडावून) थ्रका मावशीस कारगो कारगो ! thrakā māvsīs kārgo kārgo! [59]
कारगो कारगो ! kārgo kārgo!
असकास, थरपालडो, बसकास! baskās tharpāldo baskās!
" बसकास व वोडा " baskās va voḍā
" करली विंटो " karlī vimṭo
" मणका रण्या ढलपी ? " maṇkā rāvaṇyā ḍhalpī?
" बस करवी ढलपाक, वाले वरको. " bas karvī ḍhapāk vāle varko
' अकार दोलिता ' akār dolimṭā

" চপলাস "	caplās (for "Portotartarossa"?!)
" ‍ ভোস্কো, চিমরকো "	bhosko cimarko
" বোলুলী বিঁড়ো চিকর মরকো. "	bolalī biṃḍo cikar marko

More Wine? It all seems so bright and clear now. And how about some
Bengali magic:[60] Memories of Darkest Calcutta, 1973? Just a taste.

কার্গো, কার্গো, কার্গো, ভিলিয়ান্দা	Kargo, kargo, kargo, villianda
পার কার্বো, কার্গো ।	par corbo kargo
বঙ্কস্ থোরোমালুড়ো বঙ্কস্ ।	basks thromoldo basks
কেরেলি বণ্টো	kereli banto
অসকর্বিডালকোস ভলিভরকো ।	akarbidalkos valivarko
ববলিবিণ্ডো চিকারমারকো ।	Bablibindo čikarmarko

Hello! There's that *Bablibindo* again! By George, *now* we're talking. O my
God! Hand me that serviette, would you, this one is — damn it all, anyway
— this one is leaking. Thanks. Thank you very. No, it's OK.

So, what do you think now, girls? Who needs *Shakespeare* Babel? —
please excuse myWill you? I just hateit when I have to speak with mymou
thfull— We have the wherewithal to build our *own* Towers of Bablibindo!
Big Towers. Bablibablibindo. *Really* Big Babli Towers. BABLIBABLI-
BABLIBUILDO. *Infinitely* Big Bingo Towers. **And they can mean — they
can mean *ANY* damn BABLI thing you want.**

COME ON JOANNA, COME ON BERNICE.

THIS IS NO TIME FOR ~~EDITING.~~ *DIETING*

GATHER ALL THE PEOPLE, & LET'S **EAT**!

© Random Cloud, 1994, 1995,But1996 hand me another serviette, would
you? This is just too much for words. No, you're right, I can't hold it by
myself. Thanks. Boy, if my mother could see me now. 1997Please, please
everybody, just help yourselves. Don't worry about a thing. *Bem está oque
bem achaba.* You know what *that* means? I can't say it any clearer, can I?
Totu-i bine cînd sfîrșeste bine. We'll clean up this mess in the morning. And
there's sure to be more than enough for a *dozen* essays in the scraps alone.
Bablibanter Sennaar Yoseloo palatin. Longhornaidom kalinas troublanter.
Spastikosmo albertizi masqueradas ticamentali. Yawhey chronucrapia dan-

NOTES

1.   My thanks to the Folger Shakespeare Library, where the early research for this paper was carried out, and especially to its Reference Librarian, Georgiannna Ziegler. For help in graphics, photography and formatting, my thanks to Brandon Besharah, Alison Dias, Steve Jaunzems and Margot Thomas of Erindale College, University of Toronto.

Extracts from the first folio are reproduced by permission of the Fisher Rare Book Library, University of Toronto. I have used the Through Line Numbers devised by Charlton Hinman for his Norton Facsimile edition of the first folio.

Versions of this paper were presented in 1995 to the Renaissance Doctoral Colloquium of the English Department, Harvard University (at the invitation of Susan Phillips and Eric Wilson) and to the Cambridge University Faculty of English Renaissance Graduate Seminar (at the invitation of Anne Barton and John Kerrigan); and in 1996 to the 27th International Shakespeare Conference, Stanley-upon-Avon.

My thanks to Pape McLeod for help with Dutch Chough.

2.   The quoted phrases come from lines 1914, 1923 and 1931, in the first two dozen lines of 4.1. The quotation later in the paragraph comes from lines 1928-9.

3.   Of course, Shakespeare would merely have *copied* this speech, if it was originally ad-libbed in rehearsal.

4.   "The Howard Shakespeare" (London: T. Nelson & Sons, 1876) offers *movo-/usus*. Does that suggest a different pronunciation than yours?

5.   V is the upper-case shape in the first folio. U began regularly to supplement V after 1630. (At first, it often seems, the upper-case U was really just a large point-size u.) In this paradoxical example from the Contents of the first edition of George Herbert's *The Temple*, 1633, V is both the generic and consonant form of the letter, and U is its vowel form. This alphabetic styling is found in Herbert indexes down at least to 1809.

	V	
V	*Anitie*	77.104
	Vertue	18
	Ungratefulneſſe	74
	Unkindneſſe	86

W — or Double-U, in which term the V shape reveals its original name — is anomalous. If w and W ran short (or were not in the bill, as they might well not be in type supplied from France, where this letter was not part of the alphabet), they were set as vv and VV (the right edge of the left V often being kerned, to integrate it with the following typeface, as in this example (Sonnet 84 from *Shake-speares Sonnets*, 1609, which is contrasted with Sonnet 2). (After 1630, one occasionally sees vu for w in English books.)

WHo is Then In whoſe   **VV**Hen And Thy youthes

6.   4.13, 30.5, 9.12.

7.   The rule for s is this: *long-s (ſ) at the start and middle of a word, but round-s (s) at the end*. Hence, the long-s in this setting specifies *middle*. Happily, the kerning of the long-s over the v argues continuity. But the v shape right after it proclaims *beginning*, and therefore redefines the preceding *middle* as *end*, its kern notwithstanding. (Q2 (H3r) offers a long-s followed by an unexceptional u.) (The modern dictionary offers "hunt's-up" — not just a word, but a sentence — short for "The hunt is up".)

8. Modern-spelling editions are not conservative; but what about the recent Oxford original-spelling edition? One must ask this question after noticing that Taylor's editing of *Lear* conserves "auoide" (in Q, Scene 1.116), but without explanation alters "avoid" to "auoid" (in F, 1.1.125). (But the folio's "avoid" recommends itself not only because it is *original*, but also because it may be deemed a learned setting, one which actively evokes the etymology, isolating the prefix (<ME & AngloFr *a-* <OFr *es-* <L *ex-*, meaning "out") from the base (<ME *voiden* <OFr *vuidier* <L *vacare*, "to be empty"). Taylor's *All's Well* does avoid this regularization; it offers *movousus*, *vauvado*, *reuania* and *voliuorco*. But it does not spell out what is crucial in a -spelling edition: that the two underlined letter-*shapes*, *u* and *v*, originally represented only one *letter*. (Page xliv of Vivian Salmon's prefatory essay, "The Spelling and Punctuation of Shakespeare's Time", would have been a good place to make clear that this single letter has two lower-case shapes. But she does not even *name* the letter. In Shakespeare's time its name was a homophone of "you" (see Note 5). Therefore, in order to *original*-spell "HENRY V" out loud, one must say "H-E-N-R-Y—U". (Of course, if *original* spelling doesn't suit you, you may prefer Ox ford's Compete *moderized* edition.)

Where F1 ascribes *movousus* to "*Lo* E.", Ox ford originates "⌈2⌉ LORD DUMAINE". But look at "DUMAINE". There *was* no upper-case U in the first folio! Ox ford's editorially original "NAME [sic] OF THE ACTORS" for this play also projects U into "COUNTESSE" and "DUKE". This anachronistic spelling is found consistently in every editorial ACTORS list in this edition but one (*Pericles* alone does not use all-cap settings for character names); and it is found in the speech-prefixes of *every* play. The headlines of all titles (a third of them) that bear this letter are marred by the same editing. Almost every page of the original-*spelling* edition thus repeats this *spelling* error. Ironically, although U is the wrong *shape*, it will lead modern readers to the correct *spelling* of DUMAINE. The *v* in *movousus*, by contrast, is the right shape, but who will know how to original-spell it? (Or, of course, how to *pronounce* it?)

9. Published by J. Debrett, London. Its titlepage gave Shakespeare more credit as a dramatist, as it claimed merely "with alterations by J. P. Kemble".

10. There are exceptions, as Brecht's theatre, which displays texts *on stage* on banners or placards. For example, the published script titles an episode, "MUTTER COURAGE SINGT DAS LIED VON DER GROSSEN KAPITULATION", and a photograph in the Modelbuch shows a banner under the place name, Polen, reading, "Mutter Courages Lied von der Grossen Kapitulation". Occasionally there are distinctly litterary functions in the midst of Renaissance dramatic scripts, as in the centred phrase "THE ARAIGNEMENT OF VITTORIA" in Webster's *The White Divel*, 1612 (E2r).

11. See my "The Marriage of Good and Bad Quartos", *SQ*, 33.4, 1982, 421-31.

12. We have it on the authority of Heminges and Condell that Shakespere's mind and hand went so together, that what he thought, he vttered so easily, that he scarce bloated a line. (Now we know what to think of *that*.)

In early editions, the redundancy in *Romeo* is found only in Q2, Q3 and F1. (It seems that only one modernizing editor prints both *Romeo* speeches, John Andrews, in his recent Everyman edition.) By contrast, that in *Loues Labours Lost* persisted unremarked until Capell (1767), who removed one stratum, but who has not been followed by the majority of later editors.

13. A corollary: The mere fact that the script of *All's Well* can be used to produce a play, does not mean that there can't be parts of the script that express an aesthetic that is not dramatic. Now, if we allow such parts to be authorial, don't we have to envision a Shakspear who was not completely A Man of the Theatre, *even* when writing plays?

14. True, the round-s in "*Muskos*"runs against my rule. As there were no ligatures at this time in long-*s* + *k* (and very few in long-*s* + *b*), setting a long-*s* before a letter with an ascender at its left side (like *k* or *b* — or like *f*, for which there likely never was an English ligature with long-*s*) would break its kern against the ascender. Hence, to avoid fouling, a round-*s* was often used in this environment (though sometimes a long-*s* was set, along with a protective space under its fore-kern, which created a "pigeon hole" in the word in which it appeared, as in this F4 setting

Int. *Bofke Chimurcho.*
Cap. *Biblibindo Chicurmurco.*

— which should be contrasted with the F1 setting on page 10. (See my "Spellbound: Typography and the Concept of Old-Spelling Editions", *Ren&Ref*, n.s., 3.1, 1979, 197-210; reprinted as "Spellbound" in G. B. Shand and Raymond C. Shady, eds., *Play-Texts in Old Spelling*, New York: AMS Press, 1984, 81-96.)

15. 5 vols., Strassburg, 1775-82, Vol. 5. (The French prose translation by Tourneur, *Tout est bien qui finit bien*, followed closely, in 1782. The introduction to vol. 17 of his *Shakespeare, traduit de l'anglais*, Paris, 1776-84, refers to "Eschemburg".) Wieland's translation of Shakespeare, *Theatralische Werke*, 8 vols., Zürich, 1762-66 predates Eschenburg, but does not translate *All's Well*.

16. See note 14, above, for a photograph of this setting.

17. John Munro, ed. and G. W. G. Wickham, intro., *The London Shakespeare, a New Annotated and Critical Edition of the Complete Works*, 6 vols. London: Eyre & Spottiswoode, 1958.

18. The most extensive editorial comment on Chough I have seen is in the German-English *Studienausgabe* edited by Christian A. Gertsch (Tübingen: Franke Verlag, 1988), who discusses the work of O. Vočadlo in *The Slavonic and East European Review*, 44, 1966, 36-50. Vočadlo regards Shakespeare's bogus language as more like Esperanto than Russian (41), but does find one unmistakably Russian expression, *oscorbi*, which Shakespeare "remembered" ("*oskorbit'* is a common Russian verb meaning to insult" (42)). Gertsch is not impressed, however: "Solche Interpretationen sind aber unnötig, das Sh. bloß mit Klangassoziationen spielt."

The most extensive note in an English edition seems to be in G. K. Hunter's 1959 Arden edition: "Cargo] This word (taken presumably from the Spanish) is used as an exclamation elsewhere. See Wilkins' *Miseries of Enforced Marriage*, sig. F4: 'But *Cargo*, my fiddlestick cannot play'."

19. At the start of the tables, the arrow specifies derivation. After Rowe's two editions of 1709, however, the chart does not attempt to show an unbroken sequence of editions and re-editions. In general, therefore, the arrow shows merely that the reading to the left is unchanged to the right.

20. Theobald is the most famous, most notorious example. He attacked Pope's text on the basis of the authority of quartos and folios that Pope had not collated. Nevertheless, he marked up Pope's second edition for the printing of his own, and thus

inherited many of Pope's errors. (This choice of copy suited Tonson, the publisher of both editions, who gave Theobald an interleaved exemplar of Pope (part of which survives) to mark up — in order, in Peter Seary's view, to extend his copy-right over Shakespeare's text (*Lewis Theobald and the Editing of Shakespeare*, Oxford: Clarendon Press, 1990, 133-35). Simon Jarvis doubts that Tonson could have hoped to extend copyright by such a means (*Scholars and Gentlemen: Shakespearian Textual Criticism and Representations of Scholarly Labour, 1725-1765*, Oxford: Clarendon Press, 1995, 95); Seary replies in a review forthcoming in *Modern Philology* (1997 or 1998).

21. Capell's Chough departs from F1 nine times. He was much influenced by F2 — in "Cargo, cargo" (1979), "revanta" and "Osceorbi dulcos"; but curiously he did not follow F2's eloquent "Baskos ... beskos".

22. There is more logic behind the scenes. Consider these "Editorial Procedures" in Stanley Wells and Gary Taylor with John Jowett and William Montgomery, *A Textual Companion*, Ox ford: Clarendon Press, 1987, 155-7: (1) "The basic function of the Textual Notes is to record substantive departures from the control-text" (*the Textual Notes do record "Porto tartarossa"*). (2) "The section headed Incidentals records non-substantive departures in the original-spelling edition from the copy-text" (*this section does not record "Porto tartarossa"*). (3) "In foreign language passages, only what seem to be scribal or compositorial errors are emended" in the original-spelling edition (*this edition does alter the folio's "Portotartarossa"*). (4) In the modern-spelling edition, "Words in a foreign language are italicized" (*"Porto tartarossa" is italicized*). (5) "The case for well-founded and long-accepted emendation is not argued" (*this edition does argue the alteration to "Porto tartarossa"*). (6) "The aim [of this edition] has been to ascribe all emendations to the edition ... in which they first appeared" (*this edition does not ascribe "Porto tartarossa" to its originator, Capell, 1767*).

65.5

Now, try to figure out (a) what Shakespeare wrote, (b) whether the splitting of "*Portotartarossa*" was substantive, or accidental, or both, (c) whether the compositor was true to copy, (d) whether Chough is a *foreign* language (and hence *a* language), and (e) whether this editorial change to it is a well-founded and long-accepted emendation — or even an emendation. Good luck. (You'll need it.)

Further on the matter of Indo-European etymology, see note 18.

Like Taylor, J. L. Styan, *All's Well that Ends Well* (in the *Shakespeare in Performance* series, Manchester, 1984, 99), sees meaning in Chough; but it is infinite, improvisa-tional meaning on stage or in the audience, rather than etymologically-, authorially- or editorially-circumsized meaning on the page: "The baiting of Parolles begins with the language game we heard before. 'Portotartarossa' is heard in the sternest voice from the Second Lord ... Threats continue — 'Bosko chimurcho ... Boblibindo chicurmurco' — and there is no limit to the meanings to be improvised with these sounds." On p. 90 he regards the scripted Chough as a mere provocation to *ad lib*: "I take it that the few words of gibberish that Shakespeare supplies are there merely to encourage the players to invent more of their own." For Styan, "improvisation" of *meaning* lies not only in the actors' rendition of scripted Chough, but also in their creation of new Chough. (See page 58, above, for a French edition that directs Parolles' guard to ad-lib Chough. The BBC production referred to on page 50 calls for "AD LIB" between the speech prefix "ALL" and "Cargo, cargo, cargo, villianda par corbo, cargo"; after Parolles' "O, ransom, ransom ..." (and the stage direction that follows it, "THEY BLINDFOLD HIM") and First Soldier's "Boskos thromuldo boskos"; and between Parolles' "If I do not, damn me" and First Soldier's "Acordo linta". (This last example is entirely deleted.) As only the first of these three ad-libs is assigned to a speaker, the latter two, technically speaking, are assigned to Parolles!)

23. New York: Funk and Wagnalls, 1897.

24. -osa and -oso are adjectival endings in Italian, respectively feminine and masculine; they correspond in French to the endings of a word like *joyeuse, joyeux*, from which English derives *joyous*. Behind these lie -$\bar{o}sa$, -$\bar{o}sus$ in Latin (with which Greek -os is cognate). Thus the change of *Portotartaros̲s̲a* to *Portotartaros̲a* looks like an assimilation of Chough to Indo-European.

25. W. G. Clark and W. A. Wright, eds., 9 vols. Cambridge, 1863-66. This benchmark work gave the most comprehensive collations of Chough to date (four notes) and set the scholarship of this language on a very firm foundation indeed.

Its first three collations are wrong.

    [1979]   62.   *cargo, cargo*] *cargo* Hanmer.
    [1982]   64.   *Boskos ... boskos*] F_1. *Baskos ... / baskos* $F_2F_3F_4$.
    [1993]   74.   *revania*] F_1. *revanta* F_2. *re-/vancha* F_3F_4.
    [1994]   76.   *Oscorbidulchos*] F1. *Osceorbi-/dulchos*] $F_2F_3F_4$.

In 1891, the surviving editor, Wright, brought out a revision. He corrected the first two notes:

    [1979]   62   *cargo, cargo*] F_1. *cargo* $F_2F_3F_4$.
    [1982]   64   *Boskos ... boskos*] F_1. *Baskos ... beskos* $F_2F_3F_4$.

And he supplemented the fourth — incorrectly, for he missed the capital *O*'s in Rowe's and Capell's editions:

    [1994]   76   *Oscorbidulchos*] F1. *Osceorbidulchos*] $F_2F_3F_4$. *osceoribi dulchos* Rowe. *osceorbi dulcos* Capell.

He made no alteration to the third note. With his interest in editions up to Capell (and the ones beyond, who obviously influenced him, even if their names do not occur in these notes), it should have looked something like this:

    [1993]   74   *revania*] Johnson-Steevens-Reed. *reuania* F1. *revanta* F_2, Capell. *revancha* F_3F_4. *ravancha* Rowe.

This 1891 edition added five collations, all correct:

    [1978]   61   *Throca*] *Throco* F_3F_4.
    [1979]   62   *villianda*] *villiando* F_4.
    [1982]   64   *thromuldo*] *thromaldo* Rowe.
    [1993]   74   *Manka*] F_1. *Mancha* $F_2F_3F_4$. *Manca* Capell.
    [2233]   119   *Boblibindo*] *Biblibindo* F_3F_4.

But there should have been four more notes to record at least the folio variants:

[1979] 62 *Cargo, cargo, cargo*] $F_1F_2F_3$. *Cargo, cargo, oargo*] F_4.
[1988] 70 *Boskos*] $F_1F_2F_3$. *Baskos*] F_4.
[1994] 76 *volivorco*] $F_2F_3F_4$. *voliuorco*] F_1.
[2233] 119 *chicurmurco*] $F_1F_2F_3$. *Chicurmurco*] F_4.

As his interest extended to Capell (and beyond), it should have shown (at least) two more, and added to one of them, line 119.

[2227] 113 *Portotartarossa*] $F_1F_2F_3F_4$ *Portotarossa* Johnson. *Porto tartarossa* Capell.
[2232] 118 *chimurcho*] Malone. *Chimurcho* $F_1F_2F_3F_4$, Rowe. *chimurco* Capell.
[2233] 119 *chicurmurco*] $F_1F_2F_3$, Capell. *Chicurmurco* F_4, Rowe.

Yes, Cambridge. Benchmark editions indeed. They show that, despite appearances, the collations were not the *foundation* for these editors' text; rather they were merely *decorations* for a text they arrived at by other, undisclosed, means.

Since Clark and Wright's variant "Portotartaro̱sa" in the body of their text likely arose by accident, it seems too much to expect them to have collated it. But when Wright corrected it to "Portotartaro̱s̲s̲a" in 1891, should there not *then* have been a collational note? Would that possibly have kept the earlier error from contaminating the Craig-Bevington line? (If only editors collated their various selves, wouldn't they offer readers wondrous insight into textual instability?)

26. The book of W. Bridges-Adams' production is #12 in the *All's Well* section of Charles Shattuck, *The Shakespeare Promptbooks*, Urbana and London: University of Illinois Press, 1965, 31.

27. "Mučidlo" is Czech for "torture", a word that appears in the First Soldier's (Interpreter's) speech in the next line of this translation (*Complete Works*, Sládek, Klášterský and Vrchlický, transs., 6 vols., Prague, 1959).

28. My thanks to Carol Armbruster, Kornelia Merdjanska and Kirilka Stavreva for help in procuring some of the texts in Cyrillic characters, and to Philip Oldfield for help in deciphering Slavic Chough.

29. When read as *ch'ia*, the logograph in the margin means "guard-house", "customs barrier", etc. But, when read as *k'a*, it means "cough". As it is the only logograph for the latter sound, it is the one that must be used for rendering the foreign sound [k], as in "calorie" — or "cargo". (See *Mathews' Chinese-English Dictionary*, rev. American ed., Cambridge, Mass.: Harvard University Press, 1966, item 616.) My thanks to Neil McMullin and Rick Guisso for help with Chinese Chough.

30. Both translators use the same four logographs to conjure up the sounds for *villianda* — *wei-li-an-da* in the newer Pinyin romanization (not the older Wade-Giles). Now, what are the odds that both translators would have chosen these four logographs by chance? *Mathews' Chinese-English Dictionary* lists 72 logographs for *wei*, 89 for *li*, 14 for *an*, and 18 for *da*. A mathematician might formulate the odds for a fortuitous grouping of these logographs by multiplying together all four of these numbers: 1 in 1,614,816 — or one in over a million and a half! This *wei*, however, is very common in transliterating foreign terms with the [v] sound (which is absent from Chinese) — in terms like "Vienna" or "Versailles". And this logograph for *an* is also standard in transliterations. But the other two choices, for *li* and *da*, seem totally arbitrary. A more conservative estimate of the odds, therefore, could be based

on choices just among the options *li* and *da*: in this style of calculation, there is 1 chance in (1 x 89 x 1 x 18) — or 1 in 1,602 — that the second translator would independently arrive at these logographs for invoking the sounds *li* and *da*. What do such long odds signify? Surely one translator must have "borrowed" the work of the other. (We can surmise, therefore, that, in his different rendering of *cargo*, the later translator toned down the *ka-go* of his predecessor.)

31. There's a problem, however, for Capell does not use this system for the French in *Henry V*. If not for French, then for Chough?

32. *Dzieła Wiliama Szekspira*, Dr. Henryka Biegeleisena, trans., Lwów, 1896. (I am grateful to Magdalena Markiewicz for Polish examples of Chough.)

33. Possibly the translator, Diego Angeli, misread *voliyorco* as *volyorko* (that is, *iv* as *w*) — but his *k* for *c*, which compounds the bizarre effect, argues that the *w* is intentional. If it weren't for that *k*, his *luita* (for *linta*) and his *O scorbidulchos* might also look like easy misreadings or typos.

34. I say that English *can* use the *h* this way, because *ch* is a digraph in English, just as it is in Italian (though with different phonetic values) — because derivatives of Greek words beginning with χ, like those from which we derive <u>Ch</u>rist and <u>Ch</u>aos, begin with a [k]. The [č] sounds in modern English, in <u>ch</u>urch, for example, derive from Greek κ — κυρος + οικος, via palatalization in Old English; but Scots retains the original velar [k], in <u>k</u>ir<u>k</u>. Modern English [č] (written *ch* since the middle ages) is more commonly an evolution of Germanic and Italic [k]. The contrast of the ancient velar with its evolutions forward in the mouth can be vividly demonstrated in cognates that entered English at different periods: for Germanic — *dike* (<ON) / *ditch* (<OE) — or *blank* (<OE) & (from Frankish via Romance tongues) *Bianca* (<It) / *Branca* (<Port) / blanch (<OFr) / *Blanche* (<OFr); for Italic — *candle* (<Lat) / *chandler* (<OFr) / *chandelier* (<Fr). *Blanche* and *chandelier* show that the French use *ch* to render the alveolar sound [š], for which English uses *sh* (a digraph not used in French): contrast the English use of *sh* in the Germanic *shipper* (<OE) (cognate with *skipper* (<ON)).

35. Assimilation of these two words is widespread in other languages too, whether under Capell's influence or *sui generis*: in German — *chimurco* / *chirurmurco* (Kessler, 1825), *chicumurro* / *chicumurro* (Benda, 1824-34), *kimurko* / *kikurmurko* (Körner, 1836), *chimurcho* / *chicur murcho* (Ortlepp, 1842), *chimurcho* / *chicurmurcho* (Vincke, 1871), *kimurka* / *kirurmurko* (the consonants are assimilated at least) (Flatter, 1955); in Danish — *chimurrcho* / *chicurmurrcho* (Beyer, 1850); in Polish — *chimurcho* / *chimurmurcho* (1948); in French — *chicurmuro* / *chicurmuro* (Letourneur, 1821-2), *chicurmurco* / *chicurmurco* (Guizot, 1861). English examples include *Chicurmurcho* / *chicurmurcho* (1795) and *Chimurco* / *chicurmurco* (Kemble, 1801).

An example of progressive assimilation in Chough is "*Manka reuania*" (F1) to "*Mancha revanta*" (F2) to "*Mancha revancha*" (F3-4) to "*Mancha ravancha*" (Rowe).

Assimilation of nearby, look-alike words contrasts to dissimilation of them. The best example of this change is "*Boskos ... boskos*" to "*Baskos ... beskos*" in F2 (which Clark and Wright mis-collate as "*Baskos ... baskos*"). Modern versions of dissimilation for these words appear in the Schlegel and Tieck translations into German, "*Barcos ... Boscos*", and in Hereford's 1902 English edition, "*Boskus ... boskos*".

36. The Arden Shakespeare, London and New York: Methuen, 1981, 152.

37. Or how does T. J. B. Spenser, the New Penguin editor of *Romeo*, know? — "to pronounce the name as 'Petrookio' because one knows that in Italian the symbol <u>ch</u> represents the 'k' sound is misapplied knowledge" (202).

38. There is also the problem of Italian dialects. Different regions of Italy evolve the Latin [k] differently, so that cognates can be found with palatal or velar reflexes: *Fanucci* or (in Lucca) *Fanucchi, boccuccia* or (in Corsica) *boccucchia. Petrucci* is also twinned (in Southern Italy) with *Petruzzi.* (See Gerhard Rohlfs, *Grammatica storica della lingua italiana e dei suoi dialetti: Sintassi e formazione delle parole,* Temistocle Franceschi and Maria Caciagli Francelli, transs., Torino: Giulio Einaudi, 1969, 377.) In Sardinia, Latin initial and intervocalic [k] is preserved, where Italian palatalized them before high front vowels. The Italian word for "bedbug", *cimice* [č ... č ...] is pronounced [k ... k ...] in Sardinia. (See Robert A. Hall, Jr., *Proto-romance Phonology: Comparative Romance Grammar,* Vol. 2, New York, Oxford, Amsterdam: Elsevier, 1976.)

39. *Textual Companion,* 171, note for 1.2.0.1.

40. Melchiori's *en face* edition styles the names just this way: "Petrucio" for the Italian page, and "Petruchio" for the English.

41. Thanks for this reference to Leslie Thomson.

42. See Margaret Maurer's essay in this volume, "The Rowe Editions of 1709/1714 and 3.1 of *The Taming of the Shrew*".

43. On L2v. Thanks for this reference to Antony Hammond. (I miss you, Tony.)

44. *Ibid.,* for Note to lines 66-7: "The two short lines in F may indicate space left clear for business."

45. The Folger Library's "Prompt All's Well, 3" is #1 in Shattuck, *Shakespeare Prompt-books,* 29. It is reproduced with permission of the Folger Shakespeare Library.

46. The Folger Library's "Prompt All's Well, 6" is #10 in Shattuck, *Shakespeare Prompt-books,* 30. It is reproduced with permission of the Folger Shakespeare Library.

47. My thanks to Gwyniver Jones and Trevor White of the BBC Written Archives Centre for correspondence about the script.

48. #13 in Shattuck, *Shakespeare Promptbooks,* 31. It is reproduced with permission of the Shakespeare Centre Library.

49. The pointing with a question mark can be found as early as the 1811 Cumberland edition, where it must reflect Kemble's staging. There was also a question mark in "Acordo linta?". (See p. 6, above, for more of Kemble's adaptation of Chough.) In modern times, the question mark can be found in the Oxford Compete edition — in its modern-spelling *All's Well,* but not its original-spelling edition (even though the editor feels free to originate a question mark elsewhere in that edition (for example: TLN 386; original-spelling 362; modern-spelling 1.3.58). He also originates many question marks in the original-spelling *Lear,* and represents many of its inverted semicolons as question marks.

Susan Snyder's more recent Ox ford *All' s Well* uses the question mark not only here, but also after "chimurcho". But Oxford offers no collational notes (even among its *own* editions under the *same* general editor) for any Chough punctuation. Snyder's text, by the way, is one of the very few English texts to offer "Accordo". (The earliest English example of "Accordo" I have observed is the Theatres-Royal text, printed for J. Harrison, 1778). This "rationalized" form is not uncommon on the continent — in German editions by Voss (1810), Kessler (1825), or Gertsch (1988) or in Danish (Beyer, 1850). But gemination reminds one of the fate of the abutting consonants not in Germanic languages, but in Latin, as in the evolution of the phrase *ad* + *cord-,* from which our own word "accord" derives. Victor Hugo's translation does not geminate in Chough, though it does evoke this Latin etymology nearby, in the French: «*Açordolinta.* — Allons, on t'açcorde un sursis.» «Açcordo» is found in French, however, in the Pierre Messiaen translation, Paris, 1943-49. (It can be found too in the Carcano translation into Italian.)

Page 116 of the printed text for the 1989 RSC production directed by Barry Kyle offers "Açordo". But three added repetitions of it all read "Açcordo". (The 1st Lord puts it as a question, and All and Parolles repeat the word without punctuation.)

50. The image on page 51 is from Accs # 6065 (f 90) — to give it its complete designation. The "other" book (Accs # 7940) reads quite differently in diction and punctuation:

$$1^{ST} \text{ SOLD}: \text{VOLIVORCO}?$$
$$1^{ST} \text{ LORD}: \text{VOLIVORCO}!$$
$$\text{ALL}. \qquad "$$

51. # 17 in Shattuck, *Shakespeare Promptbooks*, 32. It is reproduced by permission of The Shakespeare Centre Library.

52. The following directions are written in pencil over a partially erased pencilled text, presumably an earlier version of the present blocking.

53. Reproduced by permission of the Shakespeare Centre Library.

54. Reproduced by permission of the Stratford Shakespeare Festival, Stratford, Ontario. My thanks to Archivist Lisa Brant.

55. Parolles' speech is not written into the book for the subsequent European tour.

56. My thanks to Josef Škvorecký, Zdena Salivarová and Jarmila Emmerová for help with Slovak Chough.

57. My thanks to Frank Hess and to Vassya and her mother for sending me this Greek Chough. It is translated by Basile Pota and Boulas Damianakou, 1989.

58. My thanks to Iqbal and Narendra Wagle for help with Maharati Chough.

59. Can you believe this 'means' "Do it, do it to your mother's sister"?

60. My thanks to Monika Biswas for help with Bengali Chough.

rmcleod@credit.erin.utoronto.ca

"Making Him Speak True English": Grammatical Emendation in Some Eighteenth-Century Editions of Shakespeare, with Particular Reference to *Cymbeline*

Ann Thompson

B Y any standards, the grammar of Shakespeare's *Cymbeline* is decidedly odd. In his recent book, *Shakespearean Sentences: A Study in Style and Syntax,*[1] John Porter Houston sets out to explore the stylistic values of sentence structure and the development of Shakespeare's poetic syntax over the course of his career as a dramatist. In this development, *Cymbeline* is seen as marking a distinctive new phase in which Shakespeare's frequent experiments with grammatical irregularities contribute to the peculiarity of his late style which Houston compares with that of Henry James for its oddity and apparent inelegance (200). Struggling with the play's long and convoluted sentences, he comments that the unusually loose syntax "sometimes makes the very notion of dependent and independent [grammatical] units an arbitrary matter of punctuation," (204) and that the numerous parentheses are so peculiar that they "bear little relation to what one might expect to encounter in either speech or writing" (206). Indeed the "disintegration of normal sentence movement" has gone so far in this text that "A certain ideal of coherent discourse has obviously been abandoned" (208).

Yet the pedagogic tradition in general and the editorial tradition in particular have assumed an obligation to make sense of such a text, to turn it into "coherent discourse" for students and readers by intervening to relineate and repunctuate the 1623 First Folio version (the only authoritative early text for *Cymbeline*), to emend it where it seems not to make sense, and to explain or paraphrase difficult passages in notes and commentaries. I began working on this play for the new new Arden Shakespeare series (Arden 3) and I found myself worrying about the extent to which such interventions can be reductive, offering the reader a simple

71

meaning in place of a complex one, a clear but impoverished paraphrase in place of the rich if confused original.

The difficulties begin with the opening four-line speech by an anonymous First Gentleman which in the First Folio reads:

> You do not meet a man but Frownes.
> Our bloods no more obey the Heauens
> Then our Courtiers:
> Still seeme, as do's the Kings.[2]

Horace Howard Furness, editor of the 1913 Variorum edition,[3] prints this without alteration but comments:

In hearing these lines on the stage, we find no difficulty; we at once gather from them that our moods are no more dependent on the state of the weather than our courtiers are dependent on the state of the King's moods,—as the Heavens affect us so the King affects his courtiers; the King frowns and immediately all his courtiers frown. It is almost a commonplace, and parallels may be found throughout literature ancient and modern. But when, in the closet, we analyse the lines as they stand in the Folio, the case is altered, and the passage, even to Dr Johnson, becomes "so difficult that commentators may differ concerning it without animosity or shame." (8)

There follow four pages of discussion of the nature of the difficulty and a number of ingenious suggested emendations.

Later twentieth-century editors continue to differ. J. M. Nosworthy, editor of the 1955 Arden Shakespeare,[4] prints:

> You do not meet a man but frowns: our bloods
> No more obey the heavens than our courtiers
> Still seem as does the king's.

Although he has emended lineation and punctuation as well as modernizing the spelling, he comments that "To emend is to miss Shakespeare's point completely. . . . [The First Gentleman] has a strange tale to tell, and tells it breathlessly, excitedly, and, at times, rather incoherently." J. C. Maxwell, editor of the 1960 New (Cambridge) Shakespeare,[5] prints:

> You do not meet a man but frowns.
> Our bloods
> No more obey the heavens than our courtiers
> Still seem as does the king.

G. Blakemore Evans, editor of the 1974 Riverside Shakespeare,[6] prints:

> You do not meet a man but frowns. Our bloods
> No more obey the heavens than our courtiers'
> Still seem as does the King's.

While Stanley Wells and Gary Taylor, editors of the 1986 Oxford *Complete Works,*[7] print:

> You do not meet a man but frowns. Our bloods
> No more obey the heavens than our courtiers
> Still seem as does the King.

Most members of a theater audience could hardly detect any difference between these versions (an editor of the play just might notice whether the actor said "king" or "kings"), but the reader of an edition picks up from this anxious tinkering a sense that, while it is generally clear what the character means to say—no one would disagree with Furness on this—it is difficult to make the actual words on the page yield that sense without some minor adjustments.

And the opening speech is not uncharacteristic of this play whose language has always baffled and exasperated editors. Later in Act 1 Furness comments on the attempts to make sense of Iachimo's lines to Imogen:

> should I (damn'd then)
> Slauuer with lippes as common as the stayres
> That mount the Capitoll: Ioyne gripes, with hands
> Made hard with hourely falshood (falshood as
> With labour:) then by peeping in an eye
> Base and illustrious as the smoakie light
> That's fed with stinking Tallow:
>
> (716–22)

After summarizing the editorial debate on line 108 for a page or so, he weighs Johnson's suggestion "lie peeping" against Knight's "by-peeping" and opts for the least intrusive emendation in a spirit of resigned tolerance for the rule-breaking author:

> The addition of a hyphen is certainly a less violent change than the substitution of a word, and as for rejecting a participle because it is preceded by two verbs in the subjunctive, it seems to me too late a week to demand a strict sequence of tenses from Shakespeare,—a chartered libertine in a grammar which he helped us to form. (95)

Later he remarks of a problematic moment when Shakespeare follows a second-person pronoun, "thou," with a third-person verb, "hath" ("thou / Conspir'd with that Irregulous diuell *Cloten,* / Hath heere cut off my

Lord" 2636–38): "Such sentences present to us a melancholy alternative; we must sacrifice either our ears or our grammar. Shakespeare prefered grammar as the victim." Furness therefore retains "hath" while conceding that to some editors this is "a symptom of degeneracy" (331). And a little further on he launches into a two-page note (or rather essay) on the much-emended lines:

> you some permit
> To second illes with illes, each elder worse,
> And make them dread it, to the dooers thrift.
>
> (2870–72)

with a quotation from Lewis Theobald: "Here's a Relative without an antecedent Substantive; and a Genitive Case Singular, when all the other members of the sentence run in the *plural*. Both which are a Breach of Grammar" (Variorum, 352). The very confidence in Theobald's tone here is reassuring: this is the voice of a man from an age that knew its grammatical terms and rules. But how could such an age make sense of such a text?

Theobald's remarks occur in the commentary on *Cymbeline* in his 1733 edition of Shakespeare, a contribution to scholarship which was so much maligned in the eighteenth century by other editors such as Alexander Pope, William Warburton, and Samuel Johnson that its importance may still, according to Peter Seary, be underestimated.[8] Modern editors have, of course, a general obligation to acquaint themselves with the eighteenth-century tradition of presentation, emendation, and annotation of the text, but in the case of this play it seemed potentially interesting, especially in the light of the remarks by Houston quoted above, to conduct my investigation with a special focus on the question of grammar.

One might expect eighteenth-century editors to be more distressed by Shakespeare's eccentricities of grammar than we are today and that they would be more anxious to correct them. Such an expectation might be formed not so much from the eighteenth-century editors themselves as from an earlier (and today more widely read) work, John Dryden's *Essay on the Dramatique Poetry of the last Age,* which was first published as a *Defence of the Epilogue* to the Second Part of *The Conquest of Granada* in 1672. Having advanced the claim in that Epilogue that the plays of the Elizabethan and Jacobean period were "ill-written" by comparison with those of his own improved and refined time, Dryden elaborates in the *Essay* on the "improprieties in Language" he objects to and even throws out a challenge to his readers:

[L]et any man who understands *English,* read diligently the works of *Shake-spear* and *Fletcher;* and I dare undertake that he will find, in every page either some Solecism of Speech, or some flaw in Sence. . . . [I]t is not their Plots which I meant, principally to tax: I was speaking of their Sence and Language; and I dare almost challenge any man to show me a page together, which is correct in both. (205, 207)[9]

Taking his examples from *Catiline* by the supposedly "judicious" Ben Jonson, Dryden demonstrates both "extreamly perplex'd Sence" (confused or contorted syntax) and various forms of "false Grammar" such as the use of plural subjects with singular verbs, double comparatives, incorrect use of pronouns, and incorrect placing of prepositions. He concludes triumphantly:

And what correctness, after this, can be expected from *Shakespear* or from *Fletcher,* who wanted that Learning and Care that *Jonson* had? I will therefore spare my own trouble of inquiring into their faults: who had they liv'd now, had doubtless written more correctly. (210)

Dryden is supremely confident that "correctness" is the most important criterion (and his notion of correctness extends, of course, well beyond grammar to larger issues of dramatic construction). He believes that language use has improved over time (thanks, he asserts, to the influence of the Court), though he shows that he is aware of the possibility of historical changes in what is seen as acceptable usage, as when he remarks that "that gross way of two Comparatives was then, ordinary, and therefore more pardonable" (211).

Dryden did not, of course, edit Shakespeare, but a similar attitude can be found in the work of early eighteenth-century editors such as Pope and Theobald. In the Preface to his first edition of 1725, Pope employs an architectural metaphor, describing Shakespeare's works as being like "an ancient majestick piece of Gothick Architecture," not a "neat Modern building" (xxiii), and he assumes the right to make wholesale corrections, relegating many passages of which he disapproves to the foot of the page, and rewriting lines which he finds faulty in either grammar or meter. Theobald opens the Preface to his 1733 edition with an extended version of the same metaphor (as Seary notes, 46–47):

The attempt to write upon Shakespeare is like going into a large, a spacious, and splendid Dome thro' the Conveyance of a narrow and obscure Entry. . . . And as in great Piles of Building, some Parts are often finish'd up to hit the Taste of the *Connoisseur:* others more negligently put together, to strike the Fancy of a common and unlearned Beholder: Some Parts are made stupendiously magnificent and grand, to surprize with the vast Design and Execution of the Architect; others are contracted, to amuse you with his Neatness and Elegance in little. So, in *Shakespeare,* we may find *Traits* that will stand the

Test of the severest Judgment; and Strokes as carelesly hit off, to the Level of
the more ordinary Capacities. (i–ii)

The notion that Shakespeare-as-architect was negligent or careless in his
construction of parts, if not of the whole, can clearly be made to justify
some tinkering or "finishing up" on the part of his more tasteful connois-
seurs or editors.

But it is in *Shakespeare Restored,* his 1726 critique of Pope's 1725
edition, that Theobald really puts the issue of grammatical emendation
onto the agenda of eighteenth-century editors of Shakespeare. In that
book he discusses, for example, the propriety of some of Pope's corrections of pronouns in the plays when "the *Nominative* of *Pronouns* is
used, tho' Grammar requires the *Accusative.*" As usual in *Shakespeare
Restored,* Theobald takes most of his examples from *Hamlet.* A case in
point is 639: "Making night hideous, and we fools of nature." Theobald
accepts Pope's correction of "we" to "us" in this and other similar examples, remarking:

> It may be alledged from these Instances, and some few more that might be
> gather'd, that this was a Liberty which SHAKESPEARE purposely gave him-
> self, and that therefore it is not an Error of the Copies. Be this, as it will; if
> *Grammar* and the *Idiom* of the Tongue be directly against it, we have sufficient
> Warrant to make him *now,* at least, speak true *English.* (40–41)

This seems a very clear case of an eighteenth-century scholar assuming
the right to correct Shakespeare's grammar and to alter the text of the
play, even though he is aware that the "Error" is a frequent one which
Shakespeare permitted himself and that it cannot be attributed to "the
Copies." No modern editor would take such a step, and it is unusual in
Theobald. Elsewhere in this book, as his very title shows, he is anxious
to "restore" what he takes to be the authentic Shakespeare, saving him
from both the mistakes in the earliest texts and the more recent depreda-
tions of Pope. For example, when Pope prints:

> but you must fear
> His Greatness weigh'd, his Will is not his own.
>
> (479–80)

Theobald comments:

> As this is pointed, the Sense is absolutely maim'd; for *Greatness* appears the
> *Accusative Case* to the *Verb* fear: Whereas, in the Poet's Meaning, it is an
> *Ablative absolute.* Read it therefore,

> but you must fear,
> His Greatness weigh'd, his Will is not his own.

That is, his Greatness being weigh'd or consider'd by you, you must have this Fear, that his Will is not in his own Power, but subject to the State. (21)

In this case, correct grammar can be restored by the addition of a comma. Later when Pope prints:

> We would not understand what was most fit,
> But like the owner of a foul disease,
> To keep it from divulging, lets it feed
> Ev'n on the pith of life.
>
> (2607–10)

Theobald comments: "The *Syntax* of this Passage is evidently bad, for WE is the *Nominative* to both *Verbs,* and therefore they both must be *Plural*" (106). He consequently suggests emending "lets" to "let."

In his own subsequent edition of the plays, Theobald attempts to make better sense of several passages in *Cymbeline* by similar grammatically based emendations. For example, in the following speech by Imogen at the end of 3.2:

> I see before me (Man) nor heere, not heere,
> Nor what ensues but have a Fog in them
> That I cannot looke through.
>
> (1548–50)

he rejects "in them" as ungrammatical and emends to "in ken" (i.e., "in prospect" or "within sight"). Two scenes later he finds a problem with Pisanio's instruction to Imogen to seek employment with Lucius:

> Present yourselfe, desire his service: tell him
> Wherein you're happy; which will make him know,
> If that his head haue eare in Musicke, doubtlesse
> With ioy he will imbrace you.
>
> (1865–68)

Theobald comments: "'Which will make him know', what? What Connection has This with the Rest of the Sentence?" He emends "know" to "so" (an emendation he had suggested in *Shakespeare Restored* and which had in fact been adopted by Pope in his second edition in 1728). He frequently points out places where logical and grammatical inconsistency go together, as for example in his comment on this passage from Belarius's speech about Cymbeline's sons:

> They thinke they are mine,
> And though train'd vp thus meanely
> I'th'Cave whereon the Bowe their thoughts do hit
> The Roofes of Palaces, and Nature prompts them
> In simple and lowe things, to Prince it, much
> Beyond the tricke of others.
>
>   (1642–47)[10]

Theobald remarks "the Sentence breaks off imperfectly." Later he puzzles over the same character's lines about Cloten:

> Being scarce made vp,
> I meane to man; he had not apprehension
> Of roaring terrors: for defect of iudgement
> Is oft the cause of Feare.
>
>   (2390–93)

"But then, how does the Inference come in, built upon this?" asks Theobald, ". . . I think the Poet meant to have said the meer contrary." Similarly with Lucius's query when he finds Imogen with Cloten's headless body:

> Or who was he
> That (otherwise than noble Nature did)
> Hath alter'd that good Picture?
>
>   (2691–93)

Theobald comments:

> This is far from being strictly grammatical. For the Construction of these Words is this: *who has* alter'd *that good Picture, otherwise than Nature* alter'd *it?* But That is not the Poet's Meaning. He design'd to say, if the Text be genuine; *who hath* alter'd *that good Picture* from what noble Nature *at first* made *it?*

He suggests emending "did" to "bid" here but does not actually print "bid."

But Theobald is at the same time opposed to some kinds of grammatical emendation and he begins, in *Shakespeare Restored,* a debate on the subject amongst eighteenth-century editors which is both more sophisticated and less prescriptive than one might expect. He was a friend of the by now elderly John Dennis who had written in his 1717 *Remarks upon Mr. Pope's Translation of Homer* that "Use" was "the absolute Master of Languages" (2:157)[11] and had argued in his 1711 *Reflections Critical and Satirical, upon a Late Rhapsody, Call'd An Essay of Criticism* (i.e., Pope's *Essay on Criticism*) that language use changes over time (ibid.,

1:410). Theobald's method of dealing with difficulties in Shakespeare is drawn from classical scholarship and consists of assembling parallel passages to support or challenge a reading. This often leads him to set historical or personal usage against strict correctness, as for example when he discusses Shakespeare's verbal coinages:

> It is a Licence in our Poet, of his own Authority, to coin new *Verbs* both out of *Substantives* and *Adjectives;* and it is, as we may call it, one of the *Quidlibet audendi's* very familiar with him. (*Shakespeare Restored,* 8)

He gives examples from *Measure for Measure,* "Lord Angelo dukes it well" (1583), from *King Lear,* "to knee his throne" (1507) and from *Cymbeline,* "For wrying but a little" (2862). By early eighteenth-century standards he is a conservative editor, preferring to rewrite Shakespeare as little as possible and to restore what he honestly believes Shakespeare wrote rather than what he ought to have written.

This can be further proved from his voluminous correspondence with William Warburton, an enthusiastic contriver of ingenious emendations. At the height of their scholarly friendship, on 6 November 1729, Theobald writes to Warburton:

> I agree with you, *Cymbeline* is a most corrupt Play; and I have a great number of corrections upon it: you say, you have 30 stable ones in store. I wish earnestly I could be favoured with them, if possible, by the next post. . . . You bring back to my mind the times of a love-correspondence; and the expectation of every fresh Letter from you is the joy of a mistress to me. (257)[12]

Nevertheless, he rejects most of Warburton's suggestions for altering the text, always thoughtfully and politely: "Yet, I fancy, it may be understood as it is" (264); "I have long since cured it with a lesser change" (266); "I am apt to think, if we consider the circumstances strictly, there will be no occasion to disturb the text" (614). Peter Seary has calculated that in the surviving letters taken as a whole Theobald refuted some ninety percent of Warburton's proposed emendations, and the proportion would hold for *Cymbeline.* In his vindication of Theobald, Seary goes on to note that many of his emendations have stood the test of time: the Riverside edition preserves 153 of his suggestions, as compared with 81 of Pope's, 19 of Warburton's, and 23 of Johnson's. And this is just for "substantive textual variants"; if other changes such as punctuation are included, Seary claims that the number of Theobald's emendations "generally found in modern texts" rises to 350.[13]

Warburton himself, despite his earlier exuberance for conjecture (and despite his later bitter hostility to Theobald), writes sensibly enough in the Preface to his own edition of 1747 about the danger of emending

Shakespeare when obscurity of meaning results from "hard or ungrammatical construction," which he sees as:

> the Effect of mistaken Art and Design. The Public Taste was in its Infancy; and delighted (as it always does during that State) in the high and turgid; which leads the Writer to disguise a vulgar expression with hard and forced construction, whereby the sentence frequently becomes cloudy and dark. Here, his Criticks show their modesty, and leave him to himself. For the arbitrary change of a Word doth little towards dispelling an obscurity that ariseth, not from the licentious use of a single Term, but from the unnatural arrangement of a whole Sentence. (lxiv)

In his commentary he specifically quarrels with Theobald's emendation of *Cymbeline* 1548–50 (as quoted above on 70), remarking that "not to know that Shakespeare perpetually takes these liberties of grammar, is to know nothing of his author." And he ridicules Theobald's comment on 2691–93 (as quoted above on 78): "I suppose this editor's meaning was, that the grammatical construction would not conform to the sense; for a bad writer, like a bad man, generally says one thing, and means another." Meanwhile Thomas Edwards, entering the fray on behalf of Theobald with his *A Supplement to Mr. Warburton's Edition of Shakespeare* (1747) attacks Warburton's propensity to rewrite Shakespeare by drawing up a satirical list of twenty-five "canons of criticism" to be followed by the "Professed Critic," which includes as number VI:

> As every Author is to be corrected into all possible perfection, and of that perfection the Professed Critic is to be the sole judge; He may alter any word or phrase, which does not want amendment, or which *will do,* provided He can think of any thing, which he imagines *will do better.* (25–26)

Johnson, who openly sides with Warburton against Theobald but actually makes more substantial use of Theobald's edition than of Warburton's,[14] takes a fairly nondogmatic line on grammar, claiming in the Preface to his edition of 1765 that "The stile of Shakespeare was in itself ungrammatical, perplexed and obscure" (C7r) and he seems prepared to excuse this on account of the theatrical medium for which the plays were written. He is critical of Thomas Hanmer, the 1744 editor, for being

> solicitous to reduce to grammar, what he could not be sure that his author intended to be grammatical. Shakespeare regarded more the series of ideas, than of words; and his language, not being designed for the reader's desk, was all that he desired it to be, if it conveyed his meaning to his audience. (D2r)

In his commentary on *Cymbeline,* Johnson sometimes tries to make the characters follow the rules—at 249–51 he comments "I believe the Lord means to speak a sentence"—but he rejects two of Hanmer's emendations to the song "Hark, hark, the lark" in 2.3. The Folio text reads:

> Hearke, hearke, the Larke at Heauen's gate sings,
>   and Phoebus gins arise,
> His Steeds to water at those Springs
>   On chalic'd Flowers that lyes:
> And winking Mary-buds begin to ope their Golden eyes;
>   With every thing that pretty is, my Lady sweet arise:
>   Arise, arise.

> (982–88)

Hanmer emends "at those Springs / On chalic'd flowers that lyes" to "at those Springs / Each chalic'd flower supplies" in order to "escape a false concord," but Johnson comments that "correctness must not be obtained by such licentious alterations." Johnson approves Hanmer's emendation of "is" to "bin" for the internal rhyme with "begin" two lines later but notes that "he too grammatically reads 'With all the things that pretty bin'" instead of "With every thing that pretty bin." In 1785 John Monck Mason reverts to the "Springs . . . lyes" problem in his *Comments on the Last Edition of Shakespeare's Plays* and ridicules those commentators who

> have endeavoured with much labour to justify Shakespeare on this occasion, and to free him from the charge of having made a false concord, which appears evident to unlearned readers, by proving that the mode of expression he has adopted, is agreeable to the idiom of the English language in the days of Chaucer, and to that also of the Dane-Saxons, but these are mysteries in which Shakespeare, I fear, was but little skilled, and the truth is, that he, knowingly, sacrificed grammar to rhyme in this place, as he has done in others, when he found it convenient. (325)

Mason, whose *Comments* relate to the 1773 edition by Johnson and George Steevens, also accurately paraphrases Jupiter's line "to make my guift / The more delay'd, delighted" (3137–38): "that is, the more delightful for being delayed." He comments: "It is scarcely necessary to observe, in the ninth volume, that Shakespeare uses indiscriminately the active and passive participles" (ibid., 336–37). The debate over participles goes back to *Shakespeare Restored* where Theobald objects to Pope's following of the Folio reading "Why even in that was Heaven ordinate" (*Hamlet*, 3551)—"Why a Passive participle here, when the Sense, I think, plainly requires an Active?"—and suggests correcting to "ordinant." (Modern editors generally print "ordinant," citing as their authority the Second Quarto of 1604/5 which Theobald collated for his edition but seems not to have known about in 1726.)

Theobald is also the first to notice the curious and often syntactically confusing piling up of self-interrupting parentheses in *Cymbeline* which he comments on in his discussion of punctuation or "pointing" in *Shakespeare Restored*. He argues for a clarification of the punctuation of the following passage from Imogen's first speech to Pisanio on receiving the letter from Posthumus in 3.2:

> Let what is heere contain'd, rellish of Love,
> Of my Lords health, of his content: yet not
> That we two are asunder, let that grieve him;
> Some griefes are medcinable, that is one of them,
> For it doth physicke Love, of his content,
> All but in that.
>
> (1499–1504)

Theobald comments:

Imogen, as is very frequent with our Poet upon other Occasions, breaks in upon the Thread of her own Address to the Gods, interposes a Reflection, and moralizes upon it; and then resumes the Substance of her Prayer at the very Words where She left it off. She catches herself up in the same manner in the very next page. (*Shakespeare Restored*, 149–50)

The second passage is:

> Then true *Pisanio*,
> Who long'st like me, to see thy Lord; who long'st
> (Oh let me bate) but not like me: yet long'st,
> But in a fainter kinde. Oh not like me:
> For mine's beyond, beyond.
>
> (1520–24)

In his 1767–68 edition, Edward Capell comments on the same passage that "the huddle of [Imogen's] ideas is such as leaves no time for correctness." He also criticizes earlier editors who have been "very tender of Cloten" in 4.1, "not suffering him to knock a word out of joint, make a bull, or speak out of grammar." In both these cases, the incorrect or obscure syntax can conceivably be attributed to the character or the situation, not to Shakespeare as author, an "excuse" which is considered but finally rejected by John Porter Houston in his 1988 book where he finds himself driven to admit of more than one speech that "nothing about [the] situation particularly supports the style: we . . . must have recourse to the notion of some general design in the language of the play rather than to that of character or scene."[15]

Elsewhere, Capell rejects Hanmer's emendation of "whom, not to slander" to "which, not to slander't" at 2533 saying "the old ungrammatical reading is more in the Poet's manner," and he describes 3105–6 as "a passage in which the sense is at war with the grammar, and the grammar must yield to it." In Belarius's speech at 3644f. he finds "some expressions in this author's manner, that will not stand the test of strict reasoning but must be constru'd indulgently." And the last eighteenth-century editor, Edmond Malone, whose edition was published in 1790, remarks on instances of Shakespeare's incorrect grammar in his commentary, but often refuses to emend on the grounds that such usages are commonplace and must be admitted as authentic. Faced with the problem in 2870–72 (as discussed above on 74), for example, he comments: "However ungrammatical, I believe the old reading is the true one." (See also his note on "without less quality" at 337 of *Cymbeline* and his notes on the change of persons at 1665–66 and 2526–27). By the end of the century, then, the growth in understanding and acceptance of historical usage of forms of language which violated contemporary norms had put in place a mode of editing more akin to modern practice. Theobald had pioneered these principles in explicit opposition to the more irresponsible practice of Pope, but the editors of the mid-century, notably Hanmer and Warburton, had perpetuated the tradition of more wholesale emendation.

I found, in conclusion, that the work of the eighteenth-century editors is in some ways different from what I had expected. I was often impressed by their frequent displays of care and patience, their willingness to be descriptive as well as prescriptive. Certainly they have stronger notions of what is correct than we have today, but they do not apply arbitrary rules across the board. Much of their zeal for correction goes into correcting each other rather than into correcting Shakespeare who is often allowed to break the rules. Indeed, indulgence of this kind becomes a standard way for an editor to display his superior acquaintance with his author compared with the narrower outlook of his predecessors whose efforts can then be dismissed as "too grammatical." (Johnson's vision of commentators differing "without animosity," quoted above on 72, seems a pious hope indeed in this period.) Changes in historical usage of grammar are increasingly recognized and permitted. Other "improprieties" can be explained with reference to the theatrical medium, the character, the situation, or the necessities of rhyme.

The syntactic difficulties of *Cymbeline* remain enormous. I did not expect any of the eighteenth-century editors to have solved them all, any more than a modern editor would expect to solve them. Perhaps we should not be trying to "solve" them anyway. A similar kind of irregularity or incoherence in another of Shakespeare's late plays, *The Winter's Tale,* is discussed in Stephen Orgel's recent essay called "The Poetics of Incomprehensibility"[16] where he argues that some of the speeches in that text are quite deliberately elliptical and obscure. This could indeed be part of their meaning: "We need to remember that the Renaissance tolerated, and indeed courted, a much higher degree of ambiguity and opacity than we do; we tend to forget that the age often found in incomprehensibility a positive virtue" (436). Hence, in our attempts to elucidate the Shakespearean text, "We do it wrong when we deny that it is problematic and has always been so, and reduce it to our own brand of common sense" (437). Orgel is not then being complimentary when he refers in this context to Samuel Johnson's "characteristic genius for finding a plain prose sense in the most elaborately conceited Shakespearean verse" (431–32).

Orgel is editing *The Winter's Tale* for the Oxford Shakespeare series which has already published his excellent edition of *The Tempest*. In this context, his remarks are indicative of a new departure for the editorial tradition. Editors used to speak, or attempted to speak, with a kind of magisterial authority, dismissing all previous theories and interpretations and laying claim to their own unique ability to explicate the text. But in recent years a certain convergence has taken place in textual and critical studies whereby notions of authority have been challenged. Textual and bibliographical scholars have become prepared to accept that texts— especially dramatic texts—of this period might be provisional rather than absolute, and that Shakespeare revised his work, leaving us with two or more equally "authorial" versions in several cases. At the same time, the climate created by post-structuralist criticism has destabilized notions of meaning and interpretation, forcing us all to recognize the extent to which our readings are bound to be subjective and culture-specific. While an editor of a complex Shakespearean text still has an obligation to investigate the difficulties of the text on the behalf of the reader, the aim is more to explore the possibilities than to impose a single "correct" view, to raise questions about what Shakespeare might have made of the concept of "true English" rather than to make him speak it.

NOTES

1. Baton Rouge: Louisiana State University Press, 1988.
2. TLN 1–4. All quotations are from the First Folio (1623) except when I specify a particular eighteenth-century or modern edition. Line references are to the Through Line Numbers from Charlton Hinman, *The Norton Facsimile: The First Folio of Shakespeare* (New York: Norton and London: Paul Hamlyn, 1968).
3. Philadelphia: Lippincott.
4. London: Methuen.
5. Cambridge: Cambridge University Press, 1960.
6. Boston: Houghton Mifflin.
7. Oxford: Oxford University Press.

8. See Peter Seary, *Lewis Theobald and the Editing of Shakespeare* (Oxford: Clarendon Press, 1990).

9. *The Works of John Dryden,* edited by John Loftis et al. (Berkeley: University of California Press, 1978), 11:205, 207.

10. Modern editors generally adopt Warburton's 1747 emendation of "whereon the Bow" to "wherein they bow."

11. *The Critical Works of John Dennis* edited by Edward Niles Hooker, 2 vols. (Baltimore: John Hopkins University Press, 1943).

12. "Shakespearian Correspondence of Mr. Lewis Theobald, Dr. Thirlby, and Mr. Warburton" in *Illustrations of the Literary History of the Eighteenth Century,* edited by John Nichols, 2:189–654.

13. In Seary, *Lewis Theobald,* 108 and 167.

14. Ibid., 7–11 and 159–70.

15. Houston, *Shakespearean Sentences,* 207. I agree with Houston that character-based attempts to explain the style are misguided, though the 1955 Arden editor resorts to them quite often (as indeed in his comment on the opening speech, cited above on p. 71). For further discussion see my essay, "'Casting Sense between the Speech': Parentheses in the Oxford Shakespeare," *Analytical and Enumerative Bibliography* 4. 1 (1991): 72–90.

16. Stephen Orgel, "The Poetics of Incomprehensibility," *Shakespeare Quarterly* 42 (1991): 431–37.

"The Scene Changes"? Stage Directions in Eighteenth-Century Acting Editions of Shakespeare

Linda McJannet

Prologue

THE form of English stage directions is a distinctive verbal and visual code that developed chiefly during the Elizabethan and Jacobean eras. By the "form" of stage directions, I mean their functional differentiation, their grammar and rhetoric, and their characteristic position on the page. The scheme of functionally discrete directions (entrances, exits, speech prefixes, etc.) is now so familiar, that the phrase "Enter the King" is recognizable as a stage direction to any literate speaker of English. Paradoxically, this code has also resulted in a measure of "invisibility" for the stage directions of the period. Although many theatrical professionals ignore or reject the stage directions of later drama, they often implicitly accept those in Shakespeare and his fellows while expressing the view that classic Elizabethan drama "doesn't have any stage directions."

At once authoritative and unobtrusive, the form of Elizabethan stage directions is taken for granted as "natural" or inevitable, but it was the result of a long process of evolution from the late Middle Ages onward and was not without rivals, even in its own day. My goal in this paper is to see what happens to the verbal and visual conventions for stage directions in eighteenth-century editions of Shakespeare, particularly "acting editions" that claim a close association with the stage. In an age in which so many aspects of Shakespeare were "corrected" or "improved," how did the distinctive form for stage directions fare? Do the established forms persist or undergo fundamental changes? Do the acting editions differ in their handling of stage directions from the learned "literary" editions? A preliminary answer to these questions seems to be that while the text of the plays underwent sometimes radical alteration during the eighteenth century, the Elizabethan form of the stage directions showed remarkable durability and stability.

86

ENTER FIVE EDITIONS

My remarks will focus on five so-called acting editions of *Henry VIII* that date from 1752 to 1804, namely:

1. *King Henry VIII: A Tragedy. . . . with alterations by Dryden, as it is now acted in the Theatres Royal of London and Dublin.* Dublin: James Dalton, 1752.

I am uncertain of the relationship between this edition and a 1734 Dublin edition ascribed to Leathley that William P. Halstead describes as "the first published acting edition" of this play. (Halstead does not list the 1752 Dryden version.) According to Halstead, the major cuts in the 1734 edition are the prologue, epilogue, and the coronation; many minor cuts are scattered throughout the text.[1]

2. *King Henry VIII With the Coronation of Anne Bullen . . . With Alterations, As it is Performed at the Theatre-Royal in Drury-Lane.* London: C. Hitch and L. Hawes et al, 1762.

This is Garrick's version, at the end of the play's ten-year history of productions under his direction at the Drury-Lane; the *Dramatis Personae* is essentially that of 3 October and 5, 1762. Garrick apparently did not act in the play himself. Charles Hogan lists the major textual omissions.[2]

3. *King Henry VIII by Shakespeare. As Performed at the Theatre-Royal, Covent Garden: Regulated from the Prompt-Book. With Permission of the Managers, by Mr. Younger, Prompter. An Introduction and Notes Critical and Illustrative are added by the Authors of the Dramatic Censor.* Second Edition. London: Printed for John Bell, 1774.

This is a volume in the influential and popular *Bell's Edition of Shakespeare's Plays*. Contains *Dramatis Personae* with cast lists of both Drury Lane (essentially that of 3 October and 5, 1762) and Covent Garden (cast of January, 1773). The play was regularly performed at Covent Garden from 1772 until 1787. Francis Gentleman is the author of *The Dramatic Censor*. Of the editions examined here this is the only one to burden the page with notes and commentary of various sorts.

Hogan describes this edition as essentially "identical" to the 1762 edition (in its omissions), only "somewhat more abridged." It was the standard acting version until replaced by Kemble's (see 5 below).[3]

4. *King Henry VIII: A Tragedy . . . Adapted for Theatrical Representation, as performed at the Theatres-Royal, London.* Manchester: 1801. Widener Library, Harvard University.

This is volume 21 in *Dean's Edition of the British Theatre*. The notice "To the Public" announces that this "New Pocket Edition" is based on "Johnson and Steevens' last Edition." The *Dramatis Personae* does not list actors' names.

5. *Shakespeare's King Henry the Eighth. A Historical Play. Revised by J. P. Kemble. And Now first published as it is acted at the Theatre Royal in Covent Garden.* London: Longman, 1804.

Kemble revived the play in 1788, with Mrs. Siddons as Katherine, at Drury Lane, where it continued in the repertory until 1816. Hogan describes this edition as "identical" with Bell's, but according to Halstead, Kemble cut 16 additional passages (the longest being all of 3.1, Katherine's visitation by the Cardinals at Kimbolton) and restored 31 brief passages.[4]

Of these five editions, only this one suggests a detailed reconstruction of a particular production's staging of ceremonial entries and spectacle, a tendency that grew stronger in nineteenth-century "memorial" acting editions, such as Kean's. A copy of this edition was used as a promptbook in 1806, marked and interleaved in Kemble's hand.[5] Extracts below are from the printed text only.

As can be seen from the above, the degree of dependence upon a stage version varies, but each of these editions claims a theatrical rather than a literary or scholarly authority (except Dean's edition, which claims both).[6] These editions preserve the cuts, interpolations, and transpositions of various productions (or families of productions) and eschew the scholarly commentary that was gaining in bulk in the standard editions. Thus, they might be said to represent a "rival tradition" in the editing of Shakespeare. In Margreta de Grazia's terms,[7] they invoke the "authenticity" of communal acceptance and social (theatrical) practice, rather than that of documentary evidence, which was increasingly relied upon by scholarly editors, such as Theobald and Malone.

At the same time, although acting editions may defend the justice of theatrical cuts, they do not claim that their version is the "true" or "corrected" text.[8] In presenting frankly altered versions of the text, they implicitly admit, even enshrine, the multiplicity and variability of "Shakespeare" in their age. In some acting versions, cuts and additions to the text are indicated with inverted commas and italics, respectively. This relatively scholarly refinement, however, is not observed in the five editions listed above, which ostensibly present the text as acted.

In practice, theatrical and scholarly editions differed chiefly in the completeness of the text offered, as indicated in descriptions of the five editions above. I have not made a thorough comparison of the stage directions in scholarly and acting editions. But such as I have been able to make suggests that, until Kemble's edition in the early nineteenth century, the differences between stage directions in acting and literary editions are minor compared to the issue of textual cuts. Thus, it is possible that the remarks below apply equally to directions in literary and acting editions. Overall, it seems that the acting editions, though they seek to regularize some details, follow the conventions of the folio's directions far more often than not,[9] and that in some cases significant deviations that appear in midcentury are abandoned by the century's end. Further, insofar as directions are changed to reflect (among other things) changes in theatre architecture and scenic practice, diction, and content are altered but the grammatical and visual form are left largely intact.

SPEECH PREFIXES AND PAGE DESIGN

All these acting editions (and the standard editions with which I am familiar) observe most of the visual conventions that govern Elizabethan stage directions. To summarize quickly:

1. Directions appear in italics (proper names are sometimes in Roman), in contrast to the dialogue in Roman.

2. All the editions cited above number the acts and some number acts and scenes.[10] (Act and scene headings, although not universal in Elizabethan texts, do appear in the folio text of *Henry VIII*, set off by rules above and below.)

3. Speech prefixes appear on the left-hand side of the text column, slightly indented, one speech prefix to a line. (That is, if speakers change in the middle of a line of verse, the line is "broken," and the new speaker's name appears at the left hand of the next line.)

4. As in the folio, initial entries are prominent on the page, centered within the text column (thus set off by white space) or written across the entire column. In either case, they break the column of the dialogue and clearly announce the beginning of a new scene.

5. Midscene entries are also usually centered, highlighting the arrival of a new character upon the scene.

6. Midscene directions (other than entries) are usually set on their own line, indented to the right as far as convenient.

7. Exits generally appear to the right, even flush right, either on a separate line or at the end of a line of dialogue.

The observance of these visual conventions in these editions suggests two things. Some Elizabethan conventions, such as italicized directions and centered entries, seem to have become standard for dramatic texts of all kinds. Others, though not universal, seem retained in deference to Shakespeare. For example, the left-hand, indented speech prefix is retained by Garrick, even though when composing his own texts or printing his other plays or adaptations, he preferred a centered speech prefix, which separated each speaker by vertical white space.[11] It is true that speech prefixes are regularized and clarified. For example, the folio variously refers to Wolsey as *Wol.* and *Card.;* since there are two other cardinals in the play, this can be confusing. The acting editions tend to use *Wol.* consistently. In this they share the general tendency of eighteenth-century editions to regularize the folio text.

In their sole visual innovation, the acting editions often further differentiate brief mid-scene directions for action and some exits by adding a
half-bracket or sometimes full brackets.[12] Mid-scene entries, however,
are not bracketed in these editions.

SCENE DIVISIONS AND LOCATIONS

Directions indicating the locale of the action are not found in Shakespeare and other Elizabethan dramatists, but they are added in some—
though not all—of these acting editions. In the earliest, Dryden's 1752
version, a scene indication precedes the initial entry:

S C E N E, an Anti-chamber in the Palace.

(1.1.0)

And for subsequent scenes in each act, the formula is:

S C E N E *changes to the* Council chamber.

(1.2.0)

S C E N E *changes to* York-house.

(1.4.0)

This edition thus alternates between a introductory noun phrase, such as
those used for special effects in Elizabethan texts (*Cornets, Hoboyes*)
and a direction in which the scene is active, like a character (SCENE
changes). A similar dual practice can be found in Elizabethan plays with
respect to introducing prologues: one could use a textual heading, usually
in Roman ("The Prologue") or an italic entry direction, which treated the
prologue like a character (*Enter Prologue*).

Two of these editions, Garrick's[13] and Bell's, do not add scene-by-scene
locations. Dean's (perhaps following Johnson-Steevens) inserts a general
statement at the end of the *dramatis personae* ("*The* SCENE *lies mostly
in London and Westminster; once at Kimbolton*") and indicates the location of each scene with either a noun phrase (*The Council-Chamber*,"
1.2.0), or a combination of a scene heading and "scene change direction"
(as in the Dryden edition):

SCENE IV.
Changes to York-place.

(1.4.0)

With Kemble's edition of 1804, however, the pattern of scene heading plus a brief location seems to become the norm:

SCENE II
The Council-chamber.

(1.2.0)

This pattern is reproduced in Mrs. Inchbald's 1808 edition and retained in Kemble's edition of 1815.

Although the presence of locational directions is in itself an innovation, an important deviation embraced in Garrick (and also found to a greater extent in Pope) is not continued in the later editions. Instead of the Elizabethan convention that a clearstage signals the end of one scene and the beginning of another, Garrick's version usually observes the neoclassical or French convention. That is, a new scene is indicated when a new character or group of characters enters.

For example, act 1 scene 1 of the folio text becomes three different scenes: scene one, the opening with Buckingham and Norfolk; scene two, when Wolsey enters with his train; and scene three, when Brandon enters to arrest Buckingham. This change might matter little to a spectator, but a reader would lack the appropriate signals for the scenes that were the fundamental unit of Shakespeare's dramaturgy. This innovation, however, was not retained in later acting editions, where, as in the folio, a clearstage defines a scene.

ENTRY DIRECTIONS

Initial entries, those that begin a scene, are among the most authoritative and distinctive of Elizabethan directions. They are characterized by several striking features of language as well as the prominent page position described above. First, the verb appears in a form unique to this usage: *Enter the king*. It is uninflected (unchanging for singular and plural entries), and the word order is inverted (*Enter the king,* not *The king enters*). Second, entries elaborated with details of blocking, costume, or props observe a distinctive, highly compact, Latinate syntax: they admit participles, ablative absolutes, prepositional phrases, adverbs, and adjectives, but they avoid dependent clauses and finite verbs. In complex or ceremonial entries, after the initial direction, further details of action may be given either in elliptical fashion, or in full sentences observing normal grammar.

For example, here is the initial entry for 1.1, from the folio followed by the parallel directions in later editions:

> *Enter the Duke of Norfolke at one doore. At the other,*
> *the Duke of Buckingham, and the Lord*
> *Abergavenny.*

> *Enter the Duke of Norfolk at one door; at the other, the*
> *Duke of Buckingham, and the Lord Abergavenny.*
> (Garrick, 1762, Bell's, 1774, Dean's, 1801)

> *Enter the Duke of Norfolk and the Duke of Buckingham.*
> (1804, Kemble)

By Kemble's edition, Abergavenny has been cut and the reference to stage doors has been deleted, but the basic grammar of an Elizabethan entry direction remains.

Important mid-scene entries follow the same pattern as initial entries, and their treatment in these editions is much the same. The content may be altered, but the form is generally observed. For example:

> *Enter Cardinall Wolsey, the Purse borne before him, certaine*
> *of the Guard, and two Secretaries with Papers: The*
> *Cardinall in his passage, fixeth his eye on Buck-*
> *[ing]ham, and Buckingham on him,*
> *both full of disdaine.*
> (1623 Folio. 1.1.114)

> *Enter Cardinal Wolsey attended, Secretary with papers, the*
> *Cardinal in his passage fixeth his eye on Buckingham*
> *and Buckingham on him, both full of disdain.*
> (1752, Dryden)

> *Enter Cardinal Wolsey, and Cromwell, the purse borne*
> *before him, certain of the guard, and two secretaries*
> *with papers; the Cardinal in his passage fixeth his*
> *eye on Buckingham, and Buckingham on him, both*
> *full of disdain.*
> (1762, Garrick)

> *Enter Cardinal Wolsey, and Cromwell, the purse borne*
> *before him, certain of the guard, and two secretaries*
> *with papers; the Cardinal in his passage fixeth his*

eye on Buckingham, and Buckingham on him, both
full of disdain.

(1774, Bell)

Enter footmen—Guards—Gentlemen—one Gentleman bearing
the broad seal,—another the Cardinal's hat,—two Gentle-
men with silver pillars,—two Priests with silver crosses,—
Serjeant at Arms with mace,—two Gentleman-ushers bare-
headed with wands,—Cardinal Wolsey,—two Pages bearing
his train,— Cromwell with dispatches,—two Secretaries
with bags of papers,—Chaplains,— Gentlemen,—Foot-
men,—Guards.

Wolsey in his passages fixes his eye on Buckingham, and Buck-
ingham on him, both full of disdain.

(1804, Kemble)

Up to Kemble, the form and content (with minor excisions and substitutions) remain remarkably similar. The number of characters varies and the anonymous "secretary" is early on conflated with a named character (Cromwell), perhaps to enlarge an actor's part or save doubling. Only with Kemble does the content of the direction reflect closely his particular staging, with additions of props, supers, etc. (Comparison with his 1806 promptbook suggests that this expanded direction may still not include all the details actually realized on stage, however.) Nonetheless, although Kemble inserts dashes into the entry, and despite all the additions, the form of an entry direction remains: the initial uninflected "Enter," elaborated with the characteristic syntax (chiefly ablative absolutes).

I do not wish to underestimate the substantive changes in these editions. Without changing the essential form, they do often significantly alter the dramatic meaning of a direction. Take for example, Katherine's striking entrance in 1.2, the Council scene. In the folio, an anonymous voice announces Katherine's unexpected entrance into the council. She enters "usher'd" by two powerful lords, which gives her entrance political as well as personal significance. The scripted blocking and gestures establish both her wifely submission to the king, and his affection and respect for her:

A noyse within crying roome for the Queene, usher'd by the Duke
of Norfolke. Enter the Queene, Norfolke, and
Suffolke: she kneels. King riseth from his State,

> *takes her up, kisses and placeth*
> *her by him.*

(F1623)

The acting editions make a series of substantive changes. The anonymous voice is given a name, initially the Lord Chamberlain, then Sir Henry Guildford, who is in turn often conflated with "Griffith," Katherine's waiting gentleman. Similarly, although Norfolk and Suffolk accompany her in Dryden and Garrick, Bell has her enter solus, and Kemble gives her only Guildford, again. Thus the political implications of Katherine's entrance are sharply reduced. Similarly, her interaction with Henry (raising, kissing, placing her by him) is not specified at all in Dryden, and by Kemble's editions the kiss has been omitted. Further, by the time of Kemble, a cushion is deemed necessary for the comfort of the royal knees (or perhaps the actresses demanded it), which to me further undercuts the seriousness and strength of her presence (others may find it increases the ceremony of her petition):

> *(Within) Room for the Queen. Enter the Queen usher'd*
> *by the Duke of Norfolk and Suffolk; she kneels.*

(1752, Dryden)

> *Lord Chamberlain says,* **Room for the Queen.** *Enter the Queen,*
> *she kneels. The King riseth from his State, takes her up,*
> *kisses and placeth her by him.*

(1762, Garrick)

> *Lord Chamberlain says,* **Room for the Queen.** *Enter the Queen,*
> *she kneels. The King riseth from his State,*
> *takes her up, kisses and placeth her by him.*

(1774, Bell's)

> *[Sir Henry Guildford without.]*
> *Guil.* **Room for the Queene.**
>
> *Enter the Queen, usher'd by Guildford, who places a cushion on*
> *which she kneels.—The King rises, takes her up, and places*
> *her by him.*

(1804, Kemble)

Nonetheless, granting the important changes in content, the form is remarkably stable. There are two exceptions. The Kemble version reverses the point of view—"within" becomes "without." (This reversal was ratified and transmitted to nineteenth-century readers and actors by Mrs.

Inchbald's edition (1808) and Kemble's 1815 version.) Bell's and Garrick's editions revert to an earlier form of speech attribution (*Lord Chamberlain says*, as part of the centered direction) instead of *within* or a normal speech prefix. This method of speech attribution was common in medieval drama but rare in Elizabethan plays.

Occasionally in these editions, one finds entries in the neoclassical form or so-called "massed entries": the characters in the scene are simply listed at the beginning without use of the word "enter."[14] Such entries were not unknown in Elizabethan texts, but they were more common in academic drama and in boys' plays than in plays for the men's companies. They are extremely rare in Shakespeare's plays; none occur in the folio text of *Henry VIII*. Nonetheless, several occur in Garrick's edition and in Bell's:

> *A small table under a state for the Cardinal, a longer table*
> *for the Guests. Anne Bullen, and divers other Ladies*
> *and gentlemen, as guests. Enter Sir Henry Guilford.*
>
> (1.4.0)

> *The Queen and her Women, as at work.*
>
> (3.1.0)

But like the flirtation with the neoclassical convention of the "French scene" to replace the Elizabethan principle of the clearstage, this innovation did not catch on. The traditional Elizabethan form continued to govern entries in Shakespearean texts.

There are some other differences between the folio and the acting editions. In keeping with the different resources and practices of the eighteenth-century theatre, some "entries" become "discoveries."[15] Discoveries occur in the folios and quartos, too, of course, but usually not on this scale:

> *Discover'd at the trial. Captain, six guards behind the*
> *throne. King on the throne. Norfolk and Suffolk*
> *on each side. Lord Chamberlain and Surry on a*
> *step. Sands and Lovel on another. Two Lords.*
> *Two Cardinals, on two stools, facing the audience.*
> *Cromwell at a table, in the middle, a mace on it. . . .*
>
> (Garrick, 2.4.0)

> *A state for the Cardinal, and a Table for the Guests.*
> *Anne Bullen, Lady Denny, and other Ladies and*

> *Gentlemen, as guests, Wolsey's Servants attending*
> *them, discovered.*
>
> (Kemble, 1.4.0)

The diction of the details is non-Elizabethan, the references to a "step" on the stage and, more striking, to "facing the audience" by way of indicating the blocking. Nonetheless, the syntax remains close to that of the original: compact phrases, including one ablative absolute (*a mace on it*).

One other point regarding entries deserves mention. When characters are directed in the dialogue to fetch another character and return, the folio often leaves the exit implicit, and simply marks the characters' entrance later in the scene. All of the five acting editions do likewise, except Dean's. This edition (like Bell's 1786 edition, which is also based on Johnson-Steevens) makes the exit explicit and employs the term "re-enter" when the character returns to the stage.

> *Cardinal goes out and re-enters with Gardiner.*
>
> (2.2)

> *Re-enter Griffith, with Capucius.*
>
> (4.2)

> *Re-enter Denny and Cranmer.*
>
> (5.1)

"Re-enter" is (as far as I know) not found in Elizabethan directions, which typically observe a strict, "dramatic" decorum: they operate within the immediate moment, rather than stepping outside it. Terms such as "again" or "as before," which imply an awareness of a previous direction, as opposed to remaining within the here and now of the action, do occur, but they are very rare. To use them is to survey the temporal flow of the play from the outside, from a privileged position. This was often the case in medieval directions, but was not typical of Elizabethan practice. It suggests the perspective of a director (or editor) rather than the in-the-moment point of view of the actor/character (the Elizabethan norm). In this sample of editions, "re-enter" seems a literary innovation rather than one originating in the theatre.

To summarize, on balance, in these editions the folio conventions hold for most major entries; the **content** of the entry may be abbreviated or altered, but the form is more often than not retained.

Epilogue

If I am right in viewing these editions as preserving, for the most part, the form and voice of Elizabethan stage directions, why is preservation of these conventions significant in the transmission of Shakespeare's texts? I offer one minor and one major reason for their significance.

First, the survival (or restoration) of these conventions seems to be another indication of the increasing deference to Shakespeare's text. George Coleman's edition of Fletcher's *Bonduca* for *Bell's British Theatre,* for example, regularly changes the grammar of all the entries. The unique, unvarying verb is naturalized and inflected depending on the number of characters entering: "*Junius and Petillus enter*" (1.1.0), but "*Curius enters*" (2.1.0). Similarly, Charles Johnson's *Love in a Forest,* an 1723 adaptation of scenes from *As You Like It,* employs neoclassical entries and invents a new form: "*Orlando and Adam entring*" (1.1.0). But when representing Shakespeare's own texts, editors adhere more closely to the conventions of the original texts. The converse of this point also holds: increasing deference to Shakespeare's text seems to have contributed to the survival of the Elizabethan code for stage directions.

Second, and more important, the Elizabethan form for directions is integral to Elizabethan dramatic discourse, just as the thrust stage is suited to the scope and rhythm of its action and the often presentational mode of its language. The long, novelistic directions of Shaw would be as out of place in the plays of Shakespeare and his fellows as a rococo picture frame on a Cubist painting. Moreover, unlike a frame added to a painting, the particular layout, grammar, and rhetoric of Elizabethan directions is an integral part of the dramatic text. The self-effacing voice and efficient visual design of these directions is, I believe, a small part of the reason the plays have survived both as texts for the general reader and as scripts for the theatre. Authoritative without being intrusive, the code for Elizabethan directions creates a polyvocal but readable text that preserves, if only schematically, the decorum and "presence" of drama.[16]

Notes

1. See William P. Halstead, *Statistical History of Acting Editions of Shakespeare: A Supplement to Shakespeare as Spoken,* vol. 13, (Ann Arbor: University Press of America, 1983), 427.

2. See Charles Beecher Hogan, *Shakespeare in the Theatre, 1701–1800,* vol. 2 (Oxford: Clarendon Press, 1957), 300. A photofacsimile of this edition is available in Gerald Berkowitz, *The Plays of David Garrick* (New York: Garland, 1981).

3. Charles Shattuck, *The Shakespeare Promptbooks: A Descriptive Catalogue* (Urbana and London: University of Illinois Press, 1965), 8. According to

Shattuck, the line of acting editions continued through Mrs. Inchbald, Oxberry, and so on right up to the Modern Standard Drama, which became French's Standard Drama, still in use today.

4. See Halstead, 429.

5. See Shattuck's facsimile in *John Philip Kemble's Promptbooks* (Charlottesville: University Press of Virginia, 1974).

6. For the dependence of these editions one upon another, see the chart in Halstead, 444. The chart does not include Dryden's or Dean's editions. As far as I can tell, Dean's edition follows the Johnson-Steevens edition, as it promises. Garrick's edition seems to me very similar to Pope's, although Halstead links it to the 1734 Dublin edition, and Shattuck asserts he used an acting version derived from Betterton. See Shattuck's *Catalogue,* 8.

7. Margreta de Grazia, *Shakespeare Verbatim: The Reproduction of Authenticity and the 1790 Apparatus* (Oxford: Clarendon Press, 1991), 49–51.

8. Francis Gentleman's commentary in Bell's edition, however, sometimes crosses swords with editors of the standard editions. For example, he disagrees with Warburton regarding the alleged obscurity of Buckingham's line, "I am the shadow of poor Buckingham" in 1.1.) Elsewhere he asserts the propriety of various cuts, e.g., of the gentlemen's dialogue prior to Buckingham's entrance in act 2.

9. Since my illustrative text is *Henry VIII,* which did not appear in quarto, I shall focus on the folio conventions as a late standard. While the design of the folio differs from the quartos in some obvious respects (e.g., the double column format and greater use of Latin act and scene divisions), it preserves the essentials of the Elizabethan code for stage directions.

10. However, whereas the folio divisions are in Latin and italicized, the scene headings in these editions are in English and usually appear in Roman type, all caps. Rules are found only in Bell's edition, and then only between the acts.

11. See, for example, the printed edition of *Bon Ton: or High Life above Stairs* (1775) or the photofacsimile of his manuscript for *The Meeting of the Company,* both in Gerald Berkowitz, ed., *The Plays of David Garrick* (New York: Garland Publishing, 1981), vol. 2: paginated separately.

12. Brackets begin to appear in some quartos in the 1630's, but they do not appear in the folio text.

13. Garrick's version of *Macbeth,* as it appears in Bell's series, does have locations for each scene on the model of the Dryden edition (1.1, *Scene, an open Place,* 1.2, *Scene changes to a Palace* . . .). Unlike the 1762 *Henry VIII,* this 1774 text of *Macbeth* is rather fully annotated by Francis Gentleman, who may have added the scene indications.

14. True "massed" entries, in which the characters are all named at the opening of the scene regardless of when they enter during the scene, were very rare in Elizabethan practice.

15. Small-scale discoveries are fairly common in Elizabethan plays. Judging from existing stage directions, many playhouses had some structure (such as a large curtained bed or an alcove) enclosing a space that could be hidden from the audience's view by means of a curtain. When the curtain was opened, it could reveal a small scene—a character lying in bed, or two characters playing chess (as in *The Tempest*). Large-scale discoveries, such as those in the editions I am discussing, seem to assume architecture and machinery that came in with the Restoration and were developed in the eighteenth century: namely, a proscenium arch from which a "house curtain" might be hung, or (more likely) a system of

wings on grooves or drop-cloths across the width of the stage at various intervals from front to back, which might be opened or raised to reveal a fully "dressed" stage—i.e., backdrop, large furnishings (tables, chairs), and a large number of actors.

16. These claims are the subject of a work in progress, "The Voice of Elizabethan Stage Directions: The Evolution of a Theatrical Code." See also my essay, "Elizabethan Speech Prefixes: Page Design, Typography, and Mimesis" in *Reading and Writing in Shakespeare,* edited by David Bergeron, forthcoming from the University of Delaware Press.

Part 2
Examining the Parts:
Line-by-line Analysis and the
Redistribution of Meaning

Lewis Theobald, Edmond Malone, and Others

Peter Seary

LEWIS Theobald is, without question, the scholar whose methods and discoveries were most plundered by his successors as they sought to magnify their own achievements. The process of appropriation of Theobald's work began with Pope's second edition of *Shakespear* (November 1728). After making some one hundred and six alterations deriving from Theobald's *Shakespeare Restored* (1726), in an Appendix entitled "Various Readings or Conjectures on Passages in Shakespear" Pope acknowledges an indebtedness "amounting to about twenty five *words*."[1] At this point in the relations between the two men, Pope was sufficiently magnanimous to print *recté* next to a couple of Theobald's emendations. I suspect that Pope did not consider himself a thief in this instance: he was aware, no doubt, that some readers would take the trouble to compare *Shakespeare Restored* with his second edition, especially after the appearance of *The Dunciad* (May 1728), and his casual appropriations were in keeping with his posture of genial contempt bordering on indifference. Furthermore, Pope had the complicated pleasure of knowing that his representations of *Tibbald* in *The Dunciad* were drawn from his own experience, especially when translating Homer, so that for him confusion of his and Theobald's scholarly activities was part of an extended joke.[2] Warburton's thefts from Theobald in his *Shakespear* (1747) were of a different order: as long as Theobald's correspondence with him remained unpublished, many of them would remain undetected.[3]

Warburton did not always fully understand Theobald's concerns, and Theobald himself, of course, was capable of reveling in his own ingenuity. Early in their correspondence Theobald suggested a quite startling emendation, but at the same time he was careful to support his proposed reading (which he did not include in his edition) with parallel passages and attention to the *ductus litterarum*. Although his emendation is highly plausible, his ingenuity also suggests to him the uncertainty which may attend the use of the *ductus litterarum* as a test of emendation, given the vagaries of Elizabethan orthography. The passage concerned is omitted

103

from modern editions and comes from the Induction to *The Taming of A Shrew* (1594),[4] which in Pope's edition was conflated with *The Taming of The Shrew*. Theobald focuses on the lines:

> My lord, we must have a shoulder of mutton for a property,
> and a little vinegar to make our devil roar.[5]

Our Poet, I think, seems to forget himself. Mutton, indeed, is used in the Interlude; which, being over-roasted, Petruchio throws from the table. But then there is no Devil in the Drama. Or, if there were, or that Shakespeare designed a fling at the Old Plays, in which, as we shall see, Devils were so frequent, yet what can he allude to, by

> Vinegar to make a Devil roar?

I confess I am at a fault; and, if I should run upon the wrong scent, I cannot help it. We'll start some game, if we miss that in chace. I would scarce venture to trust any body but Mr. Warburton with the conjecture that I am going to make; because it is a little peremptory. . . . Granting our Poet only intended a *Spear* [? a barb, or jibe at the old plays], as I hinted, might he not have wrote,

> ———and a little *wooden dagger* to make our Devil roar?

The difference of *wooden dagger* and *vinegar,* seems at first glance a little startling. But then, if we may call pronunciation into our aid,[6] (*Vin,* and *Wood'n;—egar,* and *dagger*) the difference is not so considerable. And again, may not error have arisen from contraction in the written copies and current hand of those times, and so *w'n* (*wooden*) been mistaken for *vin,* and *d'gar* (*dagger*) for *egar?*

The impression is that of a scholar allowing himself in a private and protected context the luxury of unleashing his abilities and imagination without exercising the restraints he habitually observed when writing for publication:

Ne sævi, magne Sacerdos, may I not fairly say? And yet take my parallel authorities; and you may wish, perhaps, I had been right, though you should be forced to determine against me.—In the first place I am to remind you, that the Old Plays (especially in the times of Popery, whilst spirits, and witchcraft, and exorcising, held their own) are generally furnished with the character of a Devil, and Buffoon, or arch fool (called *Vice*), who was equipped with a long coat, a cap and asses ears, and a lath-dagger; and who used to skip on the Devil's back, and lay on him with a vengeance, *ad captandum populum,* and set a certain quantity of barren spectators on the grin with his *Arlequinades.*
    Proofs: I shall begin with a quotation or two from your own pamphlet of

'Popish Impostures;'[7] (which I have, as you ordered, delivered to our Friend Concanen.)

> I. It was a pretty part in the old Church Plays, when the nimble *Vice* was to skip nimbly up like a jack-an-apes into the Devil's neck, and ride the Devil a cockhorse, and belabour him with his *Wooden Dagger* till he made him *roar;* whereat the people would laugh, to see the Devil so Vice-haunted.
> Her Devils, be sure, be some of those Vice-haunted, casheer'd, *wooden-beaten* Devils, that were wont to frequent the stages, &c. who are so scared with the idea of a *Vice* and a *dagger,* as they durst never since look a paper-Vice in the face. (Cap. 19, p. 114, 5).[8]

Theobald provides further illustration from Ben Jonson's *Staple of News* (1631) and *The Devil is an Ass* (1631), which, in turn, he uses to gloss passages in *Henry V, 2 Henry IV, Hamlet* and *Richard III.* As John Nichols points out, Warburton did not entirely forget these ideas, when he came to prepare his own edition of *Shakespear* (1747). Warburton's muddle over *vinegar* may, perhaps, be taken as representative of his understanding of Theobald's textual principles:

When the acting of the *mysteries* of the old and new Testament was in vogue; at the representation of the *mystery* of the Passion, *Judas* and the Devil made a part. And the Devil, whereever [sic] he came, was always to suffer some disgrace, to make the people laugh: As here, the buffonery was to apply the gall and vinegar to make him roar. And the Passion being that, of all the *mysteries,* which was most frequently represented, vinegar b[ec]ame at length the standing implement to torment the Devil: And used for this purpose even after the *mysteries* ceased, and the *moralities* came in vogue; where the Devil continued to have a considerable part.—The mention of it here was to ridicule so absurd a circumstance in these old farces.[9]

It is difficult to comment on Warburton's adaptation of *Matthew* 27:34, for the purposes of his note, which is merely fanciful.

Until finally overcome by senility, Warburton was motivated throughout his career by naked ambition. His cultivation of Theobald, like his subsequent cultivation of Pope, was only a means to an end; he was a superficial scholar, and (like many after him) he rightly concluded that to be on the side of wit, money, and social standing was more prestigious than being identified with a *scholaris pauperis* like Theobald. The same, unfortunately, is essentially true of Johnson's alignment and subsequent disalignment with Theobald. In 1745 Johnson's initial admiration for Theobald in the *Miscellaneous Observations on Macbeth* is readily apparent: "some of his amendments are so excellent, that, even when he has failed, he ought to be treated with indulgence and respect."[10] His subsequent denigration of the man in his Preface to *Shakespeare* (1765) coincides with a concern for his own respectability once he had realized his own ambitions and escaped Grub-Street after the triumph of his *Dictionary* (1755): "a man of narrow comprehension and small acquisitions, with no native and intrinsick splendour of genius, with little of the artificial light of learning, but zealous for minute accuracy, and not negligent in pursuing it."[11] Johnson's further characterization of Theobald as weak, ignorant, mean, faithless, petulant, and ostentatious[12] perhaps reflects a repressed realization that Theobald had instituted the practice in English of providing parallel readings to explain obscure words, a practice carried a great deal further by Johnson in his *Dictionary*.

A horrified sense of recognition, followed by repression or complete rejection, seems a fairly common response to Theobald by his successors, even as they seek recognition by means of scholarly achievement. Undoubtedly mere snobbery played its part in the psychodynamics of his reputation in the eighteenth century, and the social success and prestige of Pope as poet and wit combined with Johnson's dismissal of Theobald continue to be influential, even when the importance of Theobald's methodology is recognized. As Pat Rogers has observed: "William Empson once put in a word for Bentley's Milton, but not many voices have been raised in support of Lewis Theobald. Better to be one of the slashing Bentleys than one of the piddling Tibbalds, to employ Pope's cruel distinction. But Shakespearean scholars have always realized that Theobald was far superior to his adversary in the skills of an editor."[13] Rogers himself, towards the beginning of his prolific career, published *Grub Street: Studies in a Subculture* (1972), a substantial book (pp. 430), with a severely cut (following the suggestions of a *TLS* reviewer), revised, 2nd edition, newly titled *Hacks and Dunces: Pope, Swift and Grub Street* appearing in 1980. Specialists in eighteenth-century English literature will know that to look up "Theobald" in the indexes to Rogers's two books is to be instructed to "*see* Dunces." What they will find is a representation of "Tibbald" that parallels that of Pope after he was forced by the exigencies of public dispute to supplement the hilarious rhetoric of ridicule in the original *Dunciad* (1728) with the rhetoric of evasion mixed with snobbery and misguided idealism often found in his notes to *The Dunciad Variorum* (1729).[14] But, quite apart from his uneasy sense of social disapproval of his treatment of Theobald in *The Dunciad* (as manifested in part in Theobald's subscription list), Pope was fundamentally a decent man, and, like Dryden in his old age apologizing for his pollutions of the stage, made some amends for his ridicule by deposing Theobald from his eminence and substituting Colley Cibber in the revised *Dunciad* (1743).

In *Hacks and Dunces* (1980), Rogers added a page defending his choice in the first edition, *Grub Street* (1972), "to accept the view of Swift and Pope regarding the status of the Dunces." Rogers's sympathy with Pope's early ambition and difficulties was such that he "came to feel in writing the book that students of the period made far too little allowance for the huge social and personal disadvantages which Pope had to contend with, and *per contra* that the excellent life-chances available to several of the Dunces were glossed over." As a further consequence of his sympathy for Pope, Rogers "was unable to take the view that Swift and Pope were secret sharers of the duncely agony, engaged in half-sympathetic recreation of the hack's [*sic*] world, guiltily complicit in the dirty goings-on down Smithfield alleys" (15). Rogers's view of the dunces, including Theobald (perhaps the result of scarcely realized identification of his own ambition and fears with those of the young Pope) seems another example of horrified self-recognition and repression, with the setting changed from Grub-Street to Academe. However, to the extent that Pope's portrait of Theobald in *The Dunciad* corresponds with his self-portraits in his correspondence when translating Homer, he did indeed share in the "duncely agony" rejected (or repressed) by Rogers. In fact, the evidence strongly suggests that Pope experienced far more agony (of whatever kind) than did Theobald.

Edmond Malone was both financially and socially secure when he embarked on his scholarly career. Nonetheless, his friendship with Johnson, coupled with his own ambition ensured the continuation of Johnson's denigration of Theobald, although it must be acknowledged that he did not share Johnson's prejudice in favor of Warburton: "His unbounded licence in substituting his own chimerical conceits in place of the authour's genuine text, has been so fully shewn by his revisers, that I suppose no critical reader will ever again open his volumes."[15] This attempted total obliteration of Warburton was accompanied by a continuation of Johnson's campaign against Theobald, whose Preface to *Shakespeare* Malone decided to omit from his edition because it (along with those of Hanmer and Warburton) "appeared to me to throw no light on our authour or his works. . . ."[16] This contemptuous dismissal brought along its own nemesis: Malone never lived to complete his biography of Shakespeare, but of the 287 pages of the Life attributed to him in the Third Variorum (1821), 112 pages (more than a third) are devoted to discussion of a supposed Spenserian allusion to Shakespeare. In *1790* he was not "able to form a decided opinion" whether "Our pleasaunt *Willy*, ah, is dead of late" in *Tears of the Muses* (1591) is an allusion to Shakespeare,[17] but in *1821* he finally reached the same conclusion that Theobald had in his Preface.[18] (Samuel Schoenbaum comments, without any reference to Theobald, that "Malone denies any need to apologize for his long disquisition, but surely he had committed a colossal blunder of judgment. With respect to *The Tears of the Muses* he has laboriously disproved an already discountenanced supposition. . . .")[19]

Subsequently in his Preface, Malone again makes plain his bias against Theobald:

That his work should at this day be considered of any value, only shews how long impressions will remain, when they are once made; for Theobald, though not so great an innovator as Pope, was yet a considerable innovator; and his edition being printed from that of his immediate predecessor, while a few arbitrary changes made by Pope were detected, innumerable sophistications were silently adopted. His knowledge of the contemporary authours was so scanty, that all the illustration of that kind dispersed throughout his volumes, has been exceeded by the researches which have since been made for the purpose of elucidating a single play.[20]

This denigration is continued in the body of his texts, where typically Malone tends to attribute the fruits of Theobald's scholarship to Johnson, Blackstone, Farmer, or Steevens. Malone was fully complicit with Johnson. For example, *Hamlet* (3.04.92) in Pope's edition, following a late quarto, reads "In the rank sweat of an *incestuous* bed," and Malone supplied a note on the same passage:

—*an* enseamed *bed;*] Thus the quarto, 1604, and the folio. A later quarto of no authority reads—*incestuous* bed. *Enseamed bed,* as Dr. Johnson has observed, is *greasy bed. Seam* signifies *hogslard.* MALONE.[21]

Theobald had supplied the correct reading and interpretation as early as *Shakespeare Restored* (1726): in Pope's edition he supposes that "we have a *sophisticated* Reading palmed upon us, probably, from the Players first, who did not understand the Poet's *Epithet*" and restores "ENSEAMED *bed,*" observing that "when we come to the *Etymology,* and *abstracted* Meaning of *enseam'd,* we shall have a Consonancy in the *Metaphors,* and a Reason for the Poet's calling the Bed a nasty *Sty.* In short, the Glossaries tell us, that *Seam* is properly the *Fat,* or *Grease,* of a *Hog.* . . ." In a further note on *Seam* he traces the Latin derivation of the word, using Isidore and Vossius, and says that although he recalls no other instance of Shakespeare's using the compound adjective of *seam,* the substantive form is found in *Troilus and Cressida.* He then reproduces and discusses the parallel passage in which Ulysses compares Achilles to a hog (2.03.184–89) (104–5).

There are numerous other instances of like treatment of Theobald by Malone. In *1790,* 1, pt. 2: 3, a portion of a note is attributed to Steevens, where it is observed that the beauties of *The Tempest*

could not secure it from the criticism of Ben Jonson, whose malignity appears to have been more than equal to his wit. In the induction to *Bartholomew Fair,* he says: "If there be never a *servant monster* in the fair, who can help it, nor a nest of *antiques?* He is loth to make nature afraid in his plays, like those that beget *Tales, Tempests,* and such like drolleries."

However, the same reference had been pointed out by Theobald.[22] In the same note, *1790,* there is also a reference by Farmer to Theobald's commentary:

> Mr. Theobald tells us, that the *Tempest* must have been written after 1609, because the Bermuda islands, which are mentioned in it, were unknown to the English until that year; but this is a mistake. He might have seen in Hackluyt, 1600, folio, a description of Bermuda, by Henry May, who was shipwrecked there in 1593.
> It was however one of our author's last works.[23]

A further comment, attributed to Blackstone, suggests that "This play must have been written after 1609, when Bermudas was discovered, and before 1614, when Jonson sneers at it in his *Bartholomew Fair,*" and is essentially a conflation of the information found in Theobald's notes 13 and 21.[24]

It was through maneuvers such as these that Malone sought to appropriate Theobald's methods and to denigrate his discoveries and that eventually led Isaac Reed deliberately to distort the history of Shakespearian scholarship by referring to Steevens as the editor "to whom the praise is due of having first adopted, and carried into execution, Dr. Johnson's admirable plan of illustrating Shakespeare by the study of writers of his own time."[25] In fact, as the above examples from Theobald's commentary on *The Tempest* make plain, all the editors must have been aware that the "admirable plan of illustrating Shakespeare by the study of writers of his own time" was first formulated and executed by Theobald. Indeed, Johnson once commented that "Mr. Theobald had the art of making the most of his discoveries,"[26] which prompted William Kenrick to comment: "But this remark, however true it may be in one sense, is far from being so in another: for though Dr. Johnson hath made very few discoveries of his own, he hath discovered the method of making more of Theobald's at second hand, than ever the author could do, when they were spick and span new."[27] The biases of Johnson and Malone against Theobald are in fact very readily apparent and were indignantly pointed out by John Churton Collins, a somewhat unstable champion of the underdog (if not of lost causes) who, although he never made his way back to Oxford, became for a while Chair of English at Birmingham. Collins exclaimed: "the shamelessness of the injustice with which he [Theobald] has been treated by his brother commentators on Shakespeare exceeds belief."[28] Nonetheless, Johnson's and Malone's biases against Theobald have generally been deliberately ignored, and for unsurprising reasons: alignment with them has been almost inevitably perceived as more advantageous to anyone pursuing a scholarly (not to say academic) career than alignment with the hero of *The Dunciad*—even if alignment with Pope, Johnson, and Malone in this instance necessarily produces third-rate scholarship. In 1903, David Nichol Smith published *Eighteenth Century Essays on Shakespeare* (Glasgow: J. MacLehose) and pronounced in his Preface: "On the question of Theobald's qualifications as an editor, it would appear that we must subscribe to the deliberate verdict of Johnson."[29] In the body of his Introduction, Nichol Smith observes:

> It is especially remarkable that Johnson, who is not considered to have been very strong in research, should be the first to state that Shakespeare used North's translation of Plutarch. He is the first also to point out that there was an English translation of the play on which the *Comedy of Errors* was founded, and the first to show that it was not necessary to go back to the *Tale of Gamelyn* for the story of *As You Like It*. There is no evidence how he came by this knowledge. The casual and allusive manner in which he advances his information would seem to show that it was not of his own getting.[30]

In *Lewis Theobald: His Contribution to English Scholarship with some Unpublished Letters* (New York: Columbia University Press, 1919), R. F. Jones observed that "About the only correct detail in the above quotation is the suspicion that Johnson's knowledge was second hand," and it is only fair to quote him fully:

> There is plenty of evidence how Boswell's hero came by his information. . . . In a note on Timon's epitaph Theobald says,
>
>> I once imagin'd that Shakespeare might possibly have corrected this translator's Blunder from his own acquaintance with the Greek Original: but, I find, he has transcribed the four Lines from an old *English* Version of *Plutarch,* extant in his time.[31]
>
> In the very first note on the very first page of volume three, Theobald remarks that "the *Menæchmi* of *Plautus* was translated into *English,* (which our Criticks might have known from Langbaine,) and printed in *Quarto* in the year 1515, half a century before our Author was born."[32] In the preface to his edition, while speaking of the verses in *As You Like It,* Theobald says,
>
>> Dr. Thomas Lodge, a Physician who flourished early in Queen Elizabeth's Reign, and was a great Writer of the Pastoral Songs and Madrigals, which were so much the Strain of those Times, composed a whole Volume of Poems in Praise of his Mistress, whom he calls Rosalinde. I never yet could meet with this collection; but whenever I do, I am persuaded I shall find many of our Author's Canzonets on this Subject to be scraps of the Doctor's amorous Muse.[33]

Fortunately for Johnson, Theobald did not succeed in his search for Lodge's *Rosalinde,* while the later critic, following the path so clearly pointed out by the man he slandered, met with success (188–89).[34]

The twentieth-century academic politics behind Nichol Smith's exceptionally sloppy scholarship here[35] are not irrelevant. After a chapter entitled "John Churton Collins and the Attack on Oxford," D. J. Palmer writes in *The Rise of English Studies: An Account of the Study of English Language and Literature from its Origins to the Making of the Oxford English School* (London: Published for the University of Hull by the Oxford University Press, 1965):

> De Selincourt's application for the Birmingham Chair, vacated by Churton Collins's suicide, was no doubt precipitated by his failure to obtain the Goldsmith Readership, established earlier in 1908. He was then passed over in favour of David Nichol Smith, since 1904 the Professor of English at Armstrong College, Newcastle, but formerly Raleigh's assistant at Glasgow, where Raleigh first recognized in Nichol Smith's powers of scholarship a valuable complement to his own disposition. So Nichol Smith was brought to Oxford to become Raleigh's lieutenant in directing the growing school. (133)

Nichol Smith had hitched his wagon to that star of English studies, Walter Raleigh, in 1900 Chair of English Language and Literature at Glasgow and then in 1904 Merton Professor of English at Oxford, and he would not allow mere evidence to interfere with his comfortable relationship with his mentor. It is pleasing to be able to say that Sir Walter Raleigh (as he became in 1911) had no motive in his work on Johnson, first published in 1908, other than a laudable desire to celebrate the amiable qualities of his subject and to refute Macaulay.[36] Nichol Smith in due course succeeded Raleigh in the Merton Chair. Perhaps it is not surprising that of all modern commentators, Nichol Smith should be the best disposed to Warburton, with whom he had enough in common. In contrast with Nichol Smith's acceptance of Johnson's verdict on Theobald as editor, Brian Vickers calls him "the best all-round editor of Shakespeare in this period or any other"[37] and Gary Taylor asserts that he "remains one of the finest editors of the last three centuries."[38]

Margreta de Grazia[39] for strictly theoretical reasons (I presume) distances Malone as far as possible from Theobald. She begins her study of Malone's *Shakspeare* (1790) with the acknowledgment that it "is impossible to imagine the study of Shakespeare without authentic texts for his works, historical accounts defining his period, facts about his life, chartings of his artistic and psychological development, and determinations of his meaning." Nonetheless, it is her "conviction that these requirements are not necessary in any absolute sense." Because "[a]uthenticity, peri-

odization, individuation, chronology, and even interpretation" emerged
in history, "they cannot be the timeless necessities of Shakespeare study;
rather they are the determinate needs of a specific historical situation."
Her study "does not purport to be a disinterested contribution to the
history of Shakespeare scholarship" (1), since instead of seeking the
terms of Malone's *épistème* in the aggregated work of Nicholas Rowe,
Alexander Pope, Lewis Theobald, William Warburton, Edward Capell,
Samuel Johnson, and George Steevens (although the fruits of their scholarship were evidently enough present in Malone's scholarly environment)
de Grazia sees the principal influence on Malone's editorial activity to be
those late Enlightenment schema related by Michel Foucault to the "late
eighteenth century's 'invention of man'": "The social and political principle of autonomy emerging at the end of the eighteenth century [that]
finds its philosophical equivalent in Kant's programme of self-
representation gleaned from analysis of the postulate 'my representation
is my representation', a tautology which bridges the expanse between the
phenomenal and the noumenal" (9). This splendid sentence effectively
casts an almost impenetrable pall over Malone's debts to his predecessors, especially Theobald.

Whereas most writers on the editorial tradition agree with Gary Taylor,
that "There was no break with the past; accretion triumphed. Malone,
the most characteristic editor of the second half of the eighteenth century,
was a lawyer; and the edifice of Shakespeare editing, like the edifice of
English jurisprudence, rose by progressive deposits of precedent sedi-
ment,"[40] de Grazia insists on the novelty of Malone's editorial aims and
practice in Foucauldian terms. Her attempts to sustain her view on occasion lead her into overstatement, and when, perhaps, Malone's presumed
novelty is most questionable, de Grazia tends to be most emphatic: "What
must be emphasized" (48), "what needs to be stressed" (54), "what must
be stressed" (56), *et cetera*. In short, de Grazia (like Malone himself)
minimizes the continuities of Shakespearian scholarship in the eighteenth
century and supposes (as Malone would have wished) that Malone was
the sole originator of his scholarly and editorial concerns. As a consequence of her continual emphasis on Malone's supposed difference from
his predecessors, her study concentrates on "the emergence of . . . textual and critical imperatives in the late eighteenth century, stressing their
incompatibility with earlier approaches and assuming throughout their
continuity with those that subsequently became traditional" (1). In the
process there is again considerable distortion of the history of Shakespearian scholarship—a distortion made possible only by ignoring the
evidence found in Theobald's first edition of *Shakespeare* (1733) and,
indeed, in Churton Collins's "The Porson of Shakespearian Criticism."
Precedent for this kind of disregard of inconvenient evidence is found,

however, in Nichol Smith's flagrantly false characterization of Collins's scholarship as "peculiarly inept"[41] and in his failure to address matters raised in R. F. Jones's book on Theobald, either in *Shakespeare in the Eighteenth Century* (Oxford: Clarendon Press, 1928, repr. 1968) or in the 2nd edition of *Eighteenth Century Essays on Shakespeare* (1963), notwithstanding their obvious bearing on his own arguments.[42]

De Grazia's first chapter, "The 1623 Folio and the Modern Standard Edition," is, nonetheless, a fascinating consideration of the disuniformity of the First Folio with modern editions of Shakespeare. It is acknowledged that "an account of gradual progress in both domains, of advancing print technology and increasing linguistic systemization, could explain the most salient differences between the 1623 Folio and a modern edition" (19), but de Grazia's purpose is to argue against such notions of implied progress and against an editorial ideal which seeks to recreate a supposed "stable original, Shakespeare's holograph . . . a single and fixed document" (20). Rather, she supposes an original itself "resistant to the regimes of both script and print: an original involved in the vagaries of [stage] production" (20). Malone's hope for a permanent, unchanging text has become outdated: the work of Roland Barthes, Michel Foucault, and D. F. McKenzie has resulted in "the Oxford Shakespeare's recharacterization of the Shakespearean text as malleable, permeable, and even multiple . . ." (1–2).

De Grazia's supposition, that Malone is the first to hope for a permanent, unchanging text, creates obvious difficulties. The desire to impose order and regularity on vagrant and mutable scripts by an appeal to the idea of a single, fixed document is at least as old as the First Folio itself, with its claim on the title-page that the plays are "Published according to the True Originall Copies." The Folio also intimates the complexities and uncertainties of the actual circumstances of play and book production. Heminge and Condell, of all the editors of Shakespeare, were best placed to know the realities of Shakespeare's habits of composition, the evolution of his theatrical manuscripts, the copy for quartos and the Folio, and they too had a sense of "*rashnesse in the enterprize, and feare of the successe.*" Indeed, in their dedication, Heminge and Condell seem to have found the idea of "*perfection*" inherently embarrassing ("*But . . . we must also craue our abilities to be considerd. . . . We cannot go beyond our owne powers*"),[43] although in "To the great Variety of Readers" they claim that the Folio texts are "perfect of their limbes . . ." (*v.* 102). Moreover, Pope in principle at least and Johnson to some degree in practice anticipate modern views of textual instability in their willingness to acknowledge the desirability of a variorum edition of Shakespeare (that is, an edition recording various *readings*). Together, the Folio title page, Heminge and Condell, Pope and Johnson seem to anticipate Malone's concerns with authenticity and stability and later twentieth-century views of textuality. Of course, de Grazia is aware of these considerations; she does not, however, admit that they might invalidate her argument that Malone is the first to be concerned with textual stability and authenticity, or acknowledge that earlier editors adumbrated late twentieth-century ideas of textuality. For example, as early as 3 January 1730, in his correspondence with William Warburton, Theobald supposed that differences between the quarto and Folio versions of *Lear* reflected shifting theatrical circumstances: "the Players took the liberty to retrench. . . ." He also recognized that the changes might have been made "with the Author's consent."[44]

Indeed, although Theobald made his chief life's work an attempt to recover the "authentic" text of Shakespeare and then to impose stability and order upon it, his views on quarto and folio textuality and the sociology of textual production perhaps exceeded the wildest dreams of Barthes, Foucault, and McKenzie:

[M]any Pieces were taken down in Short-hand, and imperfectly copied by Ear, from a *Representation:* Others were printed from piece-meal Parts surreptitiously obtain'd from the Theatres, uncorrect, and without the Poet's Knowledge. To some of these Causes we owe the train of Blemishes, that deform those Pieces which stole singly into the World in our Author's Life-time.

There are still other Reasons, which may be suppos'd to have affected the whole Set. When the *Players* took upon them to publish his Works intire, every Theatre was ransack'd to supply the Copy; and *Parts* collected which had gone thro' as many Changes as Performers, either from Mutilations or Additions made to them. Hence we derive many Chasms and Incoherences in the Sense and Matter. Scenes were frequently transposed, and shuffled out of their true Place, to humour the Caprice or suppos'd Convenience of some particular Actor. Hence much Confusion and Impropriety has attended, and embarras'd, the Business and Fable. For there ever have been, and ever will be in Playhouses, a Set of assuming Directors, who know better than the Poet himself the Connexion and Dependance of his Scenes; where Matter is defective, or Superfluities to be retrench'd; Persons, that have the Fountain of *Inspiration* as peremptorily in them, as Kings have That of *Honour*. To these obvious Causes of Corruption it must be added, that our Author has lain under the Disadvantage of having his Errors propagated and multiplied by Time: because, for near a Century, his Works were republish'd from the faulty Copies without the assistance of any intelligent Editor: which has been the Case likewise of many a *Classic* Writer.[45]

In chapter 4, "Individuating Shakespeare's Experience: Biography, Chronology, and the Sonnets," de Grazia argues that the "promiscuous content and presumptive attribution" of John Benson's *Poems: Written by Wil. Shake-speare* (1640) reflect "not lax regulations or unethical policies but rather a more pliable concept of book and author. Until the very notions that are the subject of this present study were fixed and legally codified, authorship—especially when posthumously assigned—was a more flexible and variable ascription having more to do than has been generally allowed with a sprawling nexus of stationers' practices and printed materials than with a direct line to the author and his holograph" (170). There is truth in this, and yet the case is overstated. As early as 1656, Abraham Cowley complained that posthumous editions of poets' works are "stuffed out . . . with *counterfeit* pieces . . . *whether this proceed from the* . . . unworthy avarice of some *Stationers,* who are content to diminish the value of the *Author,* so they may encrease the price of the *Book* . . . [t]his has been the case with *Shakespear, Fletcher, Johnson,* and many others. . . ."[46] De Grazia is surely right to maintain that "Benson's edition reflected a fidelity to a bibliographical rather than a personal entity during a time when the Stationers' Company regulations protected the bookseller's interests rather than the author's" (171). She also acknowledges that "To suggest that dead authors in the seventeenth century possessed a bibliographic rather than a personal identity is not to deny that live authors were not concerned with correct attribution" (172), but at this point it does seem fair to revert to her earlier assertion, that the "promiscuous content and presumptive attribution" of John Benson's collection reflect "not lax regulations or unethical policies but rather a more pliable concept of book and author," and simply to assert (after Cowley) that publishers such as Benson were motivated by "unworthy avarice" and did indeed take unethical advantage of the fact that those most likely to complain vigorously were dead. (Michael Dobson argues that "the retrospective invention of Shakespeare as himself a Lockean economic individualist, which conclusively establishes the Bard as the author of his own works" takes place in the early eighteenth century.)[47] Such recognitions do not, however, negate de Grazia's assertion that Malone's biography and apparatus "conferred upon Shakespeare a personal identity that both informed the works and issued from them" (173). But her further implication, that this development only begins with Malone, is again overstated. Indeed, Theobald, albeit on a relatively minute scale, had previously attempted to personalize Shakespeare "by outer and inner experiences":

The Ease and Sweetness of his Temper might not a little contribute to his Facility in Writing; as his Employment, as a *Player,* gave him an Advantage and Habit of fancying himself the very Character he meant to delineate. He used the Helps of his Function in forming himself to create and express that *Sublime,* which other Actors can only copy, and throw out, in Action and graceful Attitude.[48]

Although de Grazia has much to say about Malone's commentary and aggregation of contexts, she has relatively little detailed discussion of his actual treatment of the text. Nonetheless, she does acknowledge Malone's handling of anachronisms in Shakespeare, although Malone's practice in this instance severely compromises the title of her book and her argument that Malone was the first to be consistently concerned with textual authenticity:

> While allowing philological and cultural aberrations, he unqualifiedly judged the historical deviations 'errors', 'mistakes', and 'inconsistencies', and scrupulously corrected them, in this respect resembling the editors he most disparaged: the 'superintendor' of the Second Folio, who corrected Shakespeare's syntax and vocabulary by his own standards, and Pope, who in his 1725 edition 'licentiously' emended, highlighted, and stigmatized Shakespeare according to his own peremptory taste (127).

Her further assertion, that "Earlier, less 'conservative' editors were less disturbed by anachronisms, either blaming them on the vulgar players and correcting them, like Pope, or allowing (and even applauding) them as 'poetic License', like Theobald" (127), is especially less than satisfactory. Despite the ridicule of Pope, Theobald thought it his "Duty, to discover some *Anachronisms* in our Author; which might have slept in Obscurity. . . ."[49] As opposed to simply applauding poetic license, he wrote a brief, sophisticated essay in a footnote on the nature of Shakespeare's poetic license and anachronisms and justified his refusal to "improve" the texts:

> In all *Anachronisms,* as in other Licences of Poetry, this Rule ought certainly to be observ'd; that the Poet is to have Regard to *Verisimilitude.* But there is no *Verisimilitude,* when the *Anachronism* glares in the face of the common People. For this Falshood is, like all other Falshoods in Poetry, to be only tolerated, where the Falshood is hid under Verisimilitude. No sober Critick ever blamed *Virgil,* for instance, for making *Dido* and *Æneas* contemporary. (Such a *Prolepsis* may be justified by the examples of the greatest Poets of Antiquity.) But had he made *Æneas* mention *Hamilcar,* what Man in his Senses would have thought of an Excuse for him? For the Name of *Hamilcar,* tho a Foreigner, was too recent in the Acquaintance of the People; as he had for five Years together infested the Coast of *Italy;* and after that, begun the second *Punic* War upon them. The Case of our Author differs in his mentioning *Machiavel* in some of his Plays, the action of which was earlier than that Statesman's Birth. For *Machiavel* was a Foreigner, whose Age, we may suppose, the common Audience not so well acquainted with; as being long before their time, and, indeed, very near the Time of the Action of those Plays. Besides, He having so establish'd a Reputation, in the time of our Author, amongst the Politicians; might well be suppos'd by those, who were not Chronologers, to

be of much longer Standing than he was. This, therefore, was within the Rules of Licence; and if there was not Chronological Truth, there was at least Chronological Likelihood: without which a Poet goes out of his Jurisdiction, and comes under the Penalty of the Criticks Laws. I have only one further Remark to make upon the Topick in hand, and 'tis this: That where the Authority of all the Books makes the Poet commit a Blunder, (whose general Character it is, not to be very exact;) 'tis the Duty of an Editor to shew him as he is; and to detect all fraudulent tampering to make him better.[50]

Malone would have done well to have contemplated Theobald's last sentence more carefully. De Grazia, on the other hand, in her discussion of Pope's and Theobald's views on anachronisms, may again have been unduly influenced by David Nichol Smith's hostile account of Theobald in his Preface to *Eighteenth Century Essays on Shakespeare,* since at this point she refers to Smith's texts, rather than resorting to editions published by the earlier editors.

The faults of this study arise from a failure to integrate theory with sound scholarship, that is, from a bias against the earlier editors of Shakespeare, especially Theobald, and an unwarrantable decision to disregard their contributions to Malone's purposes and understanding. This decision is consistent with Malone's own decisions to omit, to minimize, or to denigrate the work of his predecessors where he had been anticipated. But, as de Grazia herself says on her first page, her study "does not purport to be a disinterested contribution to the history of Shakespeare scholarship." In many ways her book is testimony that disinterested scholarship remains fundamentally necessary. She declares: "My purpose in defining the modern study of Shakespeare as an historical construct rather than a universal given is to question its viability and desirability in the present." There follow four rhetorical questions: "Why does this construct emerge in England at the end of the eighteenth century? To what end? At what cost? Most urgently, why should it still prevail?" The appropriate response to the first question is that the construct does *not* emerge at the end of the eighteenth century but much earlier, albeit only partially. In fact, the construct never did appear fully formed, sprung from the head of Malone or his *épistème*, but evolved with successive discoveries and analyses of documentary evidence pertaining to the life and times of Shakespeare and the performance and printing of his plays. More precise understanding of the historical emergence of the construct is necessary before satisfactory answers can be framed in response to the other questions, and without such understanding even intelligent, entertaining theoretical studies become deeply flawed.

As for Malone, his overwhelming contribution was to the commentary. In *1790,* he followed Capell[51] and omitted "a little vinegre to make our

Divell rore" from his text of *Shrew*. In *1821,* however, he included the lines in a note, following Steevens, but added a further note (exemplifying his legendary thoroughness) to Warburton's note:

> All that Dr. Warburton has said relative to *Judas* and the vinegar, wants confirmation. I have met with no such circumstances in any mysteries, whether in MS. or in print; and yet both the Chester and Coventry collections are preserved in the British Museum. See MS. Harl. 2013, and Cotton MS. Vespasian D. viii.[52]

There follow a further forty-five lines, some more some less to the point. As for Theobald, something has been seen of his ability to provide pertinent commentary, but perhaps the younger Boswell, whose love of Malone was apparently exceeded only by his love of truth, can sum up: "Poor Theobald has scarcely had justice done to him."[53]

NOTES

1. *Shakespear,* ed. Pope, 2d ed., 8 vols., 8:sig. H2^r. In a letter to *The Daily Journal* [No. 2460 (26 November 1728)] Theobald suggested that alterations adopted by Pope, including "*material Pointings,*" came to "*about* an *Hundred.*"

2. See chapter 6, "The Hero of *The Dunciad*," Peter Seary, *Lewis Theobald and the Editing of Shakespeare* (Oxford: Clarendon Press, 1990).

3. For example, on *2 Henry VI* (2.03.62)—"Here's a cup of CHARNECO"— Theobald commented in a letter to Warburton (22 January 1730): "I do not know what liquor this might be. Our Dictionaries take no notice of it. I find it mentioned, amongst several other wines, in an old tract, called "The Discovery of a London Monster, called the Black Dog of Newgate. Imprinted at London by G. Eld, for Robert Wilson, 1612" [*Illustrations of the Literary History of the Eighteenth Century,* ed. John Nichols (1817) (hereafter cited as Nichols), 2:437]. There is no note on the passage in *Shakespeare,* ed. Theobald, 7 vols. (1733) (hereafter cited as *1733*), 4:233. After disputing Sir Thomas Hanmer's interpretation of the word, Warburton presented Theobald's information as his own: charneco was "a common name for a sort of sweet wine, as appears from a passage in a pamphlet, intitled, *The discovery of a London Monster, called the black dog of Newgate, printed* 1612" [*Shakespear,* ed. Warburton, 8 vols. (1747) (hereafter cited as *1747*), 5:37n.]. For other examples of Warburton's appropriations, see appendix D, "Warburton's Claims concerning Theobald's Preface and Notes," *Lewis Theobald and the Editing of Shakespeare.* I am preparing an edition of Theobald's correspondence.

4. See Geoffrey Bullough, ed., *Narrative and Dramatic Sources of Shakespeare,* 6 vols. (London: Routledge & Kegan Paul, 1957–66), 1:71:

> My Lord, we must Have a shoulder of mutton for a propertie,
> And a little vinegre to make our Divell rore.

(*ll.* 87–88)

5. *The Works of Shakespear,* ed. Alexander Pope, 6 vols (1725), 2:279.

6. For Theobald's theory of shorthand transcriptions as a source of copy for "bad" quartos, see *Lewis Theobald and the Editing of Shakespeare,* 140–41, 150.

7. Samuel Harsnett's *Declaration of Popish Impostures* (1603). Theobald also used this work in his commentary on *King Lear.*

8. Nichols, 2:249–50.

9. *1747,* 2:393n.

10. Note III, *Miscellaneous Observations on the Tragedy of Macbeth* in *Johnson on Shakespeare* (The Yale Edition of the Works of Samuel Johnson, vols. 7, 8), ed. Arthur Sherbo (New Haven: Yale University Press, 1968) (hereafter cited as Yale), 7:8.

11. *Shakespeare,* ed. Samuel Johnson, 8 vols. (1765) (hereafter cited as *1765*), 1:sig. D^r [Yale 7:95–96].

12. Ibid., 1:sigs. D^v-D2^r [Yale 7:96].

13. "A dunce no more," *Times Literary Supplement* (9–15 November 1990), 1200.

14. See *The Dunciad Variorum* (1729), Bk. 1, *l.* 106n., *l.* 162n., and "Remarks on Book the Second" (23).

15. Preface, *The Plays and Poems of William Shakspeare,* ed. Edmond Malone, 10 vols. (in 11) (1790) (hereafter cited as *1790*), 1, pt. 1:lxvii.

16. *1790,* 1, pt. 1:lxiii.

17. "An Attempt to Ascertain the Order in which the Plays of Shakspeare were written," *1790,* 1, pt. 1:271.

18. See *1821,* 3:178–79. Cf. Theobald's Preface, *1733,* 1:ix–x:
I know, it has been mistakenly thought by some, that *Spenser*'s *Thalia,* in his *Tears of the Muses,* where she laments the Loss of her *Willy* in the Comic Scene, has been apply'd to our Author's quitting the Stage. But *Spenser* himself, 'tis well known, quitted the Stage of Life in the Year 1598; and, five Years after this, we find *Shakespeare*'s Name among the Actors in *Ben Jonson*'s *Sejanus,* which first made its Appearance in the Year 1603. Nor, surely, could he then have any Thoughts of retiring, since, that very Year, a Licence under the Privy-Seal was granted by K. *James* I. to him and *Fletcher, Burbage, Phillippes, Hemings, Condel,* &c. authorizing them to exercise the Art of playing Comedies, Tragedies, &c. as well at their usual House call'd the *Globe* on the other Side of the Water, as in any other Parts of the Kingdom, during his Majesty's Pleasure: (a Copy of which Licence is preserv'd in *Rymer's Fœdera.*) Again, 'tis certain, that *Shakespeare* did not exhibit his *Macbeth* till after K. *James* I. had begun to touch for the *Evil:* for 'tis plain, he has inserted Compliments, on both those Accounts, upon his Royal Master in that Tragedy. Nor, indeed, could the Number of Dramatic Pieces, he produced, admit of his retiring near so early as that Period. So that what *Spenser* there says, if it relate at all to *Shakespeare,* must hint at some occasional Recess he made for a time upon a Disgust taken: or the *Willy,* there mention'd, must relate to some other favourite Poet. I believe, we may safely determine that he had not quitted in the Year 1610. For in his *Tempest,* our Author makes mention of the *Bermuda* Islands, which were unknown to the *English,* till, in 1609, Sir *John Summers* made a Voyage to *North-America,* and discover'd them: and afterwards invited some of his Countrymen to settle a Plantation there.

19. *Shakespeare's Lives* (Oxford: Clarendon Press, 1970), 242–43.

20. *1790,* 1, pt. 1:lxvii.

21. *1790,* 9:338n.

22. *1733,* 1:44 n. 21:

(21) *Servant-Monster.*] [*Tempest,* 3.02.3] The Part of *Caliban* has been esteem'd a signal Instance of the Copiousness of *Shakespeare*'s Invention; and that he had shewn an Extent of Genius, in creating a Person that was not in Nature. And for this, as well as his other *magical* and *ideal* Characters, a just Admiration has been paid him. I can't help taking notice, on this Occasion, of the Virulence of *Ben. Jonson,* who, in the Induction to his *Bartlemew Fair,* has endeavour'd to throw Dirt, not only at this single Character, but at this whole Play. "If there be never a *Servant Monster* in the *Fair,* who can help it, (he says,) nor a Nest of *Anticks?* He is loth to make Nature afraid in his Plays, like Those that beget *Tales, Tempests,* and such like *Drolleries,* to mix his Head with other Mens Heels." *Shakespeare,* as the Tradition runs, was the Person who first brought *Jonson* upon the Stage; and this is the Stab we find given in Requital for such a Service, when his Benefactor was retreated from the Scene. A circumstance, that strangely aggravates the Ingratitude. But this surly Sauciness was familiar with *Ben;* when the Publick were ever out of Humour at his Performances, he would revenge it on them, by being out of Humour with those Pieces which had best pleas'd them.————I'll only add, that his *Conduct* in This was very contradictory to his cooler *Professions,* "that if Men would impartially look towards the Offices and Functions of a Poet, they would easily conclude to themselves the *Impossibility* of any Man's being the *good Poet,* without first being a *good Man.*"

23. *1790,* 1, pt. 2:4n. Cf. *1733,* 1:13–14 n. 13:

(13) *From the still-vext* Bermoothes] [*Tempest,* 1.02.229] So this Word has hitherto been mistakenly written in all the Books. There are about 400 Islands in North *America,* the principal of which was call'd *Bermuda* from a *Spaniard* of that Name who first discover'd them. They are likewise call'd *Summer* Islands, from Sir *George Summers,* who in 1609 made that Voyage; and viewing them, probably, first brought the *English* acquainted with them, and invited them afterwards to settle a Plantation there.————But why, *still-vext* Bermudas? The Soil is celebrated for its Beauty and Fruitfulness; and the Air is so very temperate and serene, that People live there to a great Age, and are seldom troubled with Sickness. But then, on the other hand, these Islands are so surrounded with Rocks on all sides, that without a perfect Knowledge of the Passage, a small Vessel cannot be brought to Haven. Again, we are told, that they are subject to violent Storms, sometimes with terrible clattering of Thunder, and dismal flashing of Lightning. And besides, Sir *George Summers,* when he made the Discovery, was actually shipwreck'd on the Coast. This, I take it, might be a sufficient Foundation for our Author's using the Epithet *still-vext.*

24. For a discussion of Theobald and the chronology of Shakespeare's plays, see *Lewis Theobald and the Editing of Shakespeare,* 178 ff.

25. "Advertisement, prefixed by Mr. Reed to Edition 1803", repr. *1821,* 1:279–80. Cf. Theobald's Preface, *1733,* 1:xliii ff., esp. xlv–xlvi: "An Editor . . . should be well vers'd in the History and Manners of his Author's Age. . . ." Malone, of course, omitted this Preface.

26. *1765,* 3:415n.

27. *A Review of Doctor Johnson's New Edition of Shakespeare* (1765), 129–30. In a letter (31 December 1763) to Richard Farmer, Thomas Percy writes: "Oldys (in a MS Note on Langbaine) says that in the 12° Edition of Theobald's Shakesp. [1740] the editor's Notes are curtailed and retrenched. If so, be so good as to procure me the 8ᵛᵒ Edition of 1733. out of your Libraries." Percy subsequently wrote to Farmer (1 February 1766), recommending Steevens's revisal of Johnson's *Shakespeare* (1765): "You will have a most correct Text founded upon a very diligent and faithful Collation of all the Old Copies: with a new [after "better" deleted] examination of Theobald's and all the former Comments, that nothing valuable may be omitted. . . ."—*The Correspondence of Thomas Percy & Rich-*

ard Farmer, ed. Cleanth Brooks (Binghamton, N.Y.: Vail-Ballou Press for the Louisiana State University Press, 1946), 58, 102. Theobald's curtailment of his commentary in *1740* may have encouraged appropriation of materials found in *1733.* In any event, Percy was not alone in his desire for *all* Theobald's commentary, since the sixth (1767) and eighth (1773) editions of his *Shakespeare* proclaim that they are *"Printed verbatim from the octavo edition"* (i.e., the first edition of 1733).

28. "The Porson of Shakespearian Criticism" in *Essays and Studies* (London: Macmillan & Co., 1895), 266.

29. Repr. in the second edition (Oxford: Clarendon Press, 1963), πʳ.

30. xxv. Repr. 2d ed., xxvi (see also the note on the passage provided by F. P. Wilson and Herbert Davis for the 2d edition).

31. Edition of Shakespeare, vol. 5, 303. See also Nichols, *Illustrations of Literature,* vol. 2, 500, 505, 508 [Jones's note].

32. The italics in both quotations are Theobald's. Theobald made a mistake in the date; it should be 1595 [Jones's note].

33. Preface, xvii. Theobald was mistaken in the nature of the work, but not in the matter of indebtedness. For this fact, as well as for much other information, Theobald was indebted to Langbaine [Jones's note].

34. In a letter to me (20 January 1966), Dr. L. F. Powell wrote:

Prof. Jones told me that Prof. Nichol Smith had said that he 'thought I was right in what I had said about Theobald'. This must have been in conversation & not in writing. What Jones said about Theobald I take to be his statements on 167 of his book. D. N. S. charge of 'theft' was a very serious one.

Prof. Nichol Smith never discussed Theobald with me. He read my proofs of the *Life* [*of Johnson,* ed. G. B. Hill, rev. L. F. Powell, 6 vols. (Oxford: Clarendon Press, 1934–64)] & made no comment at I.329, n. 1.

I think it would be going too far to say that D. N. S. changed his opinions of Theobald's character & his contributions to Shakespearian scholarship. R. F. Jones's scholarly and thorough book may perhaps have modified his opinion.

35. See also *appendix D,* "Warburton's Claims concerning Theobald's Preface and Notes" in *Lewis Theobald and the Editing of Shakespeare.*

36. *Johnson on Shakespeare* (London: Oxford University Press, 1908); *Six Essays on Johnson* (London: Oxford University Press, 1910).

37. Introduction, *Shakespeare: The Critical Heritage Volume 2, 1693–1733* (London: Routledge & Kegan Paul, 1974), 1.

38. General Introduction, Stanley Wells, Gary Taylor, with John Jowett and William Montgomery, *William Shakespeare: A Textual Companion* (Oxford: Clarendon Press, 1987), 54.

39. *Shakespeare Verbatim: The Reproduction of Authenticity and the 1790 Apparatus* (Oxford: Clarendon Press, 1991).

40. *Reinventing Shakespeare: A Cultural History from the Restoration to the Present* (New York: Weidenfeld & Nicolson, 1989), 144.

41. Introduction, *Eighteenth Century Essays on Shakespeare,* 2d ed. (Oxford: Clarendon Press, 1963), xlviii.

42. De Grazia ignores Collins completely, but does cite Jones in her Bibliography (without discussing his work in her text). She does not cite my *Lewis Theobald and the Editing of Shakespeare,* perhaps because her book was at the printers by the time it appeared.

43. Dedication, *Mr. William Shakespeare Comedies, Histories, & Tragedies* (1623), *v.v.* 38–75, passim.

44. Nichols, 2:385. See also Grace Ioppolo, "'Old' and 'New' Revisionists: Shakespeare's Eighteenth-Century Editors," *Huntington Library Quarterly,* 52 (1989): 347–61.

45. Preface, *1733,* 1:xxxvii–xxxix. For a discussion of this passage in context, see *Lewis Theobald and the Editing of Shakespeare,* 140 ff. Johnson provides a trenchant summary of this passage in his *Proposals* (1756) [Yale, 7:52], which is quoted and discussed by Malone in *1790,* 1, pt. 1:ii ff. Indeed, Johnson's debt to Theobald may have been a contributing motive to Malone's decision to omit Theobald's Preface in *1790.*

46. Preface, *Poems* (1656), rpr. *The Works of Mr Abraham Cowley* (1668): sig. B3ᵛ.

47. In *The Making of the National Poet: Shakespeare, Adaptation and Authorship, 1660–1769* (Oxford: Clarendon Press, 1992), 61.

48. Preface, *1733,* 1:xvi. There are numerous instances in Theobald's Preface and notes where he personalizes Shakespeare, either with regard to "his peculiar manner of *Thinking*" (1:xlvi), or his interaction with his contemporaries, whether the reigning Monarch or fellow playwrights. See especially Preface, *1733,* 1:xliii.

49. Preface, *1733,* 1:xlix.

50. *1733,* 4:112n.

51. Malone's debt to Capell warrants a separate study.

52. 5:369n.

53. James Boswell, "Essay on the Phraseology and Metre of Shakspeare and his Contemporaries," *1821,* 1:508–9.

"All This Farrago": The Eighteenth-Century Shakespeare Variorum Page as a Critical Structure

Joanna Gondris

THE relentless expansion of the Shakespeare variorum edition, in the late eighteenth century, was notorious. Each edition absorbed the notes of its predecessor. The vast accretion of notes ensured the ever-increasing bulkiness of the editions, swelled them to a multiplicity of thick volumes that were mocked repeatedly in a clutch of hostile reviews published during the 1780s and 90s.[1] The tone of incredulous exasperation in which one such article is voiced is representative of this concerted anathematization of the whole variorum endeavor. This article (from *The English Review,* 1784) recounts a history of culpability for the form.[2] It charges Johnson with engendering this plenitude of commentary, and laments the consequences of his influence:

> Dr. Johnson, from an excess of candour, and perhaps from a diffidence of the industry he had employed upon the subject, adopted a multiplicity of notes from various writers into his edition. Mr. Stevens [sic] has carefully preserved all this farrago, and, beside it, we are now treated with the annotations of himself, Dr. Farmer, Mr. Tyrwhitt, Mr. Malone, &c.&c.&c.&c. So that, in the state in which the author now lies before us, Tacitus *cum notis variorum* is nothing to him. . . . Nor let the reader be so idle as to imagine, that we exaggerate the fact. The first passage at which we opened is the following line in Othello: "A fellow almost damn'd in a fair face," upon which the commentators are these, each of them contradicting him that went before him: Sir Thomas Hanmer; Bishop Warburton, Mr. Stevens; Dr. Johnson; Mr. Tollett; Mr. Tyrwhitt; Mr. Malone; and Mr. Stevens again. (178–79)

The reviewer lists the cluster of names on the page only to stress the redundancy of the variorum endeavor. Their multiplicity is proof of its failure, a failure preordained by its inauspicious origins in Johnson's sense of his own inadequacy. To the reviewer, the variorum edition's display of notes on the page flaunts its betrayal of the proper editorial function, flaunts its lack of a single, magisterial voice with which it could determine each textual crux and elucidate each difficulty.

The reviewer points to the history of the Shakespeare variorum as the shaping force of the structure of notes on the page: all succeeding editions are marked with the imprint of Johnson's original editorial misjudgment. Indeed, later eighteenth-century editors are quick to acknowledge Johnson as their progenitor. They present their editions as elaborations or revisions of his. For example, the edition that the reviewer castigates is the 1778 Steevens *Shakespeare,* a second edition, "Revised and Augmented," of the 1773 Steevens revision of the original Johnson edition. It was a self-confessed augmentation of an augmentation. The next editorial work to be published, in 1780, placed itself insistently in the same trajectory: its title proclaimed its accretive growth from the ever-expanding Johnson-Steevens edition: *Supplement to the edition of Shakespeare's Plays published in 1778 by S. Johnson and G. Steevens (with additional observations by several of the former commentators: and the genuine Poems and seven plays. With notes by editor (E. Malone) and others).*

Malone's *Supplement* was only a long and elaborate series of editorial notes (he published his first proper edition of Shakespeare in 1790), but his title captures a quality of all late eighteenth-century editions. They are essentially supplementary: they build on the bulk of the commentaries that come before them. Thus, the Steevens 1778 variorum that so exasperates the reviewer is a relatively compact work compared, for example, to the fifteen-volume Steevens edition of 1793. The series of editorial notes to which the reviewer points as exemplary of the vast, accretive commentary of the variorum edition was to continue to grow all through the subsequent editions. The 1778 edition's articulation of the controversy over the *Othello* line is absorbed into the succeeding editions, and informs and shapes the later notes. Thus, in the first note in the 1793 variorum, Malone refers to the first note in the 1778 variorum: Hanmer's explanation of his own emendation which had first established the line as a crux.

The line in question was part of Iago's sneering summary of Cassio's defects as an officer:

> "Certes," says he,
> "I have already chosen my officer,"
> And what was he?
> Foresooth, a great arithmetician,
> One Michael Cassio, a Florentine,
> (A fellow almost damn'd in a fair wife . . .)

$$(1.1.16-21)[3]$$

Hanmer thought the last line corrupt: apart from this one reference, Cassio, in the rest of the play, appears conspicuously unmarried. Hanmer changes the line to an anticipatory allusion to the evidence, scattered throughout the play, of Cassio's comeliness, and substituted "fair phiz" for "fair wife." Hanmer's emendation—although the word he suggested was unconvincingly unlike, in sound and orthography, the extant word— forced the editors who succeeded him to produce a more persuasive emendation or to account for the apparently dissonant "wife."

Six notes below this, in the 1778 variorum, after a series of attempts to reclaim the line by reading it as a parenthetical aside about Iago himself (whom Shakespeare conveniently supplies with a wife), Thomas Tyrwhitt suggests an emendation much defter than Hanmer's. Tyrwhitt emends "wife" to "life," supporting his emendation by an allusion, in *The Merchant of Venice*,[4] to the gospel judgement against those who call their brothers fools, and reading Iago's words as a comparable allusion to the gospel judgement of those of whom all men speak well: there is ample evidence in the play for Cassio's reputation for a "fair life." Malone, whose note then follows, supports "Mr. Tyrwhitt's ingenious emendation" with a passage from *The Merry Wives of Windsor*. But this series of notes in the 1778 variorum edition is completed by Steevens's own note, which attempts to reclaim the unemended text without transferring the wife to Iago: "[T]he words . . . may mean, according to Iago's licentious manner of expressing himself, no more than a man *very near being married*" (379). Steevens goes on to read the line as a reference to Cassio's entanglement with Bianca.

This oscillation between emendations and extant text is played out in succeeding editions. The 1793 Steevens commentary (15:379–82) begins with a note by Malone who reverses his role in the 1778 edition by rejecting the Tyrwhitt emendation and taking up, instead, Steevens's explanation of "wife." The notes that succeed Malone's all attempt to test or to bolster Steevens's reading by focusing on his own qualms about the lack of evidence in the play that Cassio knew Bianca before he came to Cyprus. Steevens had conceded that: "If Shakspeare, however, designed *Bianca* for a courtezan of *Cyprus*, (where Cassio had not yet been, and had therefore never seen her,) Iago cannot be supposed to allude to the report concerning his marriage with her, and consequently this part of my argument must fall to the ground" (379). Steevens's candor sets the tone for the notes that test his reading. There is an extraordinary even-handedness in these notes, a willingness to admit, or even to supply, counterevidence to an editor's own reading. Thus, Malone, in the fourth note (379–80), suggests that Cassio could have known Bianca before he came to Cyprus because Iago speaks as if he, at least, already knew Bianca well when he has just arrived from Venice. In the sixth note, however, Malone is ready to admit that Shakespeare's pervasive double time-scheme in *Othello* (in which characters repeatedly act as if they have been longer in Cyprus than the evidence in the play warrants) undermines his previous note.

The first six notes in Steevens's 1793 edition exactly reproduce the commentary in Malone's 1790 edition. Steevens, however, in the seventh note, reproaches Malone for his misguided economy in suppressing Tyrwhitt's explanation:

> Thus far our commentaries on this obscure passage are arranged as they stand in the very succinct edition of Mr. Malone. Yet I cannot prevail on myself, in further imitation of him, to suppress the note of my late friend Mr. Tyrwhitt, a note that seems to be treated with civilities that degrade its value, and with a neglect that few of its author's opinions have deserved. My inability to offer such a defence of his present one, as he himself could undoubtedly have supplied, is no reason why it should be prevented from exerting its own proper influence on the reader. (381)

Steevens, as he has promised, reproduces Tyrwhitt's explanation as his eighth note, and closes the commentary with a note from Ritson in absolute support of the emendation: "That Mr. Tyrwhitt has given us Shakspeare's genuine word and meaning I have not the least doubt" (382).

Steevens, who has selected and arranged the series of notes in both editions, the 1778 and the 1793, stage-manages two quite different performances comprising opposite patterns of events. In the 1778 edition, his own final note wrests the interpretive course away from Tyrwhitt's emendation and towards a new understanding of how the original text might be defended. In the 1793 edition, in an exact inversion of the '78 pattern of reading, Steevens insists on appending the three-note coda to the commentary, in support of the emendation, as if to wrest the interpretive course back again to the reading whose near-dislodgement his own note had set up.[5]

It is not that Steevens changes his mind from 1778 to 1793 about the correct reading—he retains "wife" in the text of both editions—but that he sees Malone's suppression of the Tyrwhitt note as a misunderstanding of the proper variorum response. The "succinctness" of Malone's edition has got in the way of that interpretive comprehensiveness which Steevens sees as the very mark of a variorum edition. It is this suggestive capaciousness of the form that Steevens, in his 1793 commentary, is determined to reestablish.

II

Steevens's implication that Malone's ten-volume edition fails in its succinctness is audacious: inscribed in his capacious, fifteen-volume variorum, it risks reminding the reader of the susceptibility of his own edition to the welter of contemporary gibes at such Shakespeare variorums far removed from all claim to succinctness. Lord Hailes, for example, wrote in the *Edinburgh Magazine* in 1786:

> [T]he various editions of this poet, with their appendages of notes and commentaries, the separate publications of his various readings, the essays, remarks, critical observations, and examinations both of separate plays and separate characters, have swelled at last to so enormous a mass, that, like the books of the Roman laws before their abridgement by Justinian, they are become literally . . . "the burden of many camels."[6]

Steevens's audacity is deliberately preemptive of the kind of sneer voiced by Lord Hailes or the mockery of the article, already quoted, from *The English Review*. His commitment to the variorum form is made in full consciousness of its vulnerability to attack. It is this commitment to the inherent expansiveness of the variorum form that the critic in *The English Review* underestimates when, lamenting Steevens's "careful preservation of all this farrago" (179), he implies, in Steevens, no more than a mechanical scrupulosity of note-retention.

"Farrago" means, literally, a mixed cattle-feed (from the Latin, "far," for grain) and, metaphorically, a miscellany, or hotchpotch. The term denies all possibility of a significant structure in the variorum commentary. It allows for a variety of response, but does not allow for the kind of structured and suggestive response that Steevens's insistent appending of the three-note coda in support of Tyrwhitt's near-abandoned emendation inscribes on the variorum page.

The critic in *The English Review* insists on the variorum response as an unmeaningful sequence of disparate interpretive acts. His exhaustive listing, between semicolons, of the separate contributors on the crux in *Othello* follows on his limning of an imaginary, but prototypical, series of variorum entries:

> One gentleman proposes an hypothesis, and a second supports it; a third refutes, and a fourth ridicules it; a fifth proposes another explanation; a sixth reconciles these explanations to each other, and a seventh sets them in opposition. (179)

Each note is represented by a separate clause, the mockingly repetitive rhythm and the relentless numbering of the notes suggesting not only an absurd voluminousness but a meaningless sequentiality in the commentary. However, running counter to this suggestion of an inanely disparate succession of notes, the contents of the clauses describe notes that are

complexly interactive. New notes test themselves against old ones: each
reading breeds the next.

This hint of a compensating dynamism in the variorum commentary is
borne out in the reviewer's confession of his own compulsive succumbing
to the all too potent allure of the notes. This confession is prompted by
the reviewer's approving citation of a passage from the Preface to Johnson's edition of Shakespeare. The passage, often quoted, rules that at
least a first reading of Shakespeare should be entirely unimpeded by the
distraction of notes:

> Parts are not to be examined until the whole has been surveyed; there is a kind
> of intellectual remoteness necessary for the comprehension of any great work
> in its full design and its true proportions; a close approach shews the smaller
> niceties, but the beauty of the whole is discerned no longer.[7]

The reviewer paraphrases Johnson's rule, and then bewails his own incapacity to heed such sound advice:

> But alas! *Monsieur le Commentateur!* where is there a man so resolute and
> stoical enough to adopt your advice? For our own part, we acknowledge, our
> eyes are continually solicited to these precious notes, our imagination is busy
> in creating to itself a thousand indescribable treasures they may contain, and
> we are unable to fly their allurement. (274)

Both Johnson and the reviewer deplore the downward glance to the commentary at the bottom of the page as a damaging displacement of the
proper critical focus. Johnson, in 1765, assumes the possibility of maintaining the requisite "intellectual remoteness" and resisting the disruptive
powers of the notes. The reviewer, examining the pages of the 1778
Steevens edition (with Johnson's name still on the title page), concludes
his strictures on the variorum response to the crux in *Othello* with an
emotive image of the impossibility of evading the inexorable pull of the
notes:

> To mend the matter, all these inestimable notes are printed at the bottom of
> the page, so that a reader, at all inquisitive, can scarcely keep his eyes from
> them, and is frequently drawn into the whirlpool, in spite of all his efforts. (179)

Johnson's insistence that a true reading of Shakespeare's plays be unde-
flected by attention to the detail of a text is here overruled by the vortex-
like power of the variorum notes to draw the intellectually responsive
reader down into compelling complexities of critical argument.

III

The complexity of critical response articulated in a variorum edition comes, in part, from a prevarication, inherent in the form itself, about how a variorum commentary should be read. The variorum page presents itself in two different ways: first, as a listing of separate editorial notes, each carefully assigned to a separate contributor; secondly, as a continuous narrative of interpretation that forms a significant structure on the page. The dynamic between these two ways of reading the page allows each interpretation an autonomous voicing within the confines of a particular note even as that interpretation is subject to modification—even rebuttal—by the context of notes that follow or surround it. It is the purpose of this essay to examine four examples of variorum response in which the dynamic between these different ways of reading the page generates a complex, and transformative, playing-out of critical argument.

The first example of this variorum dynamic (which accommodates different readings of a line, while it posits implicit relationships between them) is the variorum response to a line in *Othello*. Othello, on the brink of total belief in Iago's lies about Desdemona, laments the fate of all great men who have unfaithful wives:

> O curse of marriage,
> That we can call these delicate creatures ours,
> And not their appetites! . . .
>   Yet, 'tis the plague of great ones;
> Prerogativ'd are they less than the base:
> 'Tis destiny unshunnable, like death;
> Even then this *forked plague* is fated to us,
> When we do quicken.
>
> (3.3.268–77)

—*forked plague*—] In allusion to a *barbed* or *forked* arrow, which, once infixed, cannot be extracted. JOHNSON.

Or rather, the *forked plague* is the cuckold's horns. PERCY.

Dr. Johnson *may* be right. I meet with the same thought in Middleton's comedy of *A mad World my Masters,* 1608.

> "While the broad arrow, with the *forked head,*
> "Misses his brows but narrowly."

Again, in *King Lear:*

"—though the *fork* invade
"The region of my heart."

STEEVENS.

I have no doubt that Dr. Percy's interpretation is the true one. Let our poet speak for himself. "Quoth she," says Pandarus, in *Troilus and Cressida,* "which of these hairs is Paris, my husband? The *forked* one, quoth he; pluck it out, and give it him" [1.2.178]. Again, in *The Winter's Tale:*

"—O'er head and ears a *fork'd* one."

[1.2.186]

. . . One of Sir John Harrington's epigrams, in which our poet's very expression is found, puts the matter beyond a doubt[8]:

"Actaeon guiltless unawares espying
"Naked Diana bathing in her bowre,
"Was plagu'd with *hornes;* his dogs did him devoure;
"Wherefore take heed, ye that are curious, prying,
"With some such *forked plague* you be not smitten,
"And in your foreheads see your faults be written."

MALONE.   (Steevens 93, 15:534)

Editorial scrutiny of the two-word phrase has generated a sequence of notes that sets up an oscillation between alternative readings. First, Johnson's reading stresses the inexorability of Othello's fate: the fork of the barbed arrow is an emotive, metaphorical reworking of the more abstract allusion to a "destiny unshunnable" in the line before it. The next commentator, Percy, focuses on the matter of Othello's infliction: the fork of the cuckold's horn symbolizes the role of cheated husband that Othello so dreads. The oscillation between these different stresses in the first two notes is played out in the third and fourth notes. Thus, Steevens provides corroborating quotations for the Johnson reading, and then Malone, choosing to forget that Steevens has already called on Shakespeare (in lines from *King Lear*) to confirm his choice of reading, asks Shakespeare, again, "to speak for himself" and substantiate the Percy interpretation.

This pattern of notes—in which, like a rhyme scheme, Steevens's note chimes with Johnson's, and Malone's with Percy's—offers to repeat itself endlessly, without any finally determining swing towards one reading or the other. The effect of this oscillation is to embed both readings in the text so that Johnson's image of the barbed arrow is superimposed on Percy's image of the cuckold's horn. The double reading of "forked plague" gives in miniature the whole theme of the play: Othello's acceptance of Iago's imposition of the fork of cuckoldry is as fatal to him as a wound inflicted by a forked arrow.

IV

Just as the variorum page presents itself in two ways—as a series of disparate and autonomous notes, and as a complex structure of interacting interpretations—so the variorum editor plays two roles. He supplies the individually accredited readings in his own notes, and he is responsible, in his own edition, for arranging the pattern of multiple notes on the page. This experience of balancing (often contradictory) readings comes to be internalized by the variorum editors within their own notes. For example, Malone, in a note on a line from *Cymbeline,* provides evidence for one interpretation of a phrase while announcing his allegiance to a rival reading of the words, provided by Steevens, in the note above his. Malone's response is triggered by some words of Jachimo to Imogen. Testing her virtue with false tales of her husband's infidelity, he execrates the debauchery of the supposed villain:

Jachimo. A lady
So fair, and fasten'd to an empery
Would make the great'st king double! to be partner'd
With tomboys, hir'd with that self exhibition
Which your own coffers yield! with diseas'd ventures,
That play with all infirmities for gold
Which rottenness can lend nature! such boil'd stuff,
As well might poison poison!

(1.6.124)

The variorum encounter centers on a single word in the penultimate line:

—*such* boil'd *stuff,*] The allusion is to the ancient process of sweating in venereal cases. . . . So, in *The Old Law,* by Massinger:

"—look *parboil'd,*
"As if they came from Cupid's scalding-house."

Again, in *Troilus and Cressida:* "Sodden business! there's a *stew'd* phrase indeed." Again, in *Timon of Athens:* "She's e'en setting on water to *scald* such chickens as you are." All this stuff about *boiling, scalding,* &c. is a mere play on *stew,* a word which is afterwards used for a brothel by Imogen. STEEVENS.

The words may mean,—such *corrupted* stuff; from the substantive *boil.* So, in *Coriolanus:*
"—*boils* and plagues
" Plaster you o'er!"

But, I believe, Mr. Steevens's interpretation is the true one. MALONE.

(Steevens 93, 13:57)

Steevens explains the adjective as a double allusion to prostitution: "boil'd" describes the sweating cure for syphilis, and plays on the ambiguity in the related kitchen term, "stew." Malone provides an alternative etymology. In his reading, "boil'd" refers to an encrusted skin—a symptom, or a consequence, of the disease rather than its cure. The tentativeness with which Malone proffers his suggestion—"The words may mean"—grows into absolute self-refutation as Malone ends the note on a statement of clear preference for Steevens's interpretation.

This retraction of the reading as it is being given confers a curious status on the note. The retraction does not annul the reading, and the note is retained in a later edition. Indeed, the retention of the note is responsive to the tacit assumption, in the note itself, that a reading that is proffered in full knowledge of its incapacity to displace an established reading still demands inclusion in the commentary. The note, at some level, insists that Malone's and Steevens's different editorial responses are complementary rather than mutually defeating. The capacious variorum form engineers a conversion of interpretive differences into increments of critical response. The experience of reading the variorum commentary is of a growing sense of the extraordinary recalcitrance of apparently refuted versions of the text. Each reading, in each note, sets up a verbal impression, or an image, which simply will not fade away on the emergence of a new reading.

V

The tenacious variorum edition holds on not only to rival interpretations of the text but to graphically distinct variants of a single word. It is this tenacity that shapes the variorum commentary on an earlier line in *Cymbeline* (Steevens 93, 13:14). Imogen, forced to part with Posthumus, asks him to wear a ring until her death shall free him to woo another wife. Posthumus protests:

> *Posthumus.* How! how! another?—
> You gentle gods, give me but this I have,
> And sear up my embracements from a next
> With bonds of death!

> (1.1.114–117)

The variorum altercation turns on the word "sear."[9] There are three commentators, all of whom agree that "sear up" must involve some idea of the customary confinement of a corpse. In the first note, Steevens objects to the connotations of the soldering iron in "sear," and suggests an emendation, backed up by a parallel usage in *Hamlet,* to "cere":

And sear *up my embracements from a next*
With bonds of death!] Shakespeare may poetically call the *cere-cloths* in which
the dead are wrapp'd, the *bonds of death.* If so , we should read *cere* instead
of *sear:*

> "Why thy canoniz'd bones hearsed in death,
> "Have burst their *cerements?*" [*Hamlet*, 1.4.47]

To *sear up*, is properly to *close up by burning;* but in this passage the poet may
have dropp'd that idea, and used the word simply for to *close up.* STEEVENS.

Steevens's verb, "cere," now points precisely and aptly to the wrapping
of the dead in waxen linen.

Steevens's reading is immediately controverted on the page by the note
beneath it:

> May not *sear up,* here mean *solder up,* and the reference be to a lead coffin?
> Perhaps *cerements* in Hamlet's address to the Ghost, was used for *searments*
> in the same sense. HENLEY.

Henley has proposed a reading of the unemended "sear" that is as precisely funereal as Steevens's "cere."[10] The unwelcome allusion to a heat-
caused sealing is now felicitous: "sear" describes the soldering of a lid
onto a lead coffin. Henley goes on to undermine Steevens's supporting
quotation by appropriating it boldly for his own cause. The allusion to a
soldering of leaden coffins is read back into the words from *Hamlet.*

Henley's rebuttal of Steevens's note is followed by Malone's rebuttal
of Henley's. Malone begins his note by apparently eschewing both his
predecessors' attempts to particularize the image, but his knowledge of
the fluid state of Elizabethan spelling provides him with extra evidence
of the close kinship between the two words:

> I believe nothing more than *close up* was intended. In the spelling of the last
> age, however, no distinction was made between *cere-cloth* and *sear-cloth.* Cole
> in his Latin dictionary, 1679, explains the word *cerot* by *sear-*cloth. Shakspeare
> therefore certainly might have had that practice in his thoughts. MALONE.

Steevens, in his 1793 variorum, displays all three notes. Together, they
weave a narrative of critical response that fuses together the two senses
of the verb. Each version of the word now carries with it an implication
of the other. "Sear-cloth" is also "cere-cloth," and "cerements" "sear-
ments." In the variorum structure of notes, the layers of meaning wrap
themselves around the verb as in the text the images of the sealing of a
coffin and the embalmatory shrouding of a corpse accrete in Posthumus's
imaginings of interment.

VI

The two readings of Posthumus's protestation—the readings absorbed in the structured variorum response—diverge graphically, but the different words provided by the First Folio reading and Steevens's suggestion can be heard simultaneously by any audience well-versed in Shakespearean homophones. The variorum commentary, however, can entirely transcend any conceivable playhouse response. Thus, the variorum commentary (Steevens 93, 15:210–11) on a textual crux in *Hamlet* pushes at the fundamental limiting assumption that a play's meaning is contained in a single, definitive, playable text. The crux occurs in Claudius's vindication to Rosencrantz and Guildenstern of his decision to send Hamlet to England. The quarto version read:

> The terms of our estate may not endure
> Hazard so near's as doth hourly grow
> Out of his *brows*.

> (3.3.5–7)

Pope had replaced "brows" with "lunacies" from the second folio. Theobald, in a long note, had then suggested an emendation to a word that Shakespeare had used in *The Winter's Tale*:

> The old *Quarto's* read,—*Out of his* Brows. This was from the Ignorance of the first Editors; as is this unnecessary *Alexandrine* ["lunacies"], which we owe to the Players. The Poet, I am persuaded, wrote,

> > *as doth hourly grow*
> > *Out of his* Lunes.

> i.e. his *Madness, Frenzy.* So our Poet, before, in his *Winter's Tale* [2.2.28].

> > *These dang'rous, unsafe* Lunes *i'th'* King!
> > —*beshrew 'em*

> > *He must be told of it*, &c.

The Reader, if he pleases, may turn to my 10th Remark on that *Play*.[11]

Theobald's emendation draws on both variants. "Lunes" as "fits of Madness" is a less usual synonym of "lunacies." "Lunes" is related semantically to the folio reading and orthographically to the quarto version. The emendation to "lunes" from "browes" (the quarto spelling of the word) is graphically plausible, Peter Seary points out: the "l," for example, might well have been misread as an uncapitalised—and carelessly written—"b."[12]

Theobald finds his emendation sufficiently persuasive to allow it to radiate out into another play. His conjecture for the *Hamlet* line (supported by the *Winter's Tale* example) serves, in turn, to corroborate, a new reading of a line in *The Merry Wives of Windsor* (4.2.21–22). Theobald's note on the *Hamlet* line continues:

Perhaps, too, in the *Merry Wives of Windsor,* where all the editions read;

> *Why, Woman, your Husband is in his old Lines again.*

We ought to correct;

> *in his old* Lunes *again.*

i.e. in his old Fits of Madness, Frenzy. (7:306)

Johnson, unconvinced by "lunes," leaves "lunacies" in the text, but suggests an alternative emendation:

"Lunacies" is the reading of the folio. I take "brows" to be, properly read, "frows," which, I think, is a provincial word, for "perverse humours"; which being, I suppose, not understood, was changed to "lunacies." But of this I am not confident. (988)

Like Theobald, Johnson tries to tease out from the traces of the letters of the less explicable "brows," an orthographically similar word whose meaning approximates "lunacies."

A note by Steevens balances the accumulating textual options. He endorses the evidence for Theobald's emendation (upgrading Theobald's tentative insertion of "lunes" in the *Merry Wives of Windsor* to an authoritative piece of text that clinches the *Hamlet* "lunes"),[13] and carefully provides an instance in support of the Johnson conjecture, "frows." His note ends on a lucid and succinct explanation of the (so far unexplained) quarto reading:

[*Out of his* lunes.] I would receive Theobald's emendation, because Shakespeare uses the word *lunes* in the same sense in *The Merry Wives of Windsor* and *The Winter's Tale.*

I have met, however, with an instance in support of Dr. Johnson's conjecture;

> "—were you but as favourable as you are *frowish*—."
> *Tully's Love,* by Greene, 1616.

Perhaps, however, Shakespeare designed a metaphor from horned cattle, whose powers of being dangerous increase with the *growth of their brows.*

The final note in the variorum sequence (a note by Henley) lays insistent hold on the Theobald emendation—"lunes"—and the quarto reading—"brows"—and refuses to surrender either. The note begins:

> The two readings of *brows* and *lunes*—when taken in connection with the passages referred to by Mr. Steevens, in *The Winter's Tale* and *The Merry Wives of Windsor*—plainly figure forth the image under which the King apprehended danger from Hamlet:—viz. that of a bull, which, in his frenzy, might not only gore, but push him from his throne. (15:210–11)

Henley's note is extraordinary. It seems to deem both variants necessary (or at least usefully, satisfyingly, complementary). "Brows" and "lunes" are not textual or semantic rivals but confederates. The full projection of Claudius's image of Hamlet depends on the transmission of two different, but related, ideas, which "brows" and "lunes" together body forth: the bull's horns, Hamlet's power to harm Claudius, and the bull's frenzy, the dangerous unleashing of that power, the utter lack of proper self-restraint that is manifest in Hamlet's antic killing of Polonius. Neither "brows" nor "lunes" can by itself convey the full horror of the danger that Hamlet represents to Claudius.

Henley anchors the confederacy of the two contributory parts of the image in passages from the very plays from which Theobald had drawn his supporting evidence for ousting the "brows" reading in favor of his "lunes" emendation. Henley thus, supplements *The Winter's Tale* passage (with which Theobald had buttressed his lunes emendation) with additional evidence for the "brows" reading—an elaboration, in the same play, of the image of budding horns, in an exchange between Leontes and Mamilius:

> *Leontes:* How now, you wanton calf,
> Art thou my calf?
>
> *Mamilius:* Yes, if you will, my lord.
>
> *Leontes:* Thou want'st a rough pash and the shoots that I have,
> To be full like me. . . .[14]

Henley draws on the twin passages to establish, and to illuminate, the twin parts of the image, the horns and the frenzy:

> —"The hazard that hourly grows out of his BROWS" (according to the quartos) corresponds to *"the SHOOTS from the ROUGH PASH,"* [that is *the* TUFTED PROTUBERANCE *on the head of a bull, from whence his horns spring*] al-

luded to in *The Winter's Tale;* whilst the imputation of impending danger to "his LUNES" (according to the other reading) answers as obviously to the jealous fury of the husband that thinks he has detected the infidelity of his wife.

To Henley, the perfect correspondence of the *Winter's Tale* passages to "brows" and "lunes" is compelling evidence of the part that each reading plays in the *Hamlet* speech. The image requires their double presence in the text.

As final proof of the coalescence of the two readings, Henley quotes the parallel usage of "lunes" that Theobald had suggested in the *Merry Wives of Windsor* speech, and quotes further lines from the same speech which provide a gloss for the "brows" reading. Italicizing the crucial words, he makes plain a parallel Shakespearean compacting of the ideas of horned brows and frenzy:

Thus, in *The Merry Wives of Windsor:* "Why woman, your husband is in his old *lunes*—he so takes on yonder with my husband; so rails against all married mankind; so curses all Eve's daughters, and so buffets himself on the *forehead,* crying peer out! peer out! [Johnson explains: "That is, appear horns"[15]] That any *madness,* I have ever yet beheld, seem'd but tameness, civility, and patience, to this distemper he is now in."

Henley's note completely releases Shakespeare's texts from the constraint that the transmission of a play's meaning must be fundamentally aural. An alert audience might hear both "cere" and "sear," and respond to their twin resonance, but not "lunes" and "brows." Henley's note implies that the fullest, truest response to the image in *Hamlet* is that of a vigilant reader profiting from the textual and interpretive information that a variorum edition provides. The model of reading that Henley's note intimates is entirely at odds with Johnson's prescription that a true reading should disregard the minutiae of a text.[16] The "close approach" (that insistent editorial attention to the parts of a text—and to those parts' variant forms—whose effects on a reading Johnson so deplored) disintegrates Johnson's ideal object of critical attention, "the beauty of the whole." However, the capacity of the variorum edition to draw in—and make significant structures of—the most heterogeneous and contradictory interpretive matter generates an alternative "whole" to the one invoked by Johnson. Thus, in the example from *Hamlet,* the structure of variorum notes culminates in Henley's taking up two textual variants (that no actor could voice together in a single production) and insisting on them as complementary halves of a powerful Shakespearean image. The tenacity of the variorum edition, as if in compensation for the lost Johnsonian "whole," recreates, at the level of textual minutiae, an interpretive "whole" generated by the sweep of each tiny verbal unit's textual and interpretive history.

NOTES

1. See Brian Vickers, ed., *Shakespeare: The Critical Heritage* (London: Routledge Kegan Paul, 1981), 6:48, for a list of complaints about the voluminousness of the variorum commentaries.

2. *English Review* 3 (1784): 168–79, 272–78, 342–51.This was a review of Edward Capell's *Mr. William Shakespeare his Comedies, Histories, and Tragedies,* 10 vols. (London, 1767–8). Capell's notes were published after the edition itself; the last volume of the notes was published in 1783. The reviewer praises Capell for avoiding, in his edition, the variorum method. In a comparison between Capell's *Shakespeare* and George Steevens's *The Plays of William Shakespeare,* 10 vols. (London, 1778), he advises purchase only of the former, for the reader "will not much mend his market, by having recourse to the other edition, where the chaff so much predominates over the corn, that he will run the risque of being suffocated before he be fed" (343).

3. These line numbers, and the text are taken from G. Blakemore Evans, ed., *The Riverside Shakespeare* (Boston: Houghton Mifflin, 1974), for ease of access.

4. GRATIANO: O my Anthonio, I do know of those
   That therefore only are reputed wise
   For saying nothing; when I am very sure
   If they should speak, would *almost damn* those ears
   Which hearing them would call their brothers fools.

                                                                (1.1.95–99)

Tyrwhitt's remarks on the passage are taken from pp. 2–4 of his *Observations and Conjectures upon some Passages in Shakespeare* (1765).

5. Steevens's note from the 78 edition is reproduced as the third note of the 1793 edition.

6. "Critical Remarks on the late Editions of Shakespeare's Plays." *Edinburgh Magazine* 4 (1786): 354.

7. Arthur Sherbo, ed., *Johnson on Shakespeare,* Vols. 7 and 8 of The Yale Edition of the Works of Samuel Johnson, General Ed. John H. Middendorf, 16 vols. to date (New Haven: Yale University Press, 1958–), 111.

8. Malone's claim that he has established the correct reading "beyond a doubt" is made within the confines of a single note. On the page itself, it plays a part in a rhythm of oscillating interpretative alternatives.

9. The First Folio has "seare."

10. The Rev. Samuel Henley is one of the many "neglected Shakespeareans" Arthur Sherbo is determined to reestablish in *The Birth of Shakespeare Studies: Commentators from Rowe (1709) to Boswell-Malone (1821)* (East Lansing, Michigan: Colleagues Press, 1986), xiii.

11. The note's length led later variorum editors to quote it only in abbreviated versions, but since these editors' responses are reactive to Theobald's whole note, Theobald's lines are here quoted in their entirety.

12. Peter Seary, *Lewis Theobald and the Editing of Shakespeare* (Oxford: Clarendon Press, 1990), 165.

13. Johnson, too, finds Theobald's suggested emendation of the *Merry Wives*

of Windsor passage convincing. In a note on these lines, he uses the word, "lunes," to redirect the charge of frenzy to Shakespeare himself for so compulsively reverting, in the plays, to the subject of cuckoldry: "Shakespeare is at his old lunes." See Samuel Johnson, ed., *The Plays of William Shakespeare,* 8 vols. (London, 1765), 2:526. (Curiously, "lunes," was printed as "lanes" in Johnson's edition, and had to be corrected in the Appendix.) Johnson's jovial appropriation of the phrase shows the degree to which Theobald's emendation has taken on the status of something quintessentially Shakespearean.

14. *Riverside Shakespeare,* 1.2.126–28.
15. See Johnson, *Plays,* 2:526.
16. See page 128.

Chedworth and the Territoriality
of the Reader

Paul Nelsen

THE practice of publishing editions of Shakespeare *cum notis variorum* evolved through the second half of the eighteenth century initially as a response to territorial skirmishes over the intellectual property of successive annotators and, eventually, as a response to reader interest in assaying notable cruxes of the text. To some, like Johnson, the growing intrusion of multiple notes on the page upstaged the Bard's text in the view of the reader: "The mind is refrigerated by interruption; the thoughts are diverted from the principal subject. . . ."[1] Reacting in 1788 to the ardor of the annotators, Richard Porson sardonically quipped, "The present age may justly boast of the great improvements it has made to the art of note-writing" even if the notes may displace Shakespeare as "only an incidental object; the first and grand purpose of the critic is to display his own wit and learning."[2] However, as Margreta de Grazia observes, the editorial shift to a variorum approach signals, not so much the self-aggrandizement of the annotator(s), but a "radical uncertainty about both the source of the editor's authority and the relation of his contributions both to those of other editors and to Shakespeare's text itself."[3] Despite his dislike of the chilling obstruction caused by icebergs of annotation, Johnson acknowledged the value of variorum editions as a means of empowering the reader: "If the reader is not satisfied with the editor's determination, he may have the means of chusing for himself."[4] By the end of the eighteenth century, as de Grazia puts it, "The coveted privilege of 'perfecting' the Shakespeare text was taken from the 'dictatorial' editor and invested in the general readership unaccompanied by any principle of selection whatsoever."[5] The aim of this essay is to survey the views of a solitary, recondite reader and avid note-writer—John Howe, Baron Chedworth. As a late eighteenth-century gentleman scholar, Lord Chedworth's proprietary arbitrations of Shakespearean text—drawn largely from his "critical and laborious investigation" of the "various readings of the different commentators" that Chedworth found among the plethora of notes anchoring the pages of rival late eighteenth-century editions of the collected plays—offer an exposition of the territoriality of an autonomous reader, and a representative example of a process of "chusing" and "perfecting" a personal understanding carried on by other closet critics of that age.

The three successive multivolume editions that piqued Chedworth's interest are the 1785 descendant of Samuel Johnson's and George Steevens's *The Plays of William Shakespeare,* as revised and augmented by Steevens and Isaac Reed; Edmond Malone's monumental 1790 publication of *The Plays and Poems of William Shakespeare;* and Steevens's 1793 reedited and expanded variorum.[6] Steevens and Malone vied famously for reader approval by endeavoring to provide banquets of annotation—delineating cruxes of critical explication, Shakespeare's "Beauties and Defects," historical sources and references, variant readings, and more—for the individual reader to feast upon. The accretion of notes found in these editions reflects not only an expanded body of erudition and critical perspective but significant changes in the cultural marketplace. Jean Marsden, for example, sees the expansion of Shakespearean criticism and the evolution of the variorum editions as signaling late eighteenth-century transitions in education, social values, and consequent "Taste and Understanding" in literature:

> To the critics who came after Johnson, how an individual responded to reading the Shakespearean text was crucial. Shakespeare's text, with its irregular beauties, became proof that literature must be approached intuitively, and it provided evidence of the superiority of *feeling* over the then outmoded and incomplete notion of *reason.* . . .
> The literary world reflected these changes in new assumptions concerning the role of the critic, most notably in the fundamental assumption that the critic was an individual reader, not a social spokesman. The growing emphasis on the individual most affected the study of Shakespeare in the emphasis on the reader and the validation of individual response. . . .[7]

Furthermore, Marsden argues, these societal transformations prompted responses in the publishing industry that fostered a new basis of relationship between Shakespeare and his readers:

> Fueled by growing literacy and the expanding market for the printed word, literary production in the later eighteenth century grew exponentially. Shakespeare and his words were an important part of this industry; the eighteenth century witnessed not only the remarkable proliferation of new editions but a phenomenal growth in the number of books and essays written about him. . . . (T)he subjectivity of the reader and the forces of literary production interlocked at the text, bridging the gap between the reader and the printed page. In this new literary marketplace, the reader was the consumer of printed texts, and

dramatic literature was overwhelmingly perceived as text—not performed but printed. The result was not simply the canonization of Shakespeare but the canonization of his words. (64)

Chedworth's particular fascination with details and differences among the variorum editions of 1785, 1790, and 1793 provides considerable evidence relating a reader's taste for participatory adjudication—scrutinizing the text and critical deliberations upon it as a means of perfecting a subjective Understanding of the canon.[8]

Lord Chedworth should not be put forward as an average, late eighteenth-century consumer or reader of Shakespeare's words, but he may stand as a model of one whom publishers and editors desired most to please: a gentleman of aristocratic pedigree, educated in the Greats with a solid grasp of literary masterworks; one who was highly regarded by those who knew him best for his analytical aptitude and judicious reasoning; a reader who desired to understand Shakespeare largely for his own pleasure; and one whose critical views could be influential. Born in Ipswich in August 1754 and christened John Howe, Chedworth's boyhood schooling was at Harrow where "he gave very early proof of his inclination to the stage and turf."[9] Following Harrow, he went to Queen's college, Oxford, where he read classics and cultivated his knowledge of poetry and Shakespeare. After the normal three years at university, he returned to Ipswich where he lived with his widowed mother until she died in 1778. In 1781, he succeeded his uncle in title and estates and was admitted to the House of Lords as the fourth Baron Chedworth. Acquaintances described him as remarkably shy and reserved, having a certain peculiarity of appearance and manner, but as a man with considerable intellectual talent. He took an interest in matters of law, served as a Magistrate, and earned great respect for his legal acuity among judicial colleagues and acquaintances at coffeehouses near Lincoln's Inn Fields. Although he was not a gambler, he was celebrated by compatriots who fancied horse races at Newmarket for his acute skill and swiftness of mind in calculating odds. Chedworth eschewed fashionable society and chose to live a relatively simple, secluded existence in the Ipswich family home, rarely visiting his baronial estates in Wiltshire and Gloucestershire—the management of which he turned over to an able solicitor and eventual confrere, Richard Wilson. Chedworth never married. In his private life he most enjoyed literary conversation and he developed friendships with a few actors and actresses of the Theatre Royal Norwich—an institution to which he supplied financial support—including one William Hickey Seymour.[10] Chedworth also maintained a special, longtime companionship with a surgeon from Great Yarmouth, Thomas Penrice, with whom he resided late in life. He died after an extended illness at age fifty on 29 October 1804; the barony became extinct. Following Chedworth's death, both Seymour and Penrice figure prominently in bringing Chedworth's cloistered Shakespearean commentary into public view.

Steevens certainly prepared his 1793 variorum, with its expansive revisions and refinements, to invite comparison with Malone's and all previous editions and to compete for critical approval. Chedworth responded by undertaking a collateral analysis of the textual variants and annotational deliberations found among the volumes of the forementioned trio of editions. He recorded a multitude of reactions in manuscript notes, apparently over several years, and discussed his thoughts with literary comrades. The notes are specifically alluded to in his will but whether Chedworth himself ever had publication of his collective comments in mind is ambiguous. Chedworth's *Notes upon some of the Obscure Passages in Shakespeare's Plays; with Remarks upon the Explanations and Amendments of the Commentators in the Editions of 1785, 1790, 1793* was posthumously published in London (1805)—only ten months after his death—under the editorial supervision and personal behest of his longtime companion and substantial beneficiary, Dr. Penrice.[11] In a prefatory inscription to this privately printed volume, Penrice states that Chedworth's notes "seem to be . . . intended either for his own private information and amusement, or (as it appears from some internal evidence) with a view to their being subsequently laid before the Public in a more corrected state." Penrice disavows significant editorial intervention: "To amend or enlarge his Lordship's observations falls not within my province or ability," and further advertises, "The manuscript has been strictly followed, except in the instance of enlarging the quotations, so as to bring the disputed word or text into view with the context." There is indeed no proof that Penrice altered the substance of Chedworth's commentary. Nevertheless, the range of errata found in the text reveals Penrice's inexperience as an editor and stands as evidence that the task was managed under some pressure of time.

Penrice's motivations to rush Chedworth's private notes on Shakespeare before the public are intriguing. Certainly Penrice wished to memorialize his aristocratic friend's taste for literary excellence; the expense of private publication was a small sum compared to the vast inheritance bestowed upon the Yarmouth physician. However, Penrice's primary incentive may have had more to do with protecting the fortune that Chedworth had left him than solely with commemorating his benefactor's independent scholarship. Chedworth's will[12] provided several generous legacies for friends and theatrical chums like Seymour, servants, and certain Whig politicians he admired; but the greatest bequests from Chedworth's estate were directed to Wilson, friend and attorney, and Penrice, companion and physician, in equal sums—valued at well over one hundred thousand pounds each. Chedworth's relatives were slighted or utterly neglected. Certain of the outraged kin contested the will on grounds of insanity and their suit put Penrice's substantial inheritance at risk.

In his prefatory inscription, Penrice claims he has brought the book to publication because "I have strong reason to suppose that a part of these Notes will be offered to the world in a different way, and less perfect form, I feel it a duty, which I owe to the memory of his Lordship, to edit them entire, in order to distribute copies to our respective friends, and to those readers of taste in similar studies, who may not deem such a trifle unworthy of their acceptance." One explanation of Penrice's hurry to bring the notes into print and to distribute copies of the book to "respective friends"—particularly those who might be called upon to attest at trial—is that by publishing Chedworth's recognizably astute collation project even in its largely fragmentary form, Penrice ensured against suppression or distortion of the notes as certain evidence of Chedworth's sanity.[13] The suit was dismissed by jury; a subsequent appeal failed. An account in *Gentleman's Magazine* of the trial[14] indicates that Chedworth's knowledge of Shakespeare and command of dramatic criticism were indeed brought into testimony as evidence of his mental soundness. That Penrice should bring to a trial such scholarly musings on "the inimitable Bard" as persuasive evidence of Chedworth's sanity offers an interesting comment on eighteenth-century values. That the deliberations of the jury considering Chedworth's sanity should be influenced by the quality of his notes on Shakespeare may be regarded with some delight by latter-day Shakespeareans. Nevertheless, the report states that, "above all," the most persuasive evidence of the well-read Baron's stability of mind was that "nobody could out-calculate him at Newmarket upon the races, the very last place where an insane person, or one of dull intellect, ought to be trusted."[15]

An alternative or complementary explanation of Penrice's push to publish implicates Seymour. Seymour was one of the actors at the Theatre Royal Norwich and apparently cultivated his own standing as one of Chedworth's close intellectual companions. Chedworth's will provided Seymour with a bequest of thirteen hundred pounds; along with Penrice and two other gentlemen, a portion of his library; and, if Seymour wished, "a copy of his Lordship's Notes on Shakespeare" with the original given to Penrice. Within months of Penrice's private release of Chedworth's *Notes,* Seymour published, by subscription,[16] a two-volume opus with a fashionably convoluted title: *Remarks, Critical, Conjectural, and Explanatory, upon the Plays of Shakespeare; resulting from a Collation of the Early Copies, with that of Johnson and Steevens, edited by Isaac Reed, Esq. together with Some Valuable Extracts from the Mss. of the*

Late Right Honourable John, Lord Chedworth. Seymour includes one hundred twenty-two citations ascribed to Chedworth but the vast accumulation of comments are Seymour's own. Could Seymour's limited homage to Chedworth be the rendition of the notes—"offered to the world in a different way, and less perfect form"—that Penrice suggests persuaded him to publish and distribute the entirety of his Lordship's manuscript? It is very likely. Did Penrice have jealous cause to distrust Seymour as an interloper, intent on commandeering Chedworth's studious commentary upon the variora—critical observations that Chedworth had shared in intimate conversation with Seymour and left to him, in adumbrated form, in a copy of his manuscript—and publishing these insights as authored by himself? This proposition cannot be proved with certainty but there is varied evidence to support credibility. In any case, the issue is more a matter of intrigue than of substantive concern in the annals of Shakespearean criticism.

Despite Penrice's and Seymour's respective and possibly rival efforts to draw attention to his scholarship, Chedworth's notes do not survive among citations in latter-day criticism. Several of Furness's nineteenth-century variorum editions include mention of Chedworth's *Notes* (and Seymour's *Remarks*) among his long lists of "books consulted and quoted," but even among those tomes of annotation, actual citations of Chedworth's comments are not catalogued even if they were consulted. We must view Chedworth's observations not as *sui generis* criticism, lost and now restored, but as literate marginalia assiduously recorded by an enthusiastic reader, whose contributions have been largely forgotten but here may be reevaluated.

II

Chedworth obviously relished the rich menu of variant readings, editorial emendations, and explanations found in rival editions available to him by 1793, specifically those "superintended" by George Steevens and Isaac Reed (1785), Edmond Malone (1790), and Steevens (1793), and found the array of choice appetizing. It is difficult to determine from evidence in the *Notes* the extent of Chedworth's awareness of other editions in print, including the earlier collation work of Edward Capell and Charles Jennens, or his familiarity with the body of critical discourse on editorial cruxes which preceded his interrogation of the *fin de siècle* variorum editions.[17] Chedworth's *Notes* focus purposefully on the trio of multivolume sets and the collateral distinctions to be discovered among revisions, emendations, alterations, additions, and even erasures, from later editions, of footnotes that had appeared in previous publication.

His attention to differentiation signals his cautious awareness of editorial power and the vulnerability of Shakespeare's text; his careful examination of evidence and arguments supporting one reading or another may well reflect his affection for adjudicating issues of law.

As an eager reader in pursuit of a personally perfected Shakespearean canon, Chedworth carefully appropriates those editorial options that suit his taste and—although the emphasis is on textual choices and explanatory views with which he agrees—he rejects those that strike him as wrong, foolish, or unnecessary. In several instances, he mediates views of alternative readings, sometimes allowing the legitimacy of antithetical perspectives. With regard to certain passages, he laments that none of the commentary found in the accretion of notes provides him with a satisfactory understanding. Throughout, one may uncover discerning observations based on perspicacious readings of the plays, and discover intertextual connections drawn from a sophisticated body of learning. The remarkably idiosyncratic selection of "some of the Obscure Passages in Shakespeare's Plays" that Chedworth chooses to address may strike a modern reader as bewildering—he disregards commonly debated issues of text, including infamous differences between quarto and First Folio correlative scenes and speeches. This may be explained as an inclination to disdain reviewing conspicuous cruxes, which had already drawn wide scrutiny, and to concentrate instead on certain particulars that seemed to him to have been neglected. Overall, however, Chedworth's remarks thoroughly illustrate the notion that "perfecting" Shakespeare's text was a matter of personal arbitration of the Bard's "intent" through the delectable enterprise of studious investigation. Central to the process of that investigation was the presence of the *notis variorum,* a veritable conference of alternative perspectives, that invite and inform the reader's dialectical involvement.

Penrice organized the book to present Chedworth's comments in separate chapters, laid out to follow the sequence of the thirty-six plays in the First Folio. Beneath each play title/chapter heading, appear references to the volume number in each edition where that play may be found. For example, under "King Lear" Penrice lists, "J. and S. 1785. Vol. IX.— Malone Vol. VIII.—J. and S. 1793. Vol. X." The manner of abbreviation of editions varies under some chapters. Within each chapter, Penrice includes page numbers where the correlative passage in question may be located in the three versions above each quoted fragment of Shakespeare's text that Chedworth is examining: e.g., "P. 325.—134.—29." Passages from Shakespeare are neatly indented and printed in a smaller typeface, over Chedworth's corresponding remark. Penrice also attempts to facilitate matters for the reader by italicizing, within the cited passage from Shakespeare, the particular word(s) that prompted Chedworth's comment. The text Penrice cites consistently follows the 1793 edition; rare instances focusing only on "Malone's reading" are noted. While Penrice's system of indexing citations may seem reasonable, various inconsistencies, errors, and referencing obstacles may be discovered throughout the book's 375 pages. For *Merchant of Venice,* Chedworth's comments only address the Malone edition; under *Taming of the Shrew,* he focuses exclusively on the "J. and S. 1793." In a remarkable number of cases, Penrice's page number references were off by one or two. Penrice's system provides no allusions to act, scene, or line numbers, making cross-referencing by a modern reader—without copies of all three original editions in hand—rather cumbersome.

Without the means to cross-reference to Chedworth's original source materials, a reader attempting to grasp Chedworth's critical views will be largely frustrated. As noted earlier, Chedworth's comments are essentially marginalia, recorded by him in manuscript form, then hurriedly transposed by Dr. Penrice into formal print for reasons that had nothing to do with the intrinsic lucidity of what Chedworth left—it simply provided proof of Chedworth's scholarly inclination and some indication of his dialectical acumen. Much of the text in *Notes* appears as truncated cryptographic code or may otherwise seem to be lacking in perspicuity. Each citation from a play is followed by Chedworth's isolated comment without any transitional narrative or effort to make cogent connections between entries. In many instances, Chedworth's comment is perplexingly terse—e.g., "I disagree with Mr. Steevens" or "Malone is right"—and abandoned bereft of further explanation. In order to decode the vast majority of ciphered observations, a reader must allude to the other critics' annotations found at the bottom of the page within the reference editions that Chedworth scrutinizes. For example, responding to *notis variorum* on Macbeth's words, "Here lay Duncan, / His *silver* skin *lac'd* with his *golden* blood" (note Penrice's convention of italicizing "disputed" words which I will continue to include in citations), Chedworth offers this statement: "I am afraid the opinion delivered in Warburton's note, and in the latter part of that of Dr. Johnson, is a refinement of their own. I fear Shakespeare has no claim to the praise of judgment. I do not think the idea ever entered his mind" (135). In this case, a reading of Warburton's and Johnson's glosses on the line in question reveals that both critics generally agree that "Shakespeare put these forced unnatural metaphors into the mouth of Macbeth as a mark of artifice and dissimulation" (Johnson) and "show him to be acting a part" (Warburton). Both critics, however, are strained to make the "praise of judgment" Chedworth would dismiss. Acknowledging ambivalence about the line and his inability to amend it to clarify its intent, Johnson even suggests blotting it out entirely. Even after cross-referencing, the point of Chedworth's critical remark remains enigmatic.

Deciphering most of Chedworth's hermeneutics, therefore, involves a convoluted process of search and analysis of his specific sources. What Chedworth thinks about Shakespeare is veiled in meta-notational comments on other commentators' commentary on Shakespeare. Chedworth's dialectical process may frequently be regarded as that of a discriminating consumer or connoisseur critic who "shops for" editorial options he prefers, culls preferences from the stock of readings catalogued at the bottom of the page, and procures selectively. Although terse, fragmentary notation may be found in other eighteenth-century publications, the adumbrated nature and cryptic brevity of the vast majority of these published comments obfuscate a reader's desire to understand the pattern of his critical point of view. The book reads more like a coded index than a pastiche of critical précis. Surely, however, the point must be that Chedworth's cipher was never intended to confound readers because Chedworth did not compose these notes for others to read, he wrote them for himself.

Certain of his remarks are indeed coherent as compact self-contained pensées. The one hundred twenty-two "valuable extracts" from Chedworth's manuscript[18] that Seymour reprinted—verbatim or accurately paraphrased—in his *Remarks upon the Plays of Shakespeare* represent nearly all of Chedworth's notes that may be quoted intelligibly, without extensive explanation of their source inspiration. These cogent capsule commentaries may well be "some internal evidence" that Penrice alludes to in suggesting that his Lordship may have outlined his notes "with a view to their subsequently being laid before the Public in a more corrected state." Nevertheless, the number of pensées amount to but a fraction of the sum total of Chedworth's notes. The overriding evidence suggests that Chedworth recorded his notes for "his own private information and amusement" and not "with a view to their being subsequently laid before the Public." The plurality of his entries are not just unfinished or uncorrected; they are undeveloped, and read like spontaneous quips penned in the margin. The potential, however, for enlarging responses to textual cruxes revealed in the variorum edition into a substantive work of criticism was certainly recognized by Seymour. Seymour's two volumes may indeed owe more to Chedworth than Seymour acknowledges. The extent of Seymour's critical and intellectual debt to Chedworth may not be ascertainable; but clearly his literary conversations with his noble friend and patron, and his access to Chedworth's manuscript of notes on Shakespeare, influenced the content of his own published *Remarks*.

The preponderance of "various readings of the different commentators on Shakespeare" with which Chedworth contends are traceable to annotations recorded within the Malone and/or the two "J. and S." editions. A few of the notes Chedworth refers to appear only in the 1785 and/or Malone collections, but the dominant source was the amassed annotation heaped into Steevens's 1793 fifteen volumes. Chedworth's attributions typically only name the commentator and rarely identify precisely where he came upon the remark. The answer to whether Chedworth was, in each case, familiar with the primary source, or whether he was dependent on the variorum glosses, is ambiguous.[19] Instances where he clearly cites from primary sources of criticism are substantially outnumbered by examples definitely drawn from the variorum notes. The survey of eighteenth-century critical perspectives that Chedworth summons forth is itself engaging. The commentators to whom he alludes number nearly sixty. Although a few are mentioned only once, how frequently certain names recur is itself revealing. Chedworth makes well over 600 references to Steevens and Malone, divided nearly equally between them. Johnson is named 170 plus times, followed by John Monck Mason (110+), Lewis Theobald (90+), William Warburton (68), Thomas Tyrwhitt (36), Joseph Ritson (38), Thomas Hanmer (28+), and Alexander Pope (21). Curiously, Isaac Reed's name only surfaces twice. Edward Capell is conspicuously invisible, as are Francis Gentleman, Charles Jennens, Thomas Whately, and others one might think would merit mention. Chedworth includes a couple of quotations from Seymour which are not among those found in the variorum editions. The primary sources he most frequently and most extensively draws excerpts from are Thomas Davies's *Dramatic Miscellanies,* which is cited twenty-one times, and *Letters of Literature,* by Robert Heron Esq., which is culled from on nineteen occasions.[20] With limited exceptions, the profile of critical viewpoints included in, and missing from, Chedworth's *Notes* generally reflects the pattern of eclectic sources represented in his control texts.

Can we glean from Chedworth's comments, or from patterns revealed in his choices, any sense of an underlying editorial rubric or precepts of taste? Does his process of "perfecting" Shakespeare's text by "chusing" his own reading from the *apparatus varicus* manifested in the notes fall into libertinism, arbitrariness governed only by idiosyncratic tastes, or are his labors to perfect the canon, as de Grazia puts it, "unaccompanied by any principle of selection whatsoever"? Although Chedworth's cryptic style and undeveloped commentary make it difficult to construct conclusive responses to these questions, some relevant observations can be woven from the strands of evidence.

Chedworth does not avow a particular predisposition toward any of the "old readings," folios, or the "corrected" editions. His preference for adopting, in any specific instance, the reading of quarto, First Folio, Second Folio, or a "correction"—proposed by any one of a number of crit-

ics—of a probable "corruption" of Shakespeare's intended text, is subject
to individuated reasoning. Each case is reviewed on its own merits but
each judgment is grounded in a complex of values, influenced by taste as
well as the virtues of evidence. He demonstrates engagement with the
accumulation of eclectic notes and signals no alliance to any particular
camp of criticism. For example, he may ridicule Warburton as "an officious grammarian," in one encounter—ostensibly arguing for unre-
touched authenticity by remonstrating "we know that Shakespeare is
frequently ungrammatical"—and concur with the same editor's punctili-
ous correction of grammar in another. He may adopt Theobald's explanation of one line in a scene, and Malone's interpretation of another line in
the same scene. Importantly, Chedworth's variegated selection of readings, emendations, and explanations, reflects his certain belief that he
was entitled to understand a line without philosophical allegiance to a
single editor's explicatory disposition or stylistic strictures. Chedworth
is attracted to the variorum apparatus precisely because it allows him to
participate in the hermeneutic process: not just passively receiving an
understanding, but actively authorizing his own.

The varied array and seeming unpredictability of his choice-making
does not suggest that his selections are unprincipled or capricious. Patterns of concerns materialize; evidence of personal hobbyhorses
emerges. Chedworth takes scrupulous interest in questions of "corruption" and "revision" of text. He is most frequently inclined to adopt the
quarto reading, as long as it scans properly and is defensible in terms of
cogency. Consistently, he favors fastidious metric regulation. He does not
view the presence of certain "defects" in Shakespeare's work as compro-
mising the genius of his overall accomplishment. He makes several intertextual connections among the plays as well as with classic works that a
passage in Shakespeare puts him in mind of. As one who loved to see the
plays on stage as well as study them on the page, he pays some attention
to assignment of speeches, details of stage directions, especially regarding
entrances and exits of characters, and nuances of actorly readings. His
regard for the relative contributions of Steevens and Malone appears
balanced. Johnson is the commentator with whom Chedworth most frequently disagrees but, even here, Chedworth registers approval of Johnson's notes much more often than disapproval. Chedworth's several
citations from Davies's *Dramatic Miscellanies* and Heron's *Letters of
Literature*—the only two critics with whom Chedworth always allies himself—are curious. Davies was a famous foe of Steevens; consequently
Davies's critical insights on Shakespeare are snubbed by Steevens and
do not make it into the variora. Heron, pseudonym for John Pinkerton,
was a captious Scottish critic and notorious literary duelist. The passages
quoted from Heron sardonically critique editorial biases, presumptu-

ousness, and duplicity—much of it aimed pointedly at Steevens. It is possible that Chedworth uses Heron's sarcastic poniards to express a view of Steevens that he otherwise keeps guarded. Seymour's *Remarks* are unabashedly directed against Steevens.

Despite the myriad referrals to various commentators, Chedworth's own authority constantly asserts its egoistical presence. The subject of a striking and significant majority of his sentences is not Shakespeare, Steevens, or Malone, but "I": "I think," "I agree," "I believe," "I do not understand." For the most part, therefore, the emendations and thoughts of others are predominantly introduced to predicate Chedworth's own proprietary view.

Although at least one secondary viewpoint is identified in all but a tiny fraction of the entries, Chedworth occasionally appears to venture a solo comment. In some of these instances, Chedworth simply neglects to mention the source that inspired the comment. For example, regarding a peculiar phrase used by Mistress Quickly in *Merry Wives of Windsor*— ". . . you have brought her into such canaries as was wonderful" (2.2.60)—Chedworth asserts "By *canaries* Mrs. Quickly certainly means *quandaries*" (24, cf. *Wiv.* 2.2.60) without acknowledging Malone's note suggesting "quandaries" as a possible alternative to understanding "canaries" as a lively dance.[21] Another lapse in ascription tidiness may be found in Chedworth's comment on a portion of Chorus's opening speech from *King Henry the Fifth:* "Can this cockpit hold / The vasty fields of France? or may we cram, / Within this wooden O, the very casques, / That did affright the air at Agincourt?" (1.1.11–14). The way the note is phrased, Chedworth appears to present his own view by intertwining it with that which is printed as Mason's:

> Mr. M. Mason is indisputably right. Dr. Johnson's criticism on this expression is injudicious in the extreme. It was certainly (as Mr. M. Mason observes) the poet's intention to represent the circle in which they acted in as contemptible a light as he could. (192)

Chedworth's inspiration in this case must actually have come from Malone's note: "In this place it was evidently the poet's intention to represent the little circle in which they acted in as contemptible light as he could."[22] In this example, Penrice or the typesetter could have made the error, substituting M. Mason for Mr. Malone. Elsewhere throughout the book, conventional quotation marks signal direct citations.

Often Chedworth embroiders his own design on a preexisting tapestry of scholarly debate without mentioning specific stimuli for his thought. An example of this kind of meta-notation is found in his notes on *Hamlet* where he pauses to muse upon the meta-theatrical function of Hamlet's recitation of bombastic lines from "Æeneas's tale to Dido," in order to prompt the Player's memory of a scene he hopes will catch Claudius's conscience:

> 'The rugged Pyrrhus, he whose sable arms,
> Black as his purpose, did the night resemble
> When he lay couched in th' ominous horse,
> Hath now this dread and black complexion smear'd
> With heraldry more dismal: head to foot
> Now is he total gules, horridly trick'd
> With blood of fathers, mothers, daughters, sons,
> Bak'd and impasted with the parching streets,
> That lend a tyrannous and a damned light
> To their lords's murther. Roasted in wrath and fire,
> And thus o'er-sized with coagulate gore,
> With eyes like carbuncles, the hellish Pyrrhus
> Old grandsire Priam seeks.'

(2.2.452–64)

Chedworth would have found this passage, and other sections of gothic text of the play-within-the-play, thickly annotated in his comparative editions. Most of the notes labor to explain, in one way or another, the thumping coarseness of the verse. In one of his more fully developed notes, Chedworth offers this observation:

> I have sometimes fancied that Shakespeare has made these lines elaborately tumid for the purpose of marking a distinction between the diction of this supposed tragedy and that of the personages of the drama, whose language he would have taken to be that of real life, and by this artifice, to give the greater appearance of reality to this play. He is fond of comparing the actions of his characters to a theatrical exhibition. (351)

Examining the relevant annotation in the three editions, Chedworth would have come upon Warburton's note suggesting that Hamlet's bombast here is deliberately "ironical," and Pope's perception of the diction as "tumid." Although Chedworth's comment has a distinctive slant to it, and although he is in no way adopting the whole of Warburton's or Pope's reasoning, his failure to acknowledge the relevant bits of his predecessors' comments would certainly have been chastised by pundits. The casual use of sources is yet another indication that Chedworth penned his notes with no intent immediately in mind to publish them.

A close look at another rare example of a longer note, this one drawn from *King Richard the Third,* provides evidence that Chedworth may not have consistently scrutinized all collateral bits of text and annotation found in the three editions. The lines here in question open act 2 scene

4; the cited reading comes from Steevens's 1793 edition (10: 543). The words are spoken by the Archbishop of York: "Last night, I heard, they lay at *Stony-Stratford;* / And at *Northampton* they do rest to night: / To-morrow, or next day, they will be here." Chedworth's note follows:

I think the right reading is that of the quartos. The Archbishop is not supposed to know anything of the arrest of the lords, or of the young king's being carried back: he would of course suppose that they would not lie at a place nearer London than that at which they had rested the preceding night. The puzzle seems to have arisen from the editors' knowledge; had they known nothing of the historical fact of the young Edward's being carried back from Stony Strat-ford to Northampton, they would have found no difficulty in discovering which reading was to be preferred: had they considered that the Archbishop was ignorant of this fact, the difficulty (which their knowledge raised) would, I think, have been removed. (220)

The quarto reads: "Last night I heare they lay at Northampton, / At Stonistratford will they be to night." The "J. and S. 1793" adopts the reading of the First Folio, positing the order as first Stony-Stratford, then Northampton—presumably, Chedworth speculates, to reflect the histori-cal fact that the prince was taken back to Northampton after the arrest of Rivers, Grey, and Vaughan. Chedworth's argument is sound: from the perspective of the Archbishop, the logical journey to London would move from the more distant Northampton to a stop in "Stonistratford." Dra-matically, the Archbishop can know nothing of the historical cause of the prince being taken back to Northampton. The problem here is that Chedworth's correction, without acknowledgment, appropriates Ma-lone's choice. Malone had included the quarto version[23] and written an elaborate note examining the issue. Chedworth's note in this instance relates specifically to Steevens's 1793 version, even though his remark seems to attack the collective "editors' knowledge." Not only does his comment seem to overlook Malone's preference for the quarto reading, and Malone's erudite explanation, but Chedworth also disregards Steevens's annotated explication of the dilemma that pointedly disavows any claim to adopting the order of the First Folio for reasons of historical accuracy—Steevens states that he chose Stony-Stratford to read first because it "renders the versification smoothest."[24] Like several of Chedworth's notes, the impulsive nature of this comment is consistent with the style of private marginalia. Chedworth could never have intended to put this remark, as it stands, before the public.

Quarto versus folio variants attract frequent attention. However, in most of the sixty plus notes where he designates his preference for phraseology drawn from quartos or folios, Chedworth registers summary judgment with characteristic terseness. Commenting on Steevens's adoption of the quarto reading of the phrase from Hamlet's "rogue and peasant slave" soliloquy—"That from her working, all his visage *wann'd*" (2.2.554)—Chedworth remarks, "I prefer *warm'd*, the reading of the folio, to *wann'd*, the reading of the quarto" (351). Arguments supporting one reading or the other abound in all three editions. Virtually all of Chedworth's notes on quarto versus folio readings mark a difference of choice with text printed in Steevens's 1793 edition. In each of these instances, Steevens provides ample notes acknowledging alternative readings and contentions.

Chedworth's succinct responses to massive annotation—and, perhaps its refrigerating effect on the reader—in one instance reflects laconic wit. Examining *Much Ado about Nothing,* Chedworth quotes Steevens's printing of this obscure fragment from a speech of Leontes: "If such a one will smile, and stroke his beard; / Cry—*sorrow, wag* and hem, when he should groan; / Patch grief with proverbs|. . ." (5.1.16). Proposed emendations to "Cry—sorrow wag" dominate the pages of all three editions. Steevens's '93 variorum includes nine variant readings set forward in extensive debate. Regarding the assembled array of compendious notes, Chedworth here simply quips, "This appears to me a very difficult passage" (56).

Isolating specimens of Chedworth's critical insight that are truly original is a challenge. Certainly Seymour regarded the selection of over one hundred of his patron's comments to be noteworthy. However, given Chedworth's inconsistent care in attributing credit to sources, identifying and predicating originality among his comments can be a slippery task. One example of apparently unprecedented observation may be found in his notes on *The Winter's Tale*. Reacting to the Shepherd's description of Florizel, "His garments are rich, but he wears them not handsomely" (4.4.750), Chedworth advances the view that "Here Shakespeare seems to have forgotten that Florizel's dress was that of a shepherd, that he had obscured himself with swain's wearing" (126–27). The point turns up in later editions—Furness includes parallel observations from three nineteenth-century sources—but Chedworth may indeed be the earliest reader to record the problem. Chedworth, like the most fastidious of editors, often quibbles over words as possible corruptions of Shakespeare's intent. For instance, he contemplates an inconspicuous moment from dialogue in the final act of *Coriolanus*. The scene involves an encounter between Menenius and two of Coriolanus's guard:

1. Watch. Now, sir, is your name Menenius?

2. Watch. 'Tis a spell, you see, of much power. You know the way home again.

1. Watch. Do you hear how we are shent for keeping your greatness back?

2. Watch. What cause do you think I have to swound?

Men. I neither care for th' world nor your general; for such things as you, I can scarce think there's any, y' are so slight. He that hath a will to die by himself fears it not from another. Let your general do his worst. For you, be that you are, long; and your misery increase with your age! I say to you, as I was said to, "Away!"

[*Exit.*]

1. Watch. A noble fellow, I warrant him.

2. Watch. The worthy fellow is our general. He's the rock, the oak not to be wind-shaken. [*Exit Watch.*]

(5.2.110)

The word in question here is "worthy" and Chedworth suggests an alternative reading that proposes a subtle but significant difference: "I think the sense would be improved by reading *worthier*" (271)—thus giving greater emphasis to Coriolanus's superior nobility. His suggested emendation has merit and may be regarded, I believe, as distinctive. Evidence of Chedworth's sometime carelessness in reading annotation or acknowledging sources is counterbalanced by abundant evidence of meticulous scrutiny given to cruxes in Shakespeare's text.

III

The field of concerns revealed in Chedworth's notes reflects not only personal quiddity but certain received predilections of the age. Chedworth was not the only late eighteenth-century reader driven by a deep-seated belief that a profound knowledge of Shakespeare was central to life's joy. He was clearly cautious, however, to distinguish himself from mere Bardolatry. Like most of the serious critics of the late century, Chedworth avowed wariness of "the charge of an indiscriminating admiration of [Shakespeare], too frequently imputable to commentators" (13). In various entries, he roguishly aligns himself with Heron, that literary renegade, and "arraigns the taste" of editor-alchemists who would "dream to convert the very dirt of Shakespeare into gold" (61). On the whole, however, Chedworth's notes endeavor to maintain a balanced posture of analytical objectivity. As a sensible gentleman living in an Age of Reason, Chedworth advertizes his regard for Shakespeare's "Beauties and Faults" as complementary elements of a wonderful humanity. The purpose of revisions, suggested in Chedworth's *Notes,* was not to correct Shakespeare's Faults—by emendation, alteration, addition, or "blotting out"— in order to "restore" the Bard's perfection, but to reveal the poet's "intent" (a word frequently used by Chedworth) through tasteful selection from the menu of preexisting options. That which could not be sensibly revised had to be satisfactorily explained.

Ungoverned by restrictive precepts or public manifestos defining the relative validity of variant textual sources, Chedworth's menu of options includes not only "the old copies," but the Second, Third, and Fourth Folios; and, indeed, any fragment of any prior edition that suits his palate. Steevens, Malone, and other editors may also incorporate readings from diverse precedents, but editorial duty confines them to operate within certain strictures—exceptions to rules must be made with care and defended. Again we remember: Chedworth appropriates what pleases him; Shakespeare's "intent" is a matter divined by Chedworth's proprietary Understanding. The slippery distinction between Bardolatry's "correction" of perceived Defects, and Chedworth's selected emendations of "obscure passages," emerges as an equivocation. Ironically, he professes distaste for Bardolatry but, in his own way, he practices it by adopting that reading which most suits his "Taste" in understanding Shakespeare's "intent," thereby perfecting the object of his studies. An idealized notion that "intent" is ascertainable may be the most consistently identifiable eighteenth-century tenet reflected in the *Notes*.

Chedworth also indulges in the popular sport of criticizing other critics. He takes exception to critics who, in his view, accomplish more self-aggrandizement than scholarly exegesis by pressing forward Shakespeare's failings. In one case, he chastises Malone for overzealous annotation:

> Mr. Malone's remark is true, but there is no occasion to have recourse to it in the present instance: it is going out of the way to fix an impropriety on the poet, who has improprieties enough to answer for, without being loaded with those which are made by the ingenuity of his commentators. (9)

In another instance, he complains, "Some of the editors seem dreadfully alarmed lest the reader think Shakespeare more learned than he ought to be" (62). Chedworth sometimes rebukes unnecessary editorial interventions, contesting selected explanatory notes which he deems are tangential, or are an insult to the reader's intelligence when Shakespeare's meaning is self-evident. He occasionally records laments such as the "commentators have . . . gone too deep for the meaning" (344) or "I doubt whether the poet meant all that Dr. Johnson supposes" (44). He advances a cautionary view of conjecture. Regarding matters of anachronism or inaccurate geography, he recognizes that "Shakespeare falls into such mistakes" (193) and Chedworth castigates those who overemphasize these faults. Similarly, he chides pedants obsessed with expunging grammatical infelicities, allowing that "we know that Shakespeare is frequently ungrammatical" (78). Chedworth surely recognized all these points of contention as common grist in the critical mill; he nonetheless felt compelled to participate in the grinding process. On the whole, however, his isolated sallies of invective against other critics pale compared to the diatribes of contemporaries like the redoubtable Joseph Ritson, or even Chedworth's cohort, Seymour.

Ironically, however, evidence abounds throughout the *Notes* demonstrating Chedworth's inconsistency in following principles he would prescribe for others. A remarkable pattern of inconsistency is reflected in his remarks on Malone. While he chastises Malone for including esoteric footnotes, he soon complains that Malone has deleted a note from the 1790 edition that Chedworth had found usefully placed in the earlier edition. Here and there, Chedworth speaks as a Malonean advocate of "scrupulous reverence for the old copies" (83) and finds many opportunities to agree with Malone's observations on authentic Elizabethan custom and usage. However, although he acknowledges gratitude to Malone for introducing him to variant readings found in the quartos, Chedworth relentlessly disparages Malone's rejection of the "superintendor" of the Second Folio: "I differ much from Mr. Malone about the editor of the 2d folio" (85). Chedworth also doggedly ridicules "Mr. Malone's want of ear" (64) and complains how, in his devotion to the early copies, Malone overlooks instances where certain lines have more or less than ten beats: for example, "Mr. Malone carries his dislike to the second folio so far, that he prefers an imperfect verse in the first folio to a perfect one in the second" (205); or "Malone . . . is perfectly careless of the verse. Were Shakespeare alive he might say to Malone (in the words of Orlando to Jacques), 'I pray you mar no more my verses with your reading them ill-favouredly'" (215–16). He also takes issue with several words that Malone states were, during Shakespeare's time, pronounced with the sound of an additional syllable. In most instances, Chedworth's rejection of Malone's scansion signals approval of Steevens's regulation of verse in the 1793 edition.[25] Despite his outspoken contempt for Malone's ear, Chedworth sides with Malone on at least three hundred matters of editorial choice and annotation, and notes specific disagreement with him on less than sixty. Chedworth clearly held Malone's scholarship in high regard.

At several junctures in his examination of the plays, Chedworth announces that he "is reminded of" intertextual connections, and relates a wide range of passages: verses from the Bible; morsels from Homer, Horace, Tacitus, Terence, and others (cited in Greek and Latin); or quotations from several other prominent authors such as Spenser, Milton, Gibbon, Locke, and Congreve—a practice popular in the eighteenth century because making such connections elevated the position of both Shakespeare and the annotator.[26] Chedworth's skill at doing this impressed

Seymour; a substantial number of the passages Seymour extracts from
Chedworth's manuscript fit into this category. Following another familiar
critical mode, Chedworth periodically demonstrates his studious grasp of
Shakespeare by citing bits of parallel text to argue a lexical or phraseo-
logical matter, or to elucidate factual background. In one note on *Timon
of Athens*, for example, he employs both a parallel citation and an intertextual reference, derived in part from *variora* annotation, to comment
on lines spoken by Timon: "The sea's a thief, whose liquid surge resolves /
The moon into salt tears" (4.3.439–40). Chedworth remarks:

> That Shakespeare knew the moon is the cause of tides appears likewise from
> the First Part of *Henry the Fourth* , Act I. scene 2, "being govern'd as the sea
> is, by our noble and chaste mistress the moon." Shakespeare seems to have
> been thinking of the 19th ode of Anacreon ['H γῆ μέλαινα πίνει] of which he
> had probably seen some translation, possibly that mentioned by Puttenham.
> (256)

Chedworth slights as passé a rigid adherence to principles of neoclassical aesthetics but, in the delineation of his ideal readings of the Bard's
texts, we may find a residue of the heritage of neoclassicism. On verisi-
militude, he conspicuously disregards Shakespeare's breaches, and
pauses to comment briefly on only a few. He dismisses an emendation of
Dr. Johnson about a philosophical infelicity related to strict preservation
of the character Time in *Winter's Tale* as a concept of Time personified:
"We may suppose Shakespeare not to be so philosophically accurate as
Dr. Johnson would have him" (123). Chedworth does not directly address
issues of decorum as matters of editorial ideology. In specifying the readings he would include in his perfected collection of the plays, however,
he adopts over one hundred emendations by Theobald, Pope, and other
older generation editors who methodically cleansed the plays of perceived improprieties. Although Chedworth acknowledges that "Shakespeare frequently uses expressions . . . harsh and licentious"[27] (212), he
chooses in several instances to blot them out or distance himself from
the indelicate, the lurid, and the blasphemous. For example, he notes that
he prefers Theobald's following of the First Folio's omission of Roderigo's
"Tush" and Iago's "'Sblood" in the opening speeches of *Othello* (360).
Regarding wordplay in the Toby/Aguecheek/Maria repartee in *Twelfth
Night* (1.3.39–79), Chedworth demurs: "The notes on *accost* and *board*
might, I think, have been spared. *Board* is surely the naval term" (107).
Responding to Ritson's annotation on use of a word from *King Henry
the Eighth*—"In faith for little England / You'd venture an *emballing*"
(2.3.46–47)—Chedworth remarks, "I believe Dr. Johnson's is the true
explanation. The prurient sagacity of Mr. Ritson has, I think, found a

meaning never meant" (226).[28] Citing Hamlet's execration of Claudius (3.3.94–95)—"And that his soul may be as damn'd, and black / *As hell, whereto it goes*"—Chedworth recoils: "This horrid sentiment cannot be too strongly reprobated. There is no passage in our author's writings at which I am so much offended as this" (355).[29] Vestiges of eighteenth-century sensibilities are evident also in Chedworth's closing note on *Titus Andronicus*: "I see no reason for dissenting from the commentators, who suppose this horrid play not Shakespeare's" (309). Comments of this sort were familiar to Chedworth; they may even have been regarded by some as obligatory assertions of Class and Taste.

Nevertheless, Chedworth also finds opportunities to offer some converse perspectives. He complains, "The pains some of the editors take to translate Pistol's bombast into sober sense appear to me very curious" (199). In his chapter on *Macbeth,* Chedworth ponders the use and meaning of the word "quarry" in Rosse's trenchant speech to Macduff, presenting gruesome news about the murders of Lady Macduff and the children:

> Your castle is surpris'd; your wife, and babes,
> Savagely slaughter'd. To relate the manner,
> Were on the quarry of these murther'd deer
> To add the death of you."
>
> (4.3.204–7)

Chedworth states, "Quarry seems sometimes to have a different meaning from that which the commentators have assigned it. . . . Mr. Steevens tells us that quarry 'means the game after it has been killed.' I think that does not make very good sense in this place. May not quarry be used licentiously, by Shakespeare, for sport?" (129). The "different meaning" for "quarry"—suggesting licentious sport—that Chedworth has in mind here is not made clear. Nevertheless, that he should proffer the view that Shakespeare intended sordid innuendo in the word quarry—in the context of this dreadful report of the murder of innocents—demonstrates that Chedworth's interest in the possibilities of text is greater than his concern over matters of delicacy or propriety. Chedworth isolates and interrogates topics with singular focus on the issue at hand rather than policing the text to enforce a rigid set of rules.

Although Chedworth's notes concentrate largely on cruxes of text, he occasionally pauses to deliberate on questions of character, reflecting genuine interest in psychology. He devotes three paragraphs (a relative disquisition) to contemplating Caliban's state of mind during the final scene of *The Tempest*. Citing an argument not found among the notes in the reference editions, Chedworth rebuts the censure of Dr. Warton[30] who "thinks Shakespeare injudicious for putting into the mouth of Caliban . . .

speech which implies repentance and understanding; whereas he thinks he ought to have preserved the fierce and implacable spirit of Caliban to the end" (13). Chedworth reasons that Caliban's repentant reaction at the end of the play is a "natural" product of having been transformed by recognition of his foolishly investing devotion in drunkards, and by a born-again awe for the fearsome majesty of Prospero his master.

Chedworth's analysis may not seem particularly penetrating but encoded in it are complex signals of his view of character, society, and moral order. What "seems natural" to Chedworth is of key significance. Reacting to commentators who object to Macbeth's ambivalent irresolution in act 1 scene 7, Chedworth musters this rebuff:

> Those who consider the waverings of Macbeth, as unnatural and contradictory, are not worthy of the name of criticks. In my opinion, they constitute one of the greatest excellencies of this play. Such tasteless objections deserved not the answer Mr. Steevens has condescended to give them. (133)

Examining an "imperfect" sentence uttered by Macduff during the final fight with Macbeth, Chedworth again reproves diction-fussy critics and offers a psychological defense:

> It is natural for Macduff, amid the hurry and agitation of battle, when his thoughts, full of the loss of his wife and children, and of his revenge on Macbeth, are crowding rapidly upon him, to leave the sentence incomplete. Such imperfect sentences . . . are not uncommon in real life, and sometimes occur in Shakespeare. (145)

What may be considered "natural" or "unnatural" in understanding human behavior is always a personal arbitration of facts and feelings. Despite his inclination to tinker with the text, Chedworth would not alter one of the playwright's characters. He clearly adheres to the tenet that one of Shakespeare's greatest gifts was his psychological perspicacity, and he clearly values psychological truth of character over the propriety of superficial detail. In his closing note on Othello, Chedworth cites Johnson's observation on the dramatist's Beauties and Defects as character maker:

> 'Shakespeare always makes nature predominate over accident, and, if he preserves the essential character, is not very careful of distinctions superinduced and adventitious. His story requires Romans or kings, but he thinks only on men . . . A poet overlooks the casual distinctions of country and condition, as a painter, satisfied with the figure, neglects the drapery.' (374–75)[31]

The primary objective implicit in Chedworth's "critical and laborious investigations of that inimitable Bard" is pursuit of subjective Understanding. What enthralled him about the multiplicity of "explanations and amendments" collected in those late eighteenth-century variorum editions was access to debate, in which he—from the privacy of his study and in the context of his note-making—could feel actively engaged. Several of Chedworth's entries lament that "despite the pains bestowed upon a passage by the commentators, I do not yet understand." He frequently then beckons critics to "correct" the problem. Chedworth embraces the notion that the territory of his understanding of Shakespeare is expanded and demarcated largely by the explorations of critics and editors who vied with each other to redefine boundaries. There are no compunctions tied to a pejorative concept of derivative interpretation. On the contrary, these privately written notes and comments—as arcane as they may be—collectively underscore Chedworth's delight in a sense of readerly autonomy. He is empowered by choice and is dedicated to the belief that his perfected readings of the plays would be a perfect reflection of Shakespeare's genuine intent. Perhaps one may even infer that when Chedworth says "I agree with Mr. Steevens," he essentially induces that "Mr. Steevens agrees with me;" and, by extension: "The Bard himself agrees with me." Chedworth's understanding of Shakespeare is his proprietary dominion.

NOTES

1. Johnson's remark first appeared in his "Preface" to *The Plays of William Shakespeare, in Eight Volumes, with the Corrections and Illustrations of Various Commentators, To which are added Notes by Sam. Johnson* (London, 1765). This citation may be found in Brian Vickers, ed., *Shakespeare: The Critical Heritage,* 6 vols. (London and Boston: Routledge, 1974–81), 5:99.

2. In Vickers, 6:49.

3. Margreta de Grazia, *Shakespeare Verbatim: The Reproduction of Authenticity and the 1790 Apparatus* (Oxford: Clarendon Press, 1991), 67–68.

4. In Vickers, 4:271.

5. De Grazia, 69.

6. Samuel Johnson and George Steevens, eds., revised and augmented by Isaac Reed, *The Plays of William Shakespeare,* 10 vols. (London, 1785); Edmond Malone, ed., *The Plays and Poems of William Shakspeare,* 10 vols. (London, 1790); Samuel Johnson and George Steevens, eds., *The Plays of William Shakespeare,* 15 vols. (London, 1793).

7. Jean Marsden, "The Individual Reader and the Canonized Text: Shakespeare Criticism After Johnson," in *Eighteenth-Century Life* 17 (February 1993): 62, 63.

8. Joanna Gondris's essay, in this volume, "'All this Farrago': The Eighteenth-Century Shakespeare Variorum Page as a Critical Structure," examines this point from a different perspective. Many views put forward in my discussion of Chedworth find fascinating complements among Gondris's observations.

9. As cited in the *Dictionary of National Biography*, which draws upon Chedworth's obituary printed in *Gentleman's Magazine* 74 (1804): 1242–44.

10. Born in Ireland in 1755, William Hickey appended "Seymour" to his christened name when he arrived in England in 1785 to pursue a career on the stage. He came from a cultured family: one brother, John Hickey, was a celebrated sculptor; another sibling, Thomas, was quite well-known as a painter, traveler, and autobiographer. Seymour's association with the Theatre Royal, Norwich, began in 1790 and continued in sporadic turns until 1801. He appears to have attracted some praise for his performances, but, on the whole, may have been more highly regarded as a "gentleman" than he was as an actor. His fortunes in the theater were subject to considerable vicissitude. He died in 1819. For a capsule biography of Seymour, see Philip H. Highfill, Jr., Kalman A. Burnam and Edward A. Langhans, eds., *A Biographical Dictionary of Actors, Actresses, Musicians, Dancers, Managers & Other Stage Personnel in London, 1660–1800* (Carbondale: Southern Illinois University Press, 1991), 13:273–74.

11. Penrice was a surgeon with whom Chedworth resided in Yarmouth and to whom Chedworth left the majority of his estate.

12. The entirety of Chedworth's will appeared in print along with his obituary in *Gentleman's Magazine* 74 (1804): 1242–44.

13. A brief explanatory comment in Martin's *Bibliographical Catalogue of Books Privately Printed* (London, 1834) accompanies a record of the publication of the book: "Lord Chedworth died in 1804. A service rendered him professionally by Mr. Penrice, led to a friendship which induced him to leave that gentleman his large property. An attempt was made, on the plea of insanity, to set the will aside: this did not succeed; Penrice printed these notes with the view of affording additional proof of Lord Chedworth's sanity," 158–59.

14. See *Gentleman's Magazine* 76 (1806): 672, 1030–32.

15. Ibid., 1030.

16. Seymour inventories 211 subscribers, including the names of "Malone, Edmund [sic], Esq." and "Penrice, Thomas, Esq." At the top of the list is "The Prince of Wales" followed by several dukes, earls, and other peers. Included also are many theatrical notables: Kemble, Macready, Siddons, and Richard Brinsley Sheridan, to whom Seymour dedicates the publication.

17. Capell had published in 1768 Shakespeare's collected plays, annotated in ten volumes, and later supplemented the edition of the plays with four volumes of *Notes and Various Readings*, the first of which was published in 1774. In 1770, Jennens launched an effort to publish individual plays, "collated with the old and modern editions." He completed five volumes: *King Lear* (1770), *Macbeth* (1773), *Othello* (1773), *Hamlet* (1773), and *Julius Ceasar* (1774).

18. Seymour's title indicates that the remarks he cites from Chedworth are all extracted "from the MSS." (note the plural) of his late benefactor. A few of Seymour's citations of Chedworth—some quoted in Latin—do not appear in Penrice's published collection. Apparently, either Penrice excised them from his published edition of Chedworth's manuscript or Seymour found them in another source: perhaps among marginal inscriptions Chedworth wrote in books Seymour received as part of Chedworth's bequest. In one instance, Seymour attributes a quotation to Chedworth's correspondence.

19. The time frame during which Chedworth compiled his notes seems to have been between 1793 and his decease in 1804. All published commentaries of others that he cites are included in or appeared before the 1793 Steevens variorum.

20. Like Seymour, Thomas Davies was an erstwhile actor with literary inter-

ests. In 1784, he published in three volumes his *Dramatic Miscellanies: consisting of Critical Observations on several Plays of Shakespeare: with a Review of his principal Characters, and those of eminent Writers, as represented by Mr. Garrick, and other celebrated Comedians. With Anecdotes of Dramatic Poets, Actors, &c.* When Davies left the stage, he opened a bookshop and is said to have introduced Boswell to Johnson.

Letters of Literature was published in 1785 under the pseudonym, Robert Heron.

21. Unless otherwise noted, citations and line numbers from Shakespeare's plays are drawn from G. Blakemore Evans, ed., *The Riverside Shakespeare* (Boston: Houghton Mifflin, 1974).

22. Malone, 5:447.

23. Ibid., 6:513. Capell also printed the quarto reading but, as noted earlier, Chedworth does not mention Capell even once in the entire array of notes.

24. Both Malone's and Steevens's notes may also be found in H. H. Furness, ed., *The Tragedy of Richard the Third,* 2d edition of "A new variorum edition" (Philadelphia,1909), 182–83.

25. Chedworth generally sides with Steevens's practice in the 1793 edition of restoring Second Folio scansion to readings that Malone had emended based on his contention that Elizabethan speech patterns included words pronounced with diphthongs or triphthongs, which added an additional syllable to a line's meter.

26. See de Grazia, chapter 3, especially 111–14.

27. Joanna Gondris observes in notes on an earlier draft of this essay: "This is a recognisably Johnsonian turn of phrase. Johnson uses these two epithets throughout his commentary as shorthand terms for his sense of an alternative, exclusively Shakespearean semantics."

28. For a detailed analysis of eighteenth-century editorial response to this word, see Irene Fizer's "Emballing, Empalling, Embalming, and Embailing Anne Bullen: The Annotation of Shakespeare's Bawdy Tongue After Samuel Johnson" in this volume.

29. Chedworth's sentiment here echoes expressions of indignation recorded by many of his predecessors and contemporaries. Hanmer, for example, noted that "This speech of Hamlet's has always given me great offence. There is something so very bloody in it, so inhuman, so unworthy of a hero, that I wish our poet had omitted it." See Thomas Hanmer, *Some Remarks on the Tragedy of Hamlet, Prince of Denmark* (London, 1736). Johnson was similarly repulsed: "This speech, in which Hamlet, represented as a virtuous character, is not content with taking blood for blood, but contrives damnation for the man that he would punish, is too horrible to be read or to be uttered."

30. This is Rev. Dr. Joseph Warton. Chedworth attributes the provocation of his comment to Warton's "elegant critique" of *The Tempest* printed in "*Aventurer,* Nos. 93, 97," [sic].

31. Chedworth would have found this passage in Johnson's "Preface." See Vickers, 5: 60.

Hamlet's Mousetrap and the
Play-within-the-Anecdote of Plutarch

Frank N. Clary Jr.

> When our poet's entire library shall have been discovered, and
> the fables of all his plays traced to their original source, when
> every temporary allusion shall have been pointed out, and
> every obscurity elucidated, then and not till then, let the accu-
> mulation of notes be complained of.

As genealogical research was brought to bear on Shakespeare's works
during the eighteenth century, editors exercised magisterial authority
over a rising tide of emendations and glosses that all but inundated the
playtexts themselves. As early as Nicholas Rowe's 1709 edition, these
editors supervised not only the transmission of Shakespeare's plays but
also the transformation of scholarly discourse. As they did so, their adju-
dications among competing claims concerning the relevance of a particular anecdote from Plutarch to a soliloquy by Hamlet led them to overlook,
marginalize, and erase the contributions of several of their scholarly
predecessors. In so doing, Shakespeare's eighteenth-century editors progressively compromised the analogical relevance of Plutarch's anecdote
until it was effectively excluded from consideration as a confirming historical instance. In the 1773 edition of *The Plays of William Shakespeare*,
George Steevens credits Sir John Hawkins as the first to recognize this
particular allusion to Plutarch.[1] However, in the 1790 edition, Edmond
Malone credits John Upton in place of Sir John Hawkins as the originator
of the scholarly opinion that had hitherto prevailed: namely, that Hamlet's
expression "What's Hecuba to him, or he to Hecuba," alludes "plainly"
to Plutarch's *Life of Pelopidas*.[2] Malone, in an interesting reversal of his
endorsement, already quoted, of the minutest and most comprehensive
registering of Shakespeare's allusions, summarily dismisses the relevance
of Plutarch's anecdote altogether. Subsequent editions of the Steevens-
Johnson *Plays* follow his lead.[3]

As eighteenth-century editors had excluded Plutarch's anecdote from annotations supplied for the opening section of Hamlet's soliloquy in Act 2, so twentieth-century editors have excluded it from annotations supplied for the closing section of the same soliloquy. During the twentieth century Shakespeare's editors have generally provided introductory remarks concerning the genealogy of the plot in *Hamlet* and some offer source-related citations for local passages. No editor, however, provides as much information about the playwright's sources, analogues, and influences as Geoffrey Bullough in his *Narrative and Dramatic Sources of Shakespeare*. In fact, Bullough's monumental collection of text transcriptions, all in English translation, has become the canonical supplement in a tradition of scholarly publications that began with Charlotte Lennox's first assembly of "the Novels and Histories on which the plays of Shakespear [sic] are founded" (1753).[4] Since Bullough's publication of volume 7 in 1973,[5] editors of *Hamlet* have often conveniently cited him as their scholarly authority and quoted from his collected texts in their notes on local passages. Harold Jenkins, for example, cites Bullough eight times in his introductory essay on Shakespeare's sources for *Hamlet*.[6] In one of his own annotations, he cites Bullough's transcription from *A Warning for Faire Women* as a relevant historical model. This informative note provides an Elizabethan instance that serves to validate Hamlet's speculation concerning the probable effects of his Mousetrap play, but it also dismisses a possible allusion:

> North's Plutarch associates a 'guilty conscience' with the unsuppressible emotion which caused Alexander of Pherae to leave the theatre during a performance (cf. above, ll. 515–16 LN). But the closest analogies here are with the self-betrayal of those who witness an actual image of their own crimes (cf. ll. 590–3 and Claudius's exit at III.ii.264). Various instances are reported, which playwrights liked to cite as evidence of the drama's power. *A Warning for Fair Women* (anon., pubd. 1599) recounts how at Lynn in Norfolk a woman was so moved by watching a guilty wife in a tragedy that she confessed to having murdered her own husband (sig. H2; Bullough, p. 181). This play had been 'lately' acted by Shakespeare's company and seems to have been echoed by him, though the story was apparently well known. . . . The same incident is related in Heywood's *Apology for Actors*, 1612, Gv-G2v, which names the players as Sussex's men and the play as *Friar Francis*, which Henslowe's Diary shows Sussex's to have been acting in London in 1593.[7]

In citing Plutarch's anecdote and then dismissing it as an apt analogue for Claudius's self-incriminating interruption of the Mousetrap play, Jenkins imitates Bullough and provides the capping illustration in a modern instance of editorial history repeating itself.[8]

In general, Shakespeare's eighteenth century editors set a pattern that scholars have repeated in the last quarter of the twentieth century. Omis-

sion of this annotative reference to Plutarch's anecdote shuts out the rich
resonances available in Hamlet's soliloquy, not only to Shakespeare's
audiences but also to his many readers. William Ringler, in a scholarly
essay published in 1963, underscores the currency of Plutarch's anecdote
in the public imagination through the sixteenth century. He notes, for
example, that it was included in Brusonius's often-reprinted *Facetiarum
exemplorumque libri VII* (1559), 4.1, and that a variant version from Ae-
lian's *Varia historia,* 14.40, appeared in the chapter "De crudelitate" of
Lycosthenes's popular *Apophthegmata* (1551)."[9] In addition to these esoteric scholarly texts, popular English translations presented two versions
of this anecdote in their proper Plutarchian contexts. One version of it
appeared in Thomas North's translation of Plutarch's *Lives* (published in
three editions from 1579 to 1603), and another appeared in Philemon
Holland's English translation of Plutarch's *Morals* (1603).[10] During the
Elizabethan controversy over the moral effects of stage plays, Sir Philip
Sidney made a version of this anecdote available in his *Defence of Poesie,*
first published in two separate editions in 1595, and later reprinted several
times in publications of *Arcadia,* beginning with the 1598 edition. John
Florio likewise made available Montaigne's retelling of a version of Plutarch's anecdote in his translation of the *Essays* in 1603.[11] In light of the
popular familiarity that Plutarch's anecdote enjoyed by the time Shakespeare's play was performed and published, dismissal of it as a pertinent
editorial reference diminishes a sense of its potential meaningfulness to
contemporary audiences and readers of *Hamlet.*

The following investigation will illustrate a facet of editorial practice
as it emerged and developed during the eighteenth century. Furthermore,
by examining one instance in which editorial practice effectively disen-
gaged Shakespeare's text from a relevant classical antecedent, this present study will assess the interpretive consequences of resisting the
possible relationships between the playwright's work and the texts that
his characters call to mind, and suggest a cause of that resistance.

II

In the 1773 edition of *The Plays of William Shakespeare,* George
Steevens provides the following annotation in connection with Hamlet's
line concerning the reactions of guilty creatures sitting at a play: "A
number of these stories are collected together by Tho. Heywood, in his
Actors Vindication. STEEVENS."[12] The editor's citation of himself here
may appear to be redundant. It is more understandable, however, in light
of Samuel Johnson's pronouncement of his criterion for assigning scholarly recognition. In his Preface to the 1765 edition, Johnson writes: "I

am willing that the honour, be it more or less, should be transferred to
the first claimant, for his right, and his alone, stands above dispute."[13] If
the editor's practice here respects Johnson's pronounced criterion, then
Steevens's self-crediting may be taken to signify that he was the first
to identify Thomas Heywood as a resource for contemporary English
anecdotes relevant to Hamlet's musing:

> I have heard
> That guilty creatures sitting at a play
> Have, by the very cunning of the scene,
> Been struck so to the soul that presently
> They have proclaim'd their malefactions.
>
> (2.2.584–88)

Nearly two decades earlier, however, Zachary Grey had already published
his observation on the relevance to *Hamlet* of a particular anecdote from
"Mr. T. Haywood's [sic] *Apology for Actors,* book ii. publ. 1612."[14] Grey's
account of the pertinence of his citation is decidedly genealogical. Shakespeare, he opines, "probably had in view" a particular incident of self-
betrayal, "which happened in his own time" and "of which many
witnessed":

> The old history of *Friar Francis,* being acted by the then Earl of Sussex's
> players, at Lynn, in Norfolk, wherein a woman was present, who, doating upon
> a young gentleman, had (the more securely to enjoy his affection) secretly
> murdered her husband, whose ghost haunted her, and at diverse times in her
> most solitary retirements stood before her. There was a town's woman, till then
> of good repute, who finding her conscience at this time extremely troubled,
> suddenly shriek'd, and cry'd out, "O my husband! my husband! I see the ghost
> of my husband, fiercely threatening and menacing me. . . ."[15]

Grey's absence from Steevens's note may well have been a simple oversight in 1773. The inclusion of Grey's book in a selected list of thirty-
eight "Detached Pieces of Criticism on Shakespeare," however, indicates
that Grey's work was known to the editors by 1778.[16] Nonetheless,
Steevens's self-crediting note is retained in its original form in their revised edition.[17] Despite the fact that considerable genealogical research
has broadened the base of historical contextualization, Steevens continues to be credited by editors and scholars alike as the first to cite Heywood in connection with Hamlet's musing on the power of a dramatic
performance to provoke "guilty creatures" to proclaim their "malefac-
tions."[18] Though an instance unavailable to Hamlet's own memory, this
anecdote in Heywood's *Apology* stands as confirmation of a contemporary commonplace requiring from Shakespeare's musing Prince no further specification.[19]

In the 1773 edition, however, Steevens also furnishes a precise antecedent text as relevant to Hamlet's opening lines in the same soliloquy:

> The expression of Hamlet, "What's Hecuba to him, or he to Hecuba," is plainly
> an allusion to a passage in Plutarch's "Life of Pelopidas," so exquisitely beauti-
> ful, and so pertinent, that I wonder it has never yet been taken notice of.[20]

In this particular note, Steevens goes on to quote at length from North's
translation of Plutarch:

> "And another time, being in a theatre where the tragedy of *Troades of Euripides*
> was played, he went out of the theatre, and sent word to the players notwith-
> standing, that they should go on with their play, as if he had been still among
> them; saying, that he came not away for any misliking he had of them or of
> the play, but because he was ashamed his people should see him weep, to see
> the miseries of Hecuba and Andromache played, and that they never saw him
> pity the death of any one man, of so many of his citizens as he had caused to
> be slain."[21]

Although the pertinence of this anecdote is not explicated, and the identity of the spectator in question is not specified, Steevens "honours" [Sir
John] HAWKINS as "first claimant." Such open crediting of another
scholar, in this case, may encourage the inference that Grey's exclusion
from the citation involving Heywood is not a conscious plagiarism. In
the second edition, in fact, Hawkins is again cited as the editor's source
for the relevant passage from Plutarch.[22] This time, however, the note
includes a supplementary acknowledgement: "This observation had been
already made by Mr. Upton."[23] Here Steevens credits Upton's prior
claim, yet he protects the integrity of the previous edition by attributing
an implicitly self-serving error directly to Hawkins in retaining his expressed, but now vitiated, wonder that the anecdote "has never yet been
taken notice of."[24] No longer the first claimant, Hawkins becomes the
editor's whipping boy for the earlier edition's oversight.

While Steevens rectifies the matter of scholarly crediting in his annotation for the 1778 edition, he does not adequately represent John Upton's
explication of the richness of Hamlet's allusion; nor does he alert readers
to the subtleties of his own deviations from Upton's observation and
emphasis. Upton's note, which is framed by the observation that Shakespeare here "takes an opportunity to pay a fine compliment to his own
art," is as follows:

> 'Tis plain Shakespeare alludes to a story told of Alexander the cruel tyrant of
> Pherae in Thessaly, who seeing a famous tragedian act the Troades of Euripi-
> des, was so sensibly touch'd that he left the theatre before the play was ended;

being ashamed, as he owned, that he, who never pitied those he murdered, should weep at the sufferings of HECUBA and Andromache. See Plutarch in the life of Pelopidas.[25]

There are at least three significant differences between the representation of the anecdote initially attributed to Hawkins and the one given by Upton in his own *Critical Observations* (1746). First, Upton identifies the spectator who is affected by the Euripidean play as the tyrant Alexander of Pherae; Hawkins does not identify the affected spectator by name or public position. Second, Upton defines the effect of the performance as decidedly moral, rather than cathartic, for Alexander was moved to "own" his shame and not simply ashamed to be seen weeping.[26] Third, the Variorum editor relates the anecdote to Hamlet's expressed astonishment and subsequent self-chastisement following the player's emotional display during his recitation of Aeneas's tale to Dido. Upton's interest, on the other hand, is in the anecdote's aptness as a confirming instance of a play's power to provoke confessions and as a precedent example for Hamlet's decision at the end of his soliloquy to deploy *The Murder of Gonzago* as a Mousetrap. In general, the version of the anecdote attributed to Hawkins and published by Steevens shifts the emphasis away from the psychological consequences of guilt for atrocities already committed. By emphasizing the embarrassed self-consciousness of an unspecified spectator, the Variorum editor's adjusted version of the anecdote better suits it as an analogue for Hamlet's experience following the player's passionate speech. For this reason, Steevens specifically links his annotation to the line: "What's Hecuba to him or he to Hecuba." Upton, on the other hand, had related it specifically to Hamlet's reflection, later in the same soliloquy, on the effects of self-recognition on "guilty creatures sitting at a play." Within the context of Hamlet's planning to use a play as a trap and given his preoccupation with an ancient Greek story of murders and revenge, Upton's nomination of Plutarch's anecdote is both consistent with Hamlet's mental movements and implicitly available to him as a classical commonplace. Hamlet's own faulty remembering, which had stumbled on the passage recited by the Player, makes understandable his own nonspecificity, while Upton's unqualified identification implies a currency of the commonplace in contemporary Elizabethan memory. Rather than recognize an organic connectedness in Plutarch's anecdote, the editor cites a 1612 reference work that gathers together several contemporary English illustrations. By substituting familiar current instances for a classical commonplace, however, Steevens fully anachronizes Hamlet's memory and blurs the associative motions of his troubled mind. By the end of this soliloquy, Upton's Hamlet is calmed and reassured by this remembrance; after he has been startled into self-chastisement by the player's weeping, he has settled with new confidence on a strategy to entrap.

Hawkins's contribution, which had been honored in 1773 and then denigrated in 1778 and 1790, is entirely erased in the 1793 edition.[27] Upton's contribution, however, is marginalized and maligned almost as soon as it is fully privileged, for Edmond Malone, who acknowledges Upton and also substitutes Upton's version of Plutarch's anecdote for North's translation, dismisses the likelihood of conscious allusion on the grounds that he finds no parallel in it to Hamlet's experience:

> Shakespeare, it is highly probable, had read the life of Pelopidas, but I see no ground for supposing there is here an allusion to it. Hamlet is not ashamed of being seen to weep at a theatrical exhibition, but mortified that a player, in a dream of passion, should appear more agitated by fictitious sorrow, than the prince was by a real calamity.[28]

Here Malone openly challenges the judgments of his editorial predecessors and exercises the privilege of selectivity. But by altogether dismissing Plutarch's anecdote from consideration in connection with the opening section of Hamlet's soliloquy ("What's Hecuba to him or he to Hecuba"), while maintaining the pertinence of Heywood's contemporary anecdote in connection with the closing section ("guilty creatures sitting at a play"), he further obfuscates a relevance that Steevens had already compromised by relocation.

Upton, however, had done more than identify an apparent allusion, for he went on to suggest a classical parallel to *Hamlet*: "The *Electra* of Sophocles, in many instances is not very unlike the *Hamlet* of Shakespeare."[29] In his analysis, Upton posits a broad analogy between Hamlet's story and that of Electra:

> Electra is a Grecian woman, of a masculine and generous disposition of mind; she had been a witness of the wickedness of those two miscreants [Aegysthus and Clytemnestra]; who had barbarously plotted the death of her father, the renowned Agamemnon: his Ghost called for justice; and she herself, rather than they shall escape, will be the instrument of vengeance.[30]

Although *Electra* is identified as a parallel model, Upton does not press it as a direct or indirect source for Shakespeare's own story; nor does he locate the *Troades* of Euripides, which Plutarch cites in his anecdote, along a genealogical line that leads to *Hamlet* or to *The Murder of Gonzago*.[31] Nonetheless, Upton finds the parallels illuminating and implies a rootedness of Shakespeare's play in the classical tradition. He was not, however, the first to suggest a connection like this.

In the earliest eighteenth-century collection of Shakespeare's *Works* in

1709, Nicholas Rowe posits the same parallel as the one Upton notes later in the century: "Hamlet is founded on much the same Tale with the *Electra* of Sophocles."[32] Rowe's purpose in nominating the *Electra* as a parallel model is not to establish genealogy but to offer a critical appraisal of Shakespeare relative to this classical antecedent.[33] Faulting Sophocles for "an offence against those Rules of Manners proper to the Persons that ought to be observ'd there," Rowe praises Shakespeare for restraining Hamlet "from doing Violence to his Mother" and for introducing his father's Ghost to "forbid that part of his Vengeance."[34] Charles Gildon, however, challenges Rowe's opinion in his own "Remarks on the Plays of Shakespear," printed at the end of his supplementary seventh volume to Rowe's edition, which was not published until 1710.[35] Here Gildon takes particular exception to Rowe's conclusions concerning the relative merits of *Electra* and *Hamlet:*

> Tho' I look upon this as the Master-piece of Shakspear according to our Way of writing; yet there are abundance of Errors in the Conduct and Design, which will not suffer us in Justice to prefer it to the *Electra* of Sophocles. . . . Orestes Father was commanded by the Oracle to kill his Mother and therefore all moral Duties yielding to the immediat command of the Gods, his Action according to that System of Religion under which Sophocles wrote had nothing in it of Barbarity but was entirely pious.[36]

In order to clarify the cultural context further, Gildon cites a popular ancient belief in the efficacy of plays. By way of example, he notes that the verses of Euripides' *Electra* were repeated during a time of great distress when the destruction of the city of Athens was being debated: "This shook them (says Plutarch in the *Life of Lysander*) and gave an Occasion to reflect how barbarous it wou'd appear to lay that City in Ruin, which had been renown'd for the Birth and Education of so many famous Men."[37] Sir Philip Sidney had brought this same illustration to bear in his own argument on the "sweet mysteries of poetry" in the *Defence of Poesie:*

> For only repeating certain of Euripides' verses many Athenians had their lives saved of the Syracusans. . . .[38]

This power of tragedy to shake an audience out of barbarity is precisely the point that Gildon seeks to establish when he offers the first editorial annotation of Plutarch's anecdote concerning the tyrant Alexander of Pherae. His commentary, in fact, emphasizes the specific relevance of this passage to Hamlet's own historical speculations on the miraculous power of a theatrical performance to provoke a public confession. Under the general heading "On Players and Plays," Gildon cites the following passages from *Hamlet* before introducing the anecdote that later critics and editors during the century will locate in Plutarch's *Life of Pelopidas:*

> Let them be well us'd, for they are the
> Abstracts and brief chronicles of the time, &c.
>
> I have heard that guilty creatures sitting at a play
> Have by the very cunning of the scene
> Been struck so to the soul, that presently
> They have proclaimed their malefactions, &c.[39]

Rather than claim that Shakespeare intentionally alludes to this particular anecdote, Gildon supplies it as a specific instance in support of the generalization that Hamlet pronounces as hearsay. In his own commentary, Gildon deploys the anecdote to confirm Hamlet's unspecified remembrance by reference to "undoubted History."[40]

Within the context of the scene itself, Hamlet's overactive, if somewhat faulty, memory leaves gaps for onstage as well as offstage auditors and readers to fill. For example, when he is unable to recall exactly whether a "passionate speech" he once heard was ever acted and when he misremembers the opening lines of the part he "chiefly lov'd," Hamlet depends on the better remembering of the traveling player to get it right. Then, after the player's powerful performance leads Polonius to interrupt his recitation, Shakespeare's Prince is reminded of his own passivity and moved to consider what to do. While Hamlet is vague in his own recollection, Gildon provides an appropriate illustration for his readers:

> The Power and Force of Tragedy, in this and other Particulars has been confirmed by undoubted History. Alexander Tyrant of Pherae a City of Thessaly seeing the *Hecuba* of Euripides acted, found himself so affected, that he went out before the End of the first Act, saying, That he was asham'd to be seen to weep at that Misfortune of Hecuba and Polyxena, when he daily imbrued his Hands in the Blood of his own Citizens.[41]

Sidney had earlier characterized the effects of "high and excellent tragedy" in his *Defence,* by retelling Plutarch's anecdote of "the abominable tyrant Alexander Pheraeus." His framing introduction gives the illustration a focused cogency:

> [it] maketh kings fear to be tyrants, and tyrants manifest their tyrannical humours; that with the stirring effects of admiration and commiseration teacheth the uncertainty of this world, and upon how weak foundations gilden roofs are builded.[42]

Both Gildon and Sidney foreground the specific efficacy of tragedy as a morally chastening experience for tyrannical monarchs.[43] Such an emphasis had already been overlooked by Hawkins before it was first cited in the 1773 Steevens-Johnson edition. Without this emphasis on moral efficacy, the force of the parallel is diminished. Furthermore, Sidney's specification of the lesson in tragedy's "stirring effects," echoes in the instruction that the Player King gives to the Player Queen in *The Murder of Gonzago:*

> Our wills and fates do so contrary run
> That our devices still are overthrown:
> Our thoughts are ours, their ends none of our own.
>
> (3.2.206–8)

Although Gildon does not make this latter connection, which may suggest that he had not relied directly on Sidney's *Defence* for his own commentary, the connection itself remains pertinent to the present argument: namely, that there is a structural design in the accumulation of instances and Plutarch's anecdote may be its linchpin. Furthermore, failure to assess the contemporary resonance of Plutarch's anecdote diminishes appreciation for the playwright's invocation of classical models and alters the sense of Hamlet's implied literateness.

In a few significant particulars Gildon's version of Plutarch's anecdote differs from the accounts provided later in the century by Upton, Hawkins, and the Variorum editors. In his version, Alexander's departure is advanced "before the End of the first Act," while in the other versions he leaves "before the play was ended."[44] This timing of the tyrant's departure not only intensifies the immediacy of Alexander's reaction but implicitly alters the interpretation of his reaction. In the account given by Upton, the tyrant leaves the theater after having been moved to tears, and his confession of shame is offered as a confirmation of the chastening effect of tragedy on this remorseless murderer. In Gildon's account, the tyrant leaves in order to avoid being "seen to weep," as he had in the version cited in editions from Steevens (1773) to Malone (1790). Gildon's Alexander, however, has not experienced catharsis; rather he removes himself from the occasion of unmanly weeping. Furthermore, and perhaps most tellingly, the continuing narrative is presented quite differently. In the version of the anecdote cited up to the Steevens edition in 1793, the players are encouraged to go on, and they alone are given an explanation by the tyrant for his departure (see above page 168). In this version the shame that Alexander seeks to conceal remains nearly private, and the actors are given an apology and permitted to continue with the play in the tyrant's absence. Gildon's Alexander, on the other hand, abruptly leaves but does not send an apologetic explanation to the players: in fact, he barely spares the actor's life ("The actor . . . with difficulty escap'd with his life").[45] While North's full account of this anecdote presents Alexander's fear of reprisal as a consequence of the play's effect on his "gilty conscience," commentators from Upton to Malone consistently exclude this capping assessment provided in Plutarch.[46] Gildon, on the other hand, offers a more expanded interpretation of Alexander's fear:

> He was afraid (says the admirable Dacier) that his Heart shou'd be truly molli-fied; that the Spirit of Tyranny wou'd now leave the Possession of his Breast, and that he should come a private Person out of that Theatre, into which he enter'd Master.[47]

Here Gildon displaces North's (and Upton's) emphasis on conscience, in favor of explaining his departure as a resolution to continued tyranny. Rather than risk the prospect of having his heart "truly mollified," Alexander abruptly leaves the theater so as not to be reduced to "a private Person." The rationale provided for Alexander's departure in Sidney's representation of the anecdote (he "withdrew himself from hearkening to that which might mollify his hardened heart") echoes in Gildon's. For his part, Gildon attributes the tyrant's leniency to the residual effects of mollification produced by the play: the actor's life "was secur'd by some Remains of that Pity which was the Cause of his Crime."[48] Gildon's spectator, then, is as guilty as Shakespeare's Claudius and equally fearful of losing the position he has gained and will maintain by murders. Furthermore, Claudius is as intent on reprisal as Plutarch's Alexander, though for a brief time his hardened heart is similarly mollified nearly to repentance.[49]

In Gildon's version of the anecdote, the most noticeable divergence from the account recorded in *The Life of Pelopidas* is his naming of *Hecuba* rather than *Troades* as the Euripidean play-within-the-anecdote. Neither Sidney nor North nor Florio, all of whom include this anecdote in publications printed or reprinted in 1603, had cited *Hecuba*. Gildon's displacement of *Troades,* however, is no mere creative editing, for Plutarch retold an alternate version of this anecdote in the *Morals.* In the first English translation of this work published by Philemon Holland (1603), we find the following account:

> [Alexander] suddenly left the theater, made haste away, & went faster than an ordinary pace untill he was out of sight saying withall, that it were a great indignity for him to weepe and shed teares, in compassion of the miseries and calamities of queene Hecuba or lady Polyxena, who every day caused so many citizens and subjects throats to be cut.[50]

Here Plutarch names the two central sufferers but not the play. Gildon's inference that the play in question is Euripides's *Hecuba* is perfectly reasonable in light of the identification of "lady Polyxena," rather than Andromache, as Hecuba's co-sufferer.

In *Hecuba* the execution of Polyxena is narrated in graphic detail by Talthybius. This execution is a gesture of retribution by the avenging son of Achilles (i.e., Pyrrhus) and is expressly intended to deliver his father's ghost from the pit of the dead. As such, it provides an apt analogue for the narrative delivered by Aeneas to Dido recited by the First Player in *Hamlet.* Furthermore, the executioner's momentary pause as described by Shakespeare's Player ("Pyrrhus stood / And like a neutral to his will and matter / Did nothing," 2.2.474–78),[51] has a parallel in Talthybius's account in *Hecuba:* "Torn between pity and duty, / Achilles' son stood hesitating, and then slashed her throat with the edge of his sword."[52] Not only is the horror of the moment intensified in each account by this momentary suspension of the action, but Plutarch's version of Alexander's crimes (he "caused so many citizens and subjects throats to be cut") is echoed in Euripides version of Pyrrhus's act (he "slashed her throat"). By identifying the play as *Hecuba,* Gildon implies a theory in Plutarch's substitution of Polyxena for Andromache in this second version of the anecdote. Gildon's emphasis on Polyxena's suffering as a central element within the anecdote enriches the analogy and lends a unifying amplitude to the classical references nested at the center of Shakespeare's play, which organize Hamlet's mental progress from the time the traveling players arrive until they leave Elsinore.[53]

Twentieth-century scholars have recognized a paradigm in *Hecuba* that further illuminates the appropriateness of Gildon's decision to specify it as the Euripidean text within his version of the anecdote as it appears in Plutarch's *Morals.* G. M. A. Grube, for example, relates a central theme in Euripidean drama to the structural design of *Hecuba:* namely, "the growing of sorrow and of lamentation into a desire for vengeance."[54] In the particular case of this play, as the dramatic action shifts from the dominance of sorrow to the dominance of vengeance, Hecuba undergoes a dramatic change from passive *ethopeia* to active planning of a private revenge.[55] Emrys Jones describes Hecuba's "decisive move from passivity to activity" as occurring in "a short interval of silent self-communing and withdrawal":

> Hecuba speaks to herself in a long aside, during which Agamemnon tries to make her answer him; but she is entirely self-absorbed, conceiving her plan of revenge.[56]

This moment of dramatic self-communing has its correlative in Hamlet's soliloquy at the end of Act 2. Recognition of this parallel serves to clarify the curve of thinking within the soliloquy and describes Hamlet's own transformation from a John-a-Dreams who does nothing to a resolute planner of a revenge device. The capping sentence in North's translation of the anecdote in Plutarch's *Life of Pelopidas,* which no eighteenth-century editor or commentator addresses, includes a curious contextual reference at the end: "The gilty conscience therefore of this cruell and heathen tyran [sic], did make him tremble at the only name and reputacion of Epaminondas."[57] This Greek hero is the friend and ultimate rescuer of Pelopidas, who had been captured and would probably have been executed by Alexander.[58] In 1603, North added a translation of *The Life of Epaminondas* to his collection of *Lives.* While no mention is made of the theater anecdote in this account, Plutarch describes Epaminondas's delay and his dissembling "device" as follows: by "refrain[ing] to set on [Alexander] in earnest," he sought to delude this "bloud-sucker" into thinking that he was not in imminent "daunger to be ouerthrowne."[59] Delay and dissembling color the stories of revenge in *Hecuba* as well as *Hamlet.* Shakespeare's Fortinbras, and not Hamlet, delays and dissembles in a fashion that near literally parallels in apparency the non-invasion ruse of Epaminondas. And it is only Fortinbras who achieves positive results for himself in a restoration of order. Hamlet's delay and dissembling, on the other hand, have decidedly tragic implications.

The Euripidean fusion of dark tragic irony and complex political didacticism is discernible in the allusive shadows of Shakespeare's play. Hamlet's revenge, in thoroughly Euripidean fashion, bears witness to the ironies of tragic necessity. It may also serve notice to the mighty, as Justina Gregory insists *Hecuba* had, "that it is dangerous for them to overreach themselves, for retribution may be forthcoming not from the gods but from the abused victims themselves."[60] Shakespeare and his audiences may very well have known Euripides's play. Judging from F. L. Lucas's record of the number of translations in Latin, Italian, French, and Spanish, it is clear that *Hecuba* was exceptionally popular in the sixteenth century.[61] While Greek themes most often found their ways into the English imagination by way of Seneca, H. B. Charlton notes that *Hecuba* was the only play included in all thirteen editions of Euripides's plays that appeared in England in Latin translations. William Arrowsmith, furthermore, describes the rising authority of Euripides as the prime exemplar in tragedy, noting how *Hecuba* "became one of the favorite plays of the Byzantine schoolbooks."[62] Arrowsmith also calls attention to the fact that Erasmus translated this play into Latin. This translation by Erasmus is an especially compelling fact. Emrys Jones, for example, underscores the importance of this translation because of Erasmus's unique position as "the presiding genius of Tudor school education": "it is hardly too much to say that Tudor literary culture until the third quarter of the sixteenth century is overwhelmingly Erasmian in inspiration. His influence is everywhere."[63] Certainly Roger Ascham's adulation of Erasmus, "the ornament of learning in our tyme," is unmistakable in *The Scholemaster* (1570), where he cites Erasmus in the context of his own recommendation of imitation as a method of instruction. With Erasmus, he wishes that "some man of learning and diligence would take the paines [when studying parallel texts in Greek and in Latin] to write out and ioyne together where the one doeth imitate the other."[64] Ascham goes on to outline six steps in a careful strategy of instruction, both in the principles of imitation and in the practice of comparative analysis. This outline, which requires the student to identify matters retained and then to estimate the "end and purpose" of what is left out, added, diminished, or reordered, concludes on the following step: the student is to assess what the second author "altereth and changeth, either in propertie of wordes, in forme of sentence, in substance of the matter, or in one or other conuenient circumstance of the authors present purpose."[65] Such a method of analysis may well have been adopted as a pedagogy by Elizabethan schoolmasters. Students might thereby have learned to work deliberately through textual comparisons by laying "two places [in Greek and Latin models] togither." It is not inconceivable, given the popularity and availability of Latin translations, that Euripides' *Hecuba* might have been chosen as a sample text for study. Ascham's own stated opinion, in fact, and his recommendation later in *The Scholemaster* makes it seem likely:

> In Tragedies . . . the Grecians Sophocles and Euripides far ouer match our Seneca in Latin . . . although Senecaes elocution and verse be verie commendable for his tyme. . . . his Imitation [ought to be] tryed by the same touchstone, as is spoken before.[66]

Furthermore, given the fact that Ascham names Erasmus as his lead authority in recommending comparative analysis as a pedagogical method and that there was not a Senecan version of Euripides' *Hecuba*,[67] it is not unreasonable to speculate that Elizabethan schoolmasters might examine Erasmus's own translation of the Greek original in this particular case. If this speculation is correct, then Shakespeare's readers, if not his audiences, may well have relished the audacity of a playwright who would seem to have taken up the challenge implicit in Ascham's characterization of English tragedians:

> Some in England, moe in France, Germanie, and Italie also, haue written Tragedies in our tyme: of the which not one I am sure is able to abyde the trew touch of Aristotles preceptes and Euripides examples, saue only two that euer I saw, M. Watsons *Absalon* and Georgius Buckananus *Iephthe*."[68]

In Ascham's capping examples, we may discover new resonance in Hamlet's witty pedantry when he responds to Polonius's assessment of the present state of theatrical affairs: "O Jephthah, judge of Israel, what a treasure hadst thou!" (2.2.400). In his annotation provided for Hamlet's line, Harold Jenkins provides late twentieth-century readers with precise references to the story of Jephthe in Judges. xi.30–40, and to the contemporary English ballad "Jephthah, Judge of Israel."[69] If Gildon's note on Hamlet's soliloquy leads readers back to Plutarch and Euripides, and from Plutarch and Euripides back to Sidney and Ascham, and from Sidney and Ascham back to Erasmus, then the accumulation of resonances may be far greater than biblical and pop-cultural echoes alone imply. Such tracings of an ever-broader multiplicity of references tighten the coherence at the heart of Shakespeare's play. They also lend to Hamlet's own reflections a widening gyre of instances wherein revenges revolve and histories seem to repeat themselves relentlessly.

The implications of Hamlet's education at Wittenberg, at least if readers imagined it to have occurred at about the time that Saxo's story of the legendary Amleth was first published in a Latin translation (1514), may help to account for his delays as well as his private musings and expressed fears. In 1517, Wittenberg provided the stage on which one of the most dramatic gestures in the history of the Church was enacted: Luther's posting of his ninety-five theses. During the first quarter of the sixteenth century, Luther was embroiled in the most celebrated debates of the age, and Erasmus was his adversary. Central to their debate on free will and salvation was Luther's contention that "in matters pertaining to salvation and damnation, a man has no free choice, but is a captive, subject slave either of the will of God or the will of Satan."[70] At one point in the published record of this debate, Luther turns from scripture to the things that "heathen poets and even the common people speak of":

The wise of those days were well aware of what fact and experience prove, namely that no man's plans have ever been straightforwardly realized, but for everyone things have turned out differently from what he thought they would. Vergil's Hector says, "Could Troy have stood by human arm, then it had stood by mine." Hence the very common saying on everyone's lips, "God's will be done"; and "God willing, we will do it," or "Such was the will of God." "So it pleased those above"; "Such was your will," says Vergil. From this we can see that the knowledge of God's predestination and foreknowledge remained with the common people no less than the awareness of his existence itself. But those who wished to appear wise went so far astray in their reasonings that their hearts were darkened and they became fools (Rom. 1<:21f.>), and denied or explained away the things that the poets and common people, and even their own consciences, regarded as entirely familiar, certain, and true.[71]

Poets and common people in Shakespeare's England, as well as the Hamlet of their imaginations, may well have known what Luther argues here even if they had not read the published documents. Certainly they would have heard in Hamlet's resignation of his will to Providence and in the Player King's lecture to his Queen, echoes both classical and biblical.

The common people, however, may just as well have failed to hear resonances from Luther or from other classical texts that have been sounded in this present essay. Educated readers and members of the audience with broader literary experience, on the other hand, might have heard them quite clearly. Gabriel Harvey's expressed distinction between the delights of "younger" readers and the pleasures of "the wiser sort," in fact, may lead us to appreciate both the acuity of Charles Gildon's scholarly excavations and the intellectual objective implicit in his endeavor as an editorial commentator:

> The younger sort takes much delight in Shakespeares Venus, & Adonis: but his Lucrece, & his tragedie of Hamlet, Prince of Denmarke, haue it in them, to please the wiser sort.[72]

From Rowe's edition in 1709 to Theobald's in 1733, there was a marked increase in the number and an intensification in the scholarly erudition of line-by-line annotations provided by Shakespeare's editors. On the basis of a quantitative comparison alone, it would appear that Malone's enthusiasm for the accumulation of notes, until "every temporary allusion shall have been pointed out, and every obscurity elucidated," had been anticipated by the earliest editors of the playwright's *Works*. As we have seen, however, successive editors exercised judicial authority as they discriminated among the findings of their predecessors. Gildon's questioning of Rowe's judgment concerning the relative merits of *Hamlet* when compared to a clasical antecedent, for example, as well as his own explication of the relevance of Plutarch's anecdote, reveals a tendency away from the mere accumulation of notes. Malone's imagined ideal of a community of collaborating scholars, intent on discovering "the poet's entire library," was compromised from the start by the competition for interpretive authority among eighteenth-century editors who sought to locate a text's meaning in their own annotations. Furthermore, and paradoxically, Malone's insistent validation of the most minute and intense genealogically probings is effectively contradicted by his own definitive shutting down of the allusive possibilities elaborated above. His particular exclusion of Plutarch as a relevant antecedent text is, of course, judiciously explicated in no less authoritative terms than Gildon's when he initially proposed it as an elucidating antecedent text. In this contradiction between the ideal of annnotative comprehensiveness and the practice of exclusion, an

eighteenth-century editorial resistance is discernible which is traceable
to one of Johnson's magisterial pronouncements in the Preface to his
1765 edition.

In addition to setting first-claimancy as the governing criterion for
scholarly recognition, already cited above, Johnson emphatically warns
of the damaging consequence of examining editorial commentary before
"the whole" of a great work has been surveyed. His idealization of comprehension, rather than annotational comprehensiveness, directly challenges "the close approach" practiced by editorial commentators, intent
on showing "the smaller niceties" of a text.[73] According to Johnson, readers who pay primary attention to local details will find that "the beauty
of the whole is discerned no longer." Furthermore, Johnson's recommendation of "a kind of intellectual remoteness" as the mental disposition
proper to the reading of Shakespeare's text, not only distances the activity
of reading from the practices of editorial commentators but implicitly
characterizes their annotations as repositories not of essential meaning
but of the esoteric and the arcane.

By holding up "the whole" as the repository of a great work's overriding significance, Johnson challenged the impetus that might otherwise
prompt editors to multiply the number or compound the erudition of their
annotations. Malone's supervision of the annotations that prior editors
had brought to bear on Hamlet's soliloquy gives evidence of the perva-
siveness and endurance of Johnson's magisterial influence. Furthermore,
it may help us to understand the extent to which eighteenth-century editors sought to resist, at least in part, the complicity between the accretion
of editorial notes and obscurity in a text that appears to demand allusive reference.

Although the directions taken by editors from Rowe and Gildon to
Steevens and Malone diverged considerably, pursuit of the relationship
between Shakespeare's texts and their classical antecedents was a matter
of central importance during the period. The instance here examined is an
illuminating paradigm. Curtailment of the retelling of Plutarch's anecdote,
with all of its potential resonances, not only obscures a detail in the
picture of editorial history but diminishes appreciation for Shakespeare's
conservative originality and for the recesses of Hamlet's memory. To the
extent that this instance is accurately paradigmatic, it may account for a
twentieth-century resistance to the idea of Shakespeare (and Hamlet)
partaking actively in classical learning.[74]

NOTES

Malone's assertion here, which appeared for the first time in his introduction
to the 1790 edition, was reprinted unchanged into the edition of 1821. See James

Boswell, ed., *The Plays and Poems of William Shakespeare* (London: F. C. and J. Rivington, 1821), 1:236.

1. George Steevens and Samuel Johnson, eds., *The Plays of William Shakespeare* (London: C. Bathurst, 1773), 10:228. The precise location of this note will be the focus of considerable comment later in this present essay.

2. See Edmond Malone, ed., *The Plays and Poems of William Shakespeare* (London: H. Baldwin, 1790), 9:280. In 1778, Steevens makes the following editorial correction, which Malone maintains: "This observation had been already made by Mr. Upton." See George Steevens and Samuel Johnson, eds. [rev. and aug. by Isaac Reed], *The Plays of William Shakespeare* (London: C. Bathurst, 1778), 10:268.

3. See Steevens, *Plays,* 4th ed., 1793, 9:148; Boswell, *Plays,* ed. 1821, 7:313. I am grateful to Bernice W. Kliman for clarifying the attributions of editorial credit in connection with several early and nominally collaborative editions (1773, 1778, 1793), which many regard as the first variorum editions.

4. See Charlotte Lennox, *Shakespear Illustrated* (London: A. Millar, 1753). Gerald Langbaine's systematic listing of sources for twenty-seven of the forty-six plays attributed to Shakespeare in the 1685 folio edition antedates Lennox. Langbaine, however, makes no attempt to assemble the texts in question; neither does he analyze the relationship between Shakespeare's play and the antecedent texts. See Langbaine's *An Account of the English Dramatick Poets* (Oxford: Oxford University Press, 1691), 453–69. Lewis Theobald traces his debt to him in the first note to his edition of *The Works of Shakespeare* (London: A. Bettesworth et al, 1733), 7:225–26.

5. Geoffrey Bullough, *Narrative and Dramatic Sources of Shakespeare* (New York: Columbia University Press, 1973), 7:1–189.

6. Harold Jenkins, ed., *The Arden Shakespeare Hamlet* (London: Methuen & Co., Ltd., 1982). Among recent editors of *Hamlet,* Jenkins offers the most detailed genealogical essay in his introduction as well as the most copious source-related notes throughout the text. *The Arden Shakespeare Hamlet* will be cited throughout, as it is the modern edition represented in this present argument.

7. See Jenkins, *Arden Hamlet* , 482 (LN for 2.2.585–88).

8. Eric Rasmussen has pointed out to me in an unpublished memo that Jenkins's note actually "resembles / imitates" the paragraph in Bullough and that both Bullough and Jenkins see Plutarch's anecdote as "merely an instance of a ruler not wanting to show emotion," which is, as Bullough asserts, "not quite what Hamlet meant." See Bullough, 7:38.

9. William A. Ringler, "Hamlet's Defense of the Players" in *Essays on Shakespeare and Elizabethan Drama in Honour of Hardin Craig,* ed. Richard Hosley (London: Routledge & Kegan Paul, Ltd., 1963), 205.

10. Of Plutarch's two versions of this anecdote (in *The Life of Pelopidas, Lives* 293F, and in *On the Fortune of Alexander, Morals* 334A, respectively), Ringler notes: "in both places Plutarch says that Euripides was the author of the tragedy and that the sufferings of Hecuba were the action that caused the tyrant to weep and withdraw from the theater." See Ringler, "Hamlet's Defence," 205.

11. Florio's translation was thought to have circulated in manuscript well before its first publication date in 1603. It was reprinted several times thereafter. Jenkins cites Montaigne's *Essays,* 2:27, in connection with Hamlet's reflection on the player's tears (2.2.515–16). See Jenkins, ed. 1982, 481. In this particular essay, Montaigne gives some attention to a revenger's enjoyment in not killing a man, but of "making him aware of our revenge in order to intensify his suffering."

See Montaigne, *The Complete Essays of Montaigne,* Donald M. Frame, ed. and trans. (Stanford: Stanford University Press, 1948), 523–25.

12. Steevens-Johnson, *Plays,* 1st ed., 1773, 10:230.

13. Samuel Johnson, ed., *The plays of William Shakespeare* (London: J. and R. Tonson, 1765), 1:lvii. William Warburton anticipated and shared Johnson's opinion concerning the "ownership" of emendations and annotations. For further details on "the Shakespeare Wars," see Bernice W. Kliman's "Samuel Johnson, 1745 Annotator? Eighteenth-Century Editors, Anonymity, and the Shakespeare Wars," *Analytical and Enumerative Bibliography,* NS 6 (1992): 185–207. A rewritten version of this article appears in this present volume.

14. Zachary Grey, *Critical, Historical, and Explanatory Notes on Shakespeare* (London: Richard Manby, 1754), 2:294.

15. Grey, *Critical . . . Notes,* 2:294. Two years earlier Grey had published a general attack on Warburton's editorial capabilities in support of Hanmer, under the title *An Examination of a Late Edition of Shakespear* (London: C. Norris, 1752). In the Preface, he is direct in his accusation of Warburton: "the excellent Emendations which, under the Rose and Seal of Secresy, were communicated to you by Sir Thomas, you (out of your great Regard to the Laws of Hospitality) puffed among your Friends and Acquaintances as your own, in the little Time after you had left Mildenhall, and long before Publication of the Oxford Edition." See Grey, *An Examination,* 5. Clearly Grey takes umbrage at editors who credit themselves for scholarly discoveries made by others.

16. Steevens, *Plays,* 2d ed., 1778, 1:248–52.

17. Steevens, *Plays,* 2d ed., 1778, 10:269.

18. In the 1821 Variorum edition, TODD is credited for providing the relevant passage spoken by the character "M. James" in *A Warning for Faire Women.* See Boswell, *Plays,* ed. 1821, 7:316. Bullough expands this passage in his own excerpt, and Jenkins briefly summarizes it in his note on the "guilty creatures sitting at a play" passage. See Bullough, 7:179–81; and Jenkins, *Arden Hamlet,* ed. 1982, 482. Ringler, who accurately credits Todd with the first citation of the passage from *A Warning for Faire Women,* also overlooks Grey: "Thomas Heywood repeated the anecdote in *An Apology for Actors* (1612, sigs. G1v–2—first cited by Steevens)." See Ringler, 206, n6. The *New Variorum Edition Hamlet* had set the pattern for this oversight nearly a century earlier and repeated it through ten subsequent reprintings. See Horace Howard Furness, ed., *A New Variorum Edition Hamlet* (1877; reprint, New York: Dover Publications, Inc., 1963), 1:198.

19. In the anonymous German play *Der Bestrafte Brudermord,* however, Hamlet recalls in elaborate detail an anecdote about a wife in Strasburg who confessed to murdering her husband during a performance of "a tragedy of like import," which is very much like the one that Heywood summarizes in his *Apology.* In this case, the problem noted here is transferred directly to the play and may well account for the Variorum editor's preference for an Elizabethan equivalent. See Bullough, 7:141.

20. Steevens, *Plays,* 1st ed., 1773, 10:228.

21. Steevens, *Plays,* 1st ed. 1773, 10:228, n4.

22. It should not be surprising that Steevens does not acknowledge Thomas North as the translator of Plutarch's *Life of Pelopidas,* from which he quotes directly. By the time the first and second Variorum editions are published, Richard Farmer's argument in *An Essay on the Learning of Shakespeare* (Cambridge, 1767), concerning the likelihood that Shakespeare relied principally on English translations, was widely accepted and strongly endorsed. See Karl Young, "Sam-

uel Johnson on Shakespeare: One Aspect," *University of Wisconsin Studies in Language and Literature,* 18 (1923) 146–226.

23. Steevens, *Plays,* 2d ed., 1778, 10:268. Hawkins and Steevens may well have overlooked John Upton's prior recognition of a conscious allusion to Plutarch in Hamlet's soliloquy. William Dodd, however, had identified this allusion to Plutarch less than a decade after Upton's publication, but nearly a quarter century before the 1773 Variorum. In *The Beauties of Shakespear,* in fact, Dodd implies that this recognition of Plutarch's anecdote is so commonplace that no acknowledgement of scholarly predecessor is required. Although the most cursory comparison of Dodd's language and syntax to Upton's will reveal the extent of his indebtedness to his predecessor, the point worth making is that neither Upton nor Dodd is credited with the discovery that Steevens claims for Hawkins in the 1773 edition. See John Upton, *Critical Observations on Shakespeare* (London: G. Hawkins, 1746), 62–63; and William Dodd, *The Beauties of Shakespear* (1752; reprint, New York: Augustus M. Kelley, 1971), 1:234.

24. Steevens, *Plays,* 2d ed., 1778, 10:268.

25. Upton, 62.

26. See Steevens, *Plays,* 1st ed., 1773, 10:228; and Upton, 62.

27. In the 1790 edition, Malone parenthetically identifies the unnamed spectator as "Alexander Pheraeus" in the version of the anecdote he retains from Hawkins, rather than adopt the version provided by Upton. See Malone, *Plays,* ed. 1790, 9:280. In the subsequent Variorum edition, however, Malone supplies Upton's own version and eliminates mention of Hawkins altogether. See Steevens, *Plays,* 4th ed. 1793, 9:148. Arthur Johnston's more recent study of the player's speech credits Upton in passing: "Though the transition is clear it is of interest to note a passage in Plutarch's *Life of Pelopidas,* first pointed out by John Upton in 1746." It is interesting to note that Johnston supplies the relevant passage from Plutarch by quoting from North's translation rather than from Upton, which duplicates the treatment accorded to him by Reed in the 1778 Variorum, where he credits Upton's priority while retaining Hawkins's quotation from North. See Arthur Johnston, "The Player's Speech in *Hamlet,*" *Shakespeare Quarterly,* 13 (1962) 21–30.

28. Malone's treatment of Upton, which is retained into the Boswell edition, duplicates Steevens's treatment of Hawkins and anticipates Bullough's more recent treatment of Johnston, and Jenkins of Bullough. See Malone, *Plays,* ed. 1790, 9:280; and Boswell, *Plays,* ed. 1821, 7:313.

29. Upton, 63. William Dodd, who clearly adopts Upton's language and style in devising his own comments on the anecdote from Plutarch, invites readers to compare Hamlet to Orestes in the *Electra* by Euripides (see n. 23 above). Dodd, however, emphasizes the similarity between Hamlet's condition of mind and that of Orestes, rather than stress a plot parallel between the stories of Hamlet and Electra. Taken together, however, both commentaries urge the rootedness of Shakespeare's play in the classical tradition of tragedy, rather than insist that the genealogy of *Hamlet* be traced to a single text. See Dodd, 1:234–35.

30. Upton, 63.

31. In 1733 Lewis Theobald published his discovery of Saxo Grammaticus's account of Amleth as the "ground-work" for Shakespeare's plot. See Theobald, *Works,* ed. 1733, 7:225–26. Richard Farmer would challenge this claim and nominate an English prose translation of Belleforest's French adaptation of Saxo's account, entitled *The Hystorie of Hamblet.* See Richard Farmer, *An Essay on the Learning of Shakespeare* (Cambridge: Cambridge University Press, 1767), 29. No

scholarly claim was made during the eighteenth century or since in favor of a classical dramatic play as the direct source for the *Hamlet* plot.

32. Nicholas Rowe, ed., *The Works of Mr. William Shakespear* (London: J. Tonson, 1709), 1:xxxi.

33. In the context of inviting his own readers to notice "how happily [Shakespeare] express'd himself upon the same topics" as the classical authors, Theobald cites the following declaration by Rowe : "It is without controversy, [Shakespeare] had no knowledge of the writings of the ancient poets, for that in his works we find no traces of any thing which looks like an imitation of the ancients." Theobald, who cites numerous parallel passages, leaves it to his own "Learned Readers" to determine whether or not the playwright closely imitated the classics. See Theobald, *Works,* ed. 1733, 1:xxvii–xxviii.

34. Rowe, *Works,* ed. 1709, 1:xxxii. Within two years of Rowe's edition, Joseph Addison pursues the comparison between *Hamlet* and *Electra* along slightly different lines: "It may not be unacceptable to the reader to see how Sophocles has conducted a tragedy under the like delicate circumstances. Orestes was in the same condition with Hamlet in Shakespeare. . . ." See *The Spectator* (20 April 1711), reprinted in *Shakespeare, the Critical Heritage: 1693–1733,* ed. Brian Vickers (London: Routledge & Kegan Paul, 1974), 275–77. Both Rowe and Addison, then, set a precedent for the opinion that Upton urges less tentatively by midcentury.

35. Gary Taylor, it might be noted, implies that this was a calculated misrepresentation that belies the contents of the volume: "Rowe's 1709 edition of the plays was followed in 1710 by an edition of the poems, which passed itself off as volume seven of Rowe's edition; but Charles Gildon devoted much of his introduction to berating Rowe." See Gary Taylor, *Reinventing Shakespeare* (Oxford: Oxford University Press, 1989), 72.

36. Charles Gildon, ed., *The Works of Mr. William Shakespear* (London: E. Curll et al, 1710), 7:397. Later in the century Charlotte Lennox acknowledges the cultural differences between primitive Denmark and civilized England in evaluating the playwright's deviations from the Amleth story recorded in Saxo's Danish history, which she claims to have read in translation. By then Theobald's establishment of Saxo as the direct source for Shakespeare's play had become commonplace. See Lennox, 2:241–74.

37. Gildon, *Works,* ed. 1710, 7:400. In this anecdote the Spartans were specifically dissuaded by a Phocian quoting from the parados of Euripides' *Electra.* As in the case of the Alexander of Pherae anecdote, however, Plutarch offers two versions of the anecdote that Gildon cites here: a second version appeared in Plutarch's *Life of Nicias.* The following translation of this latter version is John Dryden's, as revised by A. L. Clough in 1906:

> Several were saved for the sake of Euripides, whose poetry, it appears, was in request among the Sicilians. . . . Many of the captives who got safe back to Athens are said, after they reached home, to have gone and made their acknowledgements to Euripides, relating how some of them had been released from their slavery by teaching what they could remember of his poems, and others, when straggling after the fight, had been relieved with meat and drink for repeating some of his lyrics.

The effect of Euripides' verses, however, remains the same and serves to reinforce a cultural commonplace. See Justina Gregory, *Euripides and the Instruction of the Athenians* (Ann Arbor: The University of Michigan Press, 1991), 179.

38. See Sir Philip Sidney, *The Defence of Poesy,* in *Prose of the English Renais-*

sance, ed. J. William Hebel, et al (1595; reprint mainly based on William Posonby's edition, New York: Appleton-Century-Crofts, Inc., 1952), 293; and *An Apologie for Poetrie,*in *English Literary Criticism: The Renaissance,* ed. O. B. Hardison, Jr. (1595; reprint of Henry Olney's edition, New York: Appleton-Century-Crofts, 1963), 132.

39. Gildon, *Works,* ed. 1710, 7:399.

40. Gildon had earlier added a small number of new source identifications in his revision of Gerald Langbaine's *Account of the English Dramatick Poets,* under the new title *The Lives and Characters of the English Dramatic Poets* (Oxford: Oxford University Press, 1698). Here he echoes Langbaine's expressed interest in history as a basis for verification. Langbaine, for his own part, had sought to verify "whether this story [*Hamlet*] be true or false" by turning to historians "that have written of the affairs of Denmark and Norway." See Langbaine, 457.

41. Gildon, *Works,* ed. 1710, 7:399–400.

42. Sidney's introduction to the anecdote not only describes the effect of a tragedy on tyrants but also points to a moral lesson very much like the one that the Player King articulates in *The Murder of Gonzago* before his own murder becomes its ironic confirmation. See Sidney, *Defence,* 285; or *Apologie,* 122.

43. As will be noted later in this present study, Justina Gregory identifies an edge in Euripides's customary didacticism. Speaking specifically of Hecuba's revenge, she maintains that it "serves notice to the mighty that it is dangerous for them to overreach themselves, for retribution may be forthcoming not from the gods but from the abused victims themselves. The beacon of Cynossema signals that the desire for justice is rooted deep in human nature and cannot be torn out by force." See Gregory, 112.

44. See Gildon, *Works,* ed. 1710, 7:399; and Upton, 62.

45. Gildon, *Works,* ed. 1710, 7:400.

46. See Plutarch, *The Lives of the Noble Grecians and Romanes,* Thomas North, trans. (London: Thomas Vautroullier, 1579), EE1.

47. Gildon, *Works,* ed. 1710, 7:400.

48. Gildon, *Works,* ed. 1710, 7:400.

49. Sidney had similarly emphasized the limited duration of the tragedy's effect on this particular tyrant: "if it wrought no further good in him, it was that he in despite of himself withdrew himself from hearkening to that which might mollify his heardened heart." See Sidney, *Defence,* 285; *Apologie,* 122.

50. Plutarch, *The Morals,* Philemon Holland, trans. (London: Arnold Hatfield, 1603), 1273. With respect to dating, it may be worth noting that in his list of "Ancient Translations from Classic Authors," Reed provides the following note for the item "Plutarch's *Morals,* by Dr. Philemon Holland 1603*": "On the Stationers' books in the year 1600 is the following entry: 'A booke to be translated out of Frenche into Englishe, and so printed, called the Morall Workes of Plutarque.' Again it 1602. Again in the same year, 'The morral worke of Plutarque, being translated out of French into English.'" See Reed, ed. 1778, 1:90.

51. As Arthur Johnston notes, this pause was Shakespeare's "addition to the traditional accounts." See Johnston, 27.

52. Euripides, *Hecuba,* William Arrowsmith, trans., in *Euripides III,* David Grene and Richmond Lattimore, eds. (1958; reprint, New York: Washington Square Press, 1972), 35.

53. It is perhaps worth noting that in the anonymous German play *Der Bestrafte Brudermord,* the Mousetrap play is not *The Murder of Gonzago* but an unnamed "piece" that Hamlet had seen acted "in Wittenberg" about the poisoning

of "the great King Pyrrhus." In this respect the allusive pattern is more nearly uniform, but thereby less transformational in its progress than in the three earliest extant editions of *Hamlet*. See Bullough, 7: 140–42. For easy comparison of details, see *The Three-Text Hamlet: Parallel Texts of the First and Second Quartos and First Folio*. Paul Bertram and Bernice W. Kliman, eds. (New York: AMS Press, 1991).

54. Emrys Jones, who has analyzed the relationship between Euripidean and Shakespearean tragedy, cites G. M. A. Grube's finding here in connection with the assertion that *Hecuba*'s structural design turns on Polyxena's execution: "The play falls into two parts; the first is concerned with the sacrifice of Polyxena upon the tomb of Achilles, the second with the vengeance on Polymestor for killing Polydorus." See Jones, *The Origins of Shakespeare* (Oxford: Clarendon Press, 1977), 98. Furthermore, Jones credits Grube for refining Madeleine Doran's description of *Hecuba*'s structure as "a loose play of two independent actions." See *Origins*, 98–100.

55. Emrys Jones cites C. O. McDonald's analysis of Aphthonius's use of Hecuba as an example of passive *ethopeia*, noting that he calls Hecuba "the cliche examplar of tragic emotionality." See Jones, 86. William Arrowsmith describes Hecuba's metamorphosis as a transformation from the "*mater dolorosa* of Troy" to the "bitch of Cynossema." See Arrowsmith, Introduction to *Hecuba*, 4.

56. In his own argument, Jones pursues a direct comparison between *Hecuba* and *Titus Andronicus*. See Jones, 100.

57. North, Plutarch's *Lives*, ed. 1579, EE1.

58. James A. Freeman, though he does not explore Plutarch's *Life of Epaminondas*, sees relevance in the capping reference to Epaminondas in the anecdote as it appears in North's translation of *Life of Pelopidas*. Freeman, in fact, draws a parallel between Pelopidas and the Ghost in *Hamlet*, suggesting that each is in confinement. He goes on to posit the following claim: "Presumably the tyrant views Epaminondas as an embodiment of Nemesis who has come to punish crimes. . . . The example of Alexander allows Hamlet to begin his own regeneration. By staging the plays he can change from prisoner to judge, from 'John-a-dreams' (2.2.595) to avenging agent and from spectator to cunning director." Though his exploration of parallels is complex, Freeman's emphasis on this moment as the crucial turning place in Hamlet's transformation is direct. See Freeman, "Hamlet, Hecuba, and Plutarch," *Shakespeare Studies* 7 (1974) 201.

59. See North, Plutarch's *Lives*, ed. 1603, b3v.

60. Gregory, 112.

61. See Jones, 92. Here he refers to Lucas's *Euripides and his Influence* (1923).

62. Arrowsmith, *Hecuba*, ed. 1972, 4.

63. Jones, 96. In his study of the influence of Euripides on Shakespeare, Jones makes a compelling argument for the greater importance of this translation: "This needs to be stressed, since historians of the Elizabethan drama have never made any connection between Erasmus's translations and the rise of Shakespearian tragedy, nor has *Hecuba* ever figured in discussion of the Elizabethan revenge play." See Jones, 90–105.

64. Roger Ascham, *The Scholemaster*, in Hardison, *English Literary Criticism*, 62–63.

65. Ascham, *The Scholemaster*, in Hardison, 63.

66. Ascham, 65.

67. See Jones, 93.

68. Ascham, 67.

69. Jenkins, ed. 1982, 260.

70. See Martin Luther, *On the Bondage of the Will*, in *Luther and Erasmus: Free Will and Salvation*. E. Gordon Rupp and Philip S. Watson, eds. (Philadelphia: The Westminster Press, 1969), 143.

71. Martin Luther, *On the Bondage of the Will*, 121–22.

72. G. Blakemore Evans, ed., *The Riverside Shakespeare* (Boston: Houghton Mifflin Company, 1974), 1840. While this edition is a convenient reference, it might be well to point out, as Eric Rasmussen has to me in a private correspondence, that Evans does not acknowledge Steevens as the first to have pointed to Harvey's marginalia as pertinent to the dating of *Hamlet*. See Steevens's letter to Garrick dated "Hampstead, Saturday Evening, 1771," in *The Private Correspondence of David Garrick*, ed. James Boaden (London, 1831): 1:451–54, which is reprinted in Vickers, 5:456–65.

73. Samuel Johnson, ed., *The plays of William Shakespeare* (London: J. and R. Tonson, 1765), 1:111.

74. I am grateful to Joanna Gondris, Bernice W. Kliman, and Eric Rasmussen, who have made valuable suggestions during the process of revision, and to my colleagues James Conley and John Reiss for their assistance in discussing various translations that I have cited.

Lewis Theobald and Theories of Editing

Caroline Roberts

In *Textual Scholarship: An Introduction,* D. C. Greetham observes that Lewis Theobald's famous textual emendation "'a' babbled o' green fields' ('he babbled of green fields,' in Mistress Quickly's account of the death of Falstaff in *Henry V*) in place of the apparently nonsensical 'a *table* of green fields'" is an exception to the general tendency of textual criticism in two mutually exclusive directions.[1] The first situates the text and the editorial recovery of authorial intentions in the discipline of philology, where textual criticism is one aspect of *Altertumswissenschaft,* or the science of ancient times. The second direction makes textual criticism a more specialized, or technical discipline.[2] These two directions loosely define a number of editorial "schools." The Greg-Bowers "school of eclectic editing" can be regarded both as an heir of the old philology and as a leader in the newer direction towards technical concentration. Recent proponents of "a sociology of texts," such as Jerome McGann and D. F. McKenzie, may be seen as revisionists of the old philology in their concern to recover a text's entire social history. The purpose of this paper is to consider broadly Theobald's editorial theory and practice in relation to these two directions and these two schools. Instead of regarding Theobald's editing as an exception to textual criticism's general tendency in two directions, I should like to suggest that Theobald's emendations display a concern to identify authorial intentions and are technically proficient, and that his explanatory notes are not only historically inclined, but are also adumbrations of a social theory of textual criticism. In other words, Theobald's editing may be thought to participate in the two directions that Greetham considers "mutually exclusive." What is especially noteworthy is that these two tendencies of textual criticism suggest two distinct conceptions of the author. One sees Shakespeare as a natural genius, personally and necessarily connected to his art. The other emphasizes the collaborative, social nature of authorship. Theobald's editorial practice, engaging in both trends of criticism, is informed by both of these views of authorship and authority, raising questions about the genesis and attribution of textual meaning which this paper also attempts to explore.

Obviously, this paper does not claim to cover the entire corpus of writings by recent theorists, but it can point to the salient features of these writings as a means of considering the inclinations of Theobald's editorial work.

Before considering Theobald's work, it is worth discussing Greetham's account of the general tendencies which textual criticism has taken, and from which, in his view, Theobald is excluded. Greetham argues that after Scaliger textual criticism's movement towards history and technology continues with Nicolaus Heinsius's work on collation and the philological approach of the Maurists (317–18). Bentley, Pope, and Theobald, as already noted, are seen as exceptions to this historical trend, and, indeed, conjecture prevails in the editing of vernacular texts until F. J. Furnivall makes the practice historical with such inventions as the Early English Text Society (320). In the meantime *Altertumswissenschaft* dominates biblical and classical studies and is tempered in the late eighteenth century by a rejection of the quest for lost originals. Realism displaces optimism for recovery of the past and is reinforced by the Lachmannian system with its circumscribed, but realizable, goal: recovery of a supposed archetype, but not the author's fair copy. The way to achieve this goal is through recension, or the charting of variants, and emendation, or the rectification of error. Technical procedure triumphs over enlightened (or inspired) conjecture (322–23).

Although Lachmannism was criticized for logical deficiencies, Paul Maas, Dom Henri Quentin, W. W. Greg, and Vinton Dearing elaborated and modified filiation theory.[3] Their work focused on the internal features of texts for mapping family descent. It was the study of a text's "carriers," however, that was to advance most in the twentieth century.[4] The major catalysts for this trend were three enumerative/descriptive catalogues: Gordon Duff's descriptive catalogue of the type-forms of English incunabula (1896), Robert Proctor's index to the incunabula of the British Museum and the Bodleian Library (1898), and Pollard and Redgrave's *Short-Title Catalogue*. These catalogues sparked an interest in the material features of early printed books that became the "science" of analytical bibliography, or the "new bibliography." The central theorist of the "new bibliography" was W. W. Greg; and Greg's most influential ideas are found in his essay "The Rationale of the Copy-Text."[5] The purpose of Greg's "Rationale" was to address editorial problems created by printing conditions in Renaissance England, and to this end Greg recommended that substantives (a text's words) be distinguished from accidentals (spelling, punctuation, capitalization). An editor of a Renaissance text should ideally use an authorial manuscript as copy-text for accidentals and later states of the text for authorized substantive changes. This practice would prevent confusion of an author's accidentals with contaminations of those accidentals inadvertently introduced by compositors.

By advocating multiple authorities for copy-text, Greg headed a school of "eclectic" editing that has encouraged editors to conflate multiple witnesses to produce what Greetham calls "the text that never was," but that should have been (334). Indeed, to whatever extent this practice is waning, it is producing a nostalgia among even the most eminent of revisionists. Consider Donald McKenzie's remarks in his British Library lectures:

> At a moment like this, it is tempting to call in Aristotle's distinction between history and poetry as a model of the problem. History tells what was: it records the versions. Poetry—the more serious and philosophical art—tells us what *ought* to be. To my mind, there is a moral imperative in that "ought" which I personally find compelling. It can function in two ways. It may drive us, as historical scholars, to recover a "true" text from the detritus of versions; or it may direct us, as creative readers/writers, to generate the meanings that most matter to us. In either case, there is an act of creation involved.[6]

But if Greg has confused the roles of editor and poet, he has also made textual scholars more technologically aware by bringing technical information on the history of printing to bear on textual studies. In this respect, Greg's influence is apparent in the work of recent theorists like Randall McLeod, whose investigations of Renaissance typesetting problems—problems involving kerns, type spacing, and ligatures in the (mis)-representation of manuscript copy—focus on the technical aspects of the printing process: "with an eye on the original type sorts and their settings (something we cannot see in our old-spelling editions) we can divine within loose limits the compositorial options and exigencies."[7]

If eclectic editing based on a recognition of multiple textual authorities and a concern for the technical aspects of printing characterizes the "new bibliography," then one may see the "new bibliography" adumbrated in Theobald's editing of Shakespeare. As Peter Seary observes in *Lewis Theobald and the Editing of Shakespeare,* Theobald's first rule is to collate multiple witnesses of Shakespeare's texts: "I have thought it my Duty, in the first place, by a diligent and laborious Collation to take in the Assistance of all the older Copies."[8] Theobald collated quarto and folio texts, and occasionally quarto copies of the same edition when available to him, since he recognized that changes could be made to texts during the printing process. Further, Theobald considered the connections between quartos and folio in his collations and occasionally speculated about the nature of the copy-text for different witnesses. Theobald was aware, for instance, that theater companies hoped to monopolize their plays and proposes that many quartos were copied from shorthand transcriptions of performances:

> Hence, many Pieces were taken down in Short-hand, and imperfectly copied by Ear, from a *Representation:* Others were printed from piece-meal Parts surreptitiously obtain'd from the Theatres, uncorrect, and without the Poet's Knowledge. To some of these Causes we owe the train of Blemishes, that deform those Pieces which stole singly into the World in our Author's Lifetime.[9]

Theobald does not indicate, however, which texts might have originated in this way. Disregarding his reprints, Theobald possessed eight so-called "good" quartos, three quartos based on "good" quartos, and six "bad" quartos (including the "good" and "bad" quartos of *Romeo and Juliet*).[10] Unfortunately, he offers no discussion of how "good" and "bad" quartos of a play may relate to each other, and his allusion to shorthand has no counterpart either in his annotations in his edition or in his correspondence.[11] Theobald's view that some quartos were printed from parts "surreptitiously obtain'd" seems to derive from Pope, who, influenced by Heminge and Condell's address "To the Great Variety of Readers," concludes that all quartos were surreptitiously printed.

The quartos, or "many Pieces," were not the only texts of Shakespeare to undergo corruption in Theobald's opinion; he also felt that the folio had unreliable origins: "When the *Players* took upon them to publish his Works intire, every Theatre was ransack'd to supply the Copy; and *Parts* collected which had gone thro' as many Changes as Performers, either from Mutilations or Additions made to them."[12] In holding this opinion, Theobald was again influenced by Pope, who remarks that the folio is printed from copies "which had lain ever since the Author's days in the play-house, and had from time to time been cut or added to arbitrarily."[13] Theobald is, however, the first to recognize the authority of the first folio over successive editions, which were likely to multiply errors with each successive setting of type.[14] He was also the first to suggest, despite his apparent pessimism about the folio's origins, that the folio sometimes derives its text from a quarto. For instance, of the lines in *Othello* (4.2.188–90) "*You have told me, she hath receiv'd them, and return'd me Expectations and Comforts of sudden Respect and* Acquaintance," Theobald notes that "This was, first, the Reading of the Player-Editors, who, I presume, did not understand the Reading of the old *Quarto* [*acquintance*], which I take to have been the Poet's Word, *Acquittance;* i.e. a Requital, a proper Return of her Favours."[15]

Theobald not only collated multiple witnesses of Shakespeare's texts, but, adumbrating what may be called a Greg-Bowers school of eclectic editing, he also conflated them. Unlike Greg, however, Theobald did not conflate texts in order to reproduce accurately Shakespeare's accidentals—for example, like Johnson, he considered the matter of "pointing" to lie wholly within his jurisdiction. Rather, it seems that Theobald conflated the different states of Shakespeare's texts simply to bring together as much of "what Shakespeare wrote" as possible. Shakespeare's plays suffered a radical instability during the seventeenth century. As Johnson explains:

> No other authour ever gave up his works to fortune and time with so little care: no books could be left in hands so likely to injure them, as plays frequently acted, yet continued in manuscript: no other transcribers were likely to be so little qualified for their task as those who copied for the stage, at a time when the lower ranks of the people were universally illiterate: no other editions were made from fragments so minutely broken, and so fortuitously reunited; and in no other age was the art of printing in such unskilful hands.[16]

It was in response to presumed conditions like these that Theobald endeavoured a synthesis and stabilization of Shakespeare's texts.

For some recent theorists, such considerations do nothing to give conflation a better press. For "Random Cloud," an examination of editorial practices is good grounds for curtailing the practice of editing all together. Thus in "The Marriage of Good and Bad Quartos," McLeod censures editors for mangling Shakespeare's texts.[17] Far from displaying any of McKenzie's nostalgia for the text that ought to be, McLeod berates editors for reducing "definitive" texts that chop "bad" quartos "into messes," functioning "'ideally' to save the reader from the pains and pleasures of actual multiplicity" (422). The particular target of McLeod's ire is the editor of the new Arden edition of *Romeo and Juliet,* Brian Gibbons.[18] I should like to consider briefly some of McLeod's complaints with the Arden edition and compare Gibbons's treatment of the text with Theobald's as an indication of the latter's editorial habits.

In the first place, McLeod attacks Gibbons for speaking of "the Good Quarto" and "the Bad Quarto" (423). Since Theobald does not discuss the relationship of the two quartos, and certainly does not use the moral categories to which McLeod objects, one can proceed to McLeod's next problem with Gibbons, which concerns Gibbons's desire to reproduce in his edition "what Shakespeare wrote" (423). For McLeod, this is a limited goal for the editor of drama, but, allowing it, he then questions Gibbons's claim to have achieved it. McLeod begins with the "grey-ey'd morn" speech (2.2.188–91 in Gibbons), which is assigned both to Romeo and to the Friar in the second quarto (1599). Gibbons gives the speech to Romeo, arguing that Shakespeare marked the second speech for deletion and that it was mistakenly printed. McLeod claims that Gibbons curbs the play's "richness," although he acknowledges that a production of the play would use the speech only once. In this case, he continues, the first quarto (1597) should "swing sharply into prominence before the editor's scrutiny," since Q1 is held to recount an actual production. Q1 assigns the speech to the friar. McLeod scorns Gibbon for apparently considering Q1's speech assignment as "Bad Shakespeare" (426). Theobald follows Q1.[19] Theobald also follows Q1 in presenting two lines in a speech by Benvolio not found in Q2 (1.4.7–8): "Nor a without-book prologue faintly spoke / After the prompter, for our entrance."[20] Gibbons also incorporates these lines into his edition, but since this means that Gibbons conflates Q1 and Q2 in his text, McLeod charges Gibbons with confounding the aesthetic differentiation of each version of the play (429). If this is what Gibbons has done, however, Theobald too is guilty of raising content above form. Theobald follows Q2 for most of the text, including the lines (4.1.109–13) singled out by McLeod (Q2, 13ᵛ):

> Then as the manner of our countrie is,
> In thy best robes vncouered on the Beere,
> Be borne to buriall in thy kindreds graue:
> Thou shall be borne to that same auncient vault,
> Where all the kindred of the *Capulets* lie.[21]

McLeod concentrates on this passage because Gibbons omits the third line as "a first version accidentally printed."[22] McLeod sees the friar's multiplicity as evidence of "*his* redundancy" (425). Theobald retains the third line, which meets McLeod's requirements for characterization, but by following Q2, he here produces an eclectic edition that conflates the Q1 and Q2 texts. Of course, the issue is complicated by the fact that, due to Tonson's stratagems to maintain control over the copyright of Shakespeare's plays, Theobald was required to use Pope's edition as his copy-text: Theobald follows Pope in each of the three cases considered above.[23] However, as the title page of his edition indicates, Theobald compared Pope's texts with folio and quarto versions of the plays: "The Works of Shakespeare [Pope's edition] . . . Collated with the Oldest Copies, and Corrected." Theobald is responsible for his collation and conflation of different states of Shakespeare's texts. He is responsible for providing an eclectic, "ideal" edition that passes for "what Shakespeare wrote." For McLeod, both Pope's and Theobald's editions would be, like Gibbons's, editions in which "Artifice becomes Artofficial, and Ideology covers Reality" (431).

McLeod's view is not uncommon: the ideology of editions that claim to present "what Shakespeare wrote" has received a great deal of attention from recent textual theorists. For Jerome McGann, the work of

Fredson Bowers has brought the matter to the fore. Bowers introduced
the concept of "final intentions" to Greg's "Rationale of the Copy-Text"
in order to deal with editorial problems associated with texts of modern
periods.[24] McGann acknowledges that Greg's "Rationale" lends itself to
intentionalist formulations: Greg's concern to select the "author's originals" (particularly in accidentals) in an ancestral series of monogenous
texts becomes a theory of final intentions when an editor faces numerous
authoritative documents. The problem with all such formulations for
McGann is that they propound ideas of literary production and textual
authority which privilege a Romantic concept of the author working in
isolation. Because these ideas go unexamined, they function ideologically
to "distort our theoretical grasp of the 'mode of existence of a literary
work of art.'" For McGann, this mode of existence is social rather than
personal (8).

In keeping with their production of eclectic editions of "what Shakespeare wrote," both Pope and Theobald (in one aspect of their editorial
endeavors) conceive of Shakespeare as a Romantic, solitary, autonomous
author. As Seary observes, Pope's admiration of Shakespeare emphasizes
"the man as a natural genius" whose plays reveal their author's mind
(42). Pope prefers Shakespeare to Homer: "The Poetry of *Shakespear*
was Inspiration indeed; he is not so much an Imitator, as an Instrument
of Nature." Shakespeare "seems to have known the world by Intuition,
to have look'd thro' humane nature at one glance, and to be the only
Author that gives ground for a very new opinion, That the Philosopher
and even the Man of the world, may be *Born,* as well as the Poet."[25]
Pope's striking statement on Shakespeare's genius has a precedent in
Rowe's speculation on the chronology of Shakespeare's plays: "Art had
so little, and Nature so large a Share in what he did, that, for ought I
know, the Performances of his Youth, as they were the most vigorous,
and had the most fire and strength of Imagination in 'em, were the best."[26]

In *Shakespeare Verbatim,* Margreta de Grazia argues that Edmond
Malone's edition (1790) was the first to define Shakespeare in terms of
autonomy.[27] Influenced by Michel Foucault's recognition of the "invention of man" in the late eighteenth century, de Grazia suggests that Malone initiated a reorganization of literary studies by situating the authorial
subject as the organizing principle of literary and textual scholarship. In
de Grazia's view, Malone was responding, like everyone else at the time,
to "nothing less than those 'astonishing' revolutionary circumstances" of
the late eighteenth century (7). The problem with de Grazia's argument
is its neglect of the views of earlier editors: Rowe's and Pope's views of
Shakespeare as a natural genius predate the Enlightenment and the supposed originality of Malone's ideas within it.

Theobald also considered Shakespeare a genius. He did not believe, for instance, that "a Genius like *Shakespear's* should be judg'd by the laws of Aristotle."[28] Departing from Thomas Rymer, Theobald felt that considerations of character and language supersede those of plot: his concern for character and motive in drama indicates his proto-Romantic criticism; his concern for language reveals his interest in Shakespeare's personal style of expression. For Theobald, Shakespeare's figurative language reveals his analogical thought: "The third Species of *Obscurities*, which deform our Author, as the Effects of his own Genius and Character, are Those that proceed from his peculiar Manner of *Thinking*, and as peculiar Manner of *cloathing* those *Thoughts*."[29] Theobald's sensitivity to Shakespeare's style has editorial implications. For instance, he proposes "bawds" instead of "bonds" in the following lines in *Hamlet* (1.3.130)—

> *Do not believe his vows; for they are brokers,*
> *Not of that die which their investments shew*
> *But meer implorers of unholy suits,*
> *Breathing like sanctified and pious* BONDS,
> *The better to beguile—*

because "It is usual with our Poet, as his *Critical* Readers must have observed, to give those infamous Creatures the Style and Title of Brokers. . . . [With the emendation] a Chain of the same *Metaphors* is continued to the End."[30] The note typifies Theobald's concern for Shakespeare's style in proposing emendations and tempers de Grazia's suggestion that an awareness of personalized expression emerged only in the late eighteenth century: "Socially, politically, and epistemologically enfranchised, the individual takes possession of language as well, converting a discursive and transactional mode into a personalized and self-expressive one that makes language a convoluted allegory of consciousness" (9). For Theobald, Shakespeare's relation to his art is a personal one: his idiosyncratic style is necessarily connected to his peculiar mode of thinking.

Thus far, I have suggested that Theobald adumbrates a Greg-Bowers school of eclectic editing by collating and conflating different states of Shakespeare's texts, if for slightly different reasons. Theobald is not especially concerned to reproduce Shakespeare's accidentals, although he is concerned to reproduce as much of "what Shakespeare wrote" as possible. In keeping with these aims, Theobald has a conception of the author as an autonomous figure whose texts reflect the peculiarities of their author's mind. In addition to promoting eclectic editing and suggesting a Romantic view of the author, however, Greg brought a technical understanding of the printing process to bear on textual studies. I should now like to suggest that Theobald also adumbrates these concerns with technical matters relating to transmission.

In proposing emendations, Theobald attempts "to strip the veil of print from a text."[31] As an attorney, Theobald knew Elizabethan secretary script; as an assistant to John Stede, the prompter for John Rich's theatre company, Theobald gained an understanding of theatrical practices and dramatic manuscripts.[32] Both helped Theobald to visualize manuscripts from which compositors worked, to suggest possible mistakes made by compositors, and to introduce emendations of texts based on these considerations. Theobald's "happiest" emendation, according to Seary, occurs in *Romeo and Juliet* (1.1.153), where, in response to lines found in all the quartos, folios, and Pope's editions—

> As is the Bud bit with an envious Worm,
> *E're he can spread his sweet Leaves to the Air,*
> Or dedicate his Beauty to the SAME—

Theobald comments:

> Sure all the Lovers of *Shakespeare* and Poetry will agree with me that—*to the same*—is here a very idle, dragging *Parapleromatick,* as the Grammarians style it. I do not think the Author was any ways necessitated to it, since he might by an additional *Epithet* in the foregoing Verse have avoided the Fault objected, and express'd his Thought with more Elegance: As thus,
>
> > *E're he can spread his sweet* and infant *Leaves,*
> > *Or dedicate his Beauty to the* Air.
>
> This would have been the Natural Way of conveying his Idea, without those unpleasing *Expletives:* but SHAKESPEARE generally in his *Similies* is accurate in the *Cloathing* of them; and therefore, I believe, would not have overcharg'd This so *insipidly.* When we come to consider that there is some Power else besides *balmy* Air, that brings forth, and makes the tender Buds spread Themselves, I do not think it improbable that the Poet wrote thus;
>
> > *E're He can spread his sweet Leaves to the* Air,
> > *Or dedicate his Beauty to the* SUN.*
>
> *Or Sunne, according to the old Spelling, which brings it nearer to the Traces of the corrupted Text.[33]

In the Preface to his edition of Shakespeare, Theobald indicated his concern that his emendations be "establish'd with a very high Degree of moral Certainty";[34] his use of the *ductus litterarum* or "the Traces of the Letters" was one means of alleviating doubt. Of course, he also anticipates Greg's concern for the technicalities of printing, in this instance possible compositorial misreading of manuscript copy.

Instances of Theobald's use of the *ductus litterarum* abound both in *Shakespeare Restored* and in his edition. The only other example I wish to mention here, however, is his emendation "a' babled of green fields," discussed by Greetham at the start of this paper as an exception to textual criticism's general tendency towards historical methodology and technical proficiency. Theobald suggested the emendation in response to Pope's view that "a Table of greene fields" in the folio referred to "a Table of Greenfield's"—Greenfield supposedly being the name of a property-manager.[35] Theobald objected to this explanation, first, because he knew that the names of property-men were never inserted in prompt-books; and, second, because he knew that directions for properties were always indicated in prompt-books about a page in advance of their needed appearance. In place of Pope's solution, Theobald initially proposes "*and* a' talked *of green fields*," which accords with the idea that people near death, and especially "Those in a Calenture," may talk of green fields. Further, Theobald notes that "talked" is like "table;" but he continues: "we may still come nearer to the Traces of the Letters, by restoring it thus;

—for his Nose *was as sharp as a Pen, and* a' babled *of green Fields.*

To *bable,* or *babble,* is to mutter, or speak indiscriminately, like Children that cannot yet talk, or dying Persons when they are losing the Use of Speech."[36]

Although his technical discussions are short, due chiefly to his fear of being labeled a narrow pedant, it should be noted that Theobald's considerations of compositorial misreadings of secretary script contradict Greetham's view of Theobald's emendations as exceptions to a movement towards technical proficiency. In fact, as Seary observes, it can be said of Theobald what W. W. Greg says of "new bibliographers," that he brings criticism "down from the fascinating but all too often barren heights of aesthetic and philosophic speculation to the concrete familiarities of the theatre, the scrivener's shop, and the printing house."[37]

Theobald's emendations may anticipate concerns of the "new bibliographers"; at the same time, his explanatory notes, where he rarely proposes emendations, may be thought to anticipate a social theory of textual criticism. Of the recent proponents of such a theory, McGann is one of the better known. McGann maintains that literary works are fundamentally social products whose authority is initiated within the conventions and limits of literature's prevailing institutions.[38] It is ironic that apart from a discussion (95–100) of sonnet 129 McGann tends to neglect Shakespeare, whom he seems content to leave to the "new bibliographers":

Greg's rationale represented a special variation on that theory [of the critical edition], one designed to take account of the peculiar typographical conditions which prevailed before the eighteenth century. But the theory of final intentions, though a corollary derivative from the initial theory of the critical text and its special variant, has been asked to perform the same function under conditions which are structurally far different. (35)

McGann feels that sixteenth and seventeenth-century texts, and "pre-eminently Shakespeare's texts," generate "special issues and problems," which Greg addresses, but that lie beyond the scope of his own social theory. McGann's chief interest lies with texts of post-seventeenth-century periods (18). Independently of McGann, however, McKenzie has elaborated a "sociology of texts" that is not period-specific and that "directs us to consider the human motives and interactions which texts involve at every stage of their production, transmission and consumption. It alerts us to the roles of institutions, and their own complex structures, in affecting the forms of social discourse, past and present." McKenzie claims that "until very recently," textual critics have neglected these realities.[39] Theobald may be an exception to McKenzie's generalization.

In terms of understanding the role of institutions in relation to the production of textual meaning, it has already been noted that Theobald's work with John Stede, the prompter, provided him with a knowledge of the ways of the theater. This experience enabled him to refute Pope's suggestion that "a table of Greenfield's" was a direction to a property-man and to propose his own emendation—an example, perhaps, of how an institution (the theater) does *not* affect a text. Another example of Theobald's interest in a text's operation in a theatrical context may suffice. A stage direction in the second quarto and first folio texts of *Romeo and Juliet,* "*Enter Romeo and Peter,*" receives the following note:

> But *Peter* was a Servant to the *Capulets;* besides, he brings the Mattock and Crow to wrench open *Juliet*'s Grave, an Office hardly to be intrusted with a Servant of that Family. We find a little above, at the very Beginning of this Act, *Balthazar* is the Person who brings *Romeo* the News of his Bride's Death: and yet, at the Close of the Play, *Peter* takes upon him to depose that He brought those Tidings. *Utri creditis,* therefore *Peter* is a lying Evidence, suborn'd by the blundering Editors. We must therefore cashier him, and put *Baltha-zar* on his proper Duty. The Source of this Error seems easy to be accounted for; *Peter*'s Character ending in the 4th Act, 'tis very probable the same Person might play *Balthazar,* and so be quoted on in the prompter's Book as *Peter.*[40]

In suggesting that a book-keeper's marginal note creates an inconsistent character designation, Theobald displays a sensitivity to the interactions of texts with stage-management, showing, what McKenzie calls, "the human presence in any recorded text" (20).

Theobald was also aware that reception determined forms of theatrical discourse. During the time that Theobald worked with Rich's theater company, pantomime was enjoying huge success at the box office, and Theobald devised a series of pantomimes that bolstered Rich's fortunes until his death in 1761. Theobald could be self-conscious about his role in pantomime and ascribed its popularity to the town's debased taste. At the same time, he acknowledged the enjoyment it gave audiences and, as a consequence, qualified his views on the importance of neo-Aristotelian rules for drama. For his Shakespearian criticism, this meant that Theobald retained passages that may have pleased Shakespeare's audiences, even though he disliked them personally:

> I have made it a Rule throughout this edition, to replace all those Passages, which Mr. *Pope* in his Impressions thought fit to *degrade*. As We have no Authority to call them in Question for not being genuine; I confess, as an Editor, I thought I had no Authority to displace them. Tho', I must own freely at the same time, that there are some Scenes (particularly, in this play [*Love's Labour's Lost*];) so very mean and contemptible, that One would heartily wish for the Liberty of expunging them. Whether they were really written by our Author, whether he penn'd them in his boyish Age, or whether he purposely comply'd with the prevailing Vice of the Times, when *Puns, Conundrum,* and *quibbling* Conceits were as much in Vogue, as *Grimace* and *Arlequinades* are at this wise Period, I dare not take upon me to determine.[41]

Accompanying Theobald's recognition of the importance of consumption in determining textual content is the beginning of an understanding of the author that differs sharply from his view of the artist as an autonomous figure. What Theobald seems to recognize is that sometimes the location of the authority of texts, as McGann writes, "becomes dispersed beyond the author" (84). That the "Vice of the Times" may be responsible for certain passages is not sufficient grounds to question those passages' authenticity.

As Theobald's reference to "Mr. *Pope*" makes clear, Pope did not share Theobald's unwillingness to displace passages he disliked. In editing *Love's Labour's Lost,* for instance, he degraded 222 lines, deleted others completely, and marked four scenes with triple daggers to signify his aversion to them. In *Romeo and Juliet,* he degraded or omitted over 200 lines. Like Theobald, Pope tended to attribute the "authority" of these passages to either Shakespeare's audiences or his fellow players: "But I think the two Disadvantages which I have mentioned (to be obliged to please the lowest of people, and to keep the worst of company) if the consideration be extended as far as it reasonably may, will appear sufficient to depress the greatest Genius upon earth."[42] In his account of the folio, he gives the players direct responsibility for "trifling and bombast passages": "For whatever had been added, since those Quarto's, by the actors, or had stolen from their mouths into the written parts, were from thence conveyed into the printed text, and all stand charged upon the Author."[43] But if Pope recognizes the "authority" of audiences or players, he does not value it, and prefers certain quarto texts, such as the first quarto of *Romeo and Juliet,* to the folio. To the extent that Pope's views cater to (or are informed by) the sensibilities of eighteenth-century audiences, who did not like the word-play in texts like *Love's Labour's Lost,* Pope's (mis)reading of Shakespeare may be, what McKenzie calls, a "historical necessity, an interesting document itself in the nature of reading and the history of the book" (17).

Theobald accepts Pope's lists of *dramatis personae,* his regularization of speech prefixes, his stage directions, and his act and scene divisions, which Pope had accepted from Rowe,[44] creating a chain of editorial "authority" in accordance with Tonson's maneuvers to maintain control over Shakespeare's plays, and thereby lending credence to McGann's view of the importance of a work's accumulated social history. That Theobald does not accept Pope's degradation of passages is explicable in terms of his desire to explain rather than to emend Shakespeare where possible. In particular, Theobald was concerned to explain words and phrases in Shakespeare made obscure by the passage of time. One form these explanations took was the use of parallel readings. Indeed, as Seary observes, Theobald was the first to use this technique in the study of an English author (8). Further, he was the first to stress the importance not only of Shakespeare's classical sources, but also of Shakespeare's reading of English texts. To give an example, Theobald was able to identify "The dreadful Sagittary" in *Troilus and Cressida* (5.5.14–15) not as Teucer, as Pope suggested, but as the beast *Sagittarye* in "the old Chronicle, containing the three Destructions of Troy, printed by Caxton in 1471, and Wynken de Werde in 1503," from which Theobald quotes liberally to demonstrate how "our Poet obtained this circumstance." Theobald's parallel readings attest to the fact that a text's "forms and meanings derive from other texts" (McKenzie, 50). They also demonstrate Theobald's concern for "the relation between past meanings and present uses of verbal texts," which is one of the most obvious concerns of textual scholarship according to McKenzie (12–13).

Theobald's use of parallel readings is part of his larger project to situate Shakespeare historically in his period. Theobald felt that obscurities in Shakespeare could be explained not only by reference to other texts, but also by reference to the cultural context of Shakespeare's plays. In this sense, Theobald may be regarded as one of the earliest "new historicists." Of course, juxtaposing Shakespeare's texts with social contexts requires a sense of the plays' chronology, and although credit for addressing the problem of chronology is usually given to Malone or to Capell, Theobald proposed dates for fifteen plays in his edition. His proposals have editorial implications. For instance, where Pope had degraded Othello's tale of "men whose heads / Do grow beneath their shoulders" (1.3.144–45),[45] Theobald was able to quote from Ralegh's *Discoverie . . . of Guiana* (1596) in support of the passage: "They are call'd *Ewaipanomaws*, they are reported to have their *Eyes* in their *Shoulders*, and their *Mouths* in the middle of their *Breasts*." Further, Theobald comments on Ralegh's status:

> Sir *Walter*, at the time that his Travels were publish'd, is styled Captain of her Majesty's Guard, Lord Warden of the *Stannaries*, and Lieutenant General of the County of *Cornwal*. If we consider the Reputation, as the ingenious *Martin Folkes* Esq; observ'd to me, any thing from such a Person, and at that time in such *Posts*, must come into the World with, we shall be of Opinion that a Passage in *Shakespeare* need not be *degraded* for the Mention of a Story, which, however strange, was countenanc'd with such an Authority. *Shakespeare*, on the other hand, has shewn a fine address to Sir *Walter*, in sacrificing so much Credulity to such a *Relation*.[46]

Once again, underlying Theobald's note is a view of the author radically at odds with his conception of Shakespeare as a solitary genius whose texts reflect the autonomous workings of his own mind. In Theobald's explication, Shakespeare's play is here the product less of an intention than of determinate social circumstances: Ralegh's voyages, his accounts of them, and his status. In this sense, it may be said that this part of Othello's story is the achieved result of Shakespeare's and Ralegh's collaboration, and, further, that this is recognized by Theobald. When Theobald turns to plays like *Macbeth* and *King Lear*, he suggests that the limits of authority become dispersed among the monarchy. Of *Macbeth* he writes:

> [I]t will not be amiss to observe, that this fine Play, tis probable, was not writ till after Q. *Elizabeth*'s Death. These Apparitions, tho very properly shewn with Regard to *Macbeth*, yet are more artfully so, when we consider the Address of the Poet in complimenting K. *James* I. here upon his uniting *Scotland* to *England*: and when we consider too, the Family of the *Stuarts* are said to be the direct Descendants from *Banquo*.[47]

When considering *King Lear*, Theobald notes Shakespeare's use of Samuel Harsnett's *Declaration of Egregious Popish Impostures* in Edgar's speeches (as Poor Tom), and concludes that the allusion to the Jesuits' fraudulent exorcisms is again a compliment to James I.[48] Theobald's observations may anticipate those of Stephen Orgel, who writes of Spenser: "Spenser continually asserts that the *authority* of his text derives not from his genius but from the poem's subject and patron, the queen. Our tendency is to dismiss this claim as flattery. Flattery it may be, but it cannot be dismissed on that account . . . the question of authority in Spenser's text is both crucial and profoundly problematic."[49] Like Orgel, Theobald seems aware that the reception of *Macbeth* and *Othello* by monarchical institutions has a role in determining textual meaning.

By examining Shakespeare's plays in relation to their historical contexts, Theobald adumbrates a "sociology of texts" that considers texts to be social products and sees "authority" as collaborative. To suggest that Theobald does not participate in textual criticism's tendency towards historical methodology, as Greetham suggests, does not seem much to the point.[50] Neither does it seem particularly apt to perceive Theobald's emendations as an exception to technical proficiency, as I have also maintained. It may still be fair to suggest, nonetheless, that the two directions are incompatible, and, further, that they are founded on incompatible assumptions about the status of the author. In the second of his British Library lectures, McKenzie refers to the phrase "The broken phial" in *Areopagitica,* where Milton describes books as preserving "as in a violl the purest efficacie and extraction of that living intellect which bred them" (22). Theobald's opinion of Shakespeare as a genius and his production of an eclectic text that presents "what Shakespeare characteristically wrote" encourages us to view his edition as a phial, which "heightens the ideas of enclosure, of the text as contained, determined, stable, of the author within, both clearly visible and enduringly present" (23). But if Theobald was among the first to conceive of the author as a Romantic figure, as an autonomous person whose modes of thoughts determined his habits of expression, or, in short, his text's meanings, he was also among the first to suggest that texts interact with social contexts and are influenced, if not "authored," by them. If Theobald's edition of Shakespeare is, in one view, like a phial, and therefore closed, stable, and determinate, in another view, it is also open, unstable, and multiform. Poststructuralists were not the first to produce (if not revel in) multiplicity.

NOTES

1. D. C. Greetham, *Textual Scholarship: An Introduction* (New York: Garland Publishing Inc., 1992), 319.

2. Ibid, 314.

3. A. E. Housman, Joseph Bédier, Giorgio Pasquali, George Kane, and E. Talbot Donaldson were among those who criticized Lachmannism for its logical shortcomings and promotion of editorial timidity. See Greetham, 323–26.

4. Greetham, 330.

5. W. W. Greg, "The Rationale of the Copy-Text," *The Collected Papers of Sir Walter W. Greg,* ed. J. C. Maxwell (Oxford: Clarendon Press, 1966), 374–91.

6. D. F. McKenzie, *Bibliography and the Sociology of Texts,* The Panizzi Lectures 1985 (London: The British Library, 1986), 30.

7. Randall McLeod, "Spellbound," *Play-Texts in Old Spelling: Papers from the Glendon Conference,* ed. Raymond C. Shady and G. B. Shand (New York: AMS Press, 1983), 26–55.

8. Lewis Theobald, ed. *The Works of Shakespeare* (1733) 1:xlii (hereafter cited as *1733*). See also Peter Seary, *Lewis Theobald and the Editing of Shakespeare* (Oxford: Clarendon Press, 1990), 154–55. This paper considers issues raised by Seary's book from a theoretical perspective.

9. *1733*, 1:xxxvii–xxxviii.

10. For an account of A. W. Pollard's division of quartos into "good" and "bad" classes and the perpetuation of this binarism by twentieth-century textual critics, see Paul Werstein, "Narratives About Printed Shakespeare Texts: 'Foul Papers' and 'Bad' Quartos," *Shakespeare Quarterly* 41. 1 (Spring 1990): 65–86.

11. In *Elizabethan Shorthand and the First Quarto of* King Lear (Oxford: Basil Blackwell, 1949), G. I. Duthie argues that a system of shorthand was unavailable to Shakespeare's contemporaries. See Seary, 141, n. 34, and Werstein, 78.

12. *1733*, 1:xxxviii–xxxix.

13. Alexander Pope, ed. *The Works of Shakespear* (1725), 1:xvii (hereafter cited as *1725*).

14. Theobald's view of the different folio editions has been questioned because he lists the second edition (1632) as authoritative in his "Table" of editions. Seary argues that Theobald's table "reflects primarily his sense of their importance to him when he was engaged in forming his collection" (137).

15. *1733*, 7:470 n.

16. Samuel Johnson, *Johnson on Shakespeare* (The Yale Edition of the Works of Samuel Johnson), vol. 7, ed. Arthur Sherbo (New Haven: Yale Univ. Press, 1968), 52.

17. Random Cloud, "The Marriage of Good and Bad Quartos," *Shakespeare Quarterly,* 33. 4 (Winter 1982): 421–31.

18. (London: Methuen, 1980).

19. *1733*, 7:158–59.

20. *1733*, 7:141.

21. See *1733*, 7:199. Cf. Q1:

> O peace for shame, if not for charity.
> Your daughter liues in peace and happines,
> And it is vaine to wish it otherwise.
> Come sticke your Rosemary in this dead coarse,
> And as the custome of our Country is,
> In all her best and sumptuous ornaments,
> Conuay her where her Ancestors lie tomb'd. . . .

22. See Gibbons, 200.

23. Alexander Pope, ed. *The Works of William Shakespear,* 2d. ed. (London, 1728), 8:245, 130, 282 respectively.

24. Jerome J. McGann, *A Critique of Modern Textual Criticism* (Chicago: Univ. of Chicago Press, 1983, reissued Charlottesville: Univ. Press of Virginia, 1992), 19, 39–40.

25. *1725*, 1:ii–v.

26. Nicholas Rowe, ed. *The Works of Shakespear* (London, 1709), 1:vi–vii.

27. Margreta de Grazia, *Shakespeare Verbatim* (Oxford: Clarendon Press, 1991), 7.

28. Lewis Theobald, *The Censor* 60, 2d ed. (1717), 2:203–4.

29. *1733*, 1:xlvii. Theobald's further claim that it may be said of Shakespeare "what a celebrated Writer said of MILTON; Our *Language sunk under him, and was unequal to that Greatness of Soul which furnish'd him with such glorious Conceptions*" bears a noticeable resemblance to Shelley's observation that "When composition begins, inspiration is already on the decline, and the most glorious poetry that has ever been communicated to the world is probably a feeble shadow of the original conception of the Poet." "A Defense of Poetry," *Shelley's Prose*, rev. ed., ed. David Lee Clark (Albuquerque, 1966), 294; quoted in McGann, 102–3.

30. Lewis Theobald, *Shakespeare Restored: or, A Specimen of the Many Errors, as Well Committed, as Unamended, by Mr. Pope in his Late Edition of this Poet* (London, 1726), 118. Hereafter cited as *SR*. Theobald precedes these remarks with this exposition: "What Ideas can we form to our selves of a *breathing* BOND, or of its being *sanctified* and *pious?* Surely, so absurd a Thought could scarce come from SHAKESPEARE. The only tolerable Way of reconciling it to a Meaning without a Change, is to suppose that the Poet intends by the Word BONDS, *Verbal Obligations, Protestations;* and then, indeed, these Bonds may, in some Sense, be said to have *Breath:* But this is to make him guilty of overstraining the Word and Allusion; and it will hardly bear that Interpretation, at least, not without much Obscurity. As he, just before, is calling amorous Vows, *Brokers*, and *Implorers* of *unholy Suits;* I think, a Continuation of the plain and natural Sense directs us to an easy *Emendation,* which makes the whole Thought of a Piece, and gives it a Turn not unworthy of our Poet. I am, therefore, very willing to suspect it came from his Pen thus, tho' none of his *Editors* have been aware of it."

31. The phrase comes from Fredson Bowers, *On Editing Shakespeare and the Elizabethan Dramatists* (Philadelphia: Univ. of Pennsylvania Library, 1955), 87.

32. On the familiarity of attorneys with secretary script in the eighteenth century, see Appendix A in Seary, 213–14.

33. *SR*, 190–91; see Seary, 84.

34. *1733*, 1:xlii.

35. *1725*, 3:422.

36. *SR*, 137–38.

37. W. W. Greg, *The Editorial Problem in Shakespeare,* 3d ed. (Oxford: Clarendon Press, 1954), 3; see Seary's full discussion of this emendation, 76–82.

38. *A Critique of Modern Textual Criticism,* 48.

39. *Bibliography and the Sociology of Texts,* 6–7.

40. *1733*, 7:213–14.

41. *1733*, 2:109–10 n.

42. *1725*, 1:vi–vii.

43. *1725*, 1:xvi.

44. Rowe only provided act and scene divisions for the tragedies; Pope divided all the plays.

45. *1725*, 6:491.

46. *1733*, 7:392–93 n.

47. *1733*, 5:443–44 n.

48. Seary, 182–83. Stephen Greenblatt has considered Shakespeare's use of Harsnett in "Shakespeare and the Exorcists," *Shakespearean Negotiations* (Berkeley: Univ. of California Press, 1988), 94–128.

49. Stephen Orgel, "What is a Text?" *Research Opportunities in Renaissance Drama,* 24 (1981): 4.

50. It may also seem odd to regard social theories of textual criticism as distinct from "the old dispensation of *Altertumswissenschaft*" because the latter "finally could not sustain itself" against structuralist attacks on its linguistic core. Greetham argues that philology's diachronic assumptions were challenged by Saussure's conception of the synchronic status of language (315). If so, these assumptions have been reinstated by poststructuralists' recognition that the synchronic structure of any language is arbitrary, which makes the only worthwhile study of language a study of usages, past and present.

Part 3
Codifying Gender: The Disturbing Presence of Women

Editing Frailty in *Twelfth Night*: "Where lies your Text?"

Laurie Osborne

Detailed interest in the subsequent editing of Shakespeare's 1623 Folio arises most often when the text appears in multiple versions, like *Hamlet,* or where the Folio text is particularly littered with textual cruxes. However, *Twelfth Night*'s text in the Folio is unusually clean and free from the kinds of errors which commonly preoccupy textual bibliographers. Consequently the text of *Twelfth Night* receives little attention beyond admittedly fascinating speculations about its source text.[1] Nonetheless, the play experiences revealing emendations in the eighteenth century, changes which are all the more noticeable because of the relative clarity and accuracy of the text.

Like other Shakespearean texts, *Twelfth Night*'s textual history registers the ebb and flow of textual emendation: changes are introduced and later removed from the text as editorial opinion changes. For example, in 1747, William Warburton revised a speech in Act 1, scene 5 where Viola shows herself determined to stay and deal with Olivia, saying: "I am to hull here a little longer. Some mollification for your Giant, sweete Ladie. Tell me your minde. I am a messenger" (F, 259).[2] Concluding that the last two sentences were actually an exchange between Olivia and Viola, Warburton explained his proposed change in detail:

Viola—tell me your mind, I am a messenger.] These words must be divided between the two speakers thus,

> Oli. *Tell me your mind.*
> Vio. *I am a messenger.*

Viola growing troublesome, *Olivia* would dismiss her, and therefore cuts her short with this command, *Tell me your mind.* The other taking advantage of the ambiguity of the word *mind,* which signifies either *business* or *inclinations,* replies as if she had used it in the latter sense, *I am a messenger.*[3]

Certainly Warburton's emendation does make sense, as it fits with Olivia's insistent questions about the messenger's business. However, later editors felt that the Folio lines *could* make sense as they stood, arguing, as C. J. Sisson does, that "it is Olivia's mind that is in question, and Viola naturally couples her request for Olivia to declare her wishes with the assurance of her own authority as a messenger or herald from Orsino to hear and report that answer."[4] Therefore editors like those of the Arden, Riverside, and Oxford Shakespeare abandon Warburton's "exceptionally officious" interference, as Sisson sees it, and return both comments to Viola, as they appear in the Folio.

Perhaps more unexpectedly, the Folio *Twelfth Night* has experienced changes from the second Folio (1632) and through the eighteenth century which now appear, largely unremarked, in the body of the very modern editions which so often assure us, like Sisson, how little emendation is necessary in this particular text. This paper concentrates on one particular set of changes developed throughout the eighteenth century which typically still persists in contemporary editions. My example, which occurs in Viola's soliloquy in Act 2, scene 2, illustrates the complex origins and debates which underlie an emendation now taken as the norm. I argue that the logic of the Folio soliloquy makes more sense than its emendation in the context of the Folio and of Renaissance English stage practice.

The speech takes place in Act 2, scene 2. During the first act, after disguising herself as the boy Cesario in order to serve Illyria's Duke Orsino, Viola has revealed to the audience her love for the Duke. Orsino himself has grown so fond of Cesario that he entrusts the youth with the task of wooing the Lady Olivia on his behalf, arguing that her "constellation is right apt for this affair" (1.4.35–36).[5] Cesario does indeed prove to be a persuasive suitor; as a result, Olivia falls in love with the youth who is Viola in disguise. To reveal her feelings and insure that Cesario will return, Olivia sends her steward Malvolio to "return" a ring to Orsino's messenger. Once Malvolio leaves the ring with her, Viola gives a long soliloquy, underscoring the complications of her situation:

> I left no ring with her: what means this lady?
> Fortune forbid my outside have not charm'd her!
> She made good view of me; indeed so much
> That methought her eyes had lost her tongue,
> For she did speak in starts distractedly.
> She loves me, sure; the cunning of her passion
> Invites me in this churlish messenger.
> None of my lord's ring? Why, he sent her none.
> I am the man: If it be so, as 'tis,
> Poor lady, she were better love a dream.

Disguise, I see thou are a wickedness
Wherein the pregnant enemy does much.
How easy is it for the proper false
In women's waxen hearts to set their forms!
Alas, our frailty is the cause, not we,
For such as we are made of, such we be.
How will this fadge? My master loves her dearly,
And I, poor monster, fond as much on him;
And she, mistaken, seems to dote on me.
What will become of this? As I am man,
My state is desperate for my master's love:
As I am woman (now alas the day!),
What thriftless sighs shall poor Olivia breathe?
O time, thou must untangle this, not I,
It is too hard a knot for me t'untie.[6]

                                        (2.2.17–41)

The crucial pair of lines appear in boldface above; the Arden *Twelfth Night* offers them as emended by eighteenth-century editors. The Folio text of these lines reads quite differently: "Alas, O frailtie is the cause, not wee, / For as we are made, if such we bee" (F, 260).

The emendations to this couplet arise in two ways. The 1632 second Folio amends the Folio line "Alas, O frailtie is the cause, not wee" to read: "Alas, our frailty is the cause, not we." This transformation in the 1632 second Folio persists throughout all the eighteenth-century editions except Theobald's, meriting only a footnote to indicate the Folio version as in Steevens's 1778 edition and Malone's 1790 edition. Thus the second Folio and all subsequent texts turn a generalized "O frailtie" into "our frailty," implicitly locating weakness in the "womens waxen hearts" of the previous line more thoroughly than does the Folio. Nonetheless, the second Folio maintains the peculiarly ambiguous construction in the subsequent line: "For such as we are made, if such we bee." However, late eighteenth-century critics and editors found this comment cryptic and ultimately rewrote the statement to read: "For such as we are made of, such we be." This alteration not only moves punctuation and revises spelling, but also completely obliterates the conditional "if" clause from Viola's meditation here. Both the second Folio revision of "O" and this more complex revision have persisted through modern editions, often without much comment.[7]

Although these lines are emended regularly throughout the eighteenth century, the versions which those editors produce differ radically, disrupting in useful ways the comforting unanimity represented in the modern texts. As early as 1709, Nicholas Rowe felt obliged to revise the second line in a way which actually violates its meter: "For such as we are, we are made, if such we be."[8] Although Pope, Theobald, and Warburton stick to the Folio text version, without any note to explain the line, they, like Rowe, reproduce the second Folio emendation of "O" to "our" without comment. The second line again receives attention from Johnson in 1765, who suggests that,

> The next two lines are perhaps transposed, and should be read thus.
>
> > *For such as we are made, if such we be,*
> > *Alas, our frailty is the cause, not we.*[9]

Capell, in 1768, offers yet another version of the second line: "For, such as we are made, e'en such we be."[10] Altogether three separate though largely unexplained alternatives for emending the line appear before the version which Malone hails as, "the very happy emendation . . . suggested by Mr. Tyrwhitt."[11]

Both Styan Thirlby, in manuscript notes on two editions of Shakespeare, and Thomas Tyrwhitt, more publicly in his *Observations and Conjectures on some passages of Shakespeare's,* offer the current version, but neither supplies the logic underlying the revision.[12] The emendation which Malone adopts so enthusiastically had proven equally acceptable to Steevens in 1778, who comments extensively on both that change and the ongoing debate about "proper-false," and to Rann in 1787, who reproduces the current version without any commentary whatsoever. I quote Tyrwhitt, since his comments are cited by both Steevens and Malone:

> In the next two lines, instead of transposing them according to Mr. *Johnson's* conjecture, I am rather inclined to read the latter thus,
>
> > For such as we are made OF, such we be.[13]

Steevens augments this somewhat unrevealing statement by adding, "So, in the *Tempest:* "—we are such stuff / As dreams are *made of.*"[14] Of course, Steevens's support here is flawed since the Folio *Tempest* actually reads "we are such stuffe / As dreames are made on" (F, 15), the "of" being an emendation so common that recent textual editors never bother to remark the first instance, either simply changing it or simply noting that "on" means "of."[15] As proof that the *Twelfth Night* emendation is justified because another play ends a phrase with "made of," the line from *The Tempest* is hardly as secure a piece of evidence as one might wish. In fact, Steevens's 1778 edition completely subordinates the discussion of the two emended lines within a note that actually focuses on interpreting the "proper false." Steevens concentrates on his disagreement with Johnson's reading, only incidentally including Tyrwhitt's comments on the revision that appears in his text.

Malone takes up a more promising strategy. For one thing, he grants the line, "For such as we are made of, such we be," its own footnote. Acknowledging that the "old copy reads—made *if,*" Malone then plunges directly into Tyrwhitt's version. He then offers Steevens's reference to *The Tempest,* and the observation that "*Of* and *if* are frequently confounded in the old copies."[16] To support his own evidence, he then cites a series of examples of this printing flaw from *King John, Merchant of Venice,* and finally *As You Like It.* About the shifting punctuation he makes no comment. By omitting all of the diverse revisions offered by the earlier editors of the period and relegating Johnson's transposition to the earlier note, Malone's 1790 edition and Steevens's 1793 edition (which follows Malone's lead) start their discussions of the emended line from Tyrwhitt's emendation.[17] Malone's comments do, however, further develop Steevens's support for Tyrwhitt. Together Steevens and Malone offer explanations for changing "made, if" to "made of," and supply the logic which Tyrwhitt himself fails to give when he suggests the change. The effect in Malone's 1790 and Steevens's 1793 editions is to efface or displace the earlier alternatives and supplement the emendation after the fact with extended reasoning in support of the change.

In the case of both lines from Viola's soliloquy, we might take more seriously than C. J. Sisson does his own testy comment that "the excellence of the Folio text of this play ought to give pause to any interference with it."[18] As I will argue, the Folio text opens this speech to possible meanings beyond those dictated by the "clarification" in the later texts. The speech as it stands in the Folio makes good theatrical and even thematic sense. The couplet can certainly be read as the revised modern texts suggest—as Viola's fatalistic statement of her woman's nature and frailty held in common with Olivia. However, the Folio version offers more varied possibilities for interpretation and performance than does the revision. In fact, the emendation draws attention to the features of the speech which form its context, features that have seriously preoccupied the very editors who have changed these lines.

The soliloquy in Act 2, scene 2 is the first speech in which Viola fully confronts the problems of her male disguise. It is also one of the crucial places in the play where the presence of the boy-actress who would have played Viola on the Renaissance stage emerges from within the role, especially in her declaration, "I am the man" (F, 260). Viola follows this acknowledgement by asserting the evils of disguise, often associated with the boy-actress's usurpation of female dress on stage: "Disguise, I see thou art a wickednesse / Wherein the pregnant enemy does much." This leads in turn into an ambiguous and abstract statement about women's nature, "How easie is it, for the proper false / In womens waxen hearts to set their formes." One question here is *whose* waxen heart—Olivia's heart which has been so impressed with the false image of Cesario or Viola's heart which has succumbed to the temptation to dress and now to declare herself as a man? Another problem is what constitutes "their formes"—the women's form, the heart's form taken from the beloved or the form of the "proper false," here noticeably marked as third person plural? The various possible meanings here are amply recorded in the eighteenth-century attempts to gloss these lines in commentaries which often seem to overwhelm any attempt to discuss the considerable revision in the lines which follow.

Johnson gives the couplet, and comments: "This is obscure. The meaning is, how easy is disguise to women; how easily does *their own falsehood,* contained in their *waxen* changeable *hearts,* enable them to assume deceitful appearances."[19] For him, Viola's is the "waxen heart" impressed with the falseness of her disguise, but others vehemently disagree. Tyrwhitt objects the most strenuously, though his language is evasive in the extreme: "Mr. *Johnson* has given a strange comment, which I shall not transcribe, upon the first two lines. The sense of them, I think, is clearly this. *How easy is it for the proper false* [handsome counterfeits, beautiful outsides] *to set their forms* [to impress themselves] *in women's waxen hearts!*"[20] After refusing to quote and thus repeat Johnson's "strange comment," Tyrwhitt suggests that "it cannot be necessary to prove that *proper* signifies *handsome;* and *false* alludes to *Viola's* own case. She said just before, Fortune forbid my *outside* have not charm'd her!"(44–45). Nonetheless he does go on to prove his point in a footnote, offering several examples for each term.

Steevens at first disagrees with Johnson directly, if gently: "I am not certain that this explanation is just. Viola has been condemning those who disguise themselves, because Olivia had fallen in love with a specious appearance. How easy is it, she adds, for those who are at once *proper* (i.e., fair in appearance) and *false,* (i.e., deceitful) to make an impression on the hearts of women?" He then offers yet another possibility: "The *proper false* may be yet explained another way. Shakespeare sometimes uses *proper* for *peculiar.* So, in *Othello:* 'In my defunct and a proper satisfaction.' The *proper false* will then mean those who are *peculiarly false,* through premeditation and art. *To set their forms* means, to plant their images, that is to make an impression on their easy minds."[21] Steevens's double possibility here may overtly contradict Johnson's comment about disguise and women, but the emphasis both Tyrwhitt and Steevens place on Viola's appearance as the "proper-false" leaves open the implicit criticism which Johnson is leveling at the disguised and therefore deceitful Viola.

In this case as well, Malone supports Steevens, taking up the same technique of offering several analogs throughout the canon, including *Lucrece* and *Measure for Measure*. He is also careful to remove any taint which might attach to Viola's deceptions, closing his note with this observation from Mason: "Viola's reflection, how easy it was for those who are handsome to make an impression on the waxen hearts of women, is a natural sentiment for a girl to utter, who was herself in love."[22] While all of this meditation on the relationship between the "proper-false" and "women's waxen hearts" preoccupies the editors, they barely explain the next couplet's emendations. Nonetheless, the debate about the syntax and significance of the first two lines opens up interpretive possibilities and provides the context and strategies for questioning Tyrwhitt's emendation of the two lines which follow.

From the moment of her declaration of her "maleness" early in this soliloquy, Viola's meditation becomes more and more ambiguous through a series of statements which expose the boy-actress's disguise and comment upon his/her general seductiveness to both male and female playgoers.[23] At the same time, Viola's self-reference becomes more multiple, moving from "I" to "we," from "I am the man" to an imagined invocation of both her maleness and her femaleness at the end of the speech. Thus, within Viola's generalized meditation on the wickedness of disguise and its effect on "women's waxen hearts," an ambiguity in her invocation of frailty and, especially, in her own place within that commentary fits well with the unsettled identity which she experiences throughout the speech.

The first Folio's generalized statement, "Alas, O frailtie is the cause, not wee" (F, 260), distances "womens waxen hearts" from the new "we," maintaining the uncertainty of her position and gender within the abstract argument rather than anchoring Viola or frailty as only female. The directness of reference and implied antecedent of the second Folio's "our frailty" identifies Viola with those women in a speech which more often invokes the ambivalence of Viola's sexual identity. "Our frailty," as such, cannot grammatically refer to the ambiguous "proper false" since "they" have set "*their* formes" (emphasis mine). Thus, the shift to the personal "our" both allies "frailty" with "we" in the same line and links it to "women's waxen hearts," as the remaining available antecedent for "our." The second Folio thus forces the contrast between "their" and "our" in ways which define frailty as a female trait. In the Folio, by comparison, frailty is a general human condition that Viola invokes. As such, "frailty" can apply equally to the "proper false"—whether men or Viola's beguiling appearance as a man—and to women's hearts. These different possibilities are amply reflected in the ambivalent responses from editors about which character or rather characters are most implicated in that frailty.

In fact, despite Hamlet's all-too-influential comment, "Frailty, thy name is woman" (F, 154), most references to the term throughout the Folio concern men's frailty, particularly that of the body. Even Viola herself later in *Twelfth Night* makes it clear that *man's* frail nature is an issue, when she declares to Antonio, "I hate ingratitude in a man more / Than lying, vainnesse, babling, drunkennesse, / Or any taint of vice whose strong corruption / Inhabites our fraile blood" (F, 270). The "fraile blood" in this case is obviously identified as "in a man," although also claimed as hers with the possessive. Her assertion of male frailty is born out by Falstaff's comments on the same subject in *1 Henry 4:* "Thou see'st, I have more flesh then another man, and therefore more frailty" (F, 65). Although in *Merry Wives of Windsor* Falstaff divides his allusions to frailty between Mistress Ford and himself, he saves his generalizations for men: "bidde her thinke what a-man is: Let her consider his frailety, and then judge of my merit" (F, 52). In both plays, Falstaff both draws attention to frailty and actively embodies the concept.

However, the ways in which male and female frailty are characterized together throughout the canon resonate most usefully with Viola's meditation. In *Measure for Measure,* the term appears more frequently than in any other play, but usually with reference to man's frailty. The Duke is unsurprised by Angelo's treatment of Isabella, commenting, "but that frailty hath examples for his falling, I should wonder at him" (F, 72). Moreover, the example which the Duke offers in the very next scene is no woman, but Claudio who still mistakenly clings to life, "(by the instruction of his frailty)" (F, 74).

The relationship between male and female frailty is even more strongly suggested in the passage from *Measure for Measure* which Malone himself cites when supporting Steevens's explanation of the "proper false" setting their forms. Adopting Malone's own example and strategy while extending its context to include more of the exchange opens up the issue of masculine versus feminine frailty still further:[24]

> *Ang.* We are all fraile.
> *Isa.* Else let my brother die,
> If not a federie, but onely he
> Owe, and succeed to thy weaknesse.
> *Ang.* Nay, women are fraile too.
> *Isa.* I, as the glasses where they view themselves;
> Which are as easie broke as they make formes:
> Women? Helpe Heaven; men their creation marre
> In profiting by them: Nay call us ten times fraile,
> For we are soft, as our complexions are,
> And credulous to false prints.

                                              (F, 70)

As in Viola's speech, Isabella explicitly links frailty to the easy making of forms. However, she more clearly develops her view, in part because she speaks with Angelo. She automatically takes his initial comment as a reference to man's frailty, a general condition and therefore not exclusive to her brother Claudio. When Angelo insists that women are frail as well, Isabella acknowledges this only by asserting that men mar women, as indeed men supposedly create women—creating their form as a mirror does. In fact, her direct comments about women seem curiously tentative in the Folio punctuation though much more emphatic in many eighteenth-century versions which read "Women!—Help Heaven! Men their creation mar / In profiting by them. Nay call us ten times frail."[25] The frailty that so preoccupies the world of *Measure for Measure* is predominantly identified as a male condition, though pertaining as well to women, like Juliet, who have had their forms remade by men.

If anything, Emilia in *Othello* pursues this logic still more rigorously, arguing that women learn their frailty from men:

> . . . What is it that they do,
> When they change us for others? Is it Sport?
> I thinke it is: and doth Affection breed it?
> I thinke it doth: is't Frailty that thus erres?
> It is so too. And have not we Affections?
> Desires for Sport? and Frailty, as men have?
> Then let them use us well: else let them know,
> The illes we do, their illes instruct us so.
>
> (F, 334)

Sport, affection, and frailty are all here identified as initially male qualities, which women have as well. Thus the premise of her argument is that male frailty necessarily precedes female frailty—women may have these qualities, too, and in fact learn these "illes" from men, but male frailty is a given.

Both Isabella's and Emilia's discussions of frailty have much in common with Viola's soliloquy. Whereas Isabella likens female frailty to the mirror which can break as readily as take new forms, Viola claims the "proper-false" has set forms in women's waxen hearts. In both cases, it is ultimately the creation and destruction of forms which proves weakness. Emilia's more egalitarian argument shows women justified in sharing the actions and weaknesses of men; Viola, of course, literally embodies both male and female in her disguise. The *Twelfth Night* soliloquy, as a consequence, becomes a particularly interesting meditation on the subject.

However, Viola's situation differs from those of Isabella and Emilia in at least three important ways. First, because of her disguise, she is both male and female. Second, in her speech, she is actively acknowledging her double gender. Unlike either Isabella or Emilia, Viola's comments arise in a context where gender appears in conjunction rather than in opposition. Finally, Viola speaks alone on stage, reflecting upon and revealing her distinctive situation in soliloquy and spontaneously relating that situation to frailty. Both Isabella and Emilia address frailty within conversations where the issue has been raised by someone else. As a result of these differences, Viola presses the boundaries of performance: her soliloquy exposes the boy-actress within the role in ways that the other related speeches do not, even though those roles would also have been played by boy-actresses on the Renaissance stage.

Thus both the couplet's immediate context in Viola's soliloquy and its more general situation in the Folio suggest that "O frailtie" is as appropriate, if not more so, than "our frailtie." Since Viola's later reference to "our frail blood" is unequivocally linked to man's nature and "frailty" throughout the canon is, perhaps surprisingly, more often linked with men than women, there is no compelling reason to see the second Folio's "our frailty" as a natural correction. Obviously I would take issue with Furness's assertion that "O" is "a manifest misprint, corrected in the Second Folio."[26]

In fact, there is little reason to accept without question the second Folio's dramatic shift from a capitalized "O" to a longer and lower case "our." Even Matthew Black and Matthias Shaaber, who have collated the work of the seventeenth-century Folio editors and openly affirm the second Folio editor as "the first of Shakespeare's editors, and not the least brilliant,"[27] acknowledge that:

> The work of the revisers of the folio is guesswork; they have nothing to go on but their own intelligence, some knowledge of history, and their acquaintance with the language of the sixteenth century, the customs of the time, and the representation of Shakespeare's plays on the stage in their own day. . . . There is no clear proof that the revisers had any recourse to any printed or manuscript text other than that of the preceding folio, or to playhouse tradition. (97)

Even eighteenth-century editors, from time to time, insist that the second Folio editor's additions and changes be removed. Malone complains bitterly about a widely adopted addition in this same speech where the second Folio adds a word to the Folio line "That [sure] methought her eyes had lost her tongue": "*Sure,* which is wanting in the old copy, was added to complete the meter, by the editor of the second folio. The author of *Remarks &c on the text and notes of the last edition of Shakspeare,* very confidently asserts, that the word was *added* by our author. He speaks as if he had been at Shakspeare's elbow; and this same *addition* must have been made by the old bard sixteen years after his death. But not to dwell on such trifles, I shall only observe, that whoever shall take the trouble to compare the second folio with the first, will find proofs almost amounting to demonstration that all the additions, alterations, &c. which are found in the second folio, were made without any authority whatsoever."[28] Malone's objections about lack of authority do not extend to "our frailty" for "O frailty," which change he merely notes while keeping the unauthorized second Folio version. Obviously, retaining the "O" does not obliterate the presumed frailty Viola claims "we" have, but "our frailty" implicitly anchors that weakness as only female in a speech which generally entertains far more gender ambiguity.

Even more important is the second line of the Folio couplet: "For such as we are made, if such we bee." The conditional "if such we bee" functions as yet another of the loaded comments about Viola's own shifting gender in the speech: if we were women (although as boy-actresses, neither Olivia nor Viola would be), then we would be vulnerable. This reading requires no change in syntax, only a change in emphasis to make sense of a line which early editors have found so opaque as to need emendation: "For such as *we* are made, if such we bee" (F, 260). Here "we" includes Viola and Olivia, and also the boy-actresses who play those roles. Thus, one potential performance enabled by the Folio *Twelfe Night* allows for a much more radical exposure of the boy-actress within the role of Viola than most critics acknowledge.[29]

The Folio text also opens up a range of meanings linked to "made"; these possibilities are foreclosed, or at least limited by "made of". For example, in another context, Random Clod (a.k.a. Randall McLeod) has suggested that "made" could also be read as "mad," not because the two words sound alike in Renaissance English, but because the function of a final "e" was not so thoroughly secure during the period.[30] Indeed, in Act 1, scene 5, the Clown likens a drunken man to "a drown'd man, a foole, and a madde man" (F, 258) while Olivia herself tells the messenger that "if you be not mad, be gone" (F, 259). "For such as we are mad (or madde)" is a simpler revision than moving a comma and changing "if" to "of" and makes just as much sense of the transformations of women's hearts as does the normal emendation. Moreover, the notion of madness plays through the comedy and surfaces especially at moments when the hold on identity falters. Most tellingly Sebastian is bowled over by the jewel Olivia gives *him* and concludes "that I am mad, / Or else the Ladies mad" (F, 272). That Viola should suggest that "we are mad" is thus well in keeping with later responses to Olivia's gifts.

The Folio version also enables a pun on maid/made. Both Olivia and Viola are made maids, as boy actresses playing the roles. Just as significant is the fact that the punning on the homophones extends throughout the comedy. When Olivia is first described to Viola as a "vertuous maid,"

Viola desires that she could serve her "Till I had made mine owne occasion mellow / What my estate is" (F, 256). In the scene where Malvolio
completely remakes his appearance and behavior in accordance with the
feigned love letter dropped by Maria and Sir Toby, he quotes "Go to,
thou art made if thou desirst to be so" (F, 267). His statement echoes
"such as we are made, if such we bee" more directly than some of Malone's suggested analogs and provokes Olivia to respond "Am I made?"
Consistently the potential pun on "made/maid" occurs at points in the
play where identities are in flux, including the final scene's revelation.[31]
Sebastian, not Malvolio, has been made by Olivia's love suit and draws
attention to her error, "You are betroth'd both to a maid and man" (F,
274).[32]

Given the potential for playing upon "made," "madde," and "maid" in
the soliloquy and the prevalence of "wanton uses" of the words throughout the play, the Folio text of Viola's soliloquy offers not only a less
securely gendered version of frailty—in keeping with the boy who would
be playing the role—but also more various and more connected relationships with the other "mades" in the text. However, our current texts of
Twelfth Night leave no ambiguity about whose frailty is being discussed
(it must be women's frailty) nor about the condition and gender of the
speaker and Olivia—"For such as we are made of, such we be." These
editions offer both finality and the inescapability of women's waxen
hearts, even for the boy-actresses who might very easily disclaim them.
The crisis of identity that Viola describes throughout her speech is thus
briefly suspended before it even reaches its pinnacle in her assertions
about both her maleness and her femaleness: "As I am man . . . As I am
woman" (F, 260).

The formal annotated editions of *Twelfth Night* throughout the eighteenth century move toward an emendation which closes down both identity and performance possibilities in the comedy. In effect, the eighteenth-
century editors move Viola's speech towards a certainty of essential identity expressed nowhere else in the speech and truly nowhere else in the
play: "for such as we are made of, such we be" at one blow secures
Viola's sexual identity if "we" have been implicitly defined as women,
and expresses a fatalistic acceptance of an essential, and essentially frail,
identity in a comedy that consistently demonstrates how fluid the boundaries of the self can be. However, if the final version of this pair of lines
forecloses ambiguity and interpretive possibilities, returning to the
eighteenth-century editions as they argue for interpretations and emendations actually restores the passage's fruitful ambiguities.

Read in the context of eighteenth-century theatrical practice and
performance editions, the disturbances caused by this speech are even
clearer. If Viola's soliloquy, as spoken by a boy-actress, resonates with

Renaissance anxieties about the wickedness of theatrical cross-dressing, that same speech, when spoke by a female actress on the eighteenth-century stage, would appear to present an unambiguously female self-revelation, as when Mason suggests that Viola's comments are "a natural sentiment for a girl to offer, who was herself in love."[33] However, most of the eighteenth-century performance editions excise this entire section of the soliloquy, starting from the invocation of disguise as a wickedness. These texts, unlike the scholarly editions, offer no explanation or signal at all of the changes they make.[34] Instead, they simply cut a noticeably large segment of this speech, including the lines that so preoccupy the scholarly editors. In both the performance editions and the eighteenth-century textual history, these lines have clearly provoked sufficient uneasiness that both theatrical and scholarly revisers undertake to remove or limit the ambiguities of Viola's soliloquy. The recognition of *Twelfth Night*'s alternative ideologies of gender construction produces alternative texts, both in the cuts to those editions produced in conjunction with performance and in the emended soliloquy as ratified by Furness and adopted throughout the twentieth-century editions of *Twelfth Night*.

As these struggles with the soliloquy suggest, it is past time to reconsider and reinstate the Folio text, not as the sanctioned original text but as the version that opens up the ambiguities so often displaced and disputed in the eighteenth century. The Folio version of Viola's meditation should be set in the context of those readings and rewritings of this speech; the eighteenth-century editorial conflicts underscore the importance of Viola's articulations of gender and frailty as an index of the problematics of gender within changing cultural moments. In that spectrum of response, the range of ambiguities in Viola's soliloquy become most available, casting our own changing perceptions of both performance and text into sharp relief. As one of the few soliloquies granted a female character in the canon, Viola's speech and its playful ambiguity deserve at least as much debate and interpretation now as they received in the eighteenth century, before Tyrwhitt's changes became an accepted and uncontested norm.

NOTES

1. For both a summary of the possibilities for the source text and the textual problems that do appear in the play's Folio version, please see Robert K. Turner, Jr., "The Text of *Twelfth Night*," *Shakespeare Quarterly* 26 (1975): 128–38.

2. My references to the Folio *Twelfe Night* offer the text of Charlton Hinman's *The Norton Facsimile: The First Folio of Shakespeare* (New York: W. W. Norton & Company, Inc, 1968) and offer page numbers from that Folio.

3. William Warburton, *The Works of Shakespear* (London, 1747), n. 4, 3:135.

Later editors note that Warburton mistakenly says "latter" when he means "former" here.

4. C. J. Sisson, *New Readings in Shakespeare* (Cambridge: Cambridge University Press, 1956), 2:186.

5. This quotation is taken from *Twelfth Night: The Arden Shakespeare,* eds. J. M. Lothian and T. W. Craik (New York: Methuen, 1975). From this point on, unless I am referring to several editions, the parenthetical notes will indicate which edition I am citing, most frequently the *Arden* or the Folio.

6. I give this speech as it occurs in *Twelfth Night: The Arden Shakespeare,* eds. J. M. Lothian and T. W. Craik (New York: Methuen, 1975), but all modern editions follow this form with only minor variations in punctuation. *The Riverside Shakespeare* does note that a change has been made by bracketing off [our] and [of,].

7. Both the Arden Shakespeare *Twelfth Night* and the Oxford edition present the emended version of these lines, noting the Folio text only in the notes. Of the two, the Arden offers the lengthier explanation of the changes. Although the Riverside Shakespeare indicates there is a change from the Folio by using the brackets, that text, like the Oxford edition, offers only the Folio text in notes to the text that appear at considerable remove from the actual change and that eschew any explanations for the emendation.

8. Nicholas Rowe, *The Works of Shakespear* (London, 1709), 2:839.

9. Samuel Johnson, *The Plays of William Shakespeare* (London, 1765), 2:379.

10. Edward Capell, *The Works of Shakespeare* (London, 1768), 4:25

11. Edmond Malone, *The Plays and Poems of Shakspeare* (London, 1790), n. 7, 4:32.

12. Thirlby's annotations appear in two editions currently housed at the Folger Shakespeare Library. For more information on his editing, please see Christopher Spencer and John W. Wetz, "Styan Thirlby: A Forgotten 'Editor' of Shakespeare" *Shakespeare Studies* 7 (1970): 327–33.

13. Thomas Trywhitt, *Observations and Conjectures on some passages of Shakespeare's* (London, 1765), 45.

14. George Steevens, *The Plays of William Shakespeare* (London, 1778), n. 5, 4:187.

15. Neither the *New Variorum,* the *Oxford Textual Companion,* nor the *Arden Tempest* gives even the faintest clue where the revision of this line in *The Tempest* originates.

16. Malone, *Plays,* n. 7, 4:32.

17. George Steevens, *The Plays of William Shakespeare* (London, 1793), n. 5, 4:49.

18. Sisson, *New Readings in Shakespeare,* 2:186. Sisson restores some of the Folio *Twelfth Night,* reversing Warburton's emendation of one of Viola's speeches in Act 1, scene 5, for example, but does not mention the two lines under consideration here.

19. Johnson, *Plays,* 2:378.

20. Tyrwhitt, *Observations,* 44.

21. Steevens, *Plays,* n. 5, 4:186.

22. Malone, *Plays,* n. 5, 4:31.

23. See Lisa Jardine, "As boys and women are for the most part cattle of this colour: Female Roles and Elizabethan Eroticism" in *Still Harping on Daughters: Women and Drama in the Age of Shakespeare* (Totowa, N.J.: Barnes and Noble Books, 1983), 9–36.

24. Malone, *Plays,* n. 5, 4:31. Malone offers only part of Isabella's speech and not its context: "Nay call us ten times fraile, / For we are soft, as our complexions are, / And credulous to false prints."

25. Since the Folio typesetters occasionally used question marks for exclamation points, the exact inflection of "women" here is not wholly recoverable. Steevens has clearly decided in favor of the exclamation point in his use of the quotation (Steevens, *Plays* [1793], 4:267).

26. Howard Furness, *Twelfe Night: A New Variorum* (Philadelphia, 1901), 104.

27. Matthew W. Black and Matthias A. Shaaber, *Shakespeare's Seventeenth-Century Editors: 1632–1685* (New York: Modern Language Association of America, 1937), 96.

28. Malone, *Plays,* n. 2, 2:30.

29. See Matthew Wikander, "As Secret as Maidenhead: The Profession of the Boy-actress in *Twelfth Night," Comparative Drama* 20 (1986): 349–63.

30. Random Clod, "Information on Information," *Text: Transactions of the Society for Textual Scholarship* (New York: AMS Press, 1984), 248–50.

31. Wikander, too, notes the punning on these different "mades" ("Secret," 359), but his reading of the lines does not take into account the differences in the Folio version and accepts the fatalism of the revised text.

32. Stephen Greenblatt, in "Fiction and Friction," *Shakespearean Negotiations: The Circulation of Social Energy in Renaissance England* (Berkeley: University of California Press, 1988), 82–92, suggests that Sebastian's comment indicates that he is both virgin (maid) and man. It is also possible that he has played a maid as a youthful member of the company, and so, like Viola, appears as both man and maid.

33. Malone, quoting Mason, *Plays,* n. 5, 4:31.

34. For a thorough discussion of the various reasons for the performance editions' cuts and revisions to Viola's soliloquy and her role in general, please see my book, *The Trick of Singularity:* Twelfth Night *and the Performance Editions* (Iowa City: University of Iowa Press, 1996).

"The young, the beautiful, the harmless, and the pious": Contending with Ophelia in the Eighteenth Century

Hardin Aasand

JOHN Everett Millais's uncanny painting *Ophelia* captures in its Pre-Raphaelite manner the liminal presence that Ophelia had obtained on the English stage from the Restoration into the Victorian period.[1] Suspended between life and death, Millais's *Ophelia* inhabits a space that traverses her entrance and her exit from the scene she inhabits, an embodiment of an unseen death rendered by Shakespeare only in Gertrude's stirring narrative. Contending with Ophelia's entrance and departure in *Hamlet* has required artists and editors to make choices regarding the treatment of a figure whose brief time on the stage compels others to contend with such frailty, with such a "document in madness." In this essay, I would like to consider how the earliest modern editors dealt with this disturbing presence, for the choices made by these editors reveal their attitude towards Ophelia's madness, itself a liminal state, and its appearance on the stage.

For the eighteenth century, Ophelia's entrance resulted in a censored script that removed the bawdiness of her madness for a more refined, more operatic impression. In fact, the performance history of Ophelia shows us an ambiguous regard for her character. While she is attractive in her passiveness, she remains dangerous in her repressed sexuality:

> In order to celebrate Ophelia's helplessness as virtue and her madness as sensitivity, the eighteenth-century theater suppressed the more blatant aspects of her Renaissance bawdiness. Yet, the effects of censorship proved contradictory. While the seventeenth century marked the beginning of an 'age of repression,' the ensuing 'imposed silence' actually became a 'mechanism of increasing incitement' that helped to construct ideas of 'sexuality' to which we still adhere.[2]

An early illustration from John Bell's 1774 edition for the 1772 Theatre's Royal production gives us a refined, sensible Ophelia as portrayed by a Mrs. Lessingham. She is bedecked in flowers and holds a basket in her

"There's rue for you." From Bell's Edition of Shakespeare's Plays. **By permission of the Newberry Library, Chicago.**

left hand with her right hand outstretched. Her hair, though long, is far from disheveled and sweeps down her back in a restrained fashion.[3] Bell's editorial commentary on Ophelia's appearance enunciates this composed madness. In one note, Bell suggests,

> The transitions of this young lady's frenzy are extremely well conceived for representation, and render her a very interesting object: too much extravaganza, or a figure too much disheveled, should be avoided.[4]

On the note for Ophelia's lyrical "good night, Ladies, good night," the editor proclaims: "The author has fancied Ophelia's madness well, affectingly, and furnished it with suitable expression; we like the object, are entertained with her flights, and commiserate with the frenzy."[5] The refinement of this image, however, was not so clear in the earlier editions, as editors like Rowe, Pope, Theobald, Hanmer, Johnson, and Capell strove to incorporate an appearance that finds disparities in representation in the earlier second quarto and first folio texts.[6] These divergences reflect distinctive portraits not only of Ophelia, but also of those who attempt to decipher her madness.

Thus, editorial choices transcend mere whim; they convey the attitudes and critical acumen of the respective editors. This observation is reinforced by Randall McLeod and Margreta de Grazia, both of whom suggest that the editorial practice often alters characters and provides nuances for critical perceptions. What might seem ostensibly a neutral apparatus for an edition may implicitly affect characterization: for example, the inclusion of a *dramatis personae* that precedes the play-text, a feature of most editions since Nicholas Rowe included them for every play in his 1709 edition, inherently alters the readers' reception of the characters represented by that list. For readers of the original quartos and for the plays in the First Folio not given a dramatis personae, characters must be negotiated by a careful consideration of gender, rank, age, and acting personnel. In the words of de Grazia and Stallybrass, "Readers had to arbitrate for themselves the boundaries of identity, constructing (or failing to construct, or refusing to construct) 'individual' characters in the process of reading."[7] In brief, editorial decisions are as critical to the formation of characters as are the creative impulses provided by the author. For Jonathan Goldberg and Harry Berger, dramatic "character" is conveyed within a "locus of inscription" through which characters become the "effects rather than the causes of their language."[8]

In his provocatively entitled essay, "Five Women Eleven Ways," Steven Urkowitz reminds us that textual emendations were not confined to eighteenth-century editions and their descendants, but rather were abundant in the filiation between the quartos and folios still extant, a diversity that affects the later editors. *Apropos* of Ophelia, he notes that female characters reflect some of the most "striking instances" of variation and observes that the stage movement, physical gestures, and visible signs of a "character's social power" are all textual components that can convey sometimes subtle and sometimes explicit variants in a character's demeanor.[9] This textual grounding of "character" thus complicates the eighteenth-century notion that the dramatic personae were indeed "natural." Therefore, Alexander Pope's often cited criticism that "every single Character in Shakespeare is as much an individual as those in Life itself" acquires a layer of verbal irony unintended by the author: text is transformed into life, and life into text.

Given the already scriptive nature of drama, the eighteenth century strove to elide the text into nature, to presume that the page, the stage, and the street have a natural coalescence. This sense of character construction is given its clearest delineation in those dramatic characters who defy a superficial stereotyping and conventional formulation, characters who are aberrations and thus "must be read, made sense of, inscribed into discourse."[10] By focusing briefly on the editorial treatment of Ophelia during her mad scenes in Act 4 of *Hamlet,* we can discern eighteenth-century editors in varying ways attempting to render madness dramatically lucid and rational and make Ophelia's madness textually resonant for the readers, just as later stage productions excised and refined Ophelia's tragic, final appearance. In a sense, editors strove to expatiate upon Ophelia's madness in order to convey her madness in a textually coherent method, an editorial process that is mirrored as well in the burgeoning industry of dictionaries and linguistic classification prevalent in the eighteenth century.

In his book on Augustan notions of madness, Max Byrd conjoins eighteenth-century views on madness with the editorial practice. He reminds us of Samuel Johnson's own ambivalence towards this act of linguistic regulation even as he strove to fix and "ascertain" the English language:

> These clashes between ordering reason and exuberant imagination, between chaos and moral regulation, belong to the continuing battle that all his life Johnson fought in his own mind. But it was with a sense of inevitable failure that he regarded the finished work . . . and much of the pessimism of the preface must spring from his recognition of the intractability of the forces of unreason.[11]

The editing of texts—the duplication of Johnson's decision to disentangle perplexity, to regulate confusion, and to choose from boundless variety— was indeed incompatible with the textual confusion that Ophelia produces in her mad scenes. The passionate means by which editors strove to fix and restrain Shakespeare's text violates the unreason of Ophelia's character, just as the excision of several of her mad songs in performance makes her madness more confined and controlled. Therefore, when Edward Capell writes in his 1768 edition of the neglected state of Shakespeare's text, its "corrupt" and "licentious" production, one must recuperate the moral imperative rife within these verdicts that order must be reintroduced into these texts by cautious and prudent decisions.[12]

Through a careful collation of a variety of eighteenth-century editions of the play,[13] the reader can come to see how each editor often borrows from, rejects, and modifies previous editorial practices in restoring Ophelia to the stage in her final, disruptive state. The means by which that madness is articulated textually by eighteenth-century editors speaks volumes for their perception of madness.[14] Accordingly, the editorial work of editors from Rowe (1709) to Malone (1790) attempts both to preserve and to purge Ophelia's madness through a careful explication of her language and of the language with which other characters voice her presence. Consequently, Carol Thomas Neely's notion that madness is merely a linguistic effect for Shakespeare ignores the iconographic traditions that provided editors with a language for that madness:

> Shakespeare . . . dramatizes madness primarily through a peculiar language more often than through physiological symptoms, stereotyped behaviors, or iconographic conventions. This characteristic speech is both something and nothing, both coherent and incoherent. Spectators, onstage and off, read this language, trying to make "sense" of it, translating it into the discourse of sanity.[15]

In fact, editors after Rowe begin to elucidate this madness in their notes and textual variants precisely because of the aberrant "physiological symptoms, stereotyped behaviors, or iconographic conventions" through which their society articulated that madness. As described by Michael MacDonald in his many studies of madness, the disruption produced by melancholy and incipient madness created a rupture within the social fabric of early modern England, and the attempt to reproduce that madness in dramatic terms often frustrated an editorial practice determined to fix and ascertain the intent of the author.[16]

For the eighteenth-century editors Ophelia proved more enigmatic, more a "document in madness"[17] whose distraught entrance proved as troubling and disturbing as her "maimed rites." The editors lament her treatment on the stage by Hamlet and remain critical of Shakespeare's means of disposing of her from the stage. Indeed, she resurfaces in eighteenth-century editions and treatises as a spectral presence to be mourned and eulogized over. Samuel Johnson, long after his notes are concluded in his edition, resolves to restore Ophelia once again to the forefront of his editorial apparatus. Reflecting on the "variety" of *Hamlet*'s plotting (the "interchangeabl[e] scenes "diversified with merriment and solemnity") as a structuralist critic, Johnson returns to the "mournful distraction of Ophelia [which] fills the heart with tenderness," to a paragraph later characterizing Hamlet's madness as "useless and wanton cruelty" in his treatment of Ophelia, and concluding the critique, not with Hamlet's heroic posture but rather with the "untimely death of Ophelia, the young, the beautiful, the harmless, and the pious."[18] Writing and editing over half a century later, Samuel Singer was similarly affected by Ophelia's madness. In his 1826 edition, Singer concluded his preface, not with further examination of Hamlet's madness or delay in revenge, but rather with Ophelia's spectral presence. In his close, he cites William Hazlitt's apostrophe to her:

> Ophelia is a character almost too exquisitely touching to be dwelt upon. Oh, rose of May; oh flower too soon faded! Her love, her madness, her death, are described with the truest touches of tenderness and pathos. It is a character which nobody but Shakespeare could have drawn in the way that he has done; and to the conception of which there is not the smallest approach except in some of the old romantic ballads.[19]

These sentiments had been commonplace throughout much of the eighteenth century.

The anonymous "Some remarks on the Tragedy of Hamlet," falsely attributed to Thomas Hanmer in 1736 but now attributed to George Stubbes, evokes in critical terms the tenuousness of the editorial apparatus to return Ophelia to the stage in Act 4:

> The Scenes of Ophelia's madness are to me very shocking, in so noble a Piece as this. I am not against her having been represented mad, but surely, it might have been done with less Levity and more Decency.[20]

Ophelia's madness and subsequent death troubles the author, and she appears and reappears in his critical treatise as she appears and reappears on the stage in Act 4.5, unexpectedly and abruptly. In his analysis, Ophelia's madness is paradoxically criticized for the ambiguity of its inception and lauded for its thematic necessity for the play:

> It does not appear whether Ophelia's Madness was chiefly for her Father's Death, or for the Loss of Hamlet. It is not often that young Women run mad for the Loss of their Fathers. It is more natural to suppose, that like *Chimene*

in the *Cid,* her great Sorrow proceeded from her Father's being kill'd by the Man she lov'd, and thereby making it indecent for her ever to marry him.[21]

And, yet again, in a conjunction of scenes that is as discordant as it is revealing, Ophelia's mad scenes reappear in this treatise as the author defends the variety of scenes in the play as necessary though regrettable elements in the drama:

> Even Laertes going to France, and Ophelia's Madness, however trivial they may seem (and how much soeer I dislike the Method of that last mentioned) are incidents absolutely necessary towards the concluding of all; as will appear to any one upon due Consideration.[22]

Thus, Ophelia's madness, indecorous and appalling, troubles these editors, the "Method" of its staging particularly anguishing for editors of the mid-century.[23] This editorial apprehension conveys the intensity of the fears felt by the eighteenth-century audience, and the various editions reflect an uncertainty as to how madness should be wrought upon the stage. The characterization of Ophelia offered by Laertes, "document in madness, thoughts and remembrance fitted," refers not only to Ophelia as character but also to the play-text as edited and critiqued by the various eighteenth-century editors as madness provokes an editorial uncertainty as to how it should be made visible and plangent.

II

The construction of her madness begins long before Ophelia appears on stage; indeed, her construction begins before the play is even underway. Inserting a *dramatis personae* in what is regarded as the first edited text of Shakespeare, Nicholas Rowe editorially provides the reader with a means of deciphering Ophelia's character. As is commonplace, her appearance in the list is grouped with the other female characters, appearing after Gertrude ("Queen of Denmark, and Mother to Hamlet"), and given her dramatic standing vis-à-vis the other male characters in the play: "Daughter to Polonius, belov'd by Hamlet."[24] Pope (1725), Theobald (1733), Hanmer (1744), and Warburton (1747) follow Rowe in defining Ophelia through these relationships, suggesting implicitly the two chief motivations for her subsequent madness.[25] Pope's edition goes so far as to schematize Shakespeare's entire canon by character, speech, and character traits. Ophelia's appearance in the *dramatis personae* is given a suitable frame by Pope in his "index of fictitious Persons, with the Characters ascrib'd to them": following Orlando and preceding Othello, Ophelia is characterized as "Beauty and Innocence distracted with Calamities."[26] Ophelia's condition invites both an objective and empirical treatment as editors strive to deal textually with her state.

In Act 4.5, Ophelia dominates the scene with two entrances and two exits, upstaging the royal family in one instance and the vengeful return of her brother Laertes as he confronts Claudius over his father's death. Editors were confronted by a series of choices in editing this scene because of the disparities between the folio and the quarto texts. Below are the quarto and folio readings:[27]

2744   *Enter Horatio, Gertrard, and a Gentleman.*

2745   *Quee.* I will not speake with her.

2746   *Gent.* Shee is importunat,
2747   Indeede distract, her moode will needes be pittied.

2748   *Quee.* What would she haue?

2749   *Gent.* She speakes much of her father, sayes she heares
2750   There's tricks i'th world, and hems, and beates her hart,
2751   Spurnes enuiously at strawes, speakes things in doubt
2752   That carry but halfe sence, her speech is nothing,
2753   Yet the vnshaped vse of it doth moue
2754   The hearers to collection, they yawne at it,
2755   And botch the words vp fit to theyr owne thoughts,
2756   Which as her wincks, and nods, and gestures yeeld them,
2757   Indeede would make one thinke there might be thought
2758   Though nothing sure, yet much vnhappily.
2759   *Hora.* Twere good she were spoken with, for shee may strew
2760   Dangerous coniectures in ill breeding mindes,
2761   Let her come in.

2766   *Enter Ophelia.*

2762   *Quee.* 'To my sicke soule, as sinnes true nature is,
2763   'Each toy seemes prologue to some great amisse,
2764   'So full of artlesse iealousie is guilt,
2765   'It spills it selfe, in fearing to be spylt.

                       (Second Quarto, 1604)

2744   *Enter Queene and Horatio.*
2745   *Qu.* I will not speake with her.
2746   *Hor.* She is importunate, indeed distract, her moode
2747   will needs be pittied.
2748   *Qu.* What whould she haue?

2749 *Hor.* She speakes much of her Father, saies she heares
2750 There's trickes i'th'world, and hems, and beats her heart,
2751 Spurnes enuiously at Strawes, speakes things in doubt,
2752 That carry but halfe sense: Her speech is nothing,
2753 Yet the vnshaped vse of it doth moue
2754 The hearers to Collection; they ayme at it,
2755 And botch the words vp fit to their owne thoughts,
2756 Which as her winkes, and nods, and gestures yeeld them,
2757 Indeed would make one thinke there would be thought,
2758 Though nothing sure, yet much vnhappily.
2759 *Qu.* 'Twere good she were spoken with,
2760 For she may strew dangerous coniectures
2761 In ill breeding minds. Let her come in.

2762 To my sicke soule (as sinnes true Nature is)
2763 Each toy seemes Prologue, to some great amisse,
2764 So full of Artlesse iealousie is guilt,
2765 It spill's it selfe, in fearing to be spilt.
2766   *Enter Ophelia distracted.*

                                        (First Folio, 1623)

In the quarto, the scene is populated by Horatio, Gertrard, and a Gentleman, a grouping that the folio will reduce to only Gertrude and Horatio.
While this choice has been explained away critically by later editors like
Collier, who supposed that the folio reduced the scene to save on actors,
such a conclusion was not voiced in the eighteenth century.[28] A collation
of the editorial decisions conveys the variances between editions:

Enter Queen, Horatio, and Attendants] Rowe

Enter Queen, Horatio, and a Gentleman] Pope, Theobald

Enter Queen, and a Gentleman] Hanmer

Enter Queen and Horatio] Johnson, Malone

Enter Queen, attended; Horatio, and a Gentleman] Capell

Pope and Theobald follow the quarto exactly, whereas Rowe expands
the number onstage to an ambiguous group of "Attendants." While this
direction would appear to be a matter merely of numbers, it affects the
intimacy of the scene and the means by which Ophelia's madness is
mediated for the spectator.

Madness demands, in Neely's words, "onstage characters [to] mediate this pregnant, mad discourse, showing us how to translate it."[29] While Neely considers this notion in dramaturgical terms, she fails to consider that there is a further mediation between the onstage characters and the subject of the discourse: the editor, compiler, annotator of the text. In the case of Ophelia's distressed state, the editorial decisions are as subject to the vagaries of madness as are Ophelia's thoughts. Even Neely's essay attempts to mediate the disorder that madness engenders. Citing the prologue to Ophelia's arrival

> Her speech is nothing.
> Yet the unshaped use of it doth move
> The hearers to collection; they yawn at it,
> And botch the words up fit to their own thoughts.[30]
>
> (TLN 2752–2755)

Neely follows the quarto and identifies the speaker as the "gentleman," one of the "onstage" characters she asserts must be present for the act of mediating madness. But even this speech, which would appear a lucid, sound interpretation by one of the onstage characters, is infected by the madness represented on the stage. While the quartos, which Pope, Theobald, Hanmer, Warburton, and Capell follow in this instance, record the nondescript "Gentleman" as the speaker of these lines, the folios record Horatio as the speaker, an attribution which Rowe, Johnson, and Malone record in their respective editions.

This ambiguity is redoubled textually when Ophelia is finally returned to the stage in her first entrance in her dishevelled state. Who should be credited with announcing Ophelia's return and bringing her onstage? The ambiguity of this editorial decision is answered variously by the host of editions we have. In following the folio, Rowe (followed by Malone) prefers to have Ophelia's entrance requested by the Queen, and he thus constructs a meditative queen, who articulates for Horatio exactly her understanding of Ophelia's "dangerous conjectures in ill-breeding minds." Horatio attends Gertrude in both Folio and Rowe's edition, but she herself speaks the insightful

> Twere good she were spoken with, for she may strew dangerous conjectures
> In ill-breeding minds. Let her come in.
>
> (TLN 2759–2961)

Q2, which Pope, Theobald, Warburton, and Capell typically draw on, transforms Gertrude into a pensive, quiet presence to whom Horatio acts as counsel. For Pope, Theobald, Warburton, and Capell it is Horatio's cajoling that finally brings Ophelia on the stage.[31]

The stage directions themselves in the various editions suggest the editors' attempts to rationalize Ophelia's entrance and provide textually the emotional intensity a reader needs to anticipate the scene. Following the folio, Rowe provides Ophelia with an emotional cue: she enters "distracted," and Theobald (like Hanmer and Warburton) follows Rowe rather than Q2 in this instance by having Ophelia enter "distracted" after Gertrude's brief four-line aside:

> To my sick soul, as sin's true nature is,
> Each toy seems prologue to some great amiss;
> So full of artless jealousy is guilt,
> It spills itself in fearing to be spilt.
>
> (TLN 2762–2765)

Q2 makes these lines Gertrude's first lines since her previous question "What would she have?" She has thus remained a silent presence in Q2 and for those editors who use it here: Pope, Theobald, Warburton. The power of Ophelia's presence, in more subtle ways, is equally telling by this decision. While Q2 has Ophelia appear onstage during the utterance of these lines, giving special emphasis to her presence as one of Gertrude's "toys" that are harbingers of "some great amiss," the Folio and Rowe give the queen these lines as an overture for Ophelia's entrance.

Even more suggestive are the stage directions for her entrance. Rowe and Theobald have it thus:

> Enter Ophelia, distracted.
>
> (TLN 2905)

Rowe and Theobald bring Ophelia in alone, not indicating whether the "Gentleman" or Horatio retrieves her. Indeed, there are no exits for the Gentleman to indicate his dismissal—only later would Hanmer and Capell include an exit for the "gentleman" while Johnson would provide an exit for "Horatio." In Rowe's text and the Folio, Horatio's line, "Let her come in—"is attributed to the queen. It suggests a concession to Horatio's plea. For Pope, Theobald, and Warburton this scene acquires greater trenchancy, for this line is given to Horatio and requires the reader to rationalize its delivery. Is Horatio pleading for Ophelia's appearance because of her madness, or is he giving an order on the queen's behalf? Samuel Johnson editorially excises this dilemma by having only Horatio and Gertrude appear, and it is Horatio who exits at the Queen's request, "Let her come in." In Johnson's edition, Ophelia is subsequently treated as a subordinate for Horatio's return: "Enter Horatio, with Ophelia, distracted." Capell's edition will distill all previous stage directions to a simple "Enter Ophelia, wildly."

Ophelia's second return is equally discordant in the editorial apparatus with a variety of possibilities for her entrance. Below are the quarto and folio renditions:

2903   A noyse within.
2905   Enter Ophelia.

2904   Laer. Let her come in.
2906   How now, what noyse is that?

(Second quarto, 1604)

2904   A noise within. Let her come in.
2905   Enter Ophelia.

2906   Laer. How now? what noise is that?

(First folio, 1623)

Rowe, Theobald, Hanmer, and Warburton establish the precedent for future directions in describing her appearance as follows: "Enter Ophelia fantastically drest with straws and flowers." Rowe originated this direction and inserts the "straws" without previous authority. It would seem that Rowe himself interpolates this direction by recalling the earlier references in the scene to Ophelia's insane "spurn[ing] enviously at straws." In using the folio version, these editors also credit a stage direction for Ophelia's return:

[A Noise within, Let her come in (TLN 2904)

They thus read these lines as stage directions, making Ophelia's return a dramatic punctuation of Claudius's expression of grief to Laertes.

In *Shakespeare Restored,* Theobald logically questions Pope's attempts to attribute the "Let her come in" to Laertes as in the quarto, a decision which makes illogical Laertes' subsequent question "What noise is that?"[32] Theobald also alters the position of Ophelia's entrance and Laertes' response to the noise:

[A Noise within, Let her come in.
Laer. How now, what Noise is that?
Enter Ophelia fantastically drest with straws and flowers.

(TLN 2904–2906)

In creating this progression and stage direction, Theobald disrupts Rowe's arrangement, in which Ophelia's entrance dramatically precedes Laertes' question and establishes her as the focus before Laertes' question. Theobald is thus treating the entrance with an eye to its logical staging in the theatre.

Deflecting attention from Ophelia, later editors attempt to rationalize Laertes' question by appropriating it for the voices of the offstage actors who apparently give entrance to Ophelia. Later editors like Capell and Johnson have thus attempted to reincorporate her return through offstage auditors. For Capell, it is "Danes" within who give Ophelia leave to enter with a "Let her come in." For Johnson, it is an anonymous "crowd" who announces her presence from offstage. Capell's and Johnson's decisions require them to rationalize and annotate Laertes' own entrance previous to Ophelia. In this instance, the quarto provided them with a means of rationalizing this later entrance by Ophelia. The quarto asserts merely, *Enter Laertes with others,* and it is these "others" who become Capell's "Danes" and Johnson's "Crowd." Eighteenth-century editors expend considerable critical energy on this last appearance, and there is much to be said for Rowe, Theobald, and Hanmer's decision to follow the Folio in reading "*A noise within. Let her come in*" as a stage direction. The quietude of Ophelia's return makes ironic Laertes' "What noise is that?" and juxtaposes the brashness of his entrance with her unassuming entrance.[33]

I have concentrated on these two entrances because they reflect an editorial practice attempting to deal with the disruptive appearance of a distraught Ophelia. In order to decide how to represent editorially the bringing of madness upon the stage, the editors must conceive dramatically the most effective means for the audience to mediate and read Ophelia's state. While most of the editors coalesce around either the quarto or folio readings, other editors like Johnson and Capell assert their own authorial presence by interpolating for the author and creating new characters to mediate further Ophelia's disturbed state. Eighteenth-century editors provided the reader with a subtle range of potential readings for Ophelia's madness. The movement from the first quarto to subsequent quarto, folio, and eighteenth-century editions depicts an evolution in the use of stage directions and character responses to those directions to set the tone and mood of a scenes. The interpretation of these scenes presented by Sir Joshua Reynolds and reprinted in the 1790 Malone edition becomes part of the gradual textual mediation of Ophelia in the latter part of the eighteenth-century: "There is no part of this, in its representation on the stage, more pathetick than this scene which, I suppose, proceeds from the utter insensibility Ophelia has to her own misfortunes. A great sensibility, or none at all, seems to produce the same effect. In the latter the audience supply what she wants, and with the former they sympathize."[34]

The early editors attempted to make her appearance dramatically sound and effective for the reader as they sought a clarity for her madness. The earlier anxiety of the editorial practice, rivalled by the often censored stage presentations of Ophelia's disruptive state,[35] would give way to Edmond Malone and the later-eighteenth-century empirical regard for Ophelia and her condition, as her distribution of flowers and voicing of bawdy lyrics became comprehensible and editorially grounded in literary antecedents.[36] A glimpse at the 1821 "third variorum" edition of Malone's 1790 text divulges this accretion of reason, and one example will demonstrate this process of clarification and explication.

Ophelia's final return prompts Laertes' distressful "O heat, dry up my brains!" as well as a dramatic anatomy of Ophelia's condition. He concludes, "Nature is fine in love: and, where 'tis fine, / It sends some precious instance of itself / After the thing it loves" (TLN 2914–16). This line is omitted in the quarto, but its presence in the folio leads to a variety of editorial glosses. For Pope, the line engenders a rare note:

> Or, perhaps,
> Nature is fire in loue, and where 'tis fire
> It sends some precious incense of it self
> After the thing it loues.
>
> (6:440)

Theobald disputes Pope's reading—"I own, this Conjecture to me imparts no Satisfactory Idea"—and elaborates on his rationale for rejecting it:

Nature is suppos'd to be the Fire, and to furnish the Incense too: Had Love been suppos'd the Fire, and Nature sent out the Incense, I should more readily have been reconcil'd to the Sentiment. But no Change, in my Opinion is necessary to the Text. (7: 333–4)

Furthermore, Ophelia's madness occasions an editorial paraphrase by Theobald:

In the Passion of Love, Nature becomes more exquisite of Sensation, is more delicate and refin'd; *that is,* Natural Affection, rais'd and sublim'd into a Love-Passion, becomes more inflamed and intense than usual; and where it is so, as People in Love generally send what they have of most valuable after their Lovers; so poor *Ophelia* has sent her most precious Senses after the Object of her inflamed Affection. (7: 334)

Theobald further grounds his reading by referring to similar sentiments in Shakespeare's clown in *As You Like It,* Cressida in *Troilus and Cressida,* and Iago in *Othello.* Ophelia's erotomania thus acquires a textual grounding in the creations within Shakespeare's other plays. Theobald attempts to provide a sound rebuttal to Pope's mere conjecture.

However, Warburton, in his 1747 edition of Pope's text, removes to the bottom of the page Pope's own interpretation and conjectures his own reading:

> Nature is fal'n in love, and where 'tis fal'n
> It sends some precious instance of itself
> After the thing it loves

(8: 229–30)

Warburton then expatiates for himself on the "cause" of Ophelia's madness: "grief, occasioned by the violence of her natural affection for her murder'd father." He then attempts a rational, logical clarification of the text's intended meaning, a clarification that would seem to borrow much its imagery from Theobald's own formulation:

> To distinguish the passion of *natural affection* from the passion of love between the two sexes, *i.e. Nature, or natural affection is fal'n in love.* And as a person in love is accustomed to send the most precious of his jewels to the person beloved (for the *love-tokens* which young wenches in love send to their sweethearts, is here alluded to) so when *Nature* (says *Laertes) falls in love,* she likewise sends her love-token to the object beloved. But her most precious jewel is *Reason;* she therefore sends that: And this he gives as the cause of *Ophelia's* madness, which he is here endeavouring to account for. (8:230)

By inserting his emendation within his definition, Warburton gradually enters the text of madness and explicates it, even to the point of introducing a gloss from *Romeo and Juliet* to counter Theobald's attempt at rationalizing her state. Warburton's reading of madness duplicates his own editorial methodology as espoused in his preface: "And he [Pope] was willing that *his* Edition should be melted down into *mine,* as it would, he said, afford him (so great is the modesty of an ingenuous temper) a fit opportunity of confessing his Mistakes" (I:xix). With Warburton's incorporation and dismissal of Pope's commentary on madness, Pope's editorial decision is truly "melted down" within Warburton's authoritative definition of madness.

In this textual instance, Johnson, however, expresses his preference for the quarto even as he retains the folio's lines. In his estimation, the quarto shows greater decorum and dramatic force by omitting Laertes' reaction to Ophelia's madness. The folio lines detract from her and render Laertes' emotions as affected: "These lines might have been omitted in the Folio without great loss, for they are obscure and affected; but, I think, they require no emendation" (8:265). Regardless of his aesthetic preference, Johnson follows the editorial tradition that seeks to explicate these lines for the sake of clarity; he attempts to paraphrase Laertes' own explication of Ophelia's madness, and Johnson's paraphrase contains unmistakable echoes of Theobald's own voice:

> Love (says Laertes) is the passion by which *nature is most* exalted and *refined;* and as substances, *refined* and subtilised, easily obey any impulse, or follow any attraction, some part of nature, so purified and *refined,* flies off after the attracting object, after the thing it loves:
>
>> "As into air the purer spirits flow,
>> "And separate from their kindred dregs below
>> "So flew her soul."
>
> (8:265)

By Malone's 1790 edition, the dialogic commentary of Pope, Warburton, and Theobald have vanished from the commentary as Johnson's gloss provides Steevens (who would edit Johnson's text in 1773, 1778, 1785, and 1793) with the foundation for his own closing note on these lines: "The meaning of the passage may be—that her wits, like the spirit of fine essences, flew off or evaporated" (9:367).[37]

This initial fragmentation of editorial glosses, followed by commentary that feigns a thorough elucidation, reflects the editorial practice through which editors attempted to enter into Ophelia's "unshaped" madness and fit it to a sound interpretation, an emendation which often encourages the removal and the refining of previous interpolations. If the theatrical productions attempted to mitigate Ophelia's youthful unbalance by portraying her as a sentimentalized, pathetic lover, eighteenth-century editors transformed Ophelia into an occasion for explicating and elucidating both the madness and the love that begets it. Like the onstage "hearers" of Ophelia's discourse, who "botch the words up fit to their own thoughts," eighteenth-century editors transformed Ophelia in her madness into "the young, the beautiful, the harmless, and the pious."

Notes

1. As modern critics note, Ophelia was subject to the vagaries of editorial decisions made by editors like Davenant and actors like Betterton, each of whom removed much of Ophelia's bawdiness and thus excised much of what made her madness so iconographically powerful for the Renaissance. See Bridget Lyons, "The Iconography of Ophelia," *ELH* 44 (1977): 60–74; Claris Glick, "*Hamlet* in the English Theater—Acting Texts from Betterton (1676) to Olivier (1963)," *SQ* 20, 1 (1969),: 17–34; Elaine Showalter, "Representing Ophelia: Women, Madness, and the Responsibility of Feminist Criticism" in *Hamlet,* ed. Susanne L. Wofford (Boston and New York: Bedford Books of St. Martin's Press, 1994), 220–40.

2. Mary Floyd-Wilson, "Ophelia and Femininity in the Eighteenth Century: 'Dangerous Conjectures in ill-breeding minds," in *Womens Studies* 21 (1992): 398.

3. Similar descriptions can be found for other productions during the eighteenth century. For more details, see Showalter, 225–28 and Floyd-Wilson, 398–405.

4. See *Bell's edition of Shakespeare's plays, as they are now performed at the Theatre's Royal in London; regulated from the prompt books of each house with notes critical and illustrative,* 3 vols. (London: Printed for John Bell; and C. Etherington, 1774): 3:61.

5. *Bell's edition,* 3:61.

6. Barbara Mowat has reminded us recently that except for a period of about a hundred years (1866–1980), *Hamlet* has typically been a "radically unstable, multiform" play-text. She observes that the movement from Rowe through Capell is one of a gradual interweaving of texts, such that, "One has not only this sense of occasional dislocation but also an awareness of a text that is quite unstable, shifting its terms as each editor succeeds his predecessor, pulling in an F or Q line here, dropping one there, choosing a new (or previously abandoned) variant, reaching back for an editorial emendation or substituting an emendation of his own" (113). For Mowat, *Hamlet* becomes a "[deconstructive] illusion." See her "The Forms of *Hamlet's* Fortunes," *Renaissance Drama* 19 (1988): 113.

7. Margreta de Grazia and Peter Stallybrass, "The Materiality of the Shakespearean Text" *SQ* 44 (1993): 267; see also Random Cloud, "'The Very Names of the Persons': Editing and the Invention of Dramatick Character," in *Staging the Renaissance,* ed. David Scott Kastan and Peter Stallybrass (New York and London: Routledge, 1991): 88–98; "The Psycholopathology of Everyday Art," in *Elizabethan Theatre IX,* ed. G. R. Hibbard (Port Credit, Ontario: P.D. Meany, 1981): 100–168; "UNEditing Shak-speare," *Sub-stance* 33/34 (1982): 26–55.

8. Jonathan Goldberg, "Textual Properties," *SQ* 37 (1986): 213–17; "Hamlet's Hand," *SQ* 39 (1988): 307–27; Harry Berger, "What Did the King Know and When Did He Know It? Shakespearean Discourses and Psychoanalysis," *South Atlantic Quarterly* 88 (1989): 811–62.

9. Steven Urkowitz, "Five Women Eleven Ways: Changing Images of Shakespearean Characters in the Earliest Texts," in *Images of Shakespeare,* ed. Werner Habicht, D. J. Palmer, and Roger Pringle (Newark: Univ. of Delware Press, 1988), 292–304.

10. Carol Thomas Neely, "'Documents in Madness': Reading Madness and Gender in Shakespeare's Tragedies and Early Modern Culture," *SQ* 42 (1991): 315.

11. May Byrd, *Visits to Bedlam: Madness and Literature in the Eighteenth Century* (Columbia: Univ. of South Carolina Press, 1974), 112.

12. Edward Capell, ed., *Mr. William Shakespeare his Comedies, Histories, and Tragedies,* 10 vols. (London, 1767–68), cited in Brian Vickers, ed., *Shakespeare: The Critical Heritage 1765–74,* vol. 5 (London and Boston: Routledge, 1979), 307ff. Johnson's metaphors for controlling language convey much of this moral imperative: English has been "hitherto neglected; suffered to spread, under the direction of chance, into wild exuberance; resigned to the tyranny of time and fashion; and exposed to the corruptions of ignorance, and caprices of innovation" (cited in Byrd, 112). Johnson goes on to describe classes of verbs in terms that convey the moral degeneracy of such untamed language: "the signification is so loose and general, the use so vague and indeterminate, and the senses distorted so widely from the first idea, that it is hard to trace them through the maze of variation, to catch them on the brink of utter inanity, to circumscribe them by

any limitations, or interpret them by any words of distinct and settled meaning" (cited in Byrd, 112).

13. For the purposes of this essay, I will confine my collation to Nicholas Rowe, ed., *The Works of Mr. William Shakespear*, 6 vols. (London, 1709); Alexander Pope, ed., *The Works of Shakespeare*, 6 vols. (London, 1723–25); Lewis Theobald, ed., *The Works of Shakespeare*, 7 vols. (London, 1733); Thomas Hanmer, ed., *The Works of Shakespeare*, 6 vols. (Oxford, 1744); William Warburton, ed., *The Works of Shakespeare*, 8 vols. (London, 1747); Samuel Johnson, ed., *The Plays of William Shakespeare*, 8 vols. (London, 1765); Edward Capell (see note 12); Edmond Malone, ed., *The Plays and Poems of William Shakspeare*, 10 vols. (London, 1790). All textual references to these editions will be identified by volume and page.

14. I cite Byrd's analysis here of Augustan views of madness: "Why did the English evaluation of madness change so dramatically from one of complex possibilities to one of intense hostility? . . . One reason may lie in the experience of two generations with the confusion that private values always bring to public order. . . . In his madness, [the madman] had, after all, dispensed with the older priority of reason and trusted instead to private voices and visions, unverifiable by other men; and as with every madman his privacy suggested subversion" (53). Byrd also notes that Lockean positivism also made this view of madness possible: "One implication of the Lockean model is that all minds, since they receive the same sensory information in the same way, will perceive the same reality and come to the same conclusions about it" (51).

15. Neely (see note 10), 315–38. In countering this, Maurice and Hanna Charney indeed show that "mad characters on the Elizabethan stage all have their own special language, costume, and gesture, which depend on a set of theatrical conventions about how to represent madness effectively." See their "The Language of Madwomen in Shakespeare and his Fellow Dramatists," *Signs* 3,2 (1977): 451.

16. For example, see his *Mystical Bedlam: Madness, Anxiety, and Healing in Seventeenth-Century England* (Cambridge: Cambridge Univ. Press, 1981).

17. The *OED* shows that by the eighteenth century, "document" had acquired a connotation of inscription that makes Laertes's comment especially vital for eighteenth-century editors. While it maintained its earlier sense of "a lesson" or "an admonition," it also encompassed "something written, inscribed . . . which furnishes evidence or information."

18. Johnson, 8:311. See also Samuel Johnson, *Johnson on Shakespeare, The Yale Edition of the Works of Samuel Johnson*, ed. Arthur Sherbo (New Haven and London: Yale Univ. Press, 1968), 8:1011.

19. Samuel Weller Singer, ed., *The Dramatic Works*, 10 vols. (Chiswick: Charles Whittingham, 1826), 10:155.

20. Anonymous [Thomas Hanmer], "Some Remarks on the Tragedy of Hamlet, Prince of Denmark, Written by Mr. William Shakespeare," Augustan Reprint Society 3 (1736; reprint. Ann Arbor, MI: Edwards Brothers, Inc, 1947), 45.

21. Ibid., 46.

22. Ibid., 59.

23. Note Sir Joshua Reynolds's comments on the "pathetick" nature of the staging cited in this paper on page 236.

24. Rowe, 5:2424.

25. By Malone's edition of 1790, Ophelia is characterized only as "daughter of Polonius."

26. Pope, 6:iiii2^v.

27. All quarto and folio texts are cited from *The Three-Text Hamlet,* eds., Paul Bertram and Bernice W. Kliman (New York: AMS Press, 1991).

28. See Collier's note in his 1853 edition, "The omission in the Ff of the Gentleman was, no doubt, to avoid the employment of another actor" (cited in Furness's edition, *Hamlet. A New Variorum,* 2 vols. (1877; reprint. New York: Dover Publications, 1963: 227). Collier's conclusion would be echoed by Reverend Alexander Dyce in his 1857 edition. Dyce reiterates Collier's view: "There certainly is room for suspecting that the omission of the 'Gentleman' is to be attributed to the players. But be that as it may, there can be no doubt that if a modern editor adheres to the folio in omitting the 'Gentleman' he ought to restore to Horatio (what comes very awkwardly from the Queen),—

> "'Twere good she were spoken with,
> For she may strew dangerous coniectures
> In ill breeding minds. Let her come in."

See Alexander Dyce, ed., The Works of William Shakespeare, 6 vols. (London: Edward Moxon, 1857), 5:592.

29. Neely (see note 10), 324.

30. One further disparity in this speech is in the use of "yawn" in "they yawn at it." That remains the quarto reading, but the folio asserts "they aim at it." Both words are suitable here. "Yawn" suggests a bewilderment over her meaning, while "aim" suggests an attempt to conjecture her meaning. Aptly, both words exemplify the controversy over Ophelia's madness.

31. The attribution of lines in this scene produces a ponderous note like that found in Clark and Wright's 1863 Cambridge edition, the standard modern edition for much of the nineteenth and early twentieth century:

> Rowe followed the Folios; Pope, Theobald, Warburton and Capell, the Quartos. Hanmer continues the lines "'Twere good . . . minds' to the gentleman who had spoken the previous lines, and gives 'Let her come in &c.' to the Queen. Johnson follows Hanmer's distribution of the speeches, but substitutes 'Hor.' for 'Gent.' in lines 2 and 4; the arrangement proposed by Blackstone. Steevens (1773) assigned the speech "'Twere good . . . spilt" (14–20) to Horatio, but restored it to the Queen in his next edition. Mr. Grant White follows the Folios in giving the whole Speech to the Queen, but marks "'Twere good . . . minds" as spoken aside, and "let . . . in" "To Hor."

See William George Clark and William Aldis Wright, eds., *The Works of William Shakespeare,* 8 vols. (Cambridge: Macmillian and Co, 1866), 8:194.

32. Lewis Theobald, *Shakespeare Restored: or, a Specimen of the Many Errors. . . .* (1726; reprint. New York: AMS Press, 1970), 111–12. Theobald follows Pope's scene changes here and thus renders 4.5 as 4.7 thanks to Pope's decision to begin a new scene with Ophelia's return. More recently, G. R. Hibbard has posited in his Oxford edition that Theobald perhaps too hastily revised Q2 and F1 (as well as the still unseen Q1) by failing to see Laertes's confusion as a sound dramatic reading of the scene. See his *Hamlet,* (Oxford: Oxford Univ. Press, 1987), 305–306. I owe this observation to my colleague, Alan Young.

33. One reflection of this discordancy is the note at the bottom of the page of this scene in the 1866 volume of the Cambridge edition:

149 SCENE VII. Pope.
   Danes. [Within] Capell. See note (XXVI).

151 Re-enter . . .] Collier. Enter Ophelia, fantastically drest with Straws and Flowers. Rowe. Enter Ophelia, still distraught. Collier MS.

When the reader does turn to note XXVI, one sees the following elaborate commentary (vol 8: 194):

IV.5.149. In the Quartos the passage is thus printed:

> 'A noyse within.
> Enter Ophelia.
> Laer. Let her come in.
> How now, what noyse is that?'
> In the Folios:
> 'A noise within. Let her come in.
> Enter Ophelia.
> Laer. How now? what noise is that?'

Rowe followed the Folios, Pope the Quartos, reading "Let . . . that?" as one line. Theobald first transferred the stage direction, *Enter Ophelia* to follow the first line of Laertes's speech.

34. James Boswell, ed., *The Plays and Poems of William Shakespeare,* 21 vols. (1821; rpt. New York: AMS Press, 1966), 7:358–59.

35. See Glick (see note 1), 17–34; Floyd-Wilson (see note 2), 397–409.

36. Boswell's "third variorum" of Malone's edition suggests the panoply of responses to this section of the text as rosemary, fennel, columbine, rue, and daisy generate a bouquet of responses from Steevens, Henley, Malone, Ritson, among others. See 7:439–42.

37. In Issac Reed's 1803 and James Boswell's 1821 editions, Steevens's note and textual reference to *All's Well that Ends Well* has expanded on Theobald's and Warburton's practice of referring back to Shakespeare for authority.

The Rowe Editions of 1709/1714 and 3.1 of
The Taming of the Shrew

Margaret Maurer

Mɪᴅᴡᴀʏ through the text of *The Taming of the Shrew,* just before Pe-truchio arrives to marry Kate, the little sister, Bianca, has a scene with two of her suitors, Hortensio and Lucentio, disguised respectively as Litio and Cambio. This scene, numbered 3.1 in the modern text, owes its shape to Lewis Theobald, who suggested substantial changes to it in *Shakespeare Restored* of 1726 and printed them in his edition of 1733. Theobald's justification for doing so appears in a note to the line, "In time I may believe, yet I mistrust," a line he assigns, against the authority of any of the Folios (F1 1623, F2 1632, F3 1663/4, and F4 1685) and as an improvement on the two different versions of the scene in the Nicholas Rowe editions of 1709 and 1714,[1] not to Lucentio nor to Hortensio, but to Bianca. Theobald comments,

> This and the 7 Verses, that follow, have in all the Editions been stupidly shuffled and misplac'd to wrong Speakers: so that every Word said was glaringly out of Character. I first directed the true Regulation of them in my S H A K E - S P E A R E *restor'd,* and Mr. *Pope* has since embraced it in his last Edition. I ought to take notice, the ingenious Dr. *Thirlby,* without seeing my Book, had struck out the self-same Regulation.[2]

By 1726, the year of *Shakespeare Restored,* Nicholas Rowe had been dead and buried in Westminster Abbey for eight years; and by 1728, the year of the edition in which his good friend Alexander Pope printed the text that adopted Theobald's emendations to the scene, he had been gone an even decade. These days, some 270 years later, his work on the scene has all but disappeared from the history of *Shrew*'s text. In the careful textual notes to the New Cambridge *Shrew* edited by Ann Thompson, Rowe's name appears only incidentally in 3.1.[3]

Yet changes to the scene in both of the so-called Rowe editions are valuable to recover. The 1709 and 1714 texts emend in different ways the scene as printed in F2–F4 (itself slightly changed in a substantive way

244

from its form in F1); thus they are purposefully edited texts that stop significantly short of Theobald's revision. It is the role of Bianca in the scene, as defined by the lines assigned to her, that remains constant throughout all of these early forms. Alone with two men wishing to insinuate themselves into her graces, Bianca, after Penelope, on whom she is modeled, exerts her power over men by manipulating their competing attentions to her. In all, in the century between 1623 and 1726, there were four distinct dispositions of the lines in the scene; and each version projects a wittier and more willful Bianca than appears in Theobald's text.

The scene evolves through these versions, however, in terms of how the suitors are conveyed; increasingly, Hortensio seems to give way to the newcomer Lucentio. Rowe in 1709, as well as whoever guided the revision of the edition of 1714 that also bears his name, may have been influenced in their conception of the scene by the popularly staged Restoration version of the play called *Sauny the Scot, or The Taming of the Shrew* by John Lacey. Lacey, who played Sauny (Petruchio's servant, Grumio) in his adaptation, emphasizes the Petruchio taming business in the play and revises to enhance it, correspondingly subordinating the play's other action to it. In comparison to the more protracted intrigue in the Shakespearean *Shrew,* Biancha's unmarried state at the play's start is, in Lacey's version, quickly resolved into her attraction to the Lucentio character. The successful suitor's courtship of Biancha is thus virtually concluded in the middle of Lacey's play, leaving time for the shrew to instruct her little sister in shrewish ways as an element of her final, drawn-out resistance.

In relation to its predecessors in the Folio texts and Lacey's adaptation, the 1709 and 1714 versions are then remarkable hybrids. In 1709, Rowe moves Bianca more toward rejecting Hortensio's attentions and acceding to Lucentio's in 3.1. At the same time, however, he preserves Bianca's command of the scene. Moreover, this complex sense of her persists into the 1714 edition, even though the scene is pushed still further in Lucentio's favor by having Hortensio realize early in the scene that his rival is a formidable opponent. Ultimately, of course, acknowledging that there is logic to the pre-Theobald emendations undermines the stability of Theobald's redistribution of the lines and argues for serious reexamination of the First-Folio version of 3.1. In this essay, however, I want to stop short of admiring at full length the scene's original configuration. My business here is the briefer argument of contrasting the scene's playful ambiguities in its earlier forms (when Bianca dominates it and Theobald thought its speeches "stupidly shuffled and misplac'd") to the clarity Theobald sought to impose on it when he (his word is particularly apt) regulated it in 1726.

I

As printed in the First Folio, *Shrew*'s 3.1 seems marred by a conspicuous anomaly that is now decisively eliminated from the modern text. Though editors since Theobald may be attracted to his reconstruction of the scene as a way to repair the problem, it is by no means clear that the changes of the 1709 and 1714 texts were motivated by it.

The anomalous passage (TLN 1338–56) is about 45 lines into the scene. Thus modern texts (*The Riverside Shakespeare* is convenient here because it marks substantial emendations with square brackets[4]) do not differ substantially from the First Folio in 3.1's opening sequence. Lucentio, disguised as Cambio, a teacher of grammar, and Hortensio, disguised as Litio, a music teacher, quarrel over the priority of the art each comes to teach Bianca:

> *Luc.*   Fiddler, forbear, you grow too forward, sir.
>   Have you so soon forgot the entertainment
>   Her sister Katherine welcom'd you withal?
>
> *Hor.*   But, wrangling pedant, this is
>   The patroness of heavenly harmony.
>   Then give me leave to have prerogative,
>   And when in music we have spent an hour,
>   Your lecture shall have leisure for as much.
>
> *Luc.*   Preposterous ass, that never read so far
>   To know the cause why music was ordain'd!
>   Was it not to refresh the mind of man
>   After his studies or his usual pain?
>   Then give me leave to read philosophy,
>   And while I pause, serve in your harmony.
>
> *Hor.*   Sirrah, I will not bear these braves of thine.

Bianca takes control of the situation by evenhandedly suppressing both men:

> *Bian.* Why, gentlemen, you do me double wrong
>   To strive for that which resteth in my choice.
>   I am no breeching scholar in the schools,
>   I'll not be tied to hours, nor 'pointed times,
>   But learn my lessons as I please myself.
>   And to cut off all strife, here sit we down:
>   Take you your instrument, play you the whiles,
>   His lecture will be done ere you have tun'd.

The men, Lucentio grudgingly, accept this disposition:

    Hor.   You'll leave his lecture when I am in tune?

    Luc.   That will be never, tune your instrument.

She then appoints Lucentio to begin what he says at 3.1.13 will be a philosophy lesson but is in fact a translation exercise using a passage from Ovid's *Heroides,* Penelope's letter to Ulysses describing her life under the pressure of her many suitors:

    Bian.   Where left we last?

    Luc.   Here, madam:
           "Hic ibat Simois; hic est [Sigeia] tellus;
           Hic steterat Priami regia celsa senis."

    Bian.   Conster them.

Lucentio's response is a pretext for him to reveal himself:

    Luc.   *"Hic ibat,"* as I told you before, *"Simois,"* I am Lucentio, *"hic est,"*
           son unto Vincentio of Pisa, *"[Sigeia] tellus,"* disguis'd thus to get
           your love, *"Hic steterat,"* and that Lucentio that comes a-wooing,
           "Priami," is my man Tranio, *"regia,"* bearing my port, *"celsa senis,"*
           that we might beguile the old pantaloon.

Hortensio interrupts, but Bianca dismisses him, prompting an exultant jibe by Lucentio:

    Hor.   Madam, my instrument's in tune.

    Bian.   Let's hear. O fie, the treble jars.

    Luc.   Spit in the hole, man, and tune again.

Bianca then returns to the lesson, reading into it her reaction to Lucentio's revelation:

    Bian.   Now let me see if I can conster it:
           "Hic ibat Simois," I know you not, *"hic est [Sigeia] tellus,"* I trust
           you not, *"Hic steterat Priami,"* take heed he hear us not, *"regia,"*
           presume not, *"celsa senis,"* despair not.

To anyone familiar with the text they are reading, it is obvious that neither of them attends to the actual meaning of the Latin words; but it is likewise clear how the context of the passage is relevant to the situation of Shakespeare's play.

The Latin lines, from the first epistle in Ovid's *Heroides*, begin an account of the Trojan War, such as Penelope says she has had repeatedly to endure in Ulysses's absence. In Ovid's text, the device permits him a pointedly abbreviated distillation of his epic predecessors. Penelope represents herself as having heard such things to the point of weariness, and the lines with their anaphora on the demonstrative pronoun (hic, hic, hic[5]) convey a sense of compression and abbreviation through repeated tellings. Yet the effect is only an incidental glance at the heroical hexametrical accounts of battles. Ovid's elegy primarily revises the image of Penelope from the *Odyssey*, making her housewifely and suspicious about tales she has heard of his adventures since the War. Shakespeare's scene, taking its cue from Ovid's act of imitation, translates Penelope's situation among her suitors and adapts it to his own ends.

As most readers and audiences of *Shrew* 3.1 now experience it, however, the parallel between Penelope's and Bianca's situations fades almost at once as Bianca seems decidedly interested in Lucentio. The next section of the scene, as set by editors since Theobald, has her flirtatious dialogue with Lucentio continue over Hortensio's second interruption:

> *Hor.*   Madam, 'tis now in tune.
>
> *Luc.*   All but the base.

In the modern text, Hortensio's retort slides into a suspicious aside:

> *Hor.*   The base is right, 'tis the base knave that jars.
>   [*Aside.*] How fiery and forward our pedant is!
>   Now, for my life, the knave doth court my love:
>   Pedascule, I'll watch you better yet.

Bianca says again that she is disposed to mistrust but now prefaces her admission with encouragement:

> [*Bian.*] In time I may believe, yet I mistrust.

and she and Lucentio exchange cryptic but apparently reassuring lines:

> [*Luc.*] Mistrust it not, for sure Aeacides
>   Was Ajax, call'd so from his grandfather.

[*Bian.*] I must believe my master, else, I promise you,
      I should be arguing still upon that doubt,

as the scene's emphasis passes to Hortensio:

      But let it rest. Now, Litio, to you:
      Good master, take it not unkindly, pray,
      That I have been thus pleasant with you both.

Hor.   [*To Lucentio*] You may go walk, and give me leave a while;
        My lessons make no music in three parts.

Luc.   Are you so formal, sir? Well, I must wait,
        [*Aside.*] And watch withal, for but I be deceiv'd,
        Our fine musician groweth amorous.

As the Riverside text concedes in its speech headings, the interaction of the characters here is conveyed through some significantly redistributed lines.

As the scene continues with Hortensio's lesson in a different, more sexually explicit key, the modern text is again close to the First Folio, though notes often exert a repressive influence on the bawdy importunity[6] of Hortensio's lines:

Hor.   Madam, before you touch the instrument,
        To learn the order of my fingering,
        I must begin with rudiments of art,
        To teach you gamouth in a briefer sort,
        More pleasant, pithy, and effectual,
        Than hath been taught by any of my trade;
        And there it is in writing, fairly drawn.

Bianca and Hortensio, we know from the play's earlier scenes, have a history; (Kate at 2.1.13 has even conjectured that her sister prefers him). Some acknowledgment of this past and maybe her rejection of it as she warms to Lucentio may attend her line

Bian.   Why, I am past my gamouth long ago.

If she has not already recognized him, Hortensio reveals himself at this point:

Hor.   Yet read the gamouth of Hortensio.

Bian.   [*Reads.*]

> "*Gamouth* I am, the ground of all accord:
> *A re,* to plead Hortensio's passion;
> *B mi,* Bianca, take him for thy lord,
> *C fa ut,* that loves with all affection.
> *D sol re,* one cliff, two notes have I,
> *E la mi,* show pity, or I die."
> Call you this gamouth? Tut, I like it not.
> Old fashions please me best; I am not so nice
> To [change] true rules for [odd] inventions.[7]

Bianca's response to Hortensio admits several interpretations. The "old fashions" she professes to have nostalgia for may be the reading of an antique story such as she has just concluded with Lucentio. They may also, however, be the attentions she enjoyed with Hortensio before he resorted to disguise or even the senile advances of old man Gremio (her other suitor, not present in this scene).

The scene ends with a messenger entering to call Bianca to her sister:

Enter a MESSENGER.

[*Mess.*] Mistress, your father prays you leave your books,
     And help to dress your sister's chamber up.
     You know to-morrow is the wedding-day.

Bian.   Farewell, sweet masters both, I must be gone. [*Exeunt Bianca and Messenger.*]

Luc.   Faith, mistress, then I have no cause to stay. [*Exit.*]

Hor.   But I have cause to pry into this pedant.
     Methinks he looks as though he were in love;
     Yet if thy thoughts, Bianca, be so humble
     To cast thy wand'ring eyes on every stale,
     Seize thee that list. If once I find thee ranging,
     Hortensio will be quit with thee by changing. *Exit.*

Hortensio's last lines are a statement of man's only defense against the likes of her. But just what is the like of her? The modern text's delineation of her character is manifestly reconstituted from the lines of the scene.

To be sure, in the First Folio text, there is something odd at TLN 1338–56. Two successive speeches are assigned to Hortensio:

Hort.   Madam, tis now in tune.

Luc.   All but the base.

Hort.   The base is right, 'tis the base knave that jars.

Luc.   How fiery and forward our Pedant is,
          Now for my life the knave doth court my love,
          Pedascule, Ile watch you better yet:
          In time I may beleeve, yet I mistrust.

Bian.   Mistrust it not, for sure *Aeacides*
          Was *Ajax* cald so from his grandfather.

Hort.   I must beleeve my master, else I promise you,
          I should be arguing still upon that doubt,
          But let it rest, now *Litio* to you:
          Good master take it not unkindly pray
          That I have beene thus pleasant with you both.

Hort.   You may go walk, and give me leave a while,
          My Lessons make no musicke in three parts.

Luc.   Are you so formall sir, well I must waite
          And watch withall, for but I be deceiv'd,
          Our fine Musitian groweth amorous.

                                (F1, TLN 1338–56)

Yet it is not certain that the double speech assignment indicates an error. Charlton Hinman in the introduction to his facsimile of the First Folio describes circumstances that would produce the double heading in a single speech;[8] and the scene as written in the First Folio will play quite nicely, conveying, in contrast to the modern version, a Bianca who is less engaged with Lucentio than the modern text suggests. It is Lucentio in the First Folio, not Hortensio, who is suspicious of his rival at "How fiery and forward our Pedant is"; and it is Lucentio, not Bianca, who expresses doubt about what is going on at "In time I may beleeve, yet I mistrust." Bianca, not Lucentio, makes the cryptic comment about Ajax; and Hortensio, not Bianca, delivers a response to it, seeming to have received a measure of reassurance from what she has alluded to in his master Ovid ("I must beleeve my master . . ."). Hortensio then agrees to proceed ("But let it rest, now *Litio* to you . . ."), asks pardon for his pleasantry ("Good master take it not unkindly . . ."), and dismisses Lucentio ("You may go walk . . ."). Lucentio then repeats his doubts directly to his rival ("Are you so formall sir . . .").

Some confirmation of the scene's viability as printed in the First Folio is the correction, conceivably even mechanically motivated, introduced into the Second. There the difficulty of the consecutive "Hort." speech prefixes is simply resolved by assigning Bianca the lines attributed to the second "Hort.": "You may go walke, and give me leave a while; / My Lessons make no musicke in three parts." In this form, the scene was read and presumably appreciated on some level for the nearly seventy years that F2 through F4 were the most recently printed versions of the play:

Hort. Madam, 'tis now in tune.

Luc. All but the base.

Hort. The base is right, 'tis the base knave that jars.

Luc. How fiery and forward our *Pedant* is,
Now for my life that knave doth court my love,
Pedascule, Ile watch you better yet:
In time I may beleeve, yet I mistrust.

Bian. Mistrust it not, for sure *Aeacides*
Was *Ajax* cald so from his grandfather.

Hort. I must beleeve my Master, else I promise you,
I should be arguing still upon that doubt,
But let it rest, now *Litio* to you:
Good master take it not unkindly pray
That I have beene thus pleasant with you both.

Bian. You may goe walke, and give me leave a while,
My Lessons make no musicke in three parts.

Luc. Are you so formall sir, well I must waite
And watch withall, for but I be deceiv'd,
Our fine Musitian groweth amorous.

(F2)

"You may goe walke," spoken by Bianca, is an explicit dismissal, and Lucentio appears to recover from it by responding instead to Hortensio's preceding speech. It is from this superficially trouble-free version of the scene, reprinted in the Third and Fourth Folios, that Nicholas Rowe probably worked.

II

Rowe's work on the text of the plays seems to have been motivated by a desire to represent them accurately and also, in terms of the theater as he knew it, clearly. A playwright himself, he attended to speech headings and stage directions but was generally restrained about other substantive changes. His statement of what he sets out to do in the prefatory letter to the Duke of Somerset, describes his work modestly:

> I must not pretend to have restor'd this Work to the Exactness of the Author's Original Manuscripts: Those are lost, or, at least, are gone beyond any Inquiry I could make; so that there was nothing left, but to compare the several Editions, and give the true Reading as well as I could from thence. This I have endeavour'd to do pretty carefully, and render'd very many Places Intelligible, that were not so before.[9]

The "several Editions" to which he refers might include quartos when a given play had been printed outside the Folios. In the case of *Shrew,* it likely involved no authentic texts but one or more of the Folios. With respect to which one, it is customary to observe that he likely worked only from the Fourth.[10]

Consciously or unconsciously, however, Rowe might have considered John Lacey's *Sauny the Scot, or The Taming of the Shrew* a relevant edition as well. In print or on the stage, *Sauny the Scot* would have been fairly widely available to him. Its first recorded performance was by the King's Company at Bridges Street Theater on 9 April 1667, with a later performance (November 1) that same year. It was played at the Drury Lane Theater in 1698, a production from which the surviving text of the play was printed. In the years of Rowe's career, performances are likewise recorded in 1704 (2), 1707 (3), 1708, 1711, 1712 (2), and 1714.[11]

In his adaptation of the play, Lacey rewrites dialogue, but he follows the plot of the Shakespearean text relatively closely at first. There is, however, a slight and, in terms of what is to come in 3.1, significant change to Lacey's adaptation of the early encounter between the shrew, who is named Margaret, and Biancha, a change that is consistent with the innovation later in the play whereby Margaret and Biancha become partners in shrewishness. While Shakespeare's Bianca consistently professes her indifference to men, Lacey's Biancha seems open from the start to an especially attractive one. This serves Lacey's impulse to streamline the Biancha intrigue in that it reduces the degree to which Geraldo (Hortensio) has a significant chance to succeed in his suit once a new face is on the scene.

Lacey's Biancha expresses openness to the attractions of youth and physical charm in a way that Shakespeare's Bianca does not. In what modern Shakespearean texts call 2.1, Shakespeare has Bianca reply to Kate's charge that she "tell / Whom thou lov'st best" with the ambiguous, "Believe me, sister, of all the men alive / I never yet beheld that special face / Which I could fancy more than any other." All men are equal, in other words, in her eyes. Kate then guesses she prefers Hortensio, and Bianca replies, "If you affect him, sister, here I swear / I'll plead for you myself, but you shall have him." When Kate revises her conjecture to Gremio, Bianca protests incredulity: "Is it for him you do envy me so? / Nay then you jest . . ." (2.1.8–19). Lacey's Biancha follows Bianca in saying, "Believe me, Sister, of all Men alive, I never saw that Particular Face which I cou'd Fancy more than another" and offering to "plead for you my self, but you shall have [Geraldo]"; but she goes beyond Shakespeare's Bianca in specifying why Woodall (Gremio) is not the man: "That Old Fool: Nay now I see you but Jested with me all this while; I know you are not Angry with me" (7–8). Consequently, when Lacey's version comes to the scene equivalent to the Shakespearean 3.1, the audience is ready for the dismissal of her former suitors in favor of the new man whose name foretells his success, Winlove.

Lacey's version of 3.1 (14–15) opens with Geraldo and Winlove speaking competitively, not to one another, but to Biancha:

Geral. Pray Madam, will you take out this Lesson on the Gittar.

Win. Here be de ver fine Story in de Varle of Mounsieur *Appollo,* And Madomoselle *Daphne;* Me vill Read you dat Madam.

Geral. Good Madam, mind not that Monsieur Shorthose; But Learn this Lesson first.

Win. Begar Monsieur Fideler, you be de vera fine troublesome Fellow, me vil make de great Hole in your Head wid de Gittar, as *Margaret* did.

Ger. This is no Place to Quarrel in: But Remember—

Bian. Why Gentlemen, you do me double wrong, to strive for that which Resteth in my Bare Choice: To end the Quarrel, sit down and Tune your *instrument,* and by that time his Lecture will be done.

Geraldo reacts to Biancha's choice, and Lacey has Biancha acknowledge the insecurity of his reaction, omitting Lucentio's peevish "That will be never, tune your instrument":

Gera. You'l leave his Lecture, when *I* am in Tune.

Bian. Yes, yes; Pray be satisfied: Come, Monsieur, let's see your Ode.

Winlove, who speaks with a French accent in his assumed identity, says in his own voice,

Win.   *I* do suspect that Fellow. Sure he's no Lute-Master.

In effect, Lacey gives the Lucentio suitor the equivalent of "How fiery and forward our pedant is" as a distinct aside before he conducts his lesson.

The lesson, "de ver fine Story in de Varle of Monsieur *Appollo,* And Mademoselle *Daphne,*" replaces the Penelope element in the scene with a myth that accords with other aspects of Lacey's adaptation of the Bianca intrigue—the story of a god pursuing a nymph who ultimately becomes something other than the creature who inspired his passion. The lesson unfolds harmoniously without Biancha's response to it contradicting Winlove's. What is read is the declaration of Winlove's identity:

Bian.   Here's the Place, Come Read.   [*Reads.*
       Do not Believe *I* am a *Frenchman,* my Name is *Winlove;* He that
       bears my Name about the Town, is my Man *Tranio. I* am your
       passionate Servant, and must live by your Smiles. Therefore be so
       good, to give Life to my Hopes.

Geraldo interrupts before Biancha can comment, separating her response from the "reading":

Gera.   Madam, your Gittar is in Tune.

Biancha suppresses him,

Bian.   Let's hear; fye, there's a String split.

and Winlove joins in,

Win.   Make de spit in the Whole Man, and Tune it again.

Biancha then says,

Bian.   Now let me see. *I* know not how to believe you. But if it be true,
       Noble Mr. *Winlove* deserves to be belov'd; and, in the mean time,
       keep your own Councell; and it is not impossible but your Hopes
       may be Converted into Certainties.

After this, when Geraldo interrupts again,

Gera.   Madam, now 'tis Perfectly in Tune.

and Winlove tries to suppress him again,

Win.   Fye, fye, Begar no Tune at all.

Biancha turns to him.

Bian.   Now, Sir, *I* am for you.

It is Geraldo who says,

Gera.   Mounsieur, Pray walk now, and give me leave a while, my Lesson
will make no Musick in Three Parts.

suggesting that Lacey worked from the version of the scene printed in
the First Folio, as F2–F4 give this speech to Bianca.

Winlove then repeats his suspicions, this time with a more accurate
sense of the situation than Lucentio acknowledges in the comparable
Shakespearean scene:

Win.   Me vil no trouble you Mounsieur Fiddeller. *I* am confident it is so,
this must be some Person that has taken a Disguise, like me, to
Court *Biancha*; *I*'ll watch him. (*Aside*).

As Lacey's Biancha is more receptive to Winlove than Bianca to Lucentio, so she is more clearly repressive of Geraldo than Bianca is to
Hortensio in the next phase of the scene. She may easily signify her lack
of harmony with Geraldo by distorting her accompaniment to the song.
Geraldo seems to propose his "Rules" as a comment on her performance,
and they have little of the potential for bawdy wit that enlivens Hortensio's "gamouth":

Gera.   First, Madam, be pleas'd to Sing the Last Song that *I* Taught you,
and then we'll proceed.

Bian.   I'll try, bu*t* I'm afraid *I* shall be out.

SONG.

Gera.   Madam, before you proceed any farther, there be some few Rules set
down in this Paper, in order to your Fingering, will be worth your
Perusal.

Bian.   Let's see. (*Reads.*
Tho' I appear a Lute-Master, yet know my fair Biancha, *I have but
taken this disguise to get Access to you, and tell you I am your
humble Servant, and Passionate Admirer*, Geraldo. Pish, take your

Rules again, I like 'em not the old way pleases me best, I do not care for changing old Rules, for these Foolish new Inventions.

When a servant enters to summon Biancha to help dress the bride, she exits:

Enter Servant.

Serv.   Madam my Lord calls for you to help dress the Bride.

Bian.   Farewell then Master, I must be gone. Exeunt.

using a curiously singular "master," apparently to exclude Geraldo.

Geraldo knows now what, in the Shakespearean play, he does not express until the beginning of 4.2:

Ger.   I know not what to think of her, this fellow looks, as if he were in Love, and she carresses him. These damn'd French men, have got all the trade in Town, if they get up all the handsome Women, the *English* must e'en march into *Wales* for Mistersses; well, if thy thoughts *Biancha* are grown so low, to cast thy wandring Eyes on such a kikshaw, I'me resolv'd to ply my Widow.
Exit.

It is not until 4.2 that Shakespeare's Hortensio notes, "See how they kiss and court!" (4.2.27), and "For me, that I may surely keep mine oath, / I will be married to a wealthy widow, / Ere three days pass, which hath as long lov'd me / As I have lov'd this proud disdainful haggard" (4.2.36–39). In contrast, Winlove's final words in the scene summarize the progress that, in Lacey's version, he has made:

Win.   I am glad I'me rid of him, that I may speak my Mother Tongue agen, *Biancha* has given me hopes, I dare half believe she Loves me.

Confirming this, Geraldo tells Tranio in the next scene that Winlove has betrayed the man who employed him to woo Biancha on his behalf and "has spoken one word for [old Woodall] and two for himself" (19).

III

If Rowe worked, as he most likely did, from any of the three latter Folios, the scene he encountered there showed no outward signs of needing adjustment, the doubled "Hort." prefix having been eliminated in the

Second. It is consequently somewhat momentous that Rowe's 1709 edition takes the decisive step of assigning the speech "I must believe my master, else . . ." to Bianca, in effect eliminating the "Hort." prefix that separates it from the previous two lines, "Mistrust it not. . . ." Rowe then returns the two lines "You may go walk . . ." to Hortensio, as they had been assigned in the First Folio (which Lacey follows), departing as he did so from the assignment of those lines to Bianca in the latter Folios. The passage, as printed by Rowe, in 1709, then reads,

Luc. All but the Base.

Hor. The Base is right; 'tis the base Knave that jars.

Luc. How fiery and froward our *Pedant* is!
Now for my Life that Knave doth court my Love;
Pedascule, I'll watch you better yet:
In time I may believe, yet I mistrust.

Bian. Mistrust it not, for sure *Aeacides*
Was *Ajax,* call'd so from his Grandfather.
I must believe my Master, else I promise you,
I should be arguing still upon that Doubt;
But let it rest. Now *Licio* to you:
Good Master, take it not unkindly, pray,
That I have been thus pleasant with you both.

Hor. You may go walk, and give me leave a while;
My Lessons make not Musick in three Parts.

Luc. Are you so formal, Sir? well, I must wait,
And watch withal; for, but I be deceiv'd,
Our fine Musician groweth amorous.

(Rowe, 1709)

If this is simply, as R. B. McKerrow believes, a revision of the Fourth Folio, then it is certainly, as he says of Rowe's changes generally, "an intelligent revision" (110).

Without the provocation of the double "Hort." prefix, Rowe's change must have been motivated by a sense, originating elsewhere, that the lines "I must believe my Master . . ." are appropriate to Bianca. Perhaps he was influenced by the logic implied in the modern punctuation that places "Licio" (Litio) in commas, making it a noun of address, though seen without those commas, there is no inherent difficulty in the line. If the speech is assigned to Hortensio, Hortensio is referring to himself by his assumed proper name, just as in the last lines of the scene ("If once I find thee ranging, / Hortensio will be quit with thee by changing," 3.1.91–92) he refers to himself by his actual proper name. Or perhaps the word "Master" influenced Rowe's move of assigning the speech to Bianca. It is a word that Lacey's version puts rather emphatically in her mouth; she leaves the scene addressing only Winlove as "Master" at a point where all Folio texts have her use the plural "masters." Rowe may also have been motivated by an illogic he perceived in having Lucentio say "Are you so formal, Sir" after Bianca has just spoken, so he assigns "You may go walk" to Hortensio, thereby creating for himself the anomaly of F1, which he then corrects by giving the prior Hortensio speech to Bianca.

Whatever prompted his action, however, it is interesting to compare Bianca's enlarged speech in his 1709 edition to Biancha's speech at a comparable moment in *Sauny the Scot*. As we have seen, in *Sauny the Scot*, she responds to Winlove's "lesson,"

Now let me see. *I* know not how to believe you. But if it be true, Noble Mr. *Winlove* deserves to be belov'd; and, in the mean time, keep your own Councell; and it is not impossible but your Hopes may be Converted into Certainties.

And then, when Geraldo interrupts, she says, "Now, Sir, *I* am for you." In the enlarged speech as Rowe reconstructs it, an actress can convey this same sense of Bianca working through the gradations of her response to the revelation: "Mistrust it not, for sure *Aeacides* / Was *Ajax,* call'd so from his Grandfather. / I must believe my Master, else I promise you, / I should be arguing still upon that Doubt; / But let it rest. Now *Licio. . . .*"

Five years later, in what is generally called Rowe's third edition, the passage seems to have been reconsidered in a more thoroughgoing way. In the 1714 version of this scene, the speech "How fiery and forward our pedant is" is transferred from Lucentio to Hortensio. The motive of this transference is even harder to describe in terms of an explicit textual provocation. The speech is several lines above the double "Hort." prefix of the First Folio, so that even if one assumes that the anomaly of that double prefix triggered the impulse to emend, it is hard to explain the emendation beginning at this earlier point in the scene. Moreover, there is not, in this speech, a confusing grammatical construction like "Now Litio to you." The conversion of Lucentio's speech "How fiery and forward" to a continuation of Hortensio's line "The base is right, 'tis the base knave that jars" may have been an attempt to cope with the word "pedant," which could be taken to apply more aptly to a teacher of philosophy or the literary arts than to a music teacher.[12]

After all, however, it may be more relevant to note how the 1714 change brings the scene closer to the form it takes in *Sauny the Scot*. In Lacey's version of the play, as noted above, Winlove is still the one to express doubts in the equivalent of "How fiery and forward our pedant is": "*I* do suspect that Fellow. Sure he's no Lute-Master"; but in Lacey's version, the speech has a different effect because it does not, as in the Folio, follow on Bianca's "correction" of his declaration. That element is moved by Lacey to later in the scene. Certainly Lacey's development of the scene to enhance both Winlove's (Lucentio's) sense of confidence in his position with Biancha and Geraldo's (Hortensio's) growing suspicion that he has been displaced by the Frenchman makes assigning the speech "How fiery and forward our pedant is! / Now, for my life, the knave doth court my love: / Pedascule, I'll watch you better yet" to Hortensio instead of Lucentio a logical development.

In compiling his *Shakespeare Restored* in 1726, Theobald worked from Pope's 1723 edition which, in the speech assignments of *Shrew* 3.1, follows 1714. The version of *Shrew* 3.1.46–63 that he found there read like this:

Luc.   All but the base.

Hor.   The base is right, 'tis the base knave that jars.
         How fiery and how froward is our pedant!
         Now for my life that knave doth court my love;
         Pedascule, I'll watch you better yet:
         In time I may believe, yet I mistrust.

Bian. Mistrust it not, for sure *Aeacides*
         Was *Ajax,* call'd so from his grandfather.
         I must believe my master, else I promise you,
         I should be arguing still upon that doubt;
         But let it rest. Now *Licio* to you:
         Good masters, take it not unkindly, pray,
         That I have been thus pleasant with you both.

Hor.   You may go walk, and give me leave a while;
         My lessons make no musick in three parts.

Luc.   Are you so formal, Sir? well, I must wait,
         And watch withal; for, but I be deceiv'd,
         Our fine musician groweth amorous.

                                              (Pope, 1723)[13]

Theobald's changes to this are discrete and deliberate and motivated, as he confesses in the note in his 1733 edition, by a sense of what is appropriate to the characters of the persons in the scene. He makes two crucial changes: he assigns "In time I may believe, yet I mistrust" to Bianca instead of to either of the men (all the Folios and Rowe in 1709 had given that line to Lucentio; the 1714 edition, giving the whole speech to Hortensio, gave its last line to Hortensio); and he gives "Mistrust it not,— for, sure, *Aeacides* / Was *Ajax,* call'd so from his grandfather" to Lucentio (this speech had always been assigned to Bianca). Theobald then continues the assignment, first proposed by Rowe in 1709, of "I must believe my master, else I promise you, / I should be arguing still upon that doubt; / But let it rest. Now, *Licio,* to you: / Good masters,[14] take it not unkindly, pray, / That I have been thus pleasant with you both" to Bianca (it had been Hortensio's, until Rowe 1709 assigned it to Bianca); and he keeps to the First Folio reading of "You may go walk, and give me leave a while; / My lessons make no musick in three parts" as a speech by Hortensio, following Pope who followed Rowe who, as we have seen, probably not because he knew the First Folio reading but because he followed Lacey or came to the same point incidentally, assigned it to Hortensio.

In *Shakespeare Restored,* Theobald lists this passage as one of the six examples of an error he calls "Transpositions *of* Persons Names"; and he rationalizes the emendations he proposes by describing his sense of what is going on in the scene:

> Here, indeed, the Names are so shuffled and displaced, that I must be obliged to explain the Business of the Scene, before I can convince that there has been a manifest *Transposition*. *Bianca* is courted by two Gentlemen, *Hortensio* and *Lucentio,* who make Way for their Addresses under the Disguise of Masters, the One to instruct her in *Latine,* the other in Musick. *Lucentio,* as he is teaching her Language, informs her who he is, and to what Purpose he comes: She says, She'll construe the Lesson her self, and, in so doing, she tells him, She does not know him, does not trust him, bids him take Heed that *Hortensio* do not overhear them, and neither to presume, nor to despair. *Hortensio* is jealous that *Lucentio* is, like himself, a Lover in Disguise, and says he'll watch Him. After this, *Bianca* and *Lucentio* proceed in their Discourse, under Colour of continuing the Lesson; and there is no doubt but that the Speeches ought to be distinguish'd thus. (156)

The last two sentences of this passage are particularly important. In asserting that "*Hortensio* is jealous that *Lucentio* is, like himself, a Lover in Disguise, and says he'll watch Him," Theobald justifies the assignment of "How fiery and how froward is our Pedant . . ." to Hortensio, an assignment in which he follows the 1714 text. "After this, *Bianca* and *Lucentio* proceed in their Discourse . . . and there is no doubt but that the Speeches ought to be distinguish'd thus" refers only obliquely to two significant innovations Theobald brings to the scene: Bianca is the one to express mistrust, and Lucentio refers to Ajax's lineage from Aeacus as a warrant for urging her not to mistrust him.

IV

It is important to note in concluding this description of Rowe's work on the scene in 1709 and its evolution in 1714 what, in relation to Theobald's innovations, earlier editors, who did emend the scene, did not do to it. Rowe did not convert the line "In time I may believe, yet I mistrust" from a concluding line to a speech of suspicion of one or the other man to a coquettish invitation by Bianca to Lucentio to persevere in his efforts. And he did not take from Bianca and assign to Lucentio the cryptic reference to a word in the next line of the passage from the *Heroides* from which the Latin words are taken. Even when the scene is more substantially revised in 1714 to take it further in the direction of Lacey's conception of Bianca's attraction to Lucentio, Bianca's contributions to the dialogue remain, in these respects, unchanged. Rowe keeps both men off guard in the scene; and even the 1714 editor, who ascribes uncertainty more entirely to Hortensio, appreciates the significance of it being not Bianca, but one of the men, who expresses mistrust.

This leaves the particularly subtle and delicious lines about Ajax with Bianca. Ovid's word "Aeacides" refers to someone by his patronymic, and it invites the reader to supply the particular name of one or the other of the heroes who might be called by that name. The Elizabethan George Turberville translates the lines as a reference, not to Ajax, but to Achilles. Even to someone with only an Elizabethan grammar school education, or perhaps more especially to one such, as many members of Shakespeare's audience would be some such, the lines "for sure Aeacides / Was Ajax, call'd so from his grandfather" must have recollected a memorable pedagogical moment, rendered all the more playful by the effect of Anglicized pronunciation of the names Ajax and Aeacides.

The lines use the punning patronymic to suggest that a man might be a foolish successor to the hero to whom he says he is related and whose honors he claims to inherit. All the Folios and Nicholas Rowe (and the 1714 editor and Pope, too, at first) agree in allowing Bianca, when one of her suitors says, "In time I may believe, yet I mistrust," a witty rejoinder, prompted by the ambiguity in the word "Aeacides" that she anticipates from Ovid's next line (perhaps because she sees it, but perhaps because, being no "breeching scholar," she knows it by heart): "Mistrust it not, for sure ay-ASS-i-des / Was a-JAKES, call'd so from his grandfather." If she says it this way, which of the two is she calling an ass? It would depend on who feeds her the line about mistrust in the first place. It would depend on the motion of her head when she says it. It would depend on whether she says it so that its mocking implications are to be heard by either of the men or both of them or by the audience alone.[15] And whether it is she who continues, as Rowe has her do, or Hortensio who replies, "I must believe my master, else, I promise you . . . ," the exchange would not be about revealing one's true identity by naming one's forefathers but about using Latin words as a pretext to say something else. The exchange would be in little what the scene at large is about: invention, constering, translation in an old-fashioned sense.[16]

Lacey's impulse to use French rather than Latin words to create a more superficial sense of comedy in the scene converts the emphasis on translation to a more easily accessible source of laughter at English words being spoken with a foreign tongue. His tactic is a prudent adjustment to the likelihood that, since Shakespeare's day, fewer and fewer members of the audience would appreciate the pun inherent in the Latin crux. Rowe and his 1714 successor and Pope, too, momentarily, while adopting increasingly the elements of Lacey's scene that made Bianca more and more explicit in her preference for Lucentio, nonetheless do not deny her this moment, though conceivably the pun in the line eluded them and having Bianca mistakenly see Aeacides as Ajax fit with their notion of her inferior knowledge of this passage in Ovid. Did the joke elude Theobald? Does Theobald take the speech from her so that Lucentio can say it crudely about Hortensio or straightforwardly about himself? If he did not appreciate the line's witty potential, then the most generous construction of his emendation is that he certifies Lucentio's pedantry by having him mistake Achilles for Ajax.

These days, Bianca's playfulness is linguistically remote. In most of today's modern editions, learned men ponderously explain, sometimes incorrectly, what they take to be Lucentio's gloss on Ovid's line.[17] Thoroughly regulated now, Bianca may only be imagined enjoying a little joke on them all.

NOTES

1. Actually, there are three "Rowe" editions. Two, each of six octavo volumes, attributed to Rowe appeared in 1709, virtually the same; a seventh volume for the poems was added in 1710. The plays were then reissued in eight, with the poems, nine, duodecimo volumes in 1714. R. B. McKerrow thinks it "doubtful whether Rowe had much to do with this [1714] edition. It may, indeed, have been entirely the work of a certain 'Mr. Hughes'—presumably John Hughes, the poet and editor of Spenser—to whom Tonson paid £28 7s. 0d. in connexion with it." See "The Treatment of Shakespeare's Text by his Earlier Editors, 1709–1768, "Studies in Shakespeare, British Academy Lectures, selected and introduced by Peter Alexander (New York: Oxford University Press, 1967), 115. Recently, Ber-

nice Kliman, in a paper written for a Shakespeare Association of America session in 1994, sounds a cautionary note about continually mentioning Hughes in the context of the 1714 text: "A change in the Hughes-Shakespeare narrative will produce little effect; still, looking at how assumptions harden into fact can be a salutary activity and may even provide a parable about evidence. In a spirit of inquiry about how scholars construct knowledge, I question the eighteenth-century view of Hughes as Shakespeare editor and the flowering of certainty about him."

2. AMS reprinted Lewis Theobald's *The Works of Shakespeare* in photographic facsimile of the 1733 edition in 1968 and *Shakespeare Restored* in 1970. The full title of the latter, *SHAKESPEARE restored: / OR, A / SPECIMEN / OF THE / Many ERRORS, / AS WELL /Committed, as Unamended, by Mr. POPE / In his Late / EDITION of this POET. / DESIGNED / Not only to correct the said EDITION, but to restore the True / READING of SHAKESPEARE in all the Editions / ever yet publish'd,* gives some sense of the book's concerns; but it is detailed only with respect to Pope's text of *Hamlet.* After that, it notes other kinds of errors categorically in its appendix. The passage in 3.1 of *Shrew* is example XXXV (156–57), the fifth example of the error Theobald calls "Transpositions *of* Persons Names." Theobald lists six examples of this error, and the new Oxford *Complete Works,* eds. Stanley Wells and Gary Taylor (New York: Oxford University Press, 1986) follows him in emending four of them, including the ones at 3.1 of *Shrew* under discussion here.

3. Thompson (Cambridge: Cambridge University Press, 1984) adopts five readings from the Rowe 1709 edition in 3.1. One of them is the modernization of the word "gamouth" to "gamut," a change which is, as we shall see, not universally followed by modern editors. The other four are the demarcation of this scene as the first of two in act three and three additions or rationalizations of stage directions. Thompson also notes, but does not adopt, a plural "masters" for "master," from Rowe 1714, in a line ("Good master, take it not unkindly, pray") that will be discussed below.

McKerrow (110) characterizes Rowe's editorial work: "Apart from the correction of grammatical errors Rowe was a conservative editor and seldom tampered with anything that made sense, or tried to introduce gratuitous improvements without a reasonable ground for supposing the extant text to be wrong. . . ." He supplied lists of dramatis personae, and attended to act divisions and entrances and exits and modernized the text to some extent. Gary Taylor in the "General Introduction" to the *Textual Companion* to the new Oxford Shakespeare (Oxford: Clarendon Press, 1987), seems to find Rowe's work of limited interest to a modern editor: "Textually, the 1709 edition was a reprint of the 1685 Folio, transferred to a more manageable multi–volume quarto format. Rowe made almost no use of the 1623 folio, or of the early substantive quartos, though he was aware of the existence of at least some of them. He reproduced, or conjecturally emended, many derivative readings contained in the fourth folio. But, being a poet himself, he did successfully eliminate most of the problems of mislineation in the Folio, and he did restore sense to many passages by means of obvious emendations. . . . Alexander Pope was not only a better poet than Rowe, but also a better editor" (54).

4. All modern editions print substantially the same text of this scene. *The Riverside Shakespeare,* ed. G. Blakemore Evans (Boston: Houghton Mifflin, 1974) is useful not only for its clear marking of substantial departures from the First Folio but also because it is relatively light-handed in its editorial intrusions. I

quote all passages from Shakespeare's plays from *The Riverside Shakespeare* unless indicated otherwise in my text. When I quote from the Folios and the Rowe and Pope editions, I do not reproduce ligatures nor the long *s*, and I follow modern usage with *i, j, u,* and *v.*

5. The modern text of *Heroides,* I, 33–34, differs from the Latin in this scene. The Loeb text (*Heroides and Amores,* with an English translation by Grant Showerman, 2d ed. rev. G. P. Goold, Cambridge: Harvard University Press, 1986) reads, "hac ibat Simois; haec est Sigeia tellus; / hic steterat Priami regia celsa senis." H. J. Oliver, in his edition of *The Taming of the Shrew* (Oxford: Oxford University Press, 1984), has helpful notes about the variations between the play's version of these lines and the standard modern Latin text: "Shakespeare may have intended Lucentio's Latin to be bad; or perhaps Shakespeare was quoting from a different text of Ovid. . . . or from memory." Oliver and all modern editions follow F2 in emending Folio's "*sigeria*" to "*Sigeia*." It is interesting that the Latin lesson in *The Merry Wives of Windsor,* 4.1.42–63, has a Welsh schoolmaster, Hugh Evans, put young William Page through the paces of the demonstrative pronoun: *Nominativo, hig, hag, hog . . . Accusativo,* [*hung*], *hang, hog,*" which becomes, in Mistress Quickly's hearing, "Hang-hog" for bacon as "[*Genitivo,*] *horum, harum, horum*" provokes "Vengeance of Jinney's case! Fie on her! never name her, child, if she be a whore." The *Merry Wives* scene seems to record the way a text in a foreign tongue might inspire inventive impulses. To *Love's Labour's Lost*'s schoolmaster, Holofernes, "Ovidius Naso was the man. And why indeed "Naso" but for smelling out the odiferous flowers of fancy, the jerks of invention? *Imitari* is nothing" (4.2.123–26).

6. In the Arden text (New York: Methuen, 1981), Brian Morris concedes that "Attempts have been made to find bawdy meanings in these lines," but notes also that his predecessor R. Warwick Bond (Arden, 1904) "proposes that the 'one clef' is love, and the 'two notes' Hortensio's real and assumed personalities." The Riverside text, annotated presumably by Lloyd Berry, is simply as silent as is possible, glossing, among other words, "gamouth" as "gamut, the diatonic scale," "ut" as "the lowest note, now called *do,*" and "cliff" as "cleff, key." Ann Thompson, in the new Cambridge text, devotes an appendix ("Music in the play and Hortensio's gamut," 186–88) to exploring the "ingenious double meanings which depend on a knowledge of the Elizabethan system of musical notation (186)." Her comments at last concede that "it may be intended as a joke that [Hortensio] stumbles into obscenity" on "cliff" and "there may again be an obscene undertone" on "die" (188).

7. The line in the First Folio is "To *charge* true rules for *old* inventions" (italics mine). The second Folio prints "change" for "charge." The Rowe 1714 edition replaces "old inventions" with "new inventions." Biancha in *Sauny the Scot* says, "I do not care for changing old Rules, for these Foolish new Inventions." Theobald thought "odd" inventions gave the same sense as "new inventions." See his note to the passage on 314 of his text.

8. Hinman thinks that the doubled "*Pro.*" (Proculeius) in *Antony and Cleopatra,* 5.2, which most modern editions assume is a simple repetition indicating no error, occurred because the copy from which the printer was working repeated the speech heading after an intervening stage direction which the printer omitted because the page, as cast off, was crowded. See *The Norton Facsimile of the First Folio* (New York: W. W. Norton, 1968), xvii. At this point in *Shrew,* Hortensio has just finished a casual remark and asked pardon for the liberty. He turns to Lucentio/Cambio in a different tone, a tone Lucentio acknowledges in "Are you

so formal, sir?" The column of the page in the First Folio is full, but not so crowded as the *Antony and Cleopatra* instance. Eric Rasmussen has noted to me in private correspondence that he thinks there is evidence of a compositor shift at this point in the setting of *Shrew.* There are three consecutive speech headings of "Mal." (Malvolio) at *Twelfth Night,* 3.4.20–28, which most modern editions correct by giving the second speech to Olivia. In my full-length treatment of this problem, an as-yet-unpublished essay entitled, "The Taming of Bianca: Early Adaptations and Revisions to the Text of the Shakespearean *Taming of the Shrew,*" I discuss the virtues of earlier texts of this play. In fact, I see no reason to emend 3.1 as printed in the First Folio; but assuming that the doubled speech heading must be corrected, I am struck by how neatly the Second Folio does it without substantial change to any of the characters in the scene.

9. This statement in the prefatory letter to his Grace, the Duke of Somerset, is in Vol. 1 of the 1709 edition.

10. McKerrow believed that Rowe worked from the Fourth Folio: "There seems therefore to have been little justification for Rowe's claim to have consulted all the available editions of Shakespeare in the preparation of his text. It is in fact little more—at least with the exception of *Hamlet*—than a revision of the Fourth Folio" (110). Not having systematically studied Rowe's edition, I will not dispute this, beyond observing a general tendency in all commentators on Rowe to cast aspersions on his diligence and offering the additional observation that, at a point I have examined in the last scene of *As You Like It,* Rowe is actually (though conceivably accidentally) closer to the reading of the Third than to the Fourth Folio. Yet *Shrew* 3.1, as printed in the Fourth Folio, differs in several obvious accidentals from the scene as printed in the Second and Third; and in this case, Rowe's version is closest to the form in the Fourth. The First Folio text of *Shrew* is also substantially reproduced in a quarto copy of the play dated 1631.

11. A full treatment of the stage history of *The Taming of the Shrew* is in Tori Haring-Smith, *From Farce to Metadrama: A Stage History of* The Taming of the Shrew (Westport, Conn.: Greenwood Press, 1985). See, in particular, her appendix B, "Chronological Handlist of Performances in England and North America," 173 ff. The 1698 text of the Drury Lane *Sauny the Scot* is available in facsimile from the Cornmarket Press, 1969, the version from which I quote below.

12. The 1714 edition also further rationalizes the assignment of "I must believe my master . . ." to Bianca by changing the singular *master* in line 57 "Good master, take it not unkindly . . . ,") to the plural. When Hortensio speaks this line, he seems to use the singular *master* to apologize to Lucentio while admitting that his informality was directed at both him and Bianca. Bianca, in Rowe's 1709 edition, uses the singular at first to address Hortensio before conceding that she has been informal with both men. In Bianca's mouth in 1714, the speech is more certainly directed to both men.

13. In Pope's edition of 1723–25, the *Taming of the Shrew* is in volume 2. This edition is available in facsimile (New York: AMS Press, 1969).

14. Theobald follows the 1714 text and Pope in using the plural here.

15. It could depend on all these things, but I think the line is most likely a jibe at Lucentio. It is, after all, Lucentio who has just identified himself in terms of his father. Bianca uses the reference to Aeacus to remind herself or the spectators or even, conceivably, Litio, whom she may already have recognized as Hortensio, that ancestry is no warrant of a man's greatness. Ajax's claim to the armor of Achilles on the basis of their common lineage is in Book XIII of Ovid's *Metamor-*

phoses. Ulysses reminds Ajax and the listeners to their debate that one cannot count the deeds of one's ancestors as one's own.

16. Bianca's direction that Cambio "conster" the Latin lines of Ovid's epistle is invariably glossed as "construe," and the OED cites this passage in *Shrew* as illustrative of "construe" in the sense (3.a. *Gram.*) of "To analyse or trace the grammatical construction of a sentence; to take its words in such an order as to show the meaning of the sentence; *spec.* to do this in the study of a foreign and especially a classical language, adding a word for word translation; hence, loosely, to translate orally a passage in an ancient or foreign author." Of the seven times that this word appears in the Shakespearean canon, however, only the two incidences of it in this scene are glossed in this way; the others convey something more like "construe" in the sense of "understand" or "make me to understand" (in the negative, misconstrue), senses of the word consistent with the OED's fourth sense, "4.a. *trans.* To give the sense or meaning of; to expound, explain, interpret (language); b. To expound, interpret, or take in a specified way (often apart from the real sense)." In this sense of construe, "conster" is related to "construct" and conveys, in a context like that of the *Shrew* 3.1 lesson, something more akin to what we would call free translation or translation as a species of invention. This is the sense in which Elizabethan sonneteers translated Petrarch, literally (in terms of the etymology of translate) using the terms of Petrarch's conceits to frame the very different courtly love situations in which they found themselves.

17. See H. J. Oliver's note to the line in his Oxford Shakespeare *Shrew.* He follows the explanation offered by R. Warwick Bond in the old Arden Shakespeare: "Lucentio [to whom he, of course, assigns the lines] is now pretending that he is explaining the beginning of the next line (l. 35) from Ovid (following those he pretended to construe), namely '*Illic Aeacides. . . .*' His explanation is correct as far as it goes; but perhaps Shakespeare is being very subtle. As Bond points out, Bianca's hesitation over taking Lucentio's word may be because she knows that the patronymic *Aeacides* does not necessarily designate Ajax; and indeed the very line of Ovid that Lucentio is 'explaining' more probably refers to another grandson of Aeacus, Achilles (and Turbervile translated it, 'There fierce *Achylles* pight his Tentes')" (159). Brian Morris ignores this insight by his predecessor in the Arden series. His note to the line reads, "Ajax, son of Telamon, was called Aeacides after his grandfather, Aeacus. Shakespeare might have found this in Ovid, *Met.,* xiii.25; Bianca looks no farther than the next line of the text she is studying, *Heroides,* i.35, 'illic Aeacides, illic tendebat Vlixes'" (221).

When the Culture Obtrudes: Hanmer's *Winter's Tale*

Irene G. Dash

Decorated with the illustrations of Francis Hayman, Sir Thomas Hanmer's elegant edition of Shakespeare's *Works,* the first to be published by the Oxford Press, was directed at a culture-hungry, increasingly affluent, Puritan-oriented, merchant class.[1] It was an audience that was avidly devouring the newest accomplishments in lexicography, attending performances of Shakespeare's plays on the stage, and applauding the acting of David Garrick.[2] But it was also an audience that had participated in the clamor leading to the passage of the *Licensing Act* in 1737. In external appearance Hanmer's work answered the needs and conformed to the taste of this new audience. But also in its notes and emendations, it proved to be equally responsive to the impress of the new cultural and moral forces. His edition of *The Winter's Tale* reflects these influences.

Paralleling this development was that of Shakespeare criticism. Appearing with increasing frequency in contemporary periodicals, these comments sought to reconcile the obvious popularity of Shakespeare's plays on the stage with the rigidity of the prevailing rules.[3] This criticism relied less on clearly reasoned rebuttals to neoclassical rules and more on an emotional response to the plays as theatrical entertainment. The author of an anonymous pamphlet entitled *Memoirs of the Times; in A Letter to a Friend in the Country* (London, 1737) summarized the conflict facing critics:

> A Critick may demolish Shakespeare in his Closet, but upon the Stage we shall everlastingly admire him, unless there should come a Time that we heartily despise our Ancestors, and content ourselves with laughing at those high Qualities which have never descended to us.[4]

By the late 1730s and early 1740s there could be no doubt of Shakespeare's talents as a playwright. English scholars did not seriously question this. But in the criticism beginning to appear in periodicals in the 1730s the problem which had faced Pope, and, at a much earlier date,

Dryden, remained: how to reconcile the neoclassical rules with the obvious greatness of Shakespeare's plays. Pope, in 1725, in the Preface to his edition of the *Works,* had evolved his own rationalizations just as Dryden had, in his "Essay on Dramatic Poesy."[5]

More and more by the 1740s the decision on what rules to disregard seemed to have become a pragmatic one. If a Shakespearean play had captivated theater audiences, perhaps the rule it defied was at fault. If, however, as was true of *The Winter's Tale,* the play had not been performed, the rule would seem to have been confirmed. Thus, whereas critics finally abandoned their insistence on the unities—demolished in part by the stage popularity of many of Shakespeare's works—credibility persisted as a critical yardstick. Mentioned in 1712, by Addison, as an absolute necessity for the creation of a convincing fable, the lack of credibility was cited in 1770 as a major weakness in *The Winter's Tale.*[6] In his attempt to eradicate one flaw contributing to the play's lack of credibility, Hanmer, inventing his most memorable emendation, was, I believe, responding to the emphasis in contemporary criticism.

Like Rowe, Pope, and Theobald, the 1744 editor promised, in his preface, an edition of Shakespeare's works "cleared from the corruptions with which they have hitherto abounded" (1:a2).[7] He also intended "to note the obscurities and absurdities introduced into the text, . . . and . . . to restore the genuine sense and purity of it" (1:a2). However, as we know, he did not refer to the Quartos and Folios, as this statement implies, but based his text on Pope's edition and corrected it by Theobald's, introducing several of his own variations as well.[8] The most famous, or infamous, was his substitution of "Bithynia" for Bohemia with the following explanation:

> It is probable he [Shakespeare] removed this impropriety and placed the scene in Bithynia, which the ignorance and negligence of the first transcribers or printers might corrupt and bring back again to Bohemia by a less variation in the letters than they have been guilty of in numberless other works. (2:502)

Although today we briefly note and swiftly dismiss "Bithynia," it survived as a plausible alternative for "Bohemia" during the next quarter century. Morgan in his adaptation called *The Sheep-Shearing,* Garrick in his manuscript copy of *Florizel and Perdita* (1756), and Thomas Hull in the fairly complete version of *The Winter's Tale* written for the 1771 production at the Theatre-Royal in Covent Garden retained Hanmer's invention.[9] "Bithynia" also appears in the printed edition, *The Sheep Shearing* or *Florizel and Perdita,* published by Peter Wilson (Dublin, 1755; rpt.1767) and J. Truman (London, 1762).

That confusion existed over which of the two place names was more appropriate is illustrated by the various changes made in the texts of Garrick's play. We find, for example, that in the 1758 edition the playwright, editor, or printer opted for a return to Shakespeare's "Bohemia," rejecting the manuscript copy. By 1762, however, an updating of the cast list in a new printing allowed for the insertion of the following footnote:

> The scenes of the following Play lie in "Bohemia," which Sir Thomas Hanmer, with some Reason, has changed to "Bythinia": All the Editors of Shakespeare except Sir Thomas, have followed the original.[10]

Prudence had dictated the retention of Shakespeare's form in this 1762 text; however, the ambiguity in the wording suggests that Hanmer's emendation was not condemned. Even later than this (1794), in a working promptbook, not of Garrick's *Florizel and Perdita* but of *The Winter's Tale,* "Bithynia" still appears.[11] It would seem that audiences witnessing productions during the last decade of the eighteenth century were still in Hanmer country. Today we laugh at Hanmer's invention; nevertheless the tendency to question textual incongruities and seek a unifying "logic" still occurs as de Grazia and Stallybrass point out although concentrating on other aspects of the problem.[12]

In his second emendation of Shakespeare's text, Hanmer, whether consciously or unconsciously, succumbed to the pressures of the new morality. Having survived uncut for one hundred and fifty years, *The Winter's Tale* was to experience its first amputation in the Oxford edition. The new, more widely based audience had, in two ways, contributed to the change. Because they had clamored for more Shakespeare both on the stage and in their libraries, they had been responsible indirectly for the emergence of this play from the closet. Because they were primarily the same men and women who, as early as 1735, had filed acts with Parliament aimed at reforming the theatres, they would probably not have been averse to purging the texts of "obscenities" (*LS 3,* 1:clxv).

Scouten characterizes this period as one which witnessed the "second surge of English Puritanism" (*LS 3,* 1: clxix). During the closing years of the seventeenth and opening of the eighteenth centuries, when the earlier Puritan outcry against the "wicked influence" of the drama had been heard again, *The Winter's Tale* had rested quietly in the comparative obscurity of a read but unacted text. By 1744, however, this was no longer true. Having reached the stage in 1741 and acquired a public, as well as private, audience it had also become subject to closer moral scrutiny.

Before turning to Hanmer's alteration, let me sketch in briefly the stage history of *The Winter's Tale* between 1703 and 1756. In the early years, episodes from the play appeared as drolls, as entertainment at fairs, as musical farce, and as pastoral romance.[13] The variety of these forms mirrors that of the London stage in an era when entertainment at the fairs developed in complexity, when managers of little theatres, to the applause of loudly responsive audiences, presented musical farces, when ballad opera exploded on the scene and comic opera, its less offensive offspring, trailed after. Although records are fragmentary, critics generally agree that the unabridged play also reached the stage during this period. However, if it was "unabridged," it has a curious background. Ambiguities surround that production of 1741.

Billed with the comment "Not Acted these Hundred Years," it was presented at Goodman's Fields by Giffard. Unfortunately, we know very little about what scenes it actually contained. The cast list or "dramatis personae" presents an enigma. Whereas the pattern used in the printed text is to divide the men and women, and then to follow a hierarchical order, moving from royalty down in the social scale to shepherd, Giffard's pattern is based on the importance of the role acted and the comparative fame or obscurity of the actor or actress. He therefore does not separate the male from the female roles. Thus, Giffard as Leontes, Marshall as Polixenes, Walker as Antigonus, W. Giffard as Florizel, Paget as Camillo, and Yates as Autolicus are followed by Mrs. Steel as Paulina and Miss Hippisley as Perdita before the other male characters are listed. The curious aspect of this is that Mrs. Giffard in the role of Hermione is the last name listed, following the shepherdesses, Mopsa and Dorcas. In fact, I spent a good deal of time trying to track down some other information on this production because I felt that in many ways it may have anticipated Garrick's where Hermione's role is limited to the statue scene. But I was unsuccessful. Were a pattern based on the relative importance of the role a rigid one, it would have been easy to conclude that Giffard had abbreviated Hermione's lines since many of them had begun to be embarrassing. Moreover, her strength as a character seemed to challenge the actor managers. Thus, while Scouten suggests this was the unabridged play, it may very well have anticipated Hanmer's edition as well as the later staging at midcentury.

In methodology, Hanmer had adopted Pope's approach and text, but then had "improved" upon it. This meant not only following Pope's multiple scene divisions and accepting his "laissez-faire" attitude towards Shakespeare's poetry but also removing sections of the text from their place in the sequence and placing these sections at the bottom of the page. Hanmer, however, then found lines objectionable that apparently had been inoffensive to his predecessor. Differences in the men as well as in the times played a part: Pope's responses to the text were those of a poet—an artist not easily shocked by bawdy or innuendo—Hanmer's were those of a man of taste and sensibilities who belonged to a specific culture group and who mirrored their standards in his edition.[14]

In Act I following the exit of Hermione on the arm of Polixenes, Leontes blurts out bitter words of jealousy tinged with suggestive phrases. It is from this speech, early in the play, that Hanmer excises four lines:

> Should all despaire
> That have revolted Wives, the tenth of Mankind
> Would hang themselves. Physick for't, there's none:
> It is a bawdy Planet, that will strike
> Where 'tis predominant; *and 'tis powrefull: thinke it:*
> *From East, West, North and South, be it concluded,*
> *No Barricado for a Belly. Know't,*
> *It will let in and out the Enemy,*
> *With bag and baggage:* many thousand on's
> Have the Disease, and feele't not.
>
> (my italics; 1.2.233–242)[15]

The italicized words with their inferences of sexuality and promiscuity— "No Barricado for a Belly, Know't, / It will let in and out the Enemy, / With bag and baggage"—have been tamed into smaller type at the bottom of the page. Thus, Hanmer, by retaining the "old copy," allowed reader discrimination to operate even while he became the first to raise moral fences around *The Winter's Tale.*

It was not until Warburton's edition that more stringent censorship was initiated.[16] The lines which his predecessor had reduced to a footnote, Warburton completely excluded, justifying his action with the comment:

> After this there are four lines of infamous, senseless ribaldry, stuck in by some profligate player, which I have cashier'd; and hope no learned critick, or fine lady, will esteem this a castrated edition, for our having now and then on the same necessity, and after having given fair notice, taken the same liberty. (3:287)[17]

Thomas Edwards, Warburton's most consistent critic, was quick to assert that it was indeed a "castrated edition." In Canon twenty-one of his *Canons of Criticism* he cited the note to exemplify Warburton's method of exhibiting wit by taking "every opportunity of sneering at the fair sex."[18] The passage was later restored, but the tendency to tidy a play of Shakespeare's continued, culminating in Bowdler's edition in the early nineteenth century.[19]

Hanmer also emended Camillo's speech to Leontes referring to Hermione:

> But I cannot
> Beleeve this Crack to be in my dread Mistresse
> (So soveraignely being Honorable.)
> *I have lov'd thee,*
>
> (my italics; 1.2.372–75)

Hanmer changed the italicized words to "so loved" thereby eliminating any reference to the relationship between the two men, Camillo and Leontes. Instead, he focused only on the queen.

In the theater, an interesting example of the development of this carefulness at the turn of the nineteenth century occurs in a prompt-copy of an 1802 J. P. Kemble text of *The Winter's Tale*.[20] Hanmer and Warburton had found "bawdy" or the suggestion of immorality legitimate excuse for excision. In this acting copy, simple embarrassment at discussion of the normal functions of nature appears to have motivated the emendation. Protecting the delicate sensibilities of his audience, the actor-manager has eliminated all references to Hermione's pregnancy or motherhood. In addition to the many lines already excised, however, further cuts were made, specifically for theater audiences. Thus, the following lines, originally retained by Kemble in his emended text were, on reconsideration, neatly crossed out in the prompt copy:

> The queen, your mother, rounds apace
>
> (2.1.25; p.21)

> [This child] was prisoner to the womb
>
> (2.2.71; p.29)

> The innocent milk in its most innocent mouth
>
> (3.2.107; p.39)

While the interplay of social and literary forces had broadened the audience for Shakespeare's plays so as to include the comparatively obscure *Winter's Tale*, it had also subjected this work to a censorship absent earlier. Editing for this audience, Hanmer provided the first wedge. Later editors, actors, and producers were to continue the process until much of the basic earthiness of the characters evaporated, and increasingly, the primary stress fell on the play's ethereal, pastoral, romantic qualities. These were to emerge in the midcentury versions of Morgan and Garrick. These men discarded the play's first half with its intense sexual innuendos, and concentrated instead on the sheepshearing, Garrick bringing Hermione on stage only for the breathtaking statue scene. The versions of Morgan and Garrick not only provided unity but also eliminated the strong women characters of the play's first half. Morgan reduced the play to the sheepshearing scene. Garrick included a bit more of Shakespeare's play. The net effect was to deprive audiences of Shakespeare's fascinating development of Hermione and the strong Paulina of the play's first half. (Garrick's version necessitated major textual revision, with Leontes being washed ashore in Bithynia, coming upon the sheepshearing scene, and eventually being united with Hermione—all in Polixenes' domain.) Meanwhile, Hanmer's edition began its subtle emendations of the written text.

One other characteristic, seldom noted later on because of the competition and animosity among eighteenth-century editors, distinguished this edition. As I said earlier, interest in lexicography had begun during this period. And while contemporary influences had nurtured the weeds of morally motivated excision and overzealous dedication to logic, it also had provided a ground on which cultivated plants might grow. Hardly perceivable in Hanmer's edition because no individual note or emendation was dramatically arresting, the seeds nevertheless had taken root. Appearing were small shoots of explanation and definition for words like "Motion," considered an archaic term for puppet show (4.3.98; 2:555), "Pedler's excrement" (4.4.802; 2:579), and "unrold" (4.3.123; 2:556). Less successfully, emendations were made. "Pugging" became "progging" (4.3.9; 2:552)—a term hailed by Warburton as preferable to the earlier form and discarded by Johnson who considered both words meaningless. "Clamor your tongues" became "charm your tongues" (4.4.277; 2:564) and "pound and odde" became "a pound and one odd" (4.3.36; 2:553). Hanmer also attempted to clarify the meaning of such phrases as "stamped Coyne" (4.4.813; 2:579) and "my Revennew is the silly Cheate" (4.3.29; 2:553). As a result of his concentration on these words and phrases they were further explicated by others who followed. Although seldom credited, even during the later eighteenth century, for these early observations, it was Hanmer who had first pinpointed the ambiguities in the language of Autolicus and the rustics, and had questioned some of the text's more archaic expressions.

His preoccupation with the oddities of language and the derivation of archaisms, as compared with the aims of Theobald a decade earlier, paralleled a similar development in lexicography. The first edition of Nathan Bailey's *Dictionarium Britannicum* (1730) has been described as an important predecessor of Johnson's dictionary because it "made signal advances in scope, etymology, and other lexicographical technique[s]."[21] Of the second edition (1736), in which "proverbs and other incidental features" from *The Universal Etymological English Dictionary* were reinstated, Starnes and Noyes write:

The crispness, the clarity, and the accuracy which had been gradually developing in the definitions are here wantonly sacrificed to novelty of presentation. . . . The 1736 edition, though so much larger than the 1730, is inferior to it from the point of view of lexicography. The author has here yielded to the cardinal temptations which have beset lexicographers all along: he has included too many oddities and he has drawn no clear or consistent distinction between the provinces and methods of the dictionary and the encyclopedia. In these respects, however, Bailey was merely of his time. (123,125)

Hanmer too was of his time. His objective is clearly stated in the "Preface" where he promises to limit himself to defining obscure terms "not arising from the words but from a reference to some antiquated customs now forgotten" (1:v). Jonas Barish, in his study of Jonson's comedy, has observed that the language of comedy, because it is closer to the vernacular than the language of tragedy, becomes obsolete more quickly.[22] Since archaic and obsolete terms were Hanmer's specialty, it was perhaps inevitable that he should have discovered his richest material embedded in the language of Autolicus and the rustics.

The staged play, in which the comic scenes appear to have been most successful, may also have influenced Hanmer to explicate these words. When, in his edition, Autolicus leaped into the spotlight, a new element had entered the play's history. Although the editor, living in retirement in the country, probably did not attend Giffard's production of *The Winter's Tale* at Goodman's Fields in January 1741, he must have heard about it. We know that he was in correspondence with London friends at the time.[23] Aware of his forthcoming publication of Shakespeare's *Works* they must undoubtedly have described to him the successful performance by Yates as the "snapper up of unconsidered trifles" (4.3.28).

And here we see the interaction between the work of editors and that of theatrical producers. Alexander Pope had given theater people a handle into the play through his multiple divisions of scenes into small scenic units. This was particularly true of the extremely long sheepshearing scene where he created opportunities for transposition of the order of Autolicus's speeches. Yates, entertaining audiences in 1741–42, enhanced the characterization. Hanmer, profiting from the vision of the earlier editor and probably aware, through his correspondence, of the imaginative interpretation of the actor, moved the camera in for a close-up.

Like the photographer studying the nuances of facial expression, the Oxford editor scrutinized Autolicus's speeches, paying careful attention to individual words. This more commendable aspect of Hanmer's edition has seldom been noted by later editors, although his comments stimulated them to examine the language of the rustics. Some few editors did credit Hanmer; most did not. When, for example, Hanmer moved the word "not" into the text after "were" and excised it after "would," Johnson adopted the change to "If I thought it were not a piece of honesty to acquaint the King withal, I would do't," footnoting this with:

> This is the reading of Sir T. Hanmer, instead of "if I thought it were a piece of honesty to acquaint the King withal, I'd not do't."[24]

The *Variorum* notes the change crediting "Hanmer et etc." meaning "all other editions" (11: 419). More usual, however, was what occurred to another excision of "not." Here Johnson set a precedent for later commentary:

> Let me have no lying; it becomes none but Tradesmen, and they often give us (Souldiers) the Lye, but wee pay them for it with stamped Coyne, not stabbing Steele, therefore they doe *not* give us the Lye. (my italics; 4.4.814)

In the responses which this emendation evoked appear hints of the future fate of Hanmer's edition. Warburton, in his 1747 edition, after adopting Hanmer's version as his own, added a footnote:

> Dele the negative: the sense requires it. The joke is this, they have a profit in lying to us by advancing the price of their commodities; therefore they do lie. (3:361)

Heath, not aware of Hanmer's role but always ready to criticize Warburton, noted the Bishop's failure to understand Shakespeare's text and accused him of having missed the joke.[25] To Heath the speech was pure double-talk, exemplifying the Bard's humor. Johnson was the next editor to enter the lists. Although unwilling to accept Heath's simple explanation, he too returned to the original text. His attention having been drawn to Autolicus's lines by the excision and the subsequent comments, Johnson wrestled with them:

> The meaning is, they are "paid" for lying, therefore they do not "give" us the lye, they "sell" it us.[26]

A challenging passage to eighteenth-century editors, its full meaning still eludes us. And Hanmer has disappeared.

How did this happen? The first to be concerned with the ambiguities in this speech, he has been completely obliterated by the procession of colorful personalities drawn into subsequent combat. Why are we more familiar with the Oxford editor's blunders than with his possible insights? Is it accidental or have other factors contributed to the strange fate of his edition? Giles Dawson's study of the 1745 anonymous edition of Shakespeare's *Works* suggests that Warburton may have been instrumental in erasing Hanmer's name as the originator of many emendations.[27] In that edition many of the silent emendations found in Hanmer's 1744 work have been carefully annotated. Frequently they have been attributed to Warburton. If, as Dawson claims, the work was Warburton's, the ascription of some of these emendations may be suspect. The effect, however, of the 1745 edition on contemporary readers would have been to erase Hanmer's name from many of the more interesting comments. According to Dawson:

> The advertisement from the Booksellers informs the reader that the plan followed in this reprint of the 1744 Oxford edition of Hanmer is to mark those passages in the text altered by Hanmer and to "place the discarded Readings at the bottom of the Page, as also to point out the Emendations made by Mr. Theobald, Mr. Warburton, and Dr. Thirlby, in Mr. Theobald's Edition, which are used by this Editor"—that is by Hanmer. (42–43)

Dawson then explains that the changes made by Hanmer are identified only by "a pair of small superior slanted lines, and a footnote is supplied" (43).

> If the emendation was first proposed by Thirlby or Warburton, the appropriate name is given. If by Hanmer himself, the footnote simply gives the reading and assigns it to the "old edit.", without the emendator's hand. (43)

To illustrate how this worked, below are some developments of the examples I listed earlier. Philosophizing on his present behavior and on his future rewards, the pedler says, "Let me be unrold, and my name put in the booke of Vertue" (4.3.123–24). Hanmer footnotes "unrold" as follows:

> Alluding to the societies into which the notorious cheats and gypsies inroll themselves. (2:556)

No longer attributed to Hanmer in 1745, this note appears in Warburton's 1747 edition, with only a slight variation, as that of the editor himself. Competition, rivalry, and bitterness, as well as the absence of Hanmer's name in 1745, led to elimination of any reference to him by Warburton:

> Begging gipsies, in the time of our author, were in gangs and companies, that had something of the shew of an incorporated Body. From this noble society he wishes he may be unrolled if he does not so and so. (3:336)

Hanmer's note fades into obscurity. Warburton's is adopted by subsequent editors. Unlike Theobald, whose observations have since surfaced,

Hanmer's, having been absorbed by Warburton and sometimes further transmitted by Johnson, are nowhere visible except in the original text.

The extent of this obliteration may be seen in the next example. In Johnson's 1765 edition, we read: "What he [Shakespeare] means by 'his pedler's excrement' I know not" (2:323; *J. on S.*, 7:306). Hanmer had suggested an answer in 1744, when he identified it as a reference to Autolicus's "false beard" (4.4.802; 2:576). Did Johnson later find Hanmer's note? Or did he make the same lexicographic discovery without being aware of his predecessor's comment although in his "Preface" Johnson indicates a familiarity with Hanmer's text? (cf. *J. on S.*, 7:96–98). We do not know. We do know, however, that in the appendix to the 1765 edition, with no reference to Hanmer, Johnson writes:

Pedler's "excrement" is pedler's "beard." (*J. on S.*, 7:306)

Despite the shortcomings of his edition, Hanmer had contributed to the growing interest in the later section and therefore the whole of *The Winter's Tale*.[28] While the blunder of "Bithynia," which marked the ultimately absurd extension of neoclassical rules, and the excision of lines of poetry—dictated by a growing Puritanical preciosity—revealed the inhibiting effects of contemporary aesthetic, literary, and cultural forces, the concentration on the "oddities" of language, also brought about by contemporary developments—in literature as well as in the theater—led to an expanded understanding of the play. It was Hanmer who, noting Autolicus's strange language patterns, first alerted editors to the possible complexities of this character. His edition of *The Winter's Tale* mirrors the strength and weaknesses of mid eighteenth-century culture as it impinged upon Shakespeare's work and slowly reshaped attitudes towards his plays.

NOTES

1. Sir Thomas Hanmer, ed., *Works,* by William Shakespeare (London, 1744). This edition will hereafter be cited as Hanmer. George Fisher Russell Barker, "Hanmer," *DNB*.

2. Arthur H. Scouten, ed., *The London Stage, Part 3* (Carbondale: Southern Illinois University Press, 1961), 1: cl–cli. This work will hereafter be cited as *LS 3;* DeWitt T. Starnes and Gertrude E. Noyes, *The English Dictionary From Cawdrey to Johnson 1604–1755* (Chapel Hill: University North Carolina Press, 1946), 117–26.

3. Charles Harold Gray, *Theatrical Criticism to 1795* (New York: Columbia University Press, 1931), 68–69.

4. *Memoirs of the Times; in a Letter to a Friend in the Country* (London, 1737), 46. BM, T. 1109, 1–3.

5. Alexander Pope, ed., *Works,* by William Shakespeare (London, 1725)—hereafter cited as Pope, *Shakespeare.*

6. Joseph Addison, *The Spectator,* ed. Donald F. Bond (Oxford: Oxford University Press, 1965), 3:144–46 (#315)—although this essay is on *Paradise Lost,* it expresses Addison's attitude toward the credible and the incredible in the presentation of a fable; Francis Gentleman, *Dramatic Censor; or Critical Companion* (London, 1770), 1:37.

7. Nicholas Rowe, ed., *Works,* by William Shakespeare (London, 1709), 2: 887–975; Pope, *Shakespeare,* 1725, 2; Lewis Theobald, ed., *Works,* by William Shakespeare (London, 1733), 3: 63–164.

8. David Nichol Smith, *Shakespeare in the Eighteenth Century* (1928; rpt. Oxford: Clarendon, 1967), 43.

9. MacNamara Morgan, "Florizel and Perdita" (1754), Larpent Manuscript Collection #110, Huntington Library; David Garrick, "Florizel and Perdita" (1756), Larpent Manuscript Collection #122; William Shakespeare, *The Winter's Tale,* altered by Charles Marsh (London, 1756); William Shakespeare, *The Winter's Tale,* altered by Thomas Hull, Bell's ed. (London, 1774) and J. Wenman (London, 1779).

10. David Garrick, *Florizel and Perdita* (London, 1762), Folger Prompt F24.

11. William Shakespeare, *The Winter's Tale,* a tragedy, as performed at the Theatres Royal, Regulated from the Prompt-Books by permission of the managers (London: Printed for J. Barker, 1794), Folger Prompt *WT* 16.

12. See "The Materiality of the Shakespearean Text," *SQ* 44 (1993): 255–83.

13. Emmett L. Avery, ed., *The London Stage, Part 2* (Carbondale: Southern Illinois University Press, 1960), I:xvii–xxi. This work will hereafter be cited as *LS2.*

14. Smith, 43.

15. The lineation as well as the scene and act division, unless otherwise noted, are from Horace Howard Furness, ed. *The Winter's Tale,* by William Shakespeare, New Variorum, 6th ed. (Philadelphia, 1898)—hereafter cited as *Var.*

16. William Warburton, ed., *Works,* by William Shakespeare (London, 1747).

17. Warburton's excision is of lines 238–241, "From East . . . baggage."

18. Thomas Edwards, *A Supplement to Mr. Warburton's Edition of Shakespear. Being the Canons of Criticism, and Glossary* (London, 1748), 55–56.

19. Thomas Bowdler, *Family Shakespeare* (London, 1818).

20. William Shakespeare, *The Winter's Tale,* with alterations by J. P. Kemble (London, 1802), Kemble Collection No. 2240, Lilly Library, Bloomington, Indiana. For Kemble's method of emendation see Harold Child, *The Shakespearean Production of John Philip Kemble* (London: Oxford University Press, 1935), 7–8.

21. Starnes and Noyes, 117.

22. Jonas A. Barish, *Ben Jonson and the Language of Prose Comedy* (Cambridge, Mass.: Harvard University Press, 1967), 274–75.

23. *Correspondence of Sir Thomas Hanmer with a Memoir of his Life,* ed. by Sir Henry Bunbury (London, 1838),78.

24. Samuel Johnson, ed. *Works,* by William Shakespeare, 8 vols. (London, 1765), 2:322.

25. Benjamin Heath, *A Revisal of Shakespeare's Text: Wherein the Alterations Introduced into it by the More Modern Editors and Critics, are Particularly Considered* (London, 1765), 218.

26. After having recorded Warburton's note in the 1765 edition—2: 324—the comment appears in the appendix to that edition, in volume 8. Citations from

Samuel Johnson's text may also be found in: *Johnson on Shakespeare*, ed. Arthur Sherbo (New Haven: Yale University Press, 1968), Vols. 7 and 8 of the Yale edition of the *Works of Samuel Johnson*, hereafter cited as *J. on S.*

27. Giles E. Dawson, "Warburton, Hanmer, and the 1745 Edition of Shakespeare," *Studies in Bibliography*, 2 (1949): 34–48. Arthur Sherbo disputes this attribution to Warburton, and places the 1745 edition back into the realm of uncertainty. See Sherbo, "Warburton and the 1745 Shakespeare," *JEGP* 51 (1952): 71–82. For a detailed discussion of the 1745 edition, and a suggested attribution to Samuel Johnson, see Bernice W. Kliman's "Samuel Johnson and Tonson's 1745 Shakespeare: Warburton, Anonymity and the Shakespeare Wars," in this volume.

28. In my study of Rowe's and Pope's editions, I show how both earlier editors had concentrated on the first half of the play—Rowe through his introduction of punctuation into the dramatic speeches of Hermione, Leontes, and Paulina; Pope through his inverted commas surrounding "preferred passages" in the play's first half. See also my articles "The Touch of the Poet," *Modern Language Studies* 4 (Fall, 1974); "Bohemia's 'Sea Coast' and the Babe Who Was 'Lost Forever,'" *Literary Onomastic Studies* 3 (1976); "A Penchant for Perdita on the Eighteenth-Century Stage," *Studies in Eighteenth-Century Culture*, 6 , ed. R. Rosbottom (Madison: U. of Wisconsin P, 1977), rpt. in *The Woman's Part: Feminist Criticism of Shakespeare*, eds C. Lenz et al (University of Illinois Press, 1980); and "A Glimpse of the Sublime in Warburton's Edition of *The Winter's Tale*," *Shakespeare Studies* 11 (1978).

Emballing, Empalling, Embalming, and Embailing Anne Bullen: The Annotation of Shakespeare's Bawdy Tongue after Samuel Johnson

Irene Fizer

THE English dictionary had a double genesis. In the sixteenth century, two types of lexicons emerged: "hard lists" of serious words, pertinent to readers of scripture, and classifications of cant such as Thomas Harman's *Caveat or Warening, for Common Cursetors Vulgarely called Vagabones.*[1] A taxonomic system was taking shape that continues to define the practice of lexicography. Words that could be traced to textual sources were deemed suitable for repetition and reproduction, while words taken directly from common parlance were affixed to the page with a warning or silencing finger. Although the words sanctified by the text and the words fallen from the tongue were gradually collapsed together within the frame of the secular and national dictionary, each retains a different marking through the terminology of proper versus vulgar usage. The *Webster's New World Dictionary of American English* on my desk comprises standardized and slang terms yet continues to assert a standard of decency. Unworthy words are followed by the bracketed [Slang] or the more emphatic [Vulgar].[2] The modern English dictionary persists in legislating the division between mentionable and unmentionable discourse within its own community of the faithful, the literate. The dictionary is structured and fractured by its history as a mediating form that simultaneously aims to encompass an universal order of English words ("New World") and to enforce a proper or national standard of usage ("American English").

This uneasy relation between the spoken and the written equally marks the history of another lexicographic form that emerged in the eighteenth century: the annotated Shakespeare edition. Samuel Johnson's *A Dictionary of the English Language in which the Words are Deduced from their Originals and Illustrated in their Different Significations by Examples*

281

from the Best Writers (1755), which foregrounds its reliance on textual sources, is contemporary with his editorial preparation of the variorum Shakespeare (offered for subscription in 1756 and published in 1765). Both massive projects participate in the eighteenth-century move toward linguistic standardization as the vehicle for the institutionalization of cultural standards.[3] To survey the annotated Shakespeare, beginning with the eighteenth-century editions preceding Johnson's to the current classroom editions, is to trace a discursive history in which annotations are passed down generationally in a nearly unbroken line of descent. As a consequence, the practice of Shakespearean annotation has been circumscribed, by and large, to serious or "hard" words. Slang, particularly vulgar slang, is either left without annotation—and is thus, arguably, silenced—or, even more markedly, it is reassigned a more proper meaning. This lexicographic framing has worked to tame Shakespeare's unruly and performative scripts and to ensure that the vulgar is suppressed, at least within serious readings of the plays. Yet such serious readings come to include nearly every reader, for the standard Shakespeare, read within and outside the academy since the 1760s, is an annotated Shakespeare.

Thomas Bowdler's *The Family Shakespeare* (1807), expurgated of obscenities and truncated in length, stands as a long-running cultural joke within this history of annotation.[4] Although Bowdler's edition was popular throughout the nineteenth century, it is a late eighteenth-century cultural form, rather than a Victorian one. Intending *The Family Shakespeare* to be read aloud in Regency drawing rooms, Bowdler was responding directly to the textual practices of the eighteenth-century Shakespeare editors. As his full title announces—*The Family Shakespeare, in Ten Volumes, in Which Nothing is Added to the Original Text, but Those Words and Expressions are Omitted which Cannot with Propriety Be Read in a Family*— he has not only omitted the improper words and expressions found in Shakespeare's works but also the vast editorial apparatus that had accumulated by the late 1790s. Bowdler is founding his edition upon an open admission: that Shakespeare, the transmitter of family and British values, is also a vulgarian—an issue that was otherwise treated with greater circumspection. More pointedly, he is locating the cultural contestation between the vulgar word and the proper word not within the family room (where he has effectively silenced the vulgar) but, rather, within the annotators' circle. Whereas Bowdler's answer was to censor overtly the Shakespearean plays, his immediate editorial predecessors treated vulgar words either with active indifference or—paradoxically—with abundant and overdetermined annotation.

Annotators, beginning in the late eighteenth century, disciplined the bawdiness in Shakespeare's plays with an insular logic: they deferred to their predecessors and let the majority of vulgar and bawdy words stand without emendation. Yet they also displayed a revealing reflex: they were unable to censor each other or to clamp down on their multivocality. Once an editor annotated a word, that word entered the Shakespearean lexicon and a place had to be found for it in every subsequent edition. Thus, if one editor deemed a vulgar word worthy of annotation, his successors in the editorial circle had to contend with its significations in their own apparatus. The high cultural practice of Shakespearean annotation has always been marked by the tension between its own accumulative tradition—the aim of an all-inclusive Shakespeare index—and the inadmissibility of low words. As such, the annotation of the vulgar becomes a visible symptom of the cultural industry produced around Shakespeare's plays.

Eighteenth-century editorial practices can be charted by the progressive growth of apparatus in the collected works of Shakespeare. New Shakespeare editions were published in England in every decade of the eighteenth century; multiple prefaces, engravings, the life of Shakespeare, glossaries, endnotes, and indexes added to their increasing size. Extensive footnotes were among the last supplemental matter to be added in the period. Only after Johnson granted footnotes a distinct typographical presence in his 1765 edition were they regularly included in edited volumes. Nicholas Rowe's 1709 edition, "adorn'd with cuts," and Alexander Pope's 1725 edition appeared without annotation as such. Lewis Theobald's 1733 edition included a minimal number of notes; Thomas Hanmer's editions of 1744-1745 relied upon a glossary. In his 1747 edition, William Warburton made his critical emendations to Shakespeare's works a point of distinction for the first time. As his title page declared: "The Genuine Text (collated with all the former Editions, and then corrected and emended) is here settled: Being restored from the *Blunders* of the first Editors, and the *Interpolations* of the two Last: With A Comment and Notes, Critical and Explanatory."[5]

Johnson's edition, *The Plays of William Shakespeare, in Eight Volumes, with the Corrections and Illustrations of Various Commentators; to which are added Notes by Sam. Johnson* (1765), marks the emergence of the variorum tradition with its multiple and contestatory annotations.[6] By altering the spatial layout of the collected Shakespeare edition, Johnson had also fundamentally rethought its discursive terms: he now identified the edition as a collective cultural endeavor—and also as a central lexicon of the English language. Notes, that had previously functioned as marginalia at most, now appeared on nearly every page of his edition as he reprinted most of Theobald's and Warburton's notes alongside his own footnotes. Where Johnson took issue with Warburton who, in turn, had taken issue with Theobald, the footnotes occupied one-third to one-half of the printed page. Edward Capell, in his subsequent 1767 edition of

Shakespeare's works, abstained from adding his own extensively detailed notes, preferring to publish these notes in a separate volume. He felt compelled to comment on their absence as he was departing from the new standard "paginary intermixture of text and comment":

> [A] very great part of the world, amongst whom is the editor himself, profess much dislike to this paginary intermixture of text and comment, in works meerly for entertainment . . . as also,—that he, the editor, does not possess the secret of dealing out notes by measure, and distributing them among his volumes so nicely that the equality of their bulk shall not be broke in upon the thickness of a sheet of paper.[7]

As the number of annotators increased in the last decades of the eighteenth century, so did the volume of their editorial debate. Johnson's second variorum was coedited by George Steevens in 1773, and the 1778 Johnson-Steevens reissue appeared with supplementary volumes by Edmond Malone, the preeminent Shakespeare editor at the close of the century. *Malone's Shakspeare* of 1790 incorporated, along with its extensive notes and apparatus, a Glossary claiming to contain "all the Words and Phrases" in Shakespeare's works.[8] The 1803 variorum edition, *The Plays of William Shakespeare with the Corrections and Illustrations of Various Commentators,* was a massive twenty-one-volume reediting of the Johnson-Steevens edition by Isaac Reed, who collated the Shakespearean commentaries that had rapidly accumulated since Johnson's time. Published at a moment of cultural transition, the 1803 variorum marked the closure of the eighteenth-century editorial tradition and canonized the variorum model.[9] Most of the early annotations in the subsequent nineteenth- and twentieth-century editions can be traced back to the 1803 variorum. As Capell wryly hinted, by commenting on his own inability to distribute text and footnotes evenly on the page, the Shakespeare editors of the late eighteenth century were continually renegotiating between their assertion of linguistic standardization and their own conflictual practice. The cultural project to regulate the English language through the works of Shakespeare had resulted in an increasingly unwieldy scene of competing editorial discourses.

Johnson, in his "Preface to Shakespeare," had laid out a collaborative linguistic project harnessed to the service of national culture. *The Plays of Shakespeare* and the *Dictionary of the English Language* will stand as the twin institutional pillars for a kind of Academie Anglaise—the textual edifice upon which a formerly barbaric people will chart the course of their civilization through the maturation of their language. In Johnson's linguistic history, Shakespeare began a civilizing process that rendered the primitive dialects spoken in Elizabethan England into standardized English: "The English nation, in the time of Shakespeare, was yet struggling to emerge from barbarity. . . . Nations, like individuals, have their infancy."[10] To the charge that Shakespeare nonetheless speaks in a hybrid tongue, and continually slips between "high and low" (665) and "seriousness and merriment" (667), Johnson constructs a broad lexical field and positions Shakespeare as the mediating term:

> If there be, what I believe there is, in every nation, a stile which never becomes obsolete, a certain mode of phraseology so consonant and congenial to the analogy and principles of its respective language as to remain settled and unaltered; this stile is probably to be sought in the common intercourse of life, among those who speak only to be understood, without ambition of elegance. The polite are always catching modish innovations, and the learned depart from established forms of speech, in hope of finding or making better; those who wish for distinction forsake the vulgar, when the vulgar is right; but there is a conversation above grossness and below refinement, where propriety resides, and where this poet seems to have gathered his comick dialogue. He is therefore more agreeable to the ears of the present age than any other authour equally remote, and among his other excellencies deserves to be studied as one of the original masters of our language. (668–69)

By appointing Shakespeare as "one of the original masters of our language," Johnson seeks to establish a moderating mean of English that can withstand ravaging shifts in lexical styles. Yet Johnson's own rhetoric opens up the irresolvable crux of his lexicographic project: he identifies Shakespeare not as an author but as an initiator of an ongoing "conversation" in the nation, that is "above grossness and below refinement, where propriety resides." In the very instance that Johnson is moving to standardize Shakespeare's words through the variorum edition, the changeability of common parlance inherently resists that standard of propriety.

Johnson locates his own editorial course within his cultural moment. He himself will stand as a mediator—"keeping the middle way between presumption and timidity" (705). Unlike previous editors, he will not interfere with the integrity of Shakespeare's works, subjecting none to arbitrary cuts or selective deletions. As a consequence, however, he will extend the editorial apparatus—particularly the footnote—to new lengths. The preface and the footnotes will operate as a disciplining frame for Shakespeare's text whenever it proves too "ungrammatical, perplexed, and obscure" (691). Johnson argues that "we must ascribe the praise . . . [to Shakespeare] of having first discovered to how much smoothness and harmony the English language could be softened" (689). Yet the editor or, as Johnson prefers, "the emendatory critick" is clearly the agent of the textual weave, smoothing and harmonizing its warp. Faced with a "corrupted" Shakespearean word, to which any number of significations can be ascribed, the emendatory critic plays out all the possibilities across the lexical field and then chooses one meaning out of the many:

> an emendatory critick. . . . [i]n perusing a corrupted piece . . . must have before him all possibilities of meaning, with all possibilities of expression. Such must be his comprehension of thought, and such his copiousness of language. Out of many readings possible, he must be able to select that which best suits with the state of opinions, and modes of language prevailing in every age, and with his author's particular cast of thought, and turn of expression. (693)

While offering this principle of selection as the ideal editorial practice, Johnson maintains linguistic variability within *The Plays of Shakespeare*. Indeed, he formalizes the variorum model, in which his own lexicographic work appears alongside the contrary opinions of previous eighteenth-century critics. As he readily admits: "It is no pleasure to me, in revising my volumes to observe how much paper is wasted in confutation" (697). Nonetheless, the "complete explanation of an authour not systematick and consequential, but desultory and vagrant, abounding in casual allusions and light hints, is not be expected from any single scholiast" (701–702). Thus, the cultural project to standardize the English language through Shakespeare must also admit, by its principal aim of comprehensiveness, a range of supplementary meanings to any standard definition. To the reader, therefore, Johnson leaves a final, qualifying comment about the footnote: "Notes are often necessary, but they are necessary evils. Let him, that is yet unacquainted with the powers of Shakespeare. . . read every play from the first scene to the last, with utter negligence of all his commentators" (710). Yet how was the reader to bracket out the annotations, which had steadily swelled up the pages of the eighteenth-century editions, or to mediate between their lexical shifts?

I turn to an illustrative case from the editorial history of Shakespeare's *Henry VIII* (1613). Anne Bullen and the Old Lady, a servant in the queen's quarters, are discussing Anne's place in the king's political and sexual economy. A rumor has been circulating that Henry plans to award Anne with a title, the Marchioness of Pembroke, and an annuity, as a prelude to his marriage proposal. Although Anne has willingly been to Henry's bed, she is now reluctant to accept his legal offer. Dismissing Anne's modesty as hypocritical, the Old Lady exhorts Anne to reap the profit from her sexual labors:

> *Old Lady*:   In faith, for little England
> You'ld venture an emballing: I myself
> Would for Carnarvonshire, although there long'd
> No more to th' crown but that. . . .

> (2.3.47–50)[11]

The double entendre in the Old Lady's phrase is unmistakable: if Anne agrees to be balled by Henry, she will gain the English crown, ball, and scepter. The Old Lady asserts her own readiness for such a balling, even if the only prize were to be the Welsh county of Carnarvonshire. Throughout this short scene, the Old Lady speaks in a running series of sexual puns. The inversion of the ball, as a symbol of coronation, to connote fornication arises out of this linguistic register. Within the eighteenth-century Shakespeare editions, the Old Lady's bawdy words are covertly censored via a lack of annotation and her lines are largely left without commentary in the apparatus. Once Johnson deemed "emballing" worthy of annotation, however, the word had to be admitted into the Shakespearean lexicon—however awkwardly it fit within that taxonomic order. Indeed, the word was then tailored to fit.

Johnson inaugurates the gloss of "emballing" in his 1765 edition. He annotates the Old Lady's line with the following paraphrase:

> *You'ld venture an* emballing.] You would venture to be distinguished by the *ball,* the ensign of royalty.[12]

That Johnson is canceling out the linguistic interplay between sexual initiation and ceremonial initiation in the usage of "emballing" is clear. He is also directly contravening the Old Lady's line. As the Old Lady underscores, Henry will take Anne to his bed *before* he will give her the crown. Anne's body, figured as an object to be sexually balled, is emptied by Johnson of its physicality. He transmutes Anne herself into a "distinguished" sign of royalty.

By establishing an annotation for "emballing," Johnson also sets into place its position as a problematic term. Following his lead, all of his contemporary and succeeding annotators struggle to incorporate "emballing" into their notes. With few exceptions, the notes to the bedroom scene (Act 2, Scene 3) between Anne and the Old Lady are minimal in the editions dating down from the eighteenth century. The paucity of words chosen for annotation is a signal of the editors' reluctance to deal with the Old Lady and to play out her double entendres in the public forum of the footnotes. "Emballing" is always included in these minimal notes—it inevitably intrudes because Johnson himself, as the founder of the emendatory tradition, must be acknowledged. Once he has brought "emballing" into the open, the term can no longer be suppressed by the absence of annotation.

The 1803 variorum, *The Plays of William Shakespeare with the Corrections and Illustrations of Various Commentators,* includes a myriad of footnotes on "emballing." As a collation of the preceding eighteenth-century editions, the 1803 variorum reaches a kind of exegetical saturation. (These multilayered commentaries are gradually whittled away by nineteenth- and twentieth-century editors in favor of single footnotes.) The eighteenth-century commentators who inveigh upon "emballing" alternately agree with, attempt to supersede, and contradict one another. At first glance, their contentiousness seems to leave the signification of "emballing" unfixed. The verbiage, however, becomes increasingly self-reflexive as the commentators collude to keep the vulgar meaning of "emballing" from erupting within their proper frame. Even more precisely, they collude to prevent the alignment of Shakespeare, the reigning cultural deity and "master of the language," with the scurrilous and bawdy tongue of a female servant.

Responding to Johnson's original annotation, Tollet notes:

> Dr. Johnson's explanation cannot be right, because a *queen-consort,* such as *Anne Bullen* was, is not distinguished by the *ball,* the ensign of royalty, nor has the poet expressed that she was so distinguished.[13]

Tollet is making a surreptitious reference to Anne's status as Henry's mistress; she was not a queen in her own right, only a queen consort. Yet, in refuting Johnson, Tollet does not offer a definition of "emballing" of his own. If the ball Anne receives is not an "ensign of royalty," then what is it exactly? Tollet is calling to mind the Old Lady's scenario: the king balling his queen consort.

Malone steps into the fray and shuts down the potential articulation of the vulgar term. Implicitly conceding that "emballing" evokes indiscreet associations, even if these associations remain unmentioned, Malone argues that the word itself must be incorrect. As he notes, now in response to both Johnson and Tollet:

> Might we read—"You'd venture an *empalling;*"—i.e, being invested with the *pall* or robes of state? The word occurs in the old tragedy of King Edward III. 1596: "As with this armour I *impall* thy breast—." And, in *Macbeth,* the verb to *pall* is used in the sense of *enrobe:* "And *pall* thee in the dunnest smoke of hell."[14]

In an audacious gesture, yet one that will be echoed by later annotators, Malone substitutes "emballing" with the symbolic investiture of "empalling"—and thereby blacks out the entire bawdy scene behind a ceremonial scrim. He censors the oral improprieties of the play by tracing an alternate lexicography through Elizabethan textual sources; although his replacement of *Henry VIII's* performed word with another performed word from the plays *King Edward III* and *Macbeth* already strains his logic. The Shakespeare of *Henry VIII* has proven too discomfiting; however, another Shakespeare of *Macbeth* has been found. (*King Edward III* was ascribed to Shakespeare by certain eighteenth-century editors but Malone is referencing the play here for its Elizabethan idioms.)[15] The unresolved tension between the spoken and the written word marks his own commentary. Malone does not challenge or tamper with the Shakespeare script itself, as "emballing" remains on the printed page. Rather, he enjoins the reader to *vocalize* the word differently through the footnote: to read from below. Malone stakes his annotating claim upon the lexicon that he and his fellow eighteenth-century editors are compiling from Shakespeare's texts—a lexicon into which the word "empalling" has already been inscribed and from which "emballing" can now be barred.

Steevens's subsequent footnote shores up Malone's:

The word [empalling] recommended by Mr. Malone occurs also in Chapman's version of the eighth book of Homer's *Odyssey:*
'————such a radiance as doth round *empall* / Crown'd Cytherea————'.
(377)[16]

Ostensibly, *The Odyssey,* as the founding text of the Western literary tradition, further authorizes the change of "emballing" to "empalling." Steevens cites *The Odyssey* as a transcendent lexicon, a final reference point by which all unstable meanings can be regulated. Yet Steevens is, in fact, referencing Chapman's translation of Homer, rather than the Greek text. Chapman's edition of the classical epic, composed for an elite readership, makes a highly dubious lexical analogy with Shakespeare's *Henry VIII,* composed out of the shifting and performative registers of the public stage. Steevens's citation of a printed volume contemporary with Shakespeare's plays evidences the discursive exclusions of the eighteenth-century variorum tradition. The annotators are intent on producing an etymology of proper English words based upon Elizabethan textual sources, yet categorically refuse to admit Elizabethan parlance into this lexicographic history. The problem remains: once a vulgar word is transcribed into print, it asserts a place within this history.

In Whalley's subsequent footnote, the orthography of emballing is altered yet again. He comments:

Might we not read—"an embalming?" A queen consort is *anointed* at her coronation; and in King Richard II. the word is used in that sense: 'With my own tears I wash away my balm.' Dr. Johnson properly explains it, the *oil of consecration.* (377)[17]

Again, an alternate textual source, now from Shakespeare's *Richard II,* disciplines the indiscretions of *Henry VIII.* The reference to Johnson is equally telling. Whalley cites Johnson to authorize a "proper" explanation of "emballing" that is contrary to Johnson's own. The annotators' quest for a proper definition of "emballing" turns back upon Johnson, and turns against itself. The play upon "emballing" takes on an added irony here. As the annotators rival for the new cultural power commanded by the Shakespeare editor in the eighteenth century, they are also figuratively rivaling over Anne. In *Henry VIII,* the Old Lady is usurping the king's prerogative by "emballing" Anne herself; she penetrates Anne's body repeatedly with her verbal jibes. The annotators cannot deny that Anne's body is figured in the bedroom scene. Yet, rather than annotating her sexual balling, they crown her, place the royal ball in her hands, drape her with coronation robes, and anoint her with consecrated oil. They invent means to touch Anne's body properly with their footnotes.

By this practice, the eighteenth-century annotators invert their own manifest purpose. Instead of providing definitions for Shakespeare's words, they supply new words to suit their chosen definitions. In their attempt to suppress the vulgar and enforce the proper, they further redefine their own conceptual endeavor. Rather than working as strict standardizers, they begin to engage in an elaborate textual punning. Their lexical distortions, although censorious, also inadvertently open up a play of signification—a slippage of meaning from emballing to empalling to embalming and back again. The success of their cultural industry is evidenced in nearly every subsequent Shakespeare edition, as their annotations were perpetuated from volume to volume and remain in circulation. Bowdler was, perhaps, their earliest convert, as the censored version of *Henry VIII* in *The Family Shakespeare* (1807) lets "emballing" stand, without further annotation.

Modern editions of *Henry VIII* never stray far from Johnson and this annotating circle. John Munro, editor of *The London Shakespeare: A New Annotated and Critical Edition of the Complete Works* (1957), annotates "emballing" by citing Malone directly and Johnson by inference:

> *emballing:* Malone conj. *empalling.* Usually explained as 'invested with the ball or sphere, emblem of royalty'; probably used indelicately (*NED*). Kellner proposes *embailing, i.e.* embrace.[18]

Although Munro defines Malone's "empalling" as a "conjecture" and qualifies Johnson's annotation as the "usual" one, he reauthorizes both definitions, rather than declaring them obsolete. However, Munro's footnote also marks the increasing importance of the national English dictionary, as a critical counterweight to the longstanding authority of the annotators. As the *New English Dictionary* suggests, "emballing" is "probably used indelicately" in *Henry VIII*. (Thus, while the *NED* references the vulgar usage it also does so with obvious reticence and an exaggerated diction of propriety.) This tension between the annotating tradition, which seeks to enforce a lexicon of the best English words, and the modern English dictionary, which marks both proper and vulgar usage, continues to define standard editions of Shakespeare. In turn, Malone's alteration of the spelling of "emballing" remained current for generations: Munro closes his note by offering yet another substitute term—"embailing" or embrace—to obviate the *NED*'s indelicate suggestion. Munro leaves the Old Lady's other, and obvious, double entendres, without annotation; he is compelled to acknowledge "emballing" by virtue of the eighteenth-century tradition alone. He prefers to leave the reader with the thought, however, that Anne will be properly embailed, rather than vulgarly emballed, by the king.

Despite Munro's latter attempt to misspell correctively, "emballing" took on a dual marking in the subsequent annotated editions. J. C. Maxwell, editor of *Henry VIII* in the *Cambridge Shakespeare* (1962), reluctantly references the *Oxford English Dictionary*'s definition over the annotating tradition:

> *emballing*, here only; *OED* suspects an 'indelicate sense'; usually explained as investing with the royal emblem of the 'ball.'[19]

In the New Penguin Shakespeare edition of *Henry VIII* (1971), A. R. Humphreys continues to privilege the Johnsonian annotation. In a now familiar gesture, however, Humphreys endorses this annotation by removing "emballing" from the context of *Henry VIII* and inserting it into yet another Shakespeare play, *Henry V*. The Old Lady's bawdy words are reduced to an annotator's addendum:

> *emballing:* investment with the ball, an emblem of royalty. It signified the earth, and sovereignty; compare *Henry V, IV. I. 253*, 'the balm, the sceptre, and the ball.' A bawdy quibble is implied by the Old Lady's previous indelicacies.[20]

Most editions of Shakespeare's plays now in print and in classroom use either revert back to the Johnson annotation alone, or add a parenthetical comment on the vulgar usage. The edition of *Henry VIII* in David Bevington's *The Complete Works of Shakespeare* (1992) typifies the current standard:

> *emballing:* investiture with the ball as a royal emblem (with sexual suggestion).[21]

John Margeson's New Cambridge edition of *Henry VIII* (1990) is a particular exception. He annotates the sexual meaning of "emballing" without qualification and subsumes the Johnson annotation to an afterthought:

emballing: The sexual sense is plain; there is probably also a reference to investing with the ball (and sceptre) as an emblem of royalty.[22]

Within the editorial history of *Henry VIII,* Margeson's annotation is a rare divergence. Whenever the Shakespeare annotators cannot substitute a new term for "emballing" Johnson provides the fail-safe and stabilizing reference. As the founder of both the first reputable English dictionary and the annotating tradition, Johnson continues to set the limits of inclusion and exclusion for the Shakespearean lexicon.

In the Arden edition of *Henry VIII* (1964), R. A. Foakes offered a succinct history of the "emballing" gloss, by citing Johnson's definition directly against the reciprocal authority of the *OED:*

> *emballing]* investing with the ball as the emblem of royalty (Johnson), with a quibble carrying on from the puns in II.37, 41, 45. Emendation is unnecessary; the word is recorded in *OED* as early as 1580.[23]

The *OED* reference from 1580 to "emball" occurs in a line from Sidney that plays out a series of sexually suggestive double entendres: "Thou spheare, within whose bosom play / The rest that earth emball." Of equal significance is the *OED*'s attribution of "emballing" to Shakespeare:

> *Emballing]* (Prob. used in indelicate sense; explained by commentators as 'invested with the ball as the emblem of royalty'.) 1613 SHAKS. *Hen. VIII,* II. iii. 47 For little England You'ld venture an emballing.[24]

Thus, in the *OED,* "emballing" also stands as Shakespeare's coin—it is a self-authorizing word. Yet, in homage to the annotating tradition, Johnson's definition of emballing as an "emblem of royalty" still retains its currency. According to Foakes, the sexual pun on royal ball/royal balling glossed in the *OED* is a mere "quibble"—a minor quarrel with Johnson, the master annotator. The term does not require further emendation. Through this equivocation over the annotation of the proper and the vulgar word, "emballing" remains suspended between the two massive lexicographic projects of the English language, the dictionary and the Shakespeare variorum. The ball rests in both courts.

NOTES

1. Allon White writes of the emergence of slang lexicons, such as Thomas Harman's *Caveat or Warening, for Common Cursetors Vulgarely called Vagabones* (circa 1516), and the early history of the dictionary in "The Dismal Sacred Word: Academic Language and the Social Reproduction of Seriousness," *Literature/Teaching/Politics,* 2: 4–15.

2. *Webster's New World Dictionary of American English: Third College Edition* (New York: Simon and Schuster, 1988).

3. Raymond Williams's *The Long Revolution* (New York: Harper & Row, 1961), particularly the chapter "The Growth of 'Standard English,'" and John Barrell's *English Literature in History, 1730–80: An Equal, Wide Survey* (London: Hutchinson, 1983) have informed my discussion throughout this essay. See also Peter Stallybrass and Allon White, *The Politics and Poetics of Transgression* (Ithaca, NY: Cornell University Press, 1986), especially chapter 2, "The Grotesque Body and the Smithfield Muse: Authorship in the Eighteenth Century."

4. Originally published in 1807, Thomas Bowdler's *The Family Shakespeare* went through multiple editions in the nineteenth century. I have consulted *The Family Shakespeare, in Ten Volumes, in Which Nothing is Added to the Original Text, but Those Words and Expressions are Omitted which Cannot with Propriety Be Read in a Family* (London: Longman, Hurst, Rees, Orme, and Brown, 1818). Bowdler does include very brief annotating footnotes in his edition. On Bowdler, see also Colin Franklin, *Shakespeare Domesticated: The Eighteenth-Century Editions* (England: Scolar Press, 1991), 141–43.

For contextual and critical views of eighteenth-century Shakespeare editing, see Arthur Sherbo, *The Birth of Shakespeare Studies: Commentators from Rowe (1709) to Boswell-Malone (1821)* (East Lansing, MI: Colleagues Press, 1986); Margreta De Grazia, *Shakespeare Verbatim: The Reproduction of Authenticity and the 1790 Apparatus* (Oxford: Oxford University Press, 1991); Jean Marsden, ed., *The Appropriation of Shakespeare: Post-Renaissance Reconstructions of the Works and the Myth* (Hemel Hempstead, 1991); Edward Tomarken, *Samuel Johnson on Shakespeare* (Athens and London: The University of Georgia Press, 1991); and Michael Dobson, *The Making of the National Poet: Shakespeare, Adaptation, and Authorship, 1660–1769* (Oxford: Clarendon Press, 1992).

5. I am indebted to Franklin's study, *Shakespeare Domesticated,* for the publication history of Shakespeare's collected works in the eighteenth century. I have referenced only those eighteenth-century editions that pertain to this essay's focus on the footnote and editorial apparatus: Nicholas Rowe, *The Works of Mr. William Shakespear* (London: Printed for Jacob Tonson, 1709); Alexander Pope (London: Printed for Jacob Tonson, 1725); Lewis Theobald, *The Works of Shakespeare* (London, 1733); Thomas Hanmer, *The Works of Shakespear* (Oxford: Printed at the Theatre, 1744 and London: Printed for J. Tonson, 1745); William Warburton, *The Works of Shakespear* (London: Printed for J. and P. Knapton, et. al., 1747).

6. Samuel Johnson, *The Plays of William Shakespeare, in Eight Volumes, with the Corrections and Illustrations of Various Commentators; to which are added Notes by Sam. Johnson* (London: Printed for J. and R. Tonson, et. al., 1765).

7. Edward Capell, *Mr. William Shakespeare, his Comedies, Histories and Tragedies* (London: Printed by Dryden Leach for J. and R. Tonson, 1767). Capell, quoted in Franklin, *Shakespeare Domesticated,* 28. Capell's notes were finally printed a year before his death in 1780 as *Notes and Various Readings to Shakespeare* (London, 1780; rpt. New York: AMS Press, 1973).

8. Edmond Malone, *Malone's Shakspeare* (London: Printed for Baldwin, 1790).

9. *The Plays of William Shakespeare with the Corrections and Illustrations of Various Commentators* (London: J. Plymsell, 1803). The 1803 variorum was reprinted in 1813 and again in 1821 with additional apparatus by the editor James

Boswell, the younger son of Johnson's biographer. For the publication history of the variorum editions, see Franklin, *Shakespeare Domesticated*, 34–58.

10. Samuel Johnson, "Preface to Shakespeare," in *Johnson and Boswell,* ed. Louis Kronenberger (New York: The Viking Press, 1947), 680. All subsequent quotes are to this edition and parenthetical in the text. Also see G. F. Parker, *Johnson's Shakespeare* (Oxford: Oxford University Press, 1989). The "Preface to Shakespeare" begins by underscoring that Shakespeare should command a status as an ancient, not a modern: "The Poet, of whose works I have undertaken the revision, may now begin to assume the dignity of an ancient and claim the privilege of established fame and prescriptive veneration," 659. By characterizing Shakespeare as a "Poet," rather than a playwright, Johnson is also moving to supersede the multivocality of the playwright with the supposed univocality of the poet.

11. William Shakespeare, *Henry VIII,* Arden Edition with commentary by R. A. Foakes (Cambridge, MA: Harvard University Press, 1964), 2.3.47–50.

12. Samuel Johnson, *The Plays of William Shakespeare, Volume the Fifth* (London, 1765; rpt. New York: AMS Press, 1968), *The Life of King Henry VIII,* footnote to 2.3.47–50.

13. *Henry VIII* in *The Plays of William Shakespeare with the Corrections and Illustrations of Various Commentators,* footnotes to 2.3.47–50.

A later nineteenth-century edition, *The Works of William Shakespeare* (Boston: Little, Brown, and Co., 1888), edited by Richard Grant White, subtracts all of the commentary on "emballing" added in the 1803 Variorum in favor of a new paraphrase of Johnson's definition: "an investiture with royalty, one of the signs of which was the ball so often seen in the hands of royal effigies," footnote to 2.3.47–50.

14. Ibid. See also Franklin, *Shakespeare Domesticated,* 113 regarding Capell's attribution of *King Edward III* to Shakespeare.

15. Ibid.

16. Ibid.

17. Ibid.

18. John Munro, ed., *Henry VIII,* in *The London Shakespeare: A New Annotated and Critical Edition of the Complete Works* (New York: Simon and Schuster, 1957), footnote to 2.3.47–50.

Eric Partridge's *Shakespeare's Bawdy* (London and New York: Routledge & Kegan Paul, Ltd., 1947; rpt. 1990) should also be mentioned as a pioneering lexicon of Shakespeare's vulgar words and as a commentary on issues of sexuality in the works. As the foreword to *Shakespeare's Bawdy* notes: "Partridge was writing at a time when all editions of Shakespeare intended for use in schools were bowdlerized, when editors even of scholarly editions frequently shied away from sexual glosses . . . .*Shakespeare's Bawdy* helped to lead the way towards a new freedom and honesty in acknowledging and investigating the full extent of Shakespeare's linguistic range and in responding to the sexual resonances of a substantial section of his vocabulary," vii–viii.

First printed in 1947 in a limited edition, *Shakespeare's Bawdy* was successfully reissued in the 1950s, revised and enlarged in 1968, and remains in print. Partridge's gloss on "emballing" reads: "Old Lady to Anne Bullen (affectedly bashful), 'In faith, for little England you'ld venture an *emballing*" where emballing is innuendo'd to = a *coitus,*" 98.

19. J. C. Maxwell, ed., *King Henry the Eighth* (Cambridge: Cambridge University Press, 1962), glossary note to 2.3.47–50.

20. A. R. Humphreys, ed., *King Henry the Eighth* (New Penguin Shakespeare, 1971), footnote to 2.3.47–50.

21. David Bevington, ed., *Henry VIII*, in *The Complete Works of Shakespeare* (Harper Collins, 1992), footnote to 2.3.47–50.

22. John Margeson, ed., *King Henry VIII* in *The New Cambridge Shakespeare* (Cambridge: Cambridge University Press, 1990), footnote to 2.3.47–50.

23. Arden edition of *Henry VIII*, footnote to 2.3.47–50.

24. *Oxford English Dictionary*, s.v., "emball" and "emballing," 156.

Part 4
Editing and the Marketplace

Samuel Johnson and Tonson's 1745 Shakespeare: Warburton, Anonymity, and the Shakespeare Wars

Bernice W. Kliman

Conjectures being the very stuff of eighteenth-century Shakespeare editing, perhaps one of my own will not be amiss. I would like to advance the idea that bookseller Jacob Tonson hired Samuel Johnson in 1745 to write attributive notes, anonymously, in an inexpensive reproduction of the elegant 1744 Oxford University edition. The appearance of two textually identical editions by different publishers marks a tactical scrimmage in the complex moves of competition and collaboration that distinguish the editorial work of Johnson, Alexander Pope, Lewis Theobald, Thomas Hanmer—and, above all, William Warburton, who allied himself now with one, now with another. Their editions and related editions dominate the field in the eighteenth century. Since Johnson's activities for 1745 are largely unknown, his work on the 1745 edition could fill a lacuna in his biography. Even more significantly, it would demonstrate his role in what may be called the Shakespeare Wars, the struggle for territorial rights to Shakespeare—by publishers who wanted to sell Shakespeare and by literary men who wanted to use Shakespeare to advance their careers or reputations or both.

The six-volume 1744 edition in large quarto, though also produced anonymously, was known to be by Sir Thomas Hanmer, invariably called the Oxford editor. Hanmer sidestepped Jacob Tonson and associates, who considered themselves the owners of the rights to Shakespeare, by turning to Oxford University, which published his edition embellished with illustrations that he commissioned and paid for. (Thirty-one of the frontispieces were designed by Francis Hayman and all were engraved by Gravelot.) Tonson and the other owners were understandably disturbed by Hanmer's edition, published to their detriment by Oxford.[1] Alexander Pope, in a letter to Warburton, 18 January 1742/43, expresses the threat to Tonson's interests very well:

One Good Consequence [of the publication of the Oxford Shakespeare] will attend the printing it, wch is, that it will determine ye Book to be no mansBooksellers property, if Tonson does not contest it: & ~~your~~ the way will be open to any whom you chuse to deal with, or to yᵣself, if yᵘ prefer to take yᵉ whole on yᵣself.[2]

The main point here is that Pope saw the field as potentially open. An ancillary point is that in 1743 Warburton wanted to do something with Shakespeare but, as far as his close friend Pope knew, was undecided about what it should be.

Tonson acted quickly to contest the Oxford edition and to prevent other would-be poachers from moving in on his territory. While choosing not to prosecute his claim against Hanmer and Oxford (formidable opponents), Tonson could undercut Hanmer's success and assert his claim another way by reproducing the Oxford text and selling it cheaply. Neither Hanmer nor Oxford would dare or deign to object. Though the Oxford text presented its emendations and infrequent explanatory notes without attribution of their sources, Hanmer's brief "Preface" acknowledges debts to anonymous predecessors and contemporaries.[3] Tonson's tactic was not only to duplicate, in octavo format, the Oxford text but also to assign appropriate credit for emendations. Using Hanmer's very text was a way for Tonson to lay his claim to it. The notes in his edition made it more valuable to serious readers than the almost entirely blank margins of the Oxford edition and more importantly established Tonson's right to the notes. Though the Oxford edition fell, ultimately, through the adverse opinion of other editors rather than by Tonson's reprisal edition, his counterstroke did strengthen his claim to any published Shakespeare, and his name is associated with all the major editions of the century until his death in 1767. When Warburton finally edited his version, published in 1747, he assigned all rights (including all the editorial matter) to Tonson for £500.[4] Tonson was not taking any chances even though he believed his claim was clear. No matter who edited the text, no matter how it was annotated or emended, he owned the text of Shakespeare. He renewed his claim with each republication. Thus, the textually insignificant 1745 edition is pivotal in eighteenth-century copyright claims.

My purpose here is twofold—first, by examining Warburton's role in eighteenth-century editions (especially Hanmer's) to argue the implausibility of Warburton's writing attributive notes for the 1745 edition, and second, to gather the circumstantial evidence for Johnson's involvement. Since Warburton was mentioned as recently as 1991 as the person who wrote the notes for the reprisal volume, it is time to lay that idea to rest.[5] He would not have done hack work in 1745. Possibly other literary workhorses would have been able, using resources such as Theobald's 1733 edition, to identify emendations and assign ownership to them and to Hanmer's explanatory notes, but several coincidences make Johnson an attractive candidate. His financial situation during this period forced him to do hack work—as one of his biographers asserts in entitling a chapter covering this period "The Bookseller's Hack, 1740–1745."[6] Later, of course, he edited the 1765 edition, but in 1745 he was virtually unknown, a struggling writer, with all his famous work and reputation still before him. The thread that leads to Johnson, though knotted, can be unraveled, but one must begin with the origin of the Shakespeare Wars and with William Warburton's efforts to establish himself.

* * *

The story of Warburton's correspondence, collaboration, and break with Theobald; Warburton's sudden intimacy with Alexander Pope that lasted five years, until the poet's death in 1744; Pope's bequest to Warburton of his literary remains, and Warburton's eventual publication in 1747 of an edition bearing both Pope's name and his, need only be sketched here.[7] These well-known events lead to Warburton's link to the reprisal edition and, as I conjecture, to Johnson's work on that edition.

In 1736, after many years of intense correspondence, especially during the years immediately before Theobald produced his own 1733 edition of Shakespeare, Warburton broke decisively with Theobald and asserted his claim to all the emendations and interpretations he had communicated to Theobald that the latter had not already published (and had, in his textual notes, amply credited to Warburton). Theobald responded to Warburton's letter of 4 May on the 18th, greatly surprised at Warburton's anger and his demand for the return of his letters.[8]

The usual reasons imputed for the break may have been contributing but not decisive factors, that is, Theobald's unenthusiastic response to Warburton's proposed "compleat Critic" of Shakespeare, or Theobald's edition, which left out some of the emendations Warburton had offered. The fact that the letters between Theobald and Warburton continued for two years beyond 1733 (if at a more desultory rate) shows that these explanations are incomplete.[9] No one appears to have noticed that the timing of the break suggests it occurred because Warburton had established a similar collaboration with Sir Thomas Hanmer, which by May 1736 was heating up. Hanmer solicited Warburton's ideas and urged him not only to write weekly letters but also to visit Mildenhall, Hanmer's Suffolk estate, to examine the emendations he had made in the Shakespeare texts in his personal library. For the weekly correspondence to Hanmer, Warburton needed the notes he had written to Theobald. Though with a few exceptions Warburton's letters are unrecoverable, Hanmer's from 24 Dec. 1735 to 25 May 1739 allow one to infer the tenor of Warburton's more frequent letters.[10] In the first of these letters, Hanmer alludes to a previous discussion and a visit by Warburton to

Mildenhall; thus, the genesis of the relationship is misty (and each explains it differently). By December 1736, Hanmer is so eager to have Warburton see his marginal notes that he will carry the books to London for that purpose if Warburton prefers to meet him there—for he has resolved always to keep them about him and will not loan them.[11] Hanmer's aim, he assures Warburton in this letter, is to produce for himself a "correct" copy of Shakespeare, since he is much disgusted with the editions then available to him:

> I hear with uneasiness of the expectation you say is conceived of my making publick the observations and corrections I have made upon Shakespear. Nothing was further from my thoughts when I began them, I proposed nothing but amusement in carrying them on, and no other end but my own satisfaction in getting as correct a copy as I could of an Author I hold in the highest esteem. But there is nothing to which my mind is more averse than to become an Editor; and yet I hope you will not grudge the pains taken in communicating to me your remarks upon the same subject.

Though he insists in this letter that he has no intention of becoming an editor and of producing an edition, as Warburton appears to be urging him to do, a few days later (11 Jan. 1736/37) Hanmer is prepared to be persuaded by Warburton and other people whose judgment he respects to undertake an edition if it can be made more beautiful than the others available and if upon examination his emendations and notes are found to deserve publication:

> After they have undergone your examination and that of a few others whose judgment I value, if a few of such chosen friends judge it fit that what I have done towards purifying the text of the Author should be the foundation of a new Edition they shall over-rule my averseness and we will consider of some manner in which it may be done.

Hanmer must have received the assurance he craved from Warburton that his corrections were worthy, for Warburton writes to Thomas Birch on 24 August 1737 that he has visited Hanmer:

> You are pleased to inquire about Shakespear. I believe (to tell it as a secret) I shall, after I have got the whole of this Work out of my hands which I am now engaged in, *give an Edition of it to the World*—Sir T. H. has a true critical genius & has done great things in this Author so you may expect to see a very extraordinary edition of its Kind. I intend to draw up and preface to it a just and compleat Critic on Shakespear & his works.[12]

That Warburton respected Hanmer appears in this letter to Birch—a position he reversed in the preface of his 1747 edition, after Hanmer's death in 1746: "How the Oxford editor came to think himself qualified for this office, from which his whole course of life had been so remote, is . . . difficult to conceive. For whatever parts he might have either of genius or erudition, he was absolutely ignorant of the art of criticism, as well as of the poetry of that time, and the language of his author."[13] The 1737 letter to Birch also shows that Warburton expected that he and Hanmer would be collaborating in some way, that he and Hanmer would be editing while he, Warburton, would provide the literary criticism, the "compleat Critic" he had already proposed in 1734. If Warburton were to write a complete criticism he would be the first to do so, and if admired it could have furthered his reputation, which by 1736 was already on the rise with his publication of *The Alliance between Church and State.*

Warburton hinted to Hanmer that a collaborative edition would also be monetarily helpful, for Hanmer replied that he saw no way that Warburton would benefit from association in the sort of edition Hanmer had in mind. Later, Hanmer's queries in London about the possibility of producing an edition precipitated a break between the splenetic Warburton and Hanmer. Warburton believed that Hanmer was trying to steal his conjectures and produce the edition without crediting his weekly letters. Hanmer, in his response, insists that by canvassing the printers he was merely trying to find out if Warburton *could* benefit from an edition and had learned, he says, that there was no money to be had for such a project, for copies of the large quarto edited by Pope (the edition comparable in appearance to the one Hanmer had in mind) remained to be sold.[14] With gentlemanly dignity, the nobleman apologizes to the clergyman for any misunderstanding. Hanmer agrees to return Warburton's letters containing all his notes (just as Theobald, at Warburton's insistence, had returned letters in 1736).

Shortly after, Warburton urges Birch to announce to the world in *Bayle's Dictionary* (the English text based on the French encyclopedia) that he intends to edit on his own a complete works of Shakespeare and that he also proposes to write not only a complete criticism but also to outline the laws of such a criticism, a *canon* of criticism (the very title Thomas Edwards took later in a work that caustically ridiculed Warburton and his pretensions). For Birch's essay on Shakespeare in volume nine of *Bayle's Dictionary,* Warburton provided many notes that made their way virtually verbatim into the encyclopedia.[15] In any case, though Birch published the announcement of the new Warburton Shakespeare in *Bayle's* early in 1739, Warburton's edition did not appear for years—why is obscure—and, as Pope's letter of 18 January shows, in 1743 he was unsettled about what he would do about Shakespeare. His delay seems to have encouraged Hanmer to proceed with his edition. Sir Thomas had waited some time to conclude his arrangements with Oxford, having expected, as he says, Warburton to act. Since Warburton had already written so many of his notes, the project should not have taken nine years from announcement to completion. Something may have stopped him.[16]

Warburton's new relationship with Pope could have contributed to the delay. When he determined to produce his own edition in 1738, Warburton had not yet established his friendship with Pope, based on his brilliant (Pope thought) defense of Pope's "Essay on Man" against an attack: "A Vindication of Mr. Pope's Essay on Man, from the Misrepresentations of M. de Crousaz."[17] Warburton's letters defending Pope were published individually in December 1738 and the first half of 1739 and later collected. His defense shows such a marked turnabout from his earlier views of Pope that some have suspected his motives. Earlier, Warburton had written anonymous attacks on Pope and endorsed Theobald's claims against Pope, defending Theobald against the satires by Pope in the early *Dunciad*. Theobald's letters to Warburton indicate that Warburton not only agreed with him about Pope's deficiencies as an editor but also encouraged him in snide comments. Had he published his Shakespeare early in 1738, Warburton might have censured Pope's edition at least as enthusiastically as Theobald had. Pope knew nothing of Warburton's attacks.[18] Inspired to defend Pope's poem late in 1738, having consequently become Pope's friend, the recipient of many warm protestations of love and esteem from Pope, Warburton would have to change targets in editing Shakespeare, would have to praise rather than condemn Pope. When he eventually produced his 1747 edition, by that time Pope's literary executor, Warburton credited the edition to Pope and himself— though little enough came from Pope's 1723–25 or 1728 editions.[19] The condemnation of Pope that would have been a likely feature of the edition Warburton had first planned in the mid-1730s is altogether missing in the 1747 edition.

In 1743, after years of allowing his Shakespeare project to lie dormant, he acted out of concern for his notes in Hanmer's edition, then about to be published. Pope, in the same letter to Warburton already quoted, writes,

I consulted Mr Murray on y^r Question as to writing to Sr T. H. We agreed you s^{hd} not, as it was a thing not even to be surmized, that any Man of honour c^d dream of. But I have enquird farther, & am assured from one who hath seen ye Copy, y^t there are no notes whatsoever to it, but a Removal only of one word for another, as he thinks fitting.

Curiously enough, at the beginning of their correspondence, Hanmer, who indeed was concerned only to change one word for another as he thought fit, encouraged Warburton not to bother with explanations for his changes. If they were right, they would appear so without explanation

(6 May 1736). Warburton, a prickly sort, evidently bridled at this idea, and Hanmer hastened to write him (18 May 1736) that of course he might include the explanations in his letters if he liked, that he had told Warburton to withhold the discussions out of concern for Warburton's time, and that the arguments were certainly entertaining to read. So it is not surprising that Hanmer did not include justifications of emendations but only a few explanatory notes. Like Edward Capell some time later, Hanmer primarily wanted to produce a clean edition. He saw it as graced by engravings, with handsome, large type on fine paper. The long notes that Warburton wanted to write at the bottom of pages (emulating Theobald, the first to do so discursively) would not have answered Hanmer's purpose. Seeing his own emendations unattributed in the Oxford edition, Warburton certainly would have been eager to see it brought down.

Though it is possible that Tonson asked Warburton to write the attributive notes for the 1745 reprisal, it is not likely that he accepted. Giles Dawson shows that the person was someone close to Warburton (he thinks Warburton himself), but Arthur Sherbo demonstrates that Warburton could not have been the one. The editor attributes emendations to Warburton that Warburton himself does not claim in 1747. As Sherbo says, wouldn't Warburton be likely to recognize his own emendations? Wouldn't he credit himself with them in 1747 if he had done so in 1745? That he did not argues against his being the one to attribute them.[20]

Warburton had no reason to write anonymous notes. In the 1740s, he was aggressively seeking fame as well as fortune. Through his friendship with Pope, Warburton won influential friends (Ralph Allen, 1741), an aristocratic wife related to Allen (1745 or 1746), and, through Pope's and Allen's vigorous campaigns on his behalf, preferment, becoming first Dean of Bristol (1757) and then Bishop of Gloucester (1760).[21] His career epitomizes success as he understood it and in 1745 was already flourishing with promises of more to come. He was concerned, and had been since 1736 at least, with establishing a reputation as a polymath in spite of not having a university degree, and had already published not only his work on church and state but also the electrifying *Divine Legation of Moses Demonstrated* (1738). Why should he have been willing to do such drudgery as identifying the "owner" of explanations and emendations (those belonging to Hanmer presented without a name) and noting textual variants—and anonymously at that? Perhaps the drudgery of it would account for the anonymity, but this does not seem a job suitable for Warburton's ego. In 1745 Warburton was busy with several projects. According to Nichols's list of 1745 publications for bookseller William Bowyer, Warburton produced religious sermons and a pamphlet defending his *Divine Legation*, "Remarks on several Occasional Reflections. . . ." He was also much occupied in bringing out Pope's works.[22] Even though he is likely to have been eager to further the reprisal, he would doubtless have wanted someone else do the work.

That Warburton is involved in the 1745 text is evident from the "Advertisement" in the 1745 reprisal alluding to his coming edition, which will set all right that Hanmer got so wrong:

> This Edition [i.e., the 1745 reprisal] is exactly copied from that lately printed in *Quarto* at *Oxford;* but the Editor of that not having thought proper to point out the Alterations he has made from the former Copies, we were advised to mark those Passages in the Text thus,⁀ ⁀ and place the discarded Readings at the bottom of the Page, as also to point out the Emendations made by Mr. *Theobald,* Mr. *Warburton,* and Dr. *Thirlby,* in Mr. *Theobald's* Edition, which are used by this Editor. The changes in the disposition of the Lines for the Regulation of the Metre are too numerous to be taken particular notice of. As to the other Emendations and Notes of Mr. *Warburton,* which are for the most part marked likewise in this Edition, we are only commission'd to say thus much; *"That he desires the Publick would suspend their Opinion of his Conjectures 'till they see how they can be supported: For he holds it as ridiculous to alter the Text of an Author without Reasons assigned, as it was dishonourable to publish those Alterations without leave obtained. When he asks this Indulgence for himself, if the Publick will give it too to the Honourable Editor* [Hanmer], *he will not complain; as having no objection why his [Hanmer's] too should not occupy the Place they have usurped, until they be shewn to be arbitrary, groundless, mistaken, and violating not only the Sense of the Author, but all the Rules and Canons of true Criticism: Not that the Violation of these Rules ought to be any more objected to the Editor, than the Violation of the Rules of Poetry to his Author, as both professedly wrote without any"* [emphasis in the original].

The 1745 reprisal would merely prepare the public for the new, the accurate, the final edition of Shakespeare, to be prepared by Warburton.

Into this scene steps Samuel Johnson, trying to eke out a literary subsistence, living from hand to mouth, writing both anonymous and signed articles for his friend Edward Cave, the originator and editor of *Gentleman's Magazine.* Since Johnson's father had not provided support, dying a bankrupt, and Johnson had wasted his wife's widow-pittance in a failed academy, he was desperate for income. Perhaps the idea that came to Pope in 1742/43, that is, that the way would be open for anybody to edit Shakespeare if Hanmer could do it with impunity, also occurred to Cave and Johnson. In any case, Cave's proposal for a new *inexpensive* edition appeared soon after Hanmer's edition, appended to Johnson's anonymous notes: *"Miscellaneous Observations on the Tragedy of* Macbeth: *with Remarks on Sir. T.H.'s Edition of* Shakespear. *To which is affix'd, Proposals for a New Edition of Shakeshear* [sic], *with a Specimen.* London: Printed for E. Cave . . . and sold by J. Roberts . . . , 1745," published on 6 April.[23] The sixty-four-page pamphlet, a series of notes on lines and passages in *Macbeth,* is followed by the bookseller's advertisement and then a fold-out proposal for the new edition that emphasizes its low cost (one pound and five shillings in sheets) compared with the others available, especially the Oxford at three guineas, and includes a sample of notes from the *Macbeth* pamphlet. The advertisement lists both anonymous and credited works by Johnson, including his anonymous *Life of Richard Savage;* the two essays by M. Crousaz criticizing Pope (which Johnson had recommended to Cave for publication in translation and one of which Johnson had translated for him) bound with Warburton's defense; and, by "S. Johnson," for one shilling, "A Poem, in Imitation of the Third Satire of *Juvenal.*" Both the proposal and Johnson's notes critical of Hanmer would have interested Tonson.

Johnson says he has looked a little into the Oxford editor's *Macbeth:*

> The rest of this Edition I have not read, but, from the little that I have seen, think it not dangerous to declare that, in my Opinion, its Pomp recommends it more than its Accuracy. There is no Distinction made between the ancient Reading, and the Innovations of the Editor; there is no Reason given for any of the Alterations which are made; the Emendations of former Criticks are adopted without any Acknowledgment, and few of the Difficulties are removed which have hitherto embarrassed the Readers of *Shakespear* (64).

Probably the worst aspect of Hanmer's editing was motivated by his belief that a missing syllable "is a never failing mark with me that Shakespear has suffer'd some abuse" (letter to Warburton, Oct. 25, 1736). For tinkering with meter, Hanmer earns Johnson's ridicule: most of the Oxford Editor's emendations are "too trivial to deserve Mention"; though his "harmless Industry may, surely, be forgiven, if it cannot be praised: May he therefore never want a Monosyllable, who can use it with such wonderful Dexterity" (63). He recommends that Hanmer, an esteemed public figure, should leave such petty duties as editing to others:

> I would not, however, be thought to insult the Editor, nor to censure him with too much Petulance, for having failed in little Things, of whom I have been told, that he excells in greater. But I may, without Indecency, observe, that no Man should attempt to teach others what he has never learned himself; and that those who, like *Themistocles,* have studied the Arts of Policy, and *can teach a small State how to grow great,* should, like him, disdain to labour in Trifles, and consider petty Accomplishments as below their Ambition (64).

Having suffered the publication of the Oxford edition, Tonson could not allow anyone else to publish Shakespeare without, as Pope had conjectured, jeopardizing his rights altogether. Writing immediately to Cave,

Tonson assures him that he, Tonson, has a claim to the text of Shake-speare, a claim that he will go to law to maintain. Tonson's letter to Cave was evidently persuasive:

Sir, I have seen a proposal of yours for printing an edition of Shakespear, which I own much surprized me; but I suppose you are misled by the edition lately printed at Oxford, and that you think it is a copy any one has a right to; if so, you are very much mistaken, and if you call on me any afternoon about four or five o'clock, I doubt not I can shew you such a title as will satisfy you, not only as to the original copy, but likewise to all the emendations to this time: and I will then give you my reasons why we rather chuse to proceed with the University by way of reprisal for their scandalous invasion of our right, than by law, which reasons will not hold good as to any other persons who shall take the same liberty. As you are a man of character, I had rather satisfy you of our right by argument than by the expence of a Chancery suit, which will be the method we shall take with any one who shall attack our property in this or any other copy that we have fairly bought and paid for. I am, Sir, your very humble servant,

Jacob Tonson.

Thursday. April 11, 1745[24]

To soften the disappointment of the failed project, Tonson, I conjecture, gave the impecunious Johnson the job of editing the reprisal. Perhaps Tonson, Cave, and Johnson discussed the matter at the four or five o'clock meeting.

A non-Johnsonian narrative can certainly be constructed: Tonson, at the mooted April meeting, could have revealed that he already had re-sponded to the Oxford edition, that his reprisal edition had already been typeset. Also, unlike some of Johnson's known hack work, the attributive notes provide no clue about the style of their writer.

But Tonson's reprisal edition was probably not complete in April and may have been incomplete in May, when Cave announced it in *Gentle-man's Magazine*, (15: 280). It is even possible that the idea of adding attributive notes was not part of Tonson's original plan but was added onto the project after his discussion with Cave. If, as sometimes was the case and as Thomas Kaminski believes, the Cave announcement of *his* proposed edition in April signals that Johnson was well on his way with it (193), then Johnson would certainly have been prepared to assign the attributions if Tonson asked him to do so in April. The task would not have been beyond Johnson even were he not far advanced in April on his own edition. He was able to accomplish prodigious feats of labor when necessary; and modestly noting a completed text is less arduous than editing an original text.[25]

Support for Johnson's connection comes from the fact that though *Gen-*

tleman's Magazine did not generally publish notices of Shakespeare's *Works* and had printed none for the Oxford edition itself (1744), it published an announcement of the 1745 edition. It is likely that the unusual announcement appears as a favor to Johnson, a loyal and regular anonymous contributor to *Gentleman's Magazine* (see Nichols, *Anecdotes,* 5: 1–58). That Cave helped Johnson in just this way is shown by the next announcement of a Shakespeare text, in May 1747, listed under Warburton's name (17: 252). Not coincidentally, on the same page as the notice of the Warburton 1747 edition, an advertisement announces a reprint of the Johnson pamphlet: "Just publish'd. (Price 1*s*) Miscellaneous Observations on the Tragedy of MACBETH. Printed for R. Dodsley, and sold by J. Roberts."[26] Sales of the anonymous writer's *Observations* would be enhanced by Warburton's praise: ". . . as to all those Things, which have been published under the title of *Essays, Remarks, Observations,* &c. on Shakespear, if you except some critical Notes on *Macbeth,* given as a Specimen of a projected Edition, and written, as appears, by a Man of Parts and Genius, the rest are absolutely below a serious Notice" ("Preface," I, xiii). The juxtaposition of Warburton's 1747 edition and a re-issue of Johnson's 1745 *Observations* suggests that the advertisement in 1747 is, in part, a favor to Johnson. Would any other hack that Cave is likely to have helped in 1745 have been able to work as quickly or have been as qualified? If so, such a person is not known.

The hole in what is known about Johnson's life at the time allows room for conjecture. No letters for 1745 appear in Johnson's *Complete Letters,* edited by Chapman, or in *The Letters of Samuel Johnson,* edited by Bruce Redford. James Boswell notes that "It is somewhat curious, that his literary career appears to have been almost totally suspended in the years 1745 and 1746. . . ." Joseph Wood Krutch, one of Johnson's later biographers, has little idea about what Johnson was up to in 1745. Nor does Clifford, who notes that "Throughout most of 1745 and the first half of the next year there is little evidence of what Johnson was doing. . . . [I]t is not clear what his assignments from the booksellers were. This is a period of his life about which least is known." W. Jackson Bate, discussing the absence of apparent activity after the *Miscellaneous Observations,* sympathetically ascribes the suspension to a transition of middle age.[27] But why not the 1745 edition—not a lapse into depression and lethargy, but the most wonderful preparation, in fact, for much else that would ensure Johnson's lasting fame? The month of work would have earned him a respite from further hack labors.

Some of the facts—that no one knows what else Johnson was doing in 1745, that he frequently worked anonymously, and that he had no known source of income for that time—by themselves would be insufficient ground for the claim that Johnson wrote the notes for Tonson's edition and are merely suggestive. But they help make the case when coupled to other more compelling details: his 1745 proposal, his readiness to work on Shakespeare as indicated by his *Macbeth* pamphlet, the evident efficacy of Tonson's letter to Cave, and Cave's unusual announcement in *Gentleman's Magazine* of the 1745 edition. It hardly seems reasonable that Cave would further an edition by a publisher who had thwarted his own edition—unless he had a good reason to do so. Johnson would and could take on such a job.

Furthermore, the manner of the reprisal edition—the respect for Warburton, the evidence that the editor referred randomly to a variety of sources, without using any of them consistently or throughout, accords with Johnson's practice in his own Shakespeare.[28] The note writer had the Oxford text at his disposal, obviously. He glanced at Theobald's 1733 edition to find attributions to Theobald and Warburton. Warburton, for the same reasons he cannot be the note writer, cannot have supplied the note writer with a complete and accurate list. Warburton may, however, have allowed the writer a quick perusal of his letters—documents that Warburton could not, because of what he says (and later suppressed) about Pope, Theobald, and Hanmer, allow out of his hands, or allow to be copied. Boswell asserts that Johnson was amazing in needing only to scan a text to grasp its import (1: 71); a cursory reading of Warburton's letters by the writer could account for the errors. Warburton is likely to have shown his letter, even briefly, only to someone he trusted.

In his 1765 edition, Johnson often reprinted Warburton's notes, many of which he came to deplore without giving him occasion, it seems, to change his overall opinion about the genius of the man—partly inspired by his gratitude for Warburton's praise in his 1747 preface when Johnson had most needed it.[29] Though rising occasionally to refute Warburton's explanations, more often he simply allows Warburton's notes to speak for themselves without admitting his emendations into his text. Not placated by Johnson's mostly mild response, Warburton so took umbrage at the occasional exposures of his logical fallacies and æsthetic failings that in his own copy of his 1747 edition (now at the Folger), he struck out his praise of Johnson, probably in preparation for a new edition that was never required.

A telling point is Johnson's odd change of mind about Sir Thomas Hanmer, difficult to account for in the normal course of events but plausible if Johnson worked on the Hanmer text in 1745. Johnson had dismissed Hanmer's editorial work as beneath serious consideration in *Miscellaneous Observations,* after scanning, he admits, only *Macbeth.* In his 1765 Preface, Johnson has a much kinder regard for the Oxford editor and can put aside, it seems, Hanmer's syllabic puttering. In sketching the short history of editions, Johnson says:

Our authour fell then into the hands of Sir *Thomas Hanmer*, the *Oxford*-editor, a man, in my opinion, eminently qualified by nature for such studies. He had, what is the first requisite to emendatory criticism, that intuition by which the poet's intention is immediately discovered, and that dexterity of intellect which dispatches its work by the easiest means. He had undoubtedly read much; his acquaintance with customs, opinions, and traditions, seems to have been large; and he is often learned without shew.

After some mild criticism, Johnson deplored the world's too violent censuring of Hanmer's tinkering with syllables. Johnson does fault him for not indicating his literary debts (the fault the reprisal edition rectified), but he ends by asserting that

[a]s he never writes [referring to Hanmer's few notes] without careful enquiry and diligent consideration, I have received all his notes, and believe that every reader will wish for more.[30]

The mere half-dozen notes in *Macbeth* did not display Hanmer's perspicacity, for whatever one may say about his text, his few explanations are concise and elegant. The opportunity to read all of Hanmer's notes could have led Johnson to this altered opinion; because the Hanmer text was not authoritative and had no notes about emendations, Johnson is unlikely to have read Hanmer's edition unless required to do so.

Johnson's dictionary, his next major undertaking and the one that made his reputation, naturally includes a large percentage of examples from Shakespeare. Hanmer's limited glossary—the first to appear as part of an edition of Shakespeare and of course included in the reprisal edition[31]—may have helped Johnson decide that a detailed, literary dictionary of the English language would be a viable project, and with his dazzling memory he would have gathered while working on the 1745 edition a storehouse of Shakespeare quotations. Affirming that he had thought of a dictionary before Robert Dodsley approached him (but without specifying when or how), in 1746 Johnson entered into an agreement with the publisher to compile a dictionary (Clifford, 292). Thus, the 1745 edition, a decisive element in Tonson's copyright claims, may also have been a step toward Johnson's more important works, the dictionary published in 1755, and then the 1765 edition, proposed in 1756, when it was clear that Warburton's edition would not be the last word.

Johnson entered the Shakespeare world opportunistically, without, it seems fair to say, adulation for Shakespeare but with an unclouded mind and eye that allowed him to detach himself from ownership. Thus, his 1765 text, which has been called the first variorum edition, registers a new phase in the battles for supremacy that shape the work of the first Shakespeare scholars. His 1765 notes are very unlike the intrusive ones in his 1745 *Miscellaneous Observations*. He had not yet developed his conviction that the less the text is emended the better.[32] In his preface Johnson is less than just to Theobald, disdaining the displays of exultant pedantry that Theobald sometimes allows himself. Still, Johnson's notes are generous to predecessors, including Theobald and Hanmer, and exhibit a spirit of inclusiveness.[33] Perhaps it is not too farfetched to say that the impersonal notes of the 1745 edition could have prepared him for this generosity and inclusiveness—helping him shun his predecessors' overt attacks in their notes on *their* predecessors.

What remains to be explored is the function of anonymity in editing Shakespeare—which I can touch on only briefly here. Hanmer's is the coy anonymity of one who knows he is recognized, and it can be understood as a feint of false modesty or as a gesture of dignity and status—a Sir Thomas Hanmer craves neither money nor recognition. His identity, however, and the imprimatur of Oxford University give the text an *ex cathedra* validity, the permanence and finality of a large, clean text—one seemingly untainted by marketplace strategies. Everything about the 1745 reprisal, in contrast, from the anonymity of the person who supplied its variants and attributions, to its size and price, place it firmly in the marketplace, yet it was meant to be a throw-away text, merely a scout for other texts that would come after it. The note-writer's anonymity, contrived to serve the publisher's interests, was not meant to be breached and resists exposure. The anonymity gave Johnson—if he was indeed the note writer—a useful staging point for much of the good work he accomplished thereafter as a somewhat reluctant Shakespearean.[34]

NOTES

1. Giles E. Dawson discusses not only general copyright issues but also analyzes the various moves against Tonson's claim, both before and after 1744. See "The Copyright of Shakespeare's Dramatic Works," *The University of Missouri Studies in Honor of A. H. R. Fairchild,* ed. Charles T. Prouty (Columbia, Missouri: Univ. of Missouri, 1946), 11–35, especially 26–33. I use "Jacob Tonson," the primary shareholder, as a handy metonymy for all the booksellers who had purchased an interest in Shakespeare. Tonson was the principal player. The 1745 octavo appeared in six volumes.

An earlier version of this essay appeared in *Analytical & Enumerative Bibliography* N.S. 6.3–4 (1992 [published fall 1994]): 185–207. I am grateful to its editor, William Proctor Williams, for permission to publish this revision.

2. See *The Correspondence of Alexander Pope,* 5 vols., ed. George Sherburn (Oxford: Clarendon, 1956), 4: 439. From the version in British Library, Egerton MS. 1946, ff.71–73, I show the words "mans" and "your," crossed out, followed by the words that replaced them in the ms. When transcribing manuscripts, I have silently expanded some abbreviations and adjusted other orthographic features. All British Library mss. are quoted with permission.

3. Since Hanmer's was only the fourth edition after Rowe, conventions for assigning credit had not been established. Thus, to say that Hanmer "stole" anyone's emendations goes beyond the facts.

4. 24 January 1746/47; see Folger MS. S.a. 165, reprinted in Donald W. Nichol, ed., *Pope's Literary Legacy: The Book-Trade Correspondence of William Warburton and John Knapton with other letters and documents, 1744–1780* (Oxford: The Oxford Bibliographical Society, 1992), 191–92.

5. Margreta de Grazia, *Shakespeare Verbatim: The Reproduction of Authenticity and the 1790 Apparatus* (Oxford: Clarendon, 1991), 192n.44, mentions the conjecture first advanced by Giles E. Dawson that Warburton edited the 1745 text; see "Warburton, Hanmer, and the 1745 Edition of Shakespeare," *Studies in Bibliography* 2 (1949–50): 35–48. Arthur Sherbo, "Warburton and the 1745 Shakespeare," *JEGP* 51 (1952): 71–82, has a strong argument against the claim that Warburton wrote the notes.

6. See James L. Clifford, *Young Sam Johnson* (New York: McGraw Hill, 1955). A note by O. M. Brack, Jr., and Mary Early, "Samuel Johnson's Proposals for the *Harleian Miscellany*," *Studies in Bibliography* 45 (1992): 127–30, describes other work that Johnson had in hand in 1743 and possibly later. Thomas Kaminski has a thorough investigation of Johnson's poverty, his hack work and his connection to Cave in *The Early Career of Samuel Johnson* (New York: Oxford Univ. Press, 1987).

7. Several writers have told the story in the detail it requires, especially Peter Seary, *Lewis Theobald and the Editing of Shakespeare* (Oxford: Clarendon Press, 1990). See also Richard Foster Jones, *Lewis Theobald: His Contribution to English Scholarship with Some Unpublished Letters* (New York: Columbia Univ. Press, 1919), Thomas R. Lounsbury, *The First Editors of Shakespeare (Pope and Theobald).The Story of the First Shakespearian Controversy and of the Earliest Attempt at Establishing a Critical Text of Shakespeare* (London: David Nutt, 1906), and A[rthur] W[illiam] Evans, *Warburton and the Warburtonians: A Study in Eighteenth-Century Controversies* (London: Oxford Univ. Press, 1932). Nichol discusses the bequest, xxx–xxxviii.

8. Almost the entire correspondence from Theobald to Warburton and others, and from Warburton to various people, can be found in John Nichols, *Illustrations of the Literary History of the Eighteenth Century. . . . Intended as a Sequel to* The Literary Anecdotes (London, 1817). Most of Theobald's letters are in 2: 189–647. The letter of 18 May is in the British Library, Egerton MS. 1956, and has been published by Jones, 343–44.

9. A letter from Warburton that begins "My Dear Friend," dated 2 June 1934, says, "I have sent you all I could find to cavil at in your Edition of Shakespeare. I know it will be a pleasure to you to receive it, & it is no small compliment to your Edition. For I have been so exact in my inquisitive search after Faults that I dare undertake to defend every note thro' out the whole bulkey work save these 13" (Folger W.b. 75, f.145). How different was his attack in his "Preface," *The Works of Shakespear in Eight Volumes* (London, 1747), 1: x–xi, and throughout the *Works,* where he often criticizes Theobald for ideas he had approved in the letters. Lumping together the scholarly Theobald with Hanmer, Warburton says, "They separately possessed those two qualities which, more than any other, have contributed to bring the Art of Criticism into disrepute, *Dulness of Apprehension,* and *Extravagance of Conjecture*" (1: xiii).

10. Hanmer's are in the British Library (Egerton MS. 1957); Evans published some of the letters, 151–55, including Hanmer's last letter to Warburton. Evans

also includes a letter by Hanmer to Oxford University dated 1742 that came to light in 1761 and a rejoinder to this letter by Warburton, written when it was shown to him in 1761. See also John Nichols, *Literary Anecdotes of the Eighteenth Century . . . in six volumes* (London, 1812), 5: 588–90. Robert Ryley, *William Warburton,* Twayne's English Authors Series (Boston: Twayne, 1984), 99–100, prints the letter to Hanmer by Warburton requesting the return of his notes. Neither Hanmer nor Warburton tells the whole truth in his letter about the affair—as a survey of all of their extant letters reveals.

11. Hanmer's letters (not among those published by Evans) show that Warburton is trying to insinuate himself into the nobleman's circle, but Hanmer resists turning the literary relationship into a more general friendship. For example, after making Warburton a Christmas wish, Hanmer puts Warburton in his place: "And I hope you will not think it [the greeting] improper from so distant a friend as Your very humble servant Tho: Hanmer" (British Library, Egerton MS. 1957, 13 Dec. 1736). Hanmer often says he will miss Warburton's weekly letters; he lets Warburton know that Shakespeare alone connects them. Warburton's method in ingratiating himself was to pour letters and flattery upon his object: Theobald, Hanmer, and Pope all remark on the tardiness of their replies to his very frequent letters.

12. British Library, add. MS. 4320; Nichols, *Illustrations,* 2:72–73.

13. "Preface," 1: xi–xii.

14. Pope's edition of 1723–25; its slow sales are verified by a report in *Gentleman's Magazine* 57 [1787]: 76.

15. Warburton's letter to Birch is in the British Library, Birch add. MS. 4320. See also Nichols, *Illustrations,* 2: 93, 96–97. See *Bayle's Dictionary* 9 (1739): 190. Brian Vickers has a convenient extract in his valuable collection of primary sources, *Shakespeare: The Critical Heritage,* 6 vols. (London & Boston: Routledge & Kegan Paul, 1974), 3: 81–96. Sherbo shows that Warburton's proposed emendations in Bayle's could have helped the anonymous note-writer in 1745. Birch is also a link among Warburton, Johnson and Cave, since Birch and Johnson both assisted Cave with *Gentleman's Magazine:* see Kaminski, 30, 32.

16. Or at least slowed him. In a letter to Birch on 18 January 1742/43, Warburton writes that "for my amusement, [I] from time to time go on in preparing Shakespeare for the press"; see Nichols, *Illustrations,* 2: 129. Considering the urgency with which he had solicited Birch to announce his projected edition, Warburton appears to be remarkably relaxed about the project years later. He also says in this letter that he expects Hanmer's edition will sell so poorly that the plates from drawings by Hayman will be available for his own edition. He was wrong.

17. Warburton's defense was first published anonymously in the journal *The History of the Works of the Learned,* but Pope soon broke through the anonymity; see reference in *Boswell's Life of Johnson,* ed. George Birkbeck Hill, rev. L. F. Powell, 6 vols. (Oxford: Clarendon, 1971), 5: 491, hereafter cited as *Boswell.* Warburton and Pope, whose correspondence began after Warburton's defense began, did not meet until 1740, for on 16 April 1740, Pope writes, "Let us meet, like Men who have been many years acquainted with each other, & and whose friendship is not to begin, but continue" (Sherburn, 4: 233). Samuel Johnson encouraged Cave to publish Crousaz's attack and Warburton's "Vindication." Kaminski (154) points out that Warburton's defense helped to call attention to Johnson's translation of Crousaz that Cave had published anonymously and which he reissued in 1741—another link among Cave, Johnson and Warburton.

18. Maynard Mack says that Warburton spoke and wrote against Pope as late as 1733–34. See *Alexander Pope: A Life* (New Haven: Yale Univ. Press, 1985), 744. See also Nichols, *Anecdotes,* 5: 554. I do not believe that Warburton could have confessed to the anonymous attacks and maintained Pope's friendship, though Pope knew that Warburton had helped Theobald in 1733 and had subsequently broken off with him. Lounsbury (353–62) identifies three anonymous letters by Warburton, dating them in 1729, and reproduces a good part of their texts, showing that Warburton had "spoken worse [of Pope] than ever did Theobald, or indeed any of the writers satirized in 'The Dunciad'" (362).

Johnson believed that Warburton dropped Theobald and took up the defense of Pope "seeing him [Pope] the rising man . . ." (*Boswell* 5:80). Johnson missed the intermediate attempt on Hanmer.

19. Warburton, as Paul Bertram pointed out to me orally, superficially follows Pope in scene divisions, in marking the shining passages with inverted commas (though marking many more than Pope), and with an index of noteworthy passages (again adding many more). However, Warburton often disagrees with Pope on substantive issues.

20. For Dawson and Sherbo, see n.5, above. Sherbo does not cite many examples from *Hamlet,* but the notes in that play continue the pattern he found in the six plays he examined in detail; I offer some examples from *Hamlet* that further corroborate Sherbo's assertion:

In the summary that follows, TLN refers to the numbering system in Charleton Hinman, *The Norton Facsimile: The First Folio of Shakespeare* (New York: Norton and London: Paul Hamlyn, 1968). For Claudius's line describing Fortinbras, "Coleagued with this dream of his advantage" (*Hamlet,* TLN 199), Theobald in *Shakespeare Restored* (1726) had suggested *collogued,* meaning "flattered, imposed on, cajol'd" (4–5), but omitted the emendation in his 1733 edition. In 1744, Hanmer accepted *collogued,* but in the reprint of 1745 it passes unnoted, when it should have been credited to Theobald. An editor not as familiar with Theobald's work as was Warburton might very naturally overlook the emendation and allow it to go unremarked. The reprisal edition credits Warburton with explaining "palmy" as "victorious" (*Hamlet,* TLN 124 + 6), but how could Pope's executor, Warburton, credit to himself one of the few explanations by his friend and patron that he used, and credited to Pope, in 1747? Further, in 1745 Warburton could not have been so absentminded as to credit himself for the emendation "sanity" in "The sanity and health of this whole state" (*Hamlet,* TLN 484) when Theobald suggested it in *Shakespeare Restored* (but again had changed his mind by 1733) and Warburton preferred "safety" in 1747. The 1745 editor did not use Pope 1728, which includes a note on Theobald's "sanity" from *Shakespeare Restored.*

In 1765, after retaining Warburton's note about Q2 "safety," Johnson credits Hanmer with "sanity": he may have assigned ownership by a process of elimination and never have seen *Shakespeare Restored* or systematically consulted Pope's second edition.

21. See Mack, *A Life,* 744. Mack gives the date of the marriage as 1746, Nichols as 1745, *Anecdotes,* 5: 593. From that time, says Nichols, "Prior Park, the splendid seat of Mr. Allen, became . . . [Warburton's] principal residence, and ultimately his own property" (5: 593–94).

22. *Anecdotes,* 2: 174–78; for Warburton's 1745 works, his own and his editions of Pope, published by John and Paul Knapton, see 186, 188–89.

23. Norman Page, *A Dr Johnson Chronology* (Boston: Hall, 1990), gives the publication date of *Observations* as 6 April 1745. He has no other information

about Johnson in 1745 (7–8). For an excerpt from *Observations,* see Vickers, 3: 165–85. A copy of the original is at the Folger. Cave's text was to be printed in "Ten small Volumes."

24. The text of letter is from Karl Young, "Samuel Johnson on Shakespeare: One Aspect," *Wisconsin Studies in Language and Literature* 18 (1923): 147–227, rpt. New York: Haskell House, 1975. The letter, on 176, Young transcribed from Samuel Pegge, ed. *Anonymiana* (London, 1818; 1st issue c.1766), 23–24, alerted to its presence there by Courtney's *Bibliography of Johnson* (18). Dawson, "Copyright," also reproduces the letter, 32.

25. Johnson could work quickly when he wished; he says he "wrote forty-eight of the printed octavo pages in the Life of Savage at a sitting" (*Boswell,* 1: 71n.3).

26. See Johnson's letters to Cave mentioning Dodsley in Nichols, *Anecdotes,* 5: 24–25, 26. Dodsley, Cave, and Johnson often collaborated. See Kaminski, 19.

27. Redford, *Volume I: 1731–1772* (Princeton: Princeton Univ. Press, 1992). Krutch, *Samuel Johnson* (New York: Holt, 1944), 87–88; *Boswell,* 1: 175. Clifford, 265. Bate, *Samuel Johnson* (New York: Harcourt Brace Jovanovich, 1977). Kaminski also comments on the 1745 gap in our knowledge about Johnson, 195. The mystery about how Johnson could have survived during this gap is solved if Tonson paid Johnson enough in April and May 1745 to enable him to take a sabbatical from his labors. Kaminski discusses Johnson's finances in detail throughout his book. Other hiatuses in Johnson's work history suggest that a surge of activity might be followed by a lull. Johnson was also, as is well known, subject to melancholy.

28. Robert DeMaria, Jr., in *Johnson's* Dictionary *and the Language of Learning* (Chapel Hill and London: Univ. of No. Carolina Press, 1986), discusses the fact that for *intrenchant* Johnson in his dictionary provides Hanmer's definition and his own but does not use the example in his own edition: "The fact that Johnson chose not to gloss [intrenchant] in his edition of Shakespeare suggests that he proceeded in an ad hoc way on both critical projects, rising to comment where he felt stimulated to do so, rather than on a regular principle" (197). While others certainly used similar ad hoc methods, the method is compatible with Johnson's hand. Kaminski confirms DeMaria's view about Johnson's way of working (113–14).

29. Boswell records Johnson's gratitude to Warburton: "He praised me at a time when praise was of value to me" (1: 176). In Boswell's opinion, Johnson "had done liberal justice to Warburton's edition" (4: 46). Johnson did not forget those who helped him. Robert DeMaria, Jr., points out that Johnson was more severe with Warburton in "cancelled leaves" than in the 1765 edition and that he softened still further in the edition he and Steevens jointly edited in 1773. See *The Life of Samuel Johnson: A Critical Biography* (Oxford: Blackwell, 1993), 231, 258.

30. "Preface," *The Plays of William Shakespeare . . .* to which are added notes by Sam. Johnson (London, 1765), 1: li–lii. Interestingly enough, in 1770–71 Oxford reprinted its quarto edition, with some embellishments, including a list of 1733 Theobald and 1765 Capell variants from the Hanmer readings—ignoring the textual contributions of the 1747 Warburton and the 1765 Johnson.

31. Charles Gildon produced a glossary in his edition of Shakespeare's poems published by Curll in 1710 as "volume seven" of Tonson's 6–volume, 1709 Rowe edition. A four-page glossary also appeared at the end of volume nine, which Curll, with Tonson's approval, added to the eight volumes of Rowe's 1714 edition: the glossaries, the same except for the order of the words under each letter

heading, have about 160 entries. The Gildon material appeared also in an added volume for Pope's edition, "The whole revis'd and corrected, with a preface by Dr. Sewell" (title page). Except for a few changes in spelling (e.g., *burn* becomes *bourn*) and some additions to take into account Pope's emendations (*unknelled* for Folio *unnaneld*), the Sewell glossary appears to be copied from Gildon 1714. The Oxford glossary is much longer, about 23 pages in the 1745 edition with about 450 words, and is an integral part of the edition rather than something added.

32. See Shirley Johnston on his development from the exuberant certainty of *Miscellaneous Observations* to his mature modesty in his 1765 edition, "Samuel Johnson's Macbeth: 'Fair is Foul,'" in *The Age of Johnson: A Scholarly Annual* 3, ed. Paul J. Korshin (New York: AMS Press, 1990), 189–230. She speculates on the reasons Johnson includes in his 1765 edition notes from *Miscellaneous Observations* so different from his later practice.

33. For this insight into Johnson, I am indebted to Shirley Johnston, "From Preface to Practice: Samuel Johnson's Editorship of Shakespeare," in *Greene Centennial Studies: Essays Presented to Donald Greene in the Centennial Year of the University of Southern California*, ed. Paul J. Korshin and Robert R. Allen (Charlottesville: Univ. Press of Virginia, 1984), 250–70. See also Edward Tomarken, *Samuel Johnson on Shakespeare: The Discipline of Criticism* (Athens and London: Univ. of Georgia Press, 1991), who discusses Johnson's use of the variorum method to further his critical aims, especially, 47–48, and 145–46.

I would also like to thank Kent Cartwright, David George, William Hutchings, and E. Pearlman for their help. Members of the SAA seminar on Editing Shakespeare in the Eighteenth Century, especially Frank N. Clary, Jr., Irene Dash, Joanna Gondris, Eric Rasmussen, and Peter Seary, read a later draft. Thanks also to Morris Brownell, Thomas Kaminski, and John H. Middendorf for their useful cautions.

34. To his biographer Sir John Hawkins, Johnson said (*The Life of Samuel Johnson, LL.D*, 1787, 363), "I look upon this [editing of Shakespeare] as I did upon the Dictionary: it is all work, and my inducement to it is not love or desire of fame, but the want of money, which is the only motive to writing that I know of" (quoted in *Boswell* 1: 318n.5). The question of what induced Johnson to edit Shakespeare shades into the question of Johnson's regard for his author, but perhaps the two should be kept separate.

Anonymity and the Erasure of Shakespeare's First Eighteenth-Century Editor

Eric Rasmussen

THERE has always been a certain elegant simplicity to the history of Shakespearean editing. The seventeenth century was clearly "the pre-Editorial era,"[1] an age of monolithic folios and unnamed compositors. The eighteenth century, by contrast, witnessed "the birth of editing"[2] with multiple volume octavos produced by editors with names. But now the boundaries have been crossed, the distinctions have been blurred, the teleologies have been challenged, and the elegant simplicity has been shattered by the discovery of an early eighteenth-century folio, an edition without an editor, a text literally without rules.

Some copies of the Shakespeare Fourth Folio (1685) contain seventy scattered pages that were printed without side rules and foot rules. In most copies of the Fourth Folio these same pages are boxed with rules on the sides, head, and foot. The strikingly different appearance of the partially unruled pages was noticed over a century ago,[3] but it was not until 1951 that Giles Dawson discovered that the unruled pages had actually been reset and reprinted.[4] The reprinted pages correct dozens of errors in F4, modernize hundreds of spellings and punctuations, and systematically introduce the use of apostrophes in possessives. The fact that the compositor responsible for the reprinting was apparently unaware of the practice of boxing folio pages, combined with the fact that the reprinted sheets bear a different watermark than all of the normal sheets in the volume, suggested to Dawson that the reprinting occurred at a date substantially later than the original printing in 1685, and he proposed circa 1700. Since the reprinted pages would therefore constitute a fifth folio printing, Dawson termed them F5.

The Fourth Folio was printed in three sections by three different printers. Henry Herriman was the principal if not the sole capitalist in the publication. Dawson conjectured that following the initial sales of F4, Herriman had warehoused the stacks of ungathered sheets, from which copies could then be made up and bound as the need arose. At some point it was noticed that seventeen of the stacks were nearly exhausted while the vast majority of stacks had more than two hundred sheets remaining. Dawson speculated that a calculation of costs and of the probability of future sales indicated that it would be profitable to go to the expense of reprinting the seventeen sheets required to make the remaining stock good. All of the seventeen sheets in question appear in the second section of the folio; apparently, the printer of the second section had short-sheeted Herriman. If Herriman had noticed the discrepancy when the sheets were first delivered to him, he no doubt would have insisted that the original printer reprint the sheets, in which case the reprinted pages would be technically cancels rather than later reprints.[5]

But it is difficult to imagine that the original printer in 1685 would have produced cancels so remarkably different in appearance from the original sheets. Although the evidence for later reprinting is largely inferential, the thoroughgoing modernization of punctuation and spelling in the reprinted pages does indeed suggest a date in the early eighteenth century. If Dawson's interpretation of the evidence is correct, then the F5 pages represent the first eighteenth-century edition of *King John, 2 Henry IV, Henry V, 1 Henry VI, 2 Henry VI, Henry VIII, Troilus and Cressida, Coriolanus, Titus Andronicus,* and *Romeo and Juliet.*

Curiously though, Dawson's discovery has been universally ignored. Although the standard reference works alert editors to the existence of F5,[6] not one F5 reading has been cited in the textual notes to any edition of Shakespeare that has appeared in the last four decades. Admittedly, the F5 pages are not easily accessible. They do not appear in either the Methuen facsimile or the Pollard STC microfilm of F4, but can only be found in four of the Folger's thirty-seven copies and in two copies in the New York Public Library.[7] And yet, one suspects that if Dawson could have attached a name to the F5 text, it would almost certainly not languish in obscurity. The fundamental prejudice against anonymous editors in favor of those with names is so deeply ingrained that we tend to accept without question McKerrow's assertion that "what we understand by the 'editing' of Shakespeare" began with Rowe in 1709.[8] But when a prominent scholar observes that "Rowe, as the first to scrutinize the text, had more occasions than his successors to make worthwhile alterations,"[9] he effectively erases the thousands of alterations made in the seventeenth century by the succession of editors and compositors who, of course, scrutinized the text long before Rowe did.[10]

It is generally assumed that the intentional textual changes made by the editors of the eighteenth century were different in kind from the types of alterations made by the anonymous folio compositors, but this is not necessarily the case. Renewed attention to the reprinted Fifth Folio pages reveals that the person responsible for the text of F5 behaved very much like an eighteenth-century editor.[11]

In fact, a significant number of emendations previously attributed to Rowe, Pope, and Theobald turn out to have been anticipated by F5. Of the substantive emendations adopted by the *Riverside Shakespeare,* for instance, Rowe's emendations of *2 Henry VI* (4.2.90), *Henry VIII* (1.2.179 and 1.3.59), *Troilus and Cressida* (1.2.85 and 1.2.210), *Titus Andronicus* (1.1.144), and *Romeo and Juliet* (3.2.28), Pope's emendations of *2 Henry VI* (4.2.172) and *Troilus and Cressida* (4.5.78), and Theobald's emendation of *Titus Andronicus* (2.3.291) were all anticipated in F5. Another characteristic feature of eighteenth-century editions—the restoration of readings from earlier quarto texts—is present in the Fifth Folio as well. F5 restores two Q1 readings in *Henry V* (2.1.85 and 2.2.5), a Q1 reading in *Troilus and Cressida* (1.3.168), an F1 reading in *Coriolanus* (1.2.21), a Q1 reading of *Titus Andronicus* (3.1.115) as well as a Q2 reading (2.3.140), and a Q2 reading in *Romeo and Juliet* (3.2.106).[12]

The discovery of what may be the first eighteenth-century edition of Shakespeare challenges some of our fundamental ideas about editors and editing, and leaves us with some haunting questions as well. Were folio editions of Shakespeare in such demand at the turn of the century that Herriman (or his successors) could justify the time and considerable expense of resetting and reprinting seventy folio pages? Was the reprinting undertaken *after* the copyright was sold to Jacob Tonson? Might the reprinting have been occasioned by the renewed interest in Shakespeare generated by Rowe's edition for Tonson in 1709? Was the folio intended to compete with Rowe? This Shakespeare Fifth Folio text of manifestly uncertain date, of uncertain authority, of uncertain agency, unknown to the editors of the eighteenth century and ignored by those in the twentieth clearly deserves more careful attention.

OVERVIEW OF THE REPRINTED FOURTH FOLIO PAGES

Sig.	Page number	TLN	Text affected
2B3r	5	534–677	*King John,* 2.1.228–3.1.184
2B3v	6	678–825	"
2B4r	7	826–971	"
2B4v	8	972–1112	"
2I2r	87	3324–50	Epilogue of *2 Henry IV* and Dramatis Personae for *Henry V*
I2v	88	1–85	*Henry V,* Prologue-2.4.75

2I3r	89	86–231	"
2I3v	90	232–379	"
2I4r	91	380–523	"
2I4v	92	524–671	"
2I5r	93	672–819	"
2I5v	94	820–967	"
2M1r	121	1257–404	*1 Henry VI*, 3.1.51–3.2.103
2M1v	122	1405–542	
2M6r	131	2683–826	*1 Henry VI*, 5.4.43–5.5.108
2M6v	132	2827–931	"
2N1r	133	1–101	*2 Henry VI*, 1.1.1–1.3.147
2N1v	134	102–249	"
2N2r	135	250–393	"
2N2v	136	394–540	"
2N5r	141	1115–262	*2 Henry VI*, 2.3.59–3.1.110
2N5v	142	1263–410	"
2O3r	149	2297–439	*2 Henry VI*, 4.1.129–4.9.10
2O3v	150	2440–581	"
2O4r	151	2582–721	"
2O4v	152	2722–862	"
2T3r	209	77–223	*Henry VIII*, 1.1.33–1.3.66
2T3v	210	224–366	"
2T4r	211	367–514	"
2T4v	212	515–657	"
2X2r	231	3236–376	*Henry VIII*, 5.2.199-Epilogue
2X2r	232	3377–460	"
2X3r	233	1–76	*Troilus*, Prologue-1.3.351
2X3v	234	77–224	"
2X4r	235	225–373	"
2X4v	236	374–523	"
2X5r	237	524–671	"
2X5v	238	672–818	"
2Y1r	241	1113–260	*Troilus*, 2.2.124–2.3.199
2Y1v	242	1261–406	"
2Y6r	251	2578–723	*Troilus*, 4.5.26–5.1.1
2Y6v	252	2724–871	"
2Z2r	255	3166–309	*Troilus*, 5.2.169–5.5.57
2Z2v	256	3310–459	"
2Z3r	257	3460–592	"
2Z3v	258	1–94	*Coriolanus*, 1.1.1–1.6.46
2Z4r	259	95–242	"
2Z4v	260	243–382	"
2Z5r	261	383–520	"
2Z5v	262	521–659	"
*3B2r	279	2975–3120	*Coriolanus*, 4.6.66–5.2.23
*3B2v	280	3121–261	"

*3B5r	285	1–90	*Titus*, 1.1.1–205
*3B5v	286	91–235	"
*3C2r	291	812–957	*Titus*, 2.3.73–4.3.90
*3C2v	292	958–1098	"
*3C3r	293	1099–239	"
*3C3v	294	1240–383	"
*3C4r	295	1384–529	"
*3C4v	296	1530–669	"
*3C5r	297	1670–813	"
*3C5v	298	1814–957	"
*3E3r	317	1638–1781	*Romeo and Juliet*, 3.1.93–
			3.3.107
*3E3v	318	1782–923	"
*3E6r	323	2486–616	*Romeo and Juliet*, 4.3.7–5.1.29
*3E6v	324	2617–754	"

Notes

1. Random Cloud, "'The very name of the Persons': Editing and the Invention of Dramatick Character," in *Staging the Renaissance: Reinterpretations of Elizabethan and Jacobean Drama,* eds. David Scott Kastan and Peter Stallybrass (New York: Routledge, 1991), 88–98, esp.94.

2. Ibid., 94.

3. *Contributions to a Catalogue of the Lenox Library, No. V. Works of Shakespeare, Etc.* (New York, 1880), 41.

4. Giles Dawson, "Some Bibliographical Irregularities in the Shakespeare Fourth Folio," *Studies in Bibliography* 4 (1951): 93–103.

5. On cancels, see Philip Gaskell, *A New Introduction to Bibliography* (Oxford: Clarendon Press, 1972), 134–35.

6. See Richard Hosley, Richard Knowles, and Ruth McGugan, *Shakespeare Variorum Handbook: A Manual of Editorial Practice* (New York: Modern Language Association, 1971), 57; see also T. H. Howard-Hill, *Shakespearian Bibliography and Textual Criticism, a Bibliography* (Oxford: Clarendon Press, 1971), 71.

7. Folger copies 7, 13, 28, and 33; New York Public Library copies Astor and Lenox.

8. Ronald McKerrow, "The Treatment of Shakespeare's Text by His Earlier Editors, 1709–1768," *Proceedings of the British Academy* (London, 1933), 4.

9. Peter Seary, *Lewis Theobald and the Editing of Shakespeare* (Oxford: Clarendon Press, 1990), 60n. Elsewhere, however, Seary acknowledges that the Second Folio "was subjected to a great deal of attention by an 'editor' who, without reference to any manuscript authority, made a large number of alterations in the texts of the plays" (136).

10. The Second Folio made more than 1600 deliberate changes in the text of the First; the Third Folio made over 900 changes; the Fourth Folio made over 700. See M. W. Black and M. A. Shaaber, *Shakespeare's Seventeenth-Century Editors, 1632–1685* (New York: Modern Language Association of America, 1937).

11. My analysis of possible compositorial discriminants in the reprinted F5 pages suggests that they were all set into type by the same workperson.

12. I would like to thank Jennifer Hoyer for her assistance in preparing these collations.

Johnson's Shakespeare of 1765:
A Comparison of the Two Editions of
A Midsummer Night's Dream

Richard F. Kennedy

THERE were two distinct editions of Samuel Johnson's *Plays* of Shake-speare published by Tonson and others in 1765. The first edition (JOHN1) was published on 10 October, and the second (JOHN2) "early in Novem-ber."[1] The reason that the second edition followed so swiftly on the heels of the first was that there were 750 to 1000 subscribers, and a run of 1000 copies of the first edition, which left very few—if any—copies for the twelve booksellers to offer to the public, and so the second edition was started as early as 5 October 1765, five days before the publication of the first edition. Seven hundred fifty copies of JOHN2 were printed by 4 November 1765: 250 were delivered to Tonson.[2] Did Johnson revise the second edition? Some of the New Variorum editors seem to feel that he did, for they (e.g., Black, Shaaber, Eccles) include JOHN2 among the major editions worthy of full collation, while others (e.g., Evans, Veltz, Knowles, Spevack) spurn it and deem it barely worthy of partial colla-tion.[3] Johnsonian experts like Arthur Eastman have determined that Johnson based the text of JOHN1 partly on Warburton's 1747 edition and partly on Theobald's 1757 edition.[4] Donald Eddy has studied differences in the pagination and the press figures of the two editions, and others have studied the cancels,[5] but no one seems to have considered the text itself in detail. Sherbo indeed notes that "the text [of the second edition], where it differs from the first edition, is a subject for separate study," but he does not provide this study (102).

It is the purpose of this paper to examine the differences in the texts of the two 1765 editions in one play—*A Midsummer Night's Dream*—and to show that the very strong probability is that Johnson did not revise the text of JOHN2, at least in this play.[6] There are 113 differences be-tween the texts of JOHN1 and JOHN2. Most of these are tiny and are likely compositorial slips: such things as the omission of hyphens; the misplacing or omitting a letter in a word, as in "acron" for "acorn" (TLN

323

401), or "bow-stings" for "bow-strings" (TLN 371); the replacing of an italic ligatured "[$b]" with separately lettered "sb" (in "Thisby"); and so on. A handful of changes are substantive, and these are examined in detail in the commentary in order to try to show that they are probably compositorial rather than editorial.

LIST OF SYMBOLS ETC.

[ ]	ligature as in Thi[$b]y.
$	long s.
Λ	punctuation missing
~	the word is the same but the punctuation varies
*	the variant is discussed in the commentary
TLN	Through Line Number [the lineation of Hinman's Norton facsimile First Folio]
ActSc	Act Scene Line numbering is from Riverside, 1974.

Page	TLN	ActSc	JOHN1	JOHN2
89	7	1.1.5	wanes!	~ :
90	20	16	*Hippolyta,*	~ . *
	20	16	thee	the
	42	34	sweet-meats;	~ ,
91	58	50	power	pow'er
92	77	68	youth	truth*
93	116	107	*Nedar's*	*Nedar's*
95	164	154	dreams,	~ Λ
97	201	189	melody.	~ ,
98	213	1.1.200	*He'ena*	*Helena**
	222	209	To morrow	To-morrow
	223	210	glass,	~ ;
	228	215	primrose	~ Λ
	230	217	*Lysander*	~ ,
99	236	223	'till	Λtill
101	298	1.2.30	split—	~ !—
	304	42	bellows-	bellowsΛ
102	308	46	*Qnin.*	*Quin.*
104	363	102	moon-	moonΛ
	371	110	bow-strings	bow-stings
105	382	2.1.12	Fairy-	FairyΛ
106	401	31	acorn	acron
108	430	59	mistress.	~ Λ
	432	59 + 1	*Fairies*	*Faires*
109	462	87	disturb'd	distrub'd
113	504	128	laught	laugh'd*

114	524	148	hither;	~ ,
118	604	225	alone;	~ ? *
	606	227	brakes,	~ .
119	618	239	mischief.	~ ,
	636	255	enammel'd	enamel'd*
120	658	2.2.8	Offices	offices
121	671	21	long-leg'd	long-legg'd*
	679	28	take;	~ :
122	696	44	near.	~ ,
	701	49	interchained	interchanged*
	702	50	bosoms,	~ ∧
123	715	63	life,	~ ∧
	726	73	maid.	~ ,
124	754	99	*Hermia's*	*Hermia*'s
127	859	3.1.49	*Thi[$b]y*	*Thisby*
	859	50	moon-	moon∧ *
	867	56	may you	you may *
	868	57	and the ›	and › the*
128	874	63	*Thi[$b]y*	*Thisby*
	882	71	*Thi[$b]y*	*Thisby*
	894	81	*Thi[$b]y,*	*Thisby*∧
	895	82	*Thi[$b]y*	*Thisby*
	898	85	*Thi[$b]y*	*Thisby*
129	906	93	lilly-whit	lilly-white
	908	95	brisky	briskly*
	920	105	[*The*	[~ *
130	938	121	could	can*
131	970	153	whether	whither
	981	163	3∧	3.
	983	165	gambole	gamble
132	992	174	courtesies	curtesies
133	1023	3.2.2	Then	Than
	1041	19	spy,	~ .
134	1059	37	love-juice∧	~ , *
	1061	39	*Athenian*	*Athenian* *
135	1091	68	tell true, tell true	tell true *
137	1145	121	befal	befall
	1153	128	You	Yo
138	1166	141	*Taurus'*	*Taurus* '
141	1276	248	entreat	intreat
142	1293	262	what	What
	1307	275	left me;	left / [me; *
144	1377	338	Follow	follow
145	1388	347	mistook	~ , *
146	1432	391	fiery-	fiery∧
149	1513	4.1.3	musk-	musk∧

150	1530	20	you,	~ ∧
	1544	32	Methinks,	~ ∧
151	1567	52	fragrant	flagrant ✳
152	1597	81	musick	music
153	1603	85	musick	music
154	1627	106	musick	music
	1628	107	go,	~ ∧
155	1662	138 + 1	*within;*	~ : ✳
156	1699	174	But,	~ ∧
157	1729	201	Most	most
158	1742	216	hath	has
	1749	4.2.3	doubt,	~ ?
159	1785	41	pare	pair ✳
163	1881	84 + 1	*Exit.*	~ ∧
165	1929	130	*Thi[$b]y*	*Thisby*
	1939	140	*Thi[$b]y*	*Thisby*
	1944	145	*Thi[$b]y's*	*Thisby's*
	1947	148	*Thi[$b]y,*	*Thisby∧*
166	1960	159	*Thi[$b]y*	*Thisby*
	1975	173	*Thi[$b]y's*	*Thisby's*
	1981	179	*Thi[$b]y*	*Thisby*
167	1987	185	*Thi[$b]y's*	*Thisby's*
	1996	193	*Thi[$b]y's*	*Thisby's*
	1996	194	*Thi[$b]y*	*Thisby*
	1997	194	think.	~ ,
169	2061	261	But,	~ ∧
171	2113	319	*Thi[$b]e*	*Thisbe*
	2119	322	eyes.	~ ,
172	2128	342	word:	~ ;
	2130	346	*Thi[$b]y*	*Thisby*
	2138	355	epilogue,	~ ∧
	2141	359	*Thi[$b]e's*	*Thisbe's*
	2144	362	*clowns*	*Clowns*
173	2150	368	friends,	~ ∧
	2152	370	*Exeunt.*	[*Exeunt.*
	2170	387	mouse	~ ,
174	2172	389	before,	~ .
	2177	393	sprite	spright
175	2199	415	field-	field∧
	2209	425	slumbred	slumber'd
	2212	428	dream,	~ .
	2217	433	tongue,[6]	~,∧ ✳

COMMENTARY

89   20   *Hippolyta*.] JOHN1 indented this name as a speech prefix, and JOHN2 completed the error by putting a period.

92   77   ruth] This is an interesting variant. The line in JOHN1 has three "yo-" words: "your," "youth," and "your." Perhaps the "yo" fell out of "youth" in JOHN2 and the compositor substituted "tr" because he believed he had mistakenly put too many "yo"'s in the line.

98   213   *Helena*] The lower part of the "l" is uninked in JOHN1.

118   604   alone?] This is an eyeslip: there is a query underneath the semicolon in JOHN1.

119   636   enamel'd] This reading, with only one "m", was followed by all editors after JOHN2, but it is probably more due to the modernization of spelling than to the influence of JOHN2.

121   671   long-legg'd] All editors except Capell (1767), after JOHN2, put two "g"'s in "legg'd", but here, as at 636 above, the change is due to the modernization of spelling, and not to the influence of JOHN2.

122   701   interchanged] This compositorial slip illustrates well the principle of changing from the more difficult reading to a normal one. *OED* gives "interchain" as obsolete and rare and lists only three quotations, from here, from Florio's dictionary of 1603, and from Drummond in 1659. The compositor of the first folio changed the rare word to the familiar "interchanged," and so did the compositor of JOHN2.

127   859   moonʌ] The hyphen is uninked in some copies; it is there in Yale.

127   867   you may] This inversion is a common kind of error.

868   and / the] This is not a verbal variant but I included it to show how closely JOHN2 follows JOHN1: this is the only variation in lineation in the text.

129   908   briskly] Influenced by the "-ly" in "most lilly" (906) and "most lovely" (908), and by the nine "l"'s in lines 906–8, the compositor erroneously added an "l" to normalize Shakespeare's nonce word "brisky" (only this use is cited in OED) to "briskly." Hanmer's compositor made the same mistake in the 1743–44 edition (the second edition of 1745 keeps this reading but footnotes "brisky"). With his quiet spirit of fun Gary Taylor emends to "bristly" ["brisly" in the old spelling edition] (Oxford, 1986).

920   [*The*] JOHN2 has a damaged square bracket with the lower projection missing.

130   938   can] This is an eyeslip: there is a "can" almost directly underneath the "could" in JOHN1.

134   1059   In some copies of JOHN1 the comma is uninked.

1061   There is a damaged "e" in JOHN1.

135   1091   tell true] JOHN2 probably omits "tell true," like Q2 and F1, because the compositor suspected dittography, or because he thought he

had set the text [i.e., he saw he had put "tell true" and did not notice that it was repeated in his copytext]. The line in Q1 is: "O, once tell true: tell true, euen for my sake:". This is a good example of homoeoteleuton.

142   1307   left / [me;] Turnover.

145   1388   mistook,] There is a bit of furniture on the period in JOHN1 that makes it seem a comma.

151   1567   flagrant] The compositor was influenced by the "fl" in the succeeding word "flowers."

155   1662   *within:*] Italic colon.

159   1785   pair] This may be a homonym, like "gamble" for "gambole" at 983, but it is an alternate spelling as in Q2-F2.

175   2217   tongue,ʌ] The footnote numeral is omitted in JOHN2.

AFTERNOTE

One other indication that Johnson did not revise JOHN2 is that he and George Steevens chose to print the 1773 variorum edition from a copy of JOHN1.[7] A collation of the variant readings of the two 1765 editions with the 1773 *MND* shows that in 66 places JOHN1 agrees with 1773, while in 13 places JOHN2 agrees with 1773.[8] In these 13 places there are no substantive differences but merely changes in spelling conventions or minor corrections: for example, three hyphens are omitted in "To mor-row" (TLN 222), "moon light" (TLN 363), and "Fairy favours" (TLN 382); "laugh'd" replaces "laught" (TLN 504), "slumber'd" is put for "slumberd" (TLN 2209);"lilly-white" corrects JOHN1's "lilly-whit" (TLN 906); "long-legg'd" modernizes "long-leg'd" (TLN 671); and so on. These slight changes could have been made by either Steevens or a compositor. In the more significant different readings between JOHN1 and JOHN2, such as "interchained" and "interchanged" (TLN 701) or "brisky" and "briskly" (TLN 908), the 1773 edition invariably agrees with JOHN1. This seems to be further confirmation that these substantive changes in JOHN2 are compositorial, and not editorial.

NOTES

I am very grateful to the Social Sciences and Humanities Research Council of Canada, and to St. Thomas University, for their generous financial support of this project. I am also very thankful for the help I have received from two research assistants, Ms Tracy Lutz and Ms Rachel Jones. This paper also profited from suggestions made by other members of the seminar at the Shakespeare Association meeting in Albuquerque, especially Bernice Kliman, Joanna Gondris, and Eric Rasmussen, and I thank them.

1. Donald D. Eddy, "Samuel Johnson's Editions of Shakespeare (1765)," *The Papers of the Bibliographical Society of America* 56 (1962): 430.

2. See Arthur Sherbo, *Samuel Johnson, Editor of Shakespeare,* Illinois Studies in Language and Literature, vol. 42 (Urbana: University of Illinois Press, 1956), 10, 47; and Eddy, 428, 430, 433. Since William Mickle's translation of Camoëns's *Lusiad,* published just eleven years after Johnson's *Shakespeare,* in 1776, lists 635 subscriptions (copies subscribed for), it may be that Birch underestimated Johnson's subscribers at "about seven hundred & fifty" (Sherbo, 10), just as he erroneously numbered the second edition at "five hundred" copies when it was actually 750 (Eddy, 430, end of footnote 9). Johnson had lost his subscription list.

3. See Richard Hosley, Richard Knowles, and Ruth McGugan, *Shakespeare Variorum Handbook* (New York: The Modern Language Association of America, 1971), 64, and the various New Variorum editions.

4. Arthur M. Eastman, "The Texts from which Johnson Printed his Shakespeare," *The Journal of English and Germanic Philology* 49 (1950): 182–91.

5. Eddy, 428, citing Hazen's article on cancels, and 429.

6. I ignore Johnson's commentary here. A full collation of the two commentaries of JOHN1 and JOHN2 shows only minor differences, and, mostly, changes merely in lineation. There is no evidence of any editorial revision whatsoever.

7. The main account of Johnson's revisions which appeared in 1773 is T. J. Monaghan's "Johnson's Additions to his *Shakespeare* for the Edition of 1773," *Review of English Studies,* n.s., 4 (1953): 234–48 but this study does not deal with the copytext for the 1773 edition. In the *Variorum Handbook* (66), G. B. Evans correctly notes that 1773 is printed from JOHN1

8. Because I have ignored irrelevant items such as "$b" ligatures in "Thisby", or letters uninked or partially inked in JOHN1 or JOHN2, the number of variants has diminished from 113 to 79.

Visual Images of *Hamlet,* 1709–1800

Alan R. Young

[As a preliminary to preparing a book on eighteenth- and nineteenth-century illustrations and visual representations of Hamlet, *together with an essay that will accompany the forthcoming New Variorum edition of* Hamlet, *I am creating a computer-generated database that will record information about* Hamlet *material for both the eighteenth and nineteenth centuries. Wherever possible, the database will include high-resolution scanned images of the original pictures. Leaving aside the immensely rich illustrative material of the nineteenth century, there still remains for those wishing to study the editing of Shakespeare in the eighteenth century a highly important body of material, access to which and information about which is not always easy to obtain.]*

THE eighteenth century saw the beginning of formally edited Shakespeare. Not only was this the era of the first multivolume collected editions (beginning with that of Nicholas Rowe in 1709), but it was during this century that publishers developed the highly successful market for small-sized editions of play texts. Significantly, this was also the period when libraries (public and private) proliferated and female literacy and the female reading of Shakespeare grew.[1] The cult of the actor, the revival on stage of all but one (*Love's Labour's Lost*) of Shakespeare's plays in some form or other, the growth of Shakespeare bardolatry, and the rise of the editor-critic-biographer of Shakespeare during the Restoration and the century that followed, all contributed to a phenomenal increase in attention to the works of the man who came to be recognized, or "constructed" (to use Michael Dobson's choice of terminology) as the national poet.[2] It was, too, during this same century that the first illustrated editions appeared,[3] together with the first illustrations created to have a life independent of the printed text.[4] Any study of the editing of Shakespeare in the eighteenth century must inevitably take into account the multiplic-

330

ity of all such concurrent developments, among them being that which at present is of most interest to me—the burgeoning growth during that period of the production of illustrations of Shakespeare.

Dobson's recent book about the manner in which the Restoration and Eighteenth Century "constructed" Shakespeare as an Enlightenment culture hero claims to pay careful attention to certain neglected adaptations, as well as to a body of apparently minor or ephemeral writings. Central to Dobson's purpose is the desire to treat such texts more seriously than his predecessors, who have commonly equated commercial success with historical insignificance. For Dobson, by contrast, that many adaptations of Shakespeare were designed to capitalize on popular taste makes them more useful indicators of the contemporary reception of Shakespeare's works "than some of the self-consciously 'higher' literary forms criticism has traditionally privileged."[5] Dobson's study has little to say about the role of illustrations since his argument is primarily focused upon texts. My contention (not one that I suspect Dobson would necessarily disagree with) is that the visual illustrations produced between 1709 and 1800, particularly (but not exclusively) those appearing in printed editions, offer an additional and complementary perspective.

Hitherto somewhat ignored by those primarily concerned with printed texts, the illustrations reveal how specific Shakespeare plays were perceived within the culture at large, not just by those who attended play performances, but by that much broader spectrum of the literate and not-so-literate who absorbed and responded to Shakespeare in their homes, when browsing in print shops, when reading in coffeehouses, or (a far rarer experience) when visiting an art gallery or exhibition. Scholars like Richard Altick and Moelwyn Merchant, who have written about Shakespeare and the visual arts, have tended to confine their attention to large paintings or already familiar illustrated editions (e.g., Rowe 1709 or Hanmer 1744), or have dealt with individual plays only in passing.[6] I am proposing a somewhat different though overlapping route to that taken by my predecessors. My concern will be with a single play—*Hamlet*—and the study of the broad dissemination of images of this play that occurred during the eighteenth century and on through the nineteenth. This dissemination took place through costly printed editions, together with large and expensive works of art, that may have reached only a small segment of society.[7] At the same time, however, dissemination occurred through various other media based upon reproductive techniques that led to an ever-accelerating proliferation of mass-produced works of art. These were frequently available as illustrations within printed texts whose format seems often to have been designed to access a less affluent market. Printings of individual plays, for example, are known to have been sold at playhouses. Such texts often contained illustrations. Of course, there was also a market for other illustrations that had been created independently of any text, but, then again, illustrations often were available in two forms—as illustrations bound in with a text or in a separate form.

In studying the editorial response to Shakespeare, scholars endeavoring to wrestle with a number of difficult and complex questions will be helped by the information and reproductions in the database concerning printed editions. The database, in facilitating the exploration of the interface of editing and illustration, should, for example, assist one in dealing with such teasing questions as whether different kinds of illustration in the editions are a product in some way of differently intended readerships. Is it true that the more expensive editions had fewer illustrations than cheaper publications aimed at a more popular readership? At first this would not appear to be the case. Tonson's 1709 octavo six-volume edition (with a few copies printed on large paper) had only one illustration per play. When attempting perhaps to reach a broader market with the duodecimo eight/nine-volume edition of 1714,[8] the number of illustrations remained the same. Nevertheless, it is perhaps significant that the first Theobald edition of 1733 had no illustrations except for a portrait, whereas the subsequent edition of 1740 was illustrated. However, only with the appearance much later in the century of the editions by Bell, Harding, and Bellamy, who appear to have made multiple illustrations a feature of the editions they published, can a wholly convincing argument be made to corroborate the view that the use of illustrations was a feature aimed at creating a more popular readership,[9] a phenomenon due to many social and economic causes and paralleling the burgeoning number of artworks based on Shakespeare that were to become a staple of art exhibitions. Where copies of certain editions (Hanmer's 1744 edition would be an obvious example) seem to have been destined for the private libraries of the fairly affluent and well-educated, editions of single plays (many of them directed towards playhouse audiences) often appear to have been aimed at a different readership, one for which cheap pictorial images surely offered a particular attraction, perhaps because expensive original works of art, large engravings, and the like were financially out of reach. Such an explanation is for the moment supposition, but for anyone wishing to examine editorial response to Shakespeare and the nature of the cultural artifacts produced by different editors at different dates throughout the eighteenth century, such matters are of considerable significance. Where editions of *Hamlet* are of concern, the proposed database, with its reproductions of the original illustrations for each edition, should offer a starting point for anyone wishing to explore such complex issues.

One may also use the database to explore the ways in which the illustrations accompanying printed texts of *Hamlet* tend to privilege certain scenes in the play. In spite of the memorable representation of the Play Scene in Hanmer's edition, a representation closely related to Francis Hayman's paintings of the scene, this was decidedly not a common subject in eighteenth-century printed editions. Instead, following the 1709 representation of the Closet Scene in Rowe's edition (the first ever pictorial representation of a scene from *Hamlet*), one can note a succession of playtext illustrations of the dramatic reappearance of the Ghost in Act 3, scene 4, in 1714, 1718, and 1728 (all related to the 1709 original but including the unusual addition of Gertrude's bed),[10] together with further examples in 1734, 1737, 1773, and 1798. Almost as common is Hamlet's encounter with the Ghost in Act 1, beginning with Tonson's edition in 1734 and Theobald's in 1740, with other examples occuring in 1779, 1782, 1785, 1788, and 1798. Both these scenes seem to have engendered comment among those who wrote descriptions of performances, but what about the responses of editors? And if editors do not privilege the scenes in any way, what is the effect, nonetheless, of the inclusion within an edition of such an illustration? Though its presence may have been the result of a publisher/printer's decision made independently of the editor, its existence as part of the final editorial artifact cannot be ignored in any study of the editorial response to Shakespeare.

With regard to critical and editorial commentary and the privileging of certain scenes, the material already in the database reveals that the growing fascination with Ophelia among artists at the end of the century and on into the next is matched to some extent by the first appearance in editions of illustrations depicting Ophelia. First appeared the 1774 portrait of Mrs Lessingham in the mad scene (Act 4, scene 5). This was closely followed by John Hamilton Mortimer's extraordinary portrait of the mad Ophelia in his *Shakespeare's Characters* (1775–76). Though not part of an edition at this time, his portrait was later to be redone as an illustration for an edition early in the nineteenth century. In 1790 and 1797, the respective editions by Bellamy and Harding each offered engravings of Ophelia, the former depicting her death and the latter showing her in her mad state in a densely wooded situation, perhaps just prior to her death. That the editions reflect early on what was to become an almost obsessional interest of the Romantic and Victorian periods is clearly of some import. It will be for the scholar wishing to track the editorial response to Shakespeare to reveal more fully whether the printed texts reflect the "discovery" of Ophelia. Again, the evidence of the illustrations is clearly important and can, it is to be hoped, be gleaned from the proposed database. As for whether the presence of illustrative material is related in some way to an editorial slant towards a more popular readership, it is striking that a notable feature of Bellamy and Robarts's edition is that it has no note on the text and no notes, while Harding's edition, though it contains Rowe's *Life,* Farmer's essay on Shakespeare's Learning, a glossary, and "Observations" as in Johnson and Steevens (1793), also has no notes.[11]

Such questions, and the above are only selected examples that spring most immediately to mind, should surely be part of any study of the nature of the eighteenth-century editions of Shakespeare (and specifically that of *Hamlet*) and the editorial responses they represent. It is my hope that the database that I am constructing will be a useful tool in dealing with these and other matters.

THE DATABASE

I hope to create a "stand-alone" product that could be made available to students, scholars, and libraries, thereby making widely available an immensely valuable resource for the study of Shakespeare. It would serve to make accessible (in electronic format) a portion of the incredibly rich visual material available in some of the great collections of Shakespeareana throughout the world. Two means of doing this have already presented themselves:

1. The MIT team working on the Shakespeare Interactive Research Archive Plans to incorporate the database, with its digitized images, into their final project.

2. The database will use as many digitized items from the Folger Shakespeare Library collection as possible, adding items from elsewhere only when they are not in the Folger's collections. It should then be possible to offer the library a discrete record of its entire *Hamlet* holdings. Such projects that record electronically rare or precious materials indirectly serve to help with the conservation of what are often fragile artifacts, since, in many instances, electronic access will be all that a student or scholar requires.

Present plans call for the database to contain the following fields of information:

1. Unique Number. Every item entered will be given a unique number, a useful internal feature, though not necessarily of interest to the user of the final product.

2. Act/Scene/Line Numbers. Wherever it is possible to identify precisely the subject of a particular scene, the Act, Scene, and Line numbers from *Hamlet*

are provided. These references are at present keyed to the Riverside edition of Shakespeare (but this could of course be altered). They will be expressed as a single five-figure digit. Thus, Act 1, Scene 2, Line 2 would appear in the database as "12002".

3. Through Line Numbers. In *The Norton Facsimile: The First Folio of Shakespeare* (1968), Charlton Hinman established a system of Through Line Numbers (TLN) by numbering consecutively every typograpical line in the Folio text of each play (including stage directions).[12] This to date is the closest available system to a uniform line-numbering of Shakespeare's plays independent of editorial variation. The database will follow Hinman's TLN system, but, as with the recently-published *The Three-Text* Hamlet, + or − numbers are added where the Riverside edition has different line divisions, and, where text not in the Folio text is referred to (usually material from Q2), the lines are assigned the last TLN from the First Folio text followed by +1, +2, and so forth.[13]

4. Name of Original Artist/Designer. Where the original creator or designer of a work is known, this name is given, even if the specific entry (record) is based only on a copy (e.g., engraving, lithograph, woodcut) of that original. This is an important detail, since a number of paintings have not survived, whereas reproductions of them still exist.

5. Dates of the Original Artist/Designer. (Where known)

6. Date of Orignal Work of Art. (Where known)

7. Medium of Original Work of Art/Design.

8. Name of Artist Responsible for Work Recorded in this Data Entry. This may differ from the name recorded in item 4 above. Thus, although the Original Artist/Designer for the frontispiece for the 1744 Hanmer *Hamlet* is recorded as Francis Hayman (1708–76), the engraving in Hanmer's edition was by Hubert Gravelot. Hayman's original pen and ink drawing of ca. 1740–41, from which the engraving was made and which forms part of he Folger Shakespeare Library collection, has a separate database entry.

9. Dates of Artist Responsible for Work Recorded in this Data Entry.

10. Medium of Work Recorded in this Data Entry. This may, of course, differ from item 7 above.

11. Size. This provides the dimensions of the work of art being recorded. Dimensions in both centimeters and inches are given. These dimensions, unless otherwise stated, are usually those of the image only. On occasion the full plate size of an engraving may be given, and in the case of some paintings, only the frame size is available.

12. Actor 1. If the item depicts a specific actor, his/her name is recorded.

13. Actor 2. Since some illustrations depict more than one identifiable actor, this field and the fields for Actor 3 and 4 offer further opportunities to record names in a form that can be indexed.

14. Actor 3. See comments for Actor 2.

15. Actor 4. See comments for Actor 2.

16. Production. Some illustrations depict specific productions of a play, a character in a specific production, or a design for a specific production. This field provides an opportunity to record such facts.

17. Location. A record of where the illustration is located. In the case of an engraving or print, the field entry may list a number of locations where the item may be found. Wherever possible shelf or catalogue numbers within specific locations are given. When many copies of an item exist, a selected listing is recorded. Priority will be given to listing items in the Folger Shakespeare Library collection.

18. Type. A record of the type of illustration being listed, such as Portrait (e.g., Ellen Terry as Ophelia), Scene, Imagined Scene (e.g., Hamlet as a child), Set Design, Illustrative Title-Page. This field will be indexed so that all portraits or all illustrative title-pages, for example, could be retrieved by the researcher.

19. Bibliography. This entry contains bibliographical details of relevant secondary literature and reproductions of illustrations in secondary material. Inevitably, it is selective in nature.

20. Description. A detailed description of the work of art. For the purposes for which I need the database, this is the most important field. It will be the largest field in the database. When the Image field is fully incorporated, there will be less need for a detailed verbal description. However, a verbal description will still be useful in alerting the user to important details that might be overlooked: Hamlet's "down-gyved" stocking, Ophelia's fan, a tiny portrait-miniature on the floor, Ophelia's bare feet, etc. Inevitably, selecting the details that are described will involve a degree of interpretive subjectivity.

21. Image. This field will access the digitized photographic image of the visual image. Wherever possible photographic slides are obtained of the original image. These are then recorded on Kodak Photo Compact Disks. This resolves the problem of scanning images (Kodak does that), it ensures very high resolution images (Kodak looks after that), and above all it resolves the problem of computer storage since the images are stored on the CDs and not on the hard drive of the computer. Each Kodak disk can hold up to 100 images. Already, devices (usually "towers") are available that can hold and provide access to numerous disks. Since I have tentatively estimated that I will have about 1,500 images, I should have no difficulty with storage and access.

22. Comments. This will contain notes on various relevant topics. The item on Charles Grignion's engraving (after Francis Hayman) in Charles Jennens's 1773 edition of *Hamlet,* for example, contains the following entry in the Comments field: "After painting by Hayman of Spranger Barry and Mrs. Mary Elmy (Garrick Club). The engraving substitutes Garrick's features for those of Barry."

I plan to index the following fields from among the above: 2–10, 12–15, 17, and possibly 16 (this last would permit the selection of a discrete selection of images, e.g., all those at the Folger, or all those recorded as located in the Victoria and Albert Museum). The user will thus be able to retrieve and study all the images of a particular Act, Scene, and Line (e.g., Hamlet's reaction to his first encounter with the Ghost; or all the works by an individual artist (e.g., Francis Hayman, William Nelson Gardiner, or John Hamilton Mortimer); or all the works created within a specified time period (e.g., 1760–80); or all the works created in a specific medium (e.g., all engravings, or all photographs, or all oil paintings); or the depictions of a particular actor (David Garrick, Mary Elmy, Spranger Barry, Edwin Booth, or Ellen Terry); or the depictions of a particular type of subject (e.g., set designs, or portraits).

THREE SAMPLE ENTRIES FROM THE PROPOSED *HAMLET*
DATABASE
(Note: some of the entries may not as yet be complete)

49   ACT SCENE LINE: 14084
TLN: 0671
ORIGINAL ARTIST/DESIGNER: Gravelot, Hubert François
DATE OF ORIGINAL ARTIST/DESIGNER: 1699–1773
DATE OF ORIGINAL WORK: 1740
MEDIUM OF ORIGINAL WORK:
ARTIST FOR THIS RECORD: Gucht, Gerard van der
DATES OF ARTIST FOR THIS RECORD:
DATE OF WORK IN THIS RECORD: 1740
MEDIUM OF WORK IN THIS RECORD: Engraving
SIZE OF WORK IN THIS RECORD: 13.2×7.5 cm; 5 $\frac{3}{16} \times 2\frac{15}{16}''$ (17.2×9.5 cm—full page)
ACTORS: 1)   2)   3)   4)
PRODUCTION:
LOCATION: Folger Shakespeare Library, Art File S528h1 no. 5; Copy 2: Art File S528h1 no.5 dated in pencil on rear "1752" (contains only minor differences); Folger Shakespeare Library, Art Vol. a 34 (Vol. 17, opp. p. 486). From 2d edition of Theobald's *The Works of Shakespeare* (1740), Vol. 8 (reprinted 1752, 1772, 1773). British Library 11762.b.
BIBLIOGRAPHY: Hammelmann 1975, 38–42, 43–44.[14]
TYPE: Scene
DESCRIPTION: Before a drawbridge (at right) to the castle. The Ghost to left of center in armor and plumed helmet with visor raised gestures with both arms for Hamlet to follow him off to the left. His right foot is pointing in that direction and his head is turned back towards Hamlet over his left shoulder. Hamlet in contemporary eighteenth-century dress

Hamlet about to follow the Ghost. Engraving by Gerard van der Gucht after design by Hubert François Gravelot, from the second edition of Theobald's *The Works of Shakespeare* (1740). By permission of the Folger Shakespeare Library.

still stands on the drawbridge but is restrained from following the Ghost by Horatio who gestures with his arms in front of Hamlet. Unusual is the fact that Hamlet is looking at Horatio rather than at the Ghost. Marcellus, barely visible, stands behind. The scene is illuminated by the crescent moon at top left.

COMMENTS: Cf. version signed "I Iune" in Jacob Tonson's 1734 edition of *Hamlet, Prince of Denmark; A Tragedy, as it is now acted by his Majesty's Servants* (London, 1734). Size: 12.8 × 8 cm; 5 × 3⅛". British Library 11763. ppp.52. Folger Shakespeare Library Copy 1 has "1740" in pencil on rear.

427   ACT SCENE LINE: 34103

TLN: 2484

ORIGINAL ARTIST/DESIGNER: Guernier, Louis du

DATE OF ORIGINAL ARTIST/DESIGNER: 1687–?1716

DATE OF ORIGINAL WORK: 1714

MEDIUM OF ORIGINAL WORK:

ARTIST FOR THIS RECORD: Anon. (unsigned)

DATES OF ARTIST FOR THIS RECORD:

DATE OF WORK IN THIS RECORD: 1718

MEDIUM OF WORK IN THIS RECORD: Engraving

SIZE OF WORK IN THIS RECORD: 13.7 × 7.5 cm; 5⅜ × 3"

ACTORS: 1)   2)   3)   4)

PRODUCTION:

LOCATION: Folger Shakespeare Library, PR 2807 1718 Copy 1 Sh. Coll. *Hamlet, Prince of Denmark. A Tragedy. As it is now acted by His Majesty's Servants* (London: Printed by J. Darby for M. Wellington, 1718); Folger Shakespeare Library, Art Vol. a34 (Vol. 17, after p. 536); British Library 11784.a.41 (2).

BIBLIOGRAPHY: Kliman 1993.[15]

TYPE: Scene

DESCRIPTION: Hamlet in his mother's closet. Hamlet to right raises his hands upon seeing the Ghost in armor at left. The Ghost, who holds a truncheon in his left hand, is in armor (the visor raised) and appears to address Hamlet. Gertrude, seated upon a chair between the two figures but towards the rear, looks startled and stares at Hamlet. Behind and above her on the wall are large portraits of Hamlet's father (he wears armor and carries a truncheon in his left hand) and another figure (a woman). To the left behind the Ghost is Gertrude's bed. Note that Hamlet stands in the pose described in Sprague's *Shakespeare and the Actors* with feet apart, one foot advanced before the other, his weight upon the rear foot as though he is starting back.[16] Both hands are raised before him in the direction of the Ghost, the right higher than the left. The fingers

Hamlet confronted by the Ghost in his mother's closet. Engraving by Louis du Guernier, from *Hamlet, Prince of Denmark* (London: printed by J. Darby for M. Wellington, 1718). By permission of the Folger Shakespeare Library.

of both hands are extended. He is hatless. His left stocking is "down-gyved." In the portrait of the King, the figure holds a truncheon, thereby matching that held by the Ghost.

COMMENTS: A copy in reverse with minor changes of Du Guernier's 1714 engraving in *The Works of Mr. William Shakespeare,* published by Tonson. This was the first separate *Hamlet* text to be illustrated and the first individual *Hamlet* in duodecimo (Kliman, 9).

76   ACT SCENE LINE: 47172
TLN: 3164
ORIGINAL ARTIST/DESIGNER: Richter, Henry James
DATE OF ORIGINAL ARTIST/DESIGNER: 1772–1857
DATE OF ORIGINAL WORK:
MEDIUM OF ORIGINAL WORK:
ARTIST FOR THIS RECORD: Hawkins
DATE OF ARTIST FOR THIS RECORD:
DATE OF WORK IN THIS RECORD: 1790
MEDIUM OF WORK IN THIS RECORD: Engraving
SIZE OR WORK IN THIS RECORD: 15.5 × 10 cm; 6¼ × 4"
ACTORS: 1)   2)   3)   4)
PRODUCTION:
LOCATION: Folger Shakespeare Library, Art File S528h1 no. 83. Published by Bellamy & Robarts, 1 May 1790. For *The Plays of William Shakespeare,* vol. 8 (London: Bellamy and Robarts, 1788–91). British Library has 1796 edition (British Library 11761.d.).
BIBLIOGRAPHY:
TYPE: Scene (imagined)
DESCRIPTION: A brook in the foreground. On the right beside the bank the large trunk of a willow tree that bends to the right over the bank but then bends back towards the upper center of the picture over the brook. At the extreme lower right of the picture a thin dead tree branch or trunk extends upwards towards the top center of the picture. Ophelia's left arm is wrapped around this, while her feet appear to be on the bank of the brook on the other side of the main tree trunk. She is leaning slightly out over the water, and her right arm is extended as she attempts to hang her crownet weeds upon a branch of the tree that hangs out over the brook and reaches over to the left side of the picture. Ophelia's arms are bare and she wears a white diaphanous dress. She appears to have blonde hair that is loose and hanging down behind her (thus mostly not visible to the viewer). Around her head is a wreath of flowers. Her expression seems somewhat distracted as she looks towards where she is trying to hang her garland. The setting is that of a dense forest. Clearly not based on

The death of Ophelia. Engraving by Hawkins after design by Henry James Richter, from *The Plays of William Shakespeare* (London: Bellamy and Robarts, 1788–91). By permission of the Folger Shakespeare Library.

stage practice. The picture is framed by a wall with ivy and other objects relevant to the play (e.g., a cup, a sword, a recorder, a crown, etc.). COMMENTS: This edition contained two engravings for *Hamlet.* The engraving is dated 1790.

Notes

1. Gary Taylor, *Reinventing Shakespeare: A Cultural History from the Restoration to the Present* (New York: Oxford University Press, 1989), 87–88 and 92–93.
2. Michael Dobson,*The Making of the National Poet: Shakespeare, Adaptation and Authorship, 1660–1769* (Oxford: Clarendon, 1992), 1.
3. Nicholas Rowe's edition, *The Works of Mr. William Shakespear,* 6 vols. (London, 1709), with designs believed to be by Francois Boitard and engravings by Elisha Kirkall and Michael van der Gucht, has already been mentioned. Cf. Nicholas Rowe, ed., *The Works of Mr. William Shakespear,* 8 vols. (London, 1714), with engravings by Louis du Guernier and Elisha Kirkall; Alexander Pope, ed., *The Works of Shakespeare,* 2d ed., 8 vols. (London, 1728), with engravings by du Guernier and with re-engravings of du Guernier by F. Foudrinier; Lewis Theobald, ed., *The Works of Shakespeare,* 2d ed., 8 vols. (London, 1740), with designs by Hubert Francois Gravelot with engravings by Gravelot and Gerard van der Gucht; Thomas Hanmer, ed., *The Works of Shakespeare,* 6 vols. (Oxford, 1744), with designs by Francis Hayman and Gravelot, and engravings by Gravelot; Charles Jennens, *Hamlet, Prince of Denmark . . . Collated with the Old and Modern Editions* (London, 1773), with engravings by Charles Grignion; *Bell's Edition of Shakespeare's Plays,* 9 vols. (London, 1773–74), with designs by Edward Edwards; *The Dramatick Writings of William Shakspere [Bell's Editions of Shakspere],* 20 vols. (London, 1786–88), with designs by Philippe Jacques De Loutherbourgh and engravings by Bartolozzi and Johann Heinrich Ramberg; *The Plays of William Shakspeare,* 8 vols. (London: Bellamy and Robarts, 1788–89), with designs by Richard Corbould and Henry James Richter; and *The Plays of William Shakespeare,* 38 numbers (individually dated and published by E. Harding, et. al.), or 12 vols. (London: Printed by T. Bensley for Vernor and Hood, Poultry; E. Harding, Pall-Mall; and J. Wright, Piccadilly, 1800), with engravings by William Nelson Gardiner, Thomas Stothard, and John Thurston.
4. John Runciman's 1767 painting of *King Lear in the Storm* (National Gallery of Scotland) is an early example on a grand scale of an artist's attempt to portray the imaginative spirit of the text rather than reflect staged performance or the actual words on the page.
5. Dobson, *National Poet,* 5–6.
6. Richard D. Altick, *Paintings from Books: Art and Literature in Britain, 1760–1900* (Columbus, Ohio: Ohio State University Press, 1985); W. Moelwyn Merchant, *Shakespeare and the Artist* (London: Oxford University Press, 1959) and *Shakespeare in Art: A Visual Approach to the Plays,* Exhibition at Nottingham University Art Gallery 1961 (Nottingham: Nottingham University, 1961) and *Shakespeare in Art: Paintings, Drawings and Engravings Devoted to Shakespearean Subjects,* Exhibition catalogue (London: Arts Council of Great Britain, 1964).
7. The distinction implied here between expensive artistic products available only to a monied few and cheaper more readily available material is not quite as

straightforward as it may at first seem. As Boydell and others before him discovered, whereas a painting was a unique, often large, and highly costly object, an engraving based upon it could be small, a great deal cheaper, and available in whatever quantity the market could absorb. Ironically, in many instances the original artifact has been lost or destroyed and engraved copies are all that survive.

8. For suggestions that this edition was aimed at a different readership, see Colin Franklin, *Shakespeare Domesticated: The Eighteenth-Century Editions* (Aldershot: Scolar Press, 1991), 11–12.

9. One notes, however, that although the 1744 Hanmer edition by Oxford contained one illustration for each play, other editions with scholarly pretensions often had no illustrative material other than the occasional portrait. See Alexander Pope, ed., *The Works of Shakespeare,* 6 vols. (London, 1723–25); Lewis Theobald, ed., *The Works of Shakespeare,* 7 vols. (London, 1733); William Warburton, ed., *The Works of Shakespeare,* 8 vols. (London, 1747); Samuel Johnson, ed., *The Plays of William Shakespeare,* 8 vols. (London, 1765); Samuel Johnson and George Steevens, eds., *The Plays of Wiliiam Shakespeare,* 10 vols. (London, 1773), Revised and Augmented by Isaac Reed in 1778 and1793; Edward Capell, ed., *Mr. William Shakespeare his Comedies, Histories, and Tragedies,* 10 vols. (London, 1767–68); Edmond Malone, ed., *The Plays and Poems of William Shakespeare,* 10 vols. (London, 1790).

10. For a discussion of the depiction of Gertrude's bed, see Bernice W. Kliman, "The Bed in *Hamlet*'s Closet Scene: Rowe 1709 and 1714," *Shakespeare Newsletter* 43: 1, no. 216 (1993): 8–9.

11. See Franklin, 46, 50.

12. *The Norton Facsimile: The First Folio of Shakespeare,* Prepared by Charlton Hinman (New York: Norton, 1968).

13. Paul Bertram and Bernice W. Kliman, *The Three-Text* Hamlet*: Parallel Texts of the First and Second Quartos and First Folio* (New York: AMS Press, 1991), 8–9.

14. Hanns Hammelmann, *Book Illustrators in Eighteenth-Century England,* edited and completed by T. S. R. Boase (New Haven: Yale University Press, 1975).

15. See note 10.

16. Arthur Colby Sprague, *Shakespeare and the Actors: The Stage Business in His Plays (1660–1905)* (Cambridge: Harvard University Press: 1944), 138–40.

Province of Pirates: The Editing and Publication of Shakespeare's Poems in the Eighteenth Century

Catherine M. S. Alexander

THE first eighteenth-century collected works of Shakespeare, published in 1709, excluded his poems. Nicholas Rowe, who edited the six-volume collection, and whose first profession was that of barrister, carefully explained, "There is a Book of Poems, publish'd in 1640, under the Name of *William Shakespear,* but as I have but very lately seen it, without an Opportunity of making any Judgment upon it, I won't pretend to determine, whether it be his or no."[1] This text is almost certainly John Benson's rearrangement of the sonnets with "A Lover's Complaint," and the "Passionate Pilgrim" pieces.[2] Rowe had knowledge of other Shakespearian verse (his reference to "Venus and Adonis" and "The Rape of Lucrece"' in a "late Collection of Poems" probably alludes to "Poems on Affairs of State" published in 1707, for example, rather than their many seventeenth-century reprints), but offers no reason for excluding them from his edition.[3] In ignoring the poems he was reinforcing the practice of the folio collections and prolonging the disassociation between poems and plays, and the poems one from another.

Over eighty years later, the final volume of Malone's edition of Shakespeare contained his poems in an inclusive move which was reflected in the title of the collection, *The Poems and Plays of William Shakspeare in Ten Volumes,* a specificity which contrasted with Rowe's apparent breadth but actual narrowness: *The Works of Mr.William Shakespear.*[4] Malone clearly had more time for his editorial task and access to a greater range of texts than Rowe, asserting in his Preface (which was reprinted from his 1780 supplement to Johnson and Steevens's second edition of Shakespeare), "Though above a century and a half has elapsed since the death of Shakspeare, it is somewhat extraordinary . . . that none of his various editors should have attempted to separate his genuine poetical compositions from the spurious performances with which they have been long intermixed; or have taken the trouble to compare them with the earliest and most authentick copies" (1:lxii).

345

Rowe and Malone represent the poles of eighteenth-century editorial practice not merely in terms of chronology. Rowe was reticent (he excluded the overt criticism of Shakespeare which is evident in his prologue to *The Ambitious Stepmother*,[5] for example) and, whether prompted by considerations of tradition, time, or authenticity, was tentative (he excluded Shakespeare's poems). Malone was confident, critical, and inclusive. Such differences in style and character, frequently exaggerated by personal and commercial rivalries, were to be influential features in the work on Shakespeare—particularly the publication of the poems—for much of the eight decades which separate Rowe's and Malone's editions. Yet the differences in their work was also a reflection of changes in fashion, interest, and the status of poetry, and of the growth of confidence in Shakespeare as a great poet and a national figure, which was a confining as well as liberating development. The movement from one editorial practice to another, however, was far from a steady progression and the publication of Shakespeare's verse proceeded fitfully throughout the period.

Rowe's edition of *The Works of Mr. William Shakespear* was printed for Jacob Tonson whose business retained control of Shakespeare's plays until 1744 when Oxford published Hanmer's edition and the Tonson copyright claim was ignored for the first time. Tonson never demonstrated the same control over Shakespeare's poems, however, which gave other publishers a commercial opportunity to respond to Rowe's successful presentation of the plays. Bernard Lintott clearly had an eye for the market. In 1709 he produced *A Collection of Poems, viz: I. Venus and Adonis; II. The Rape of Lucrece; III. The Passionate Pilgrim; IV. Sonnets to Sundry Notes of Musick, by Mr. William Shakespeare,* which he expanded to two volumes in the following year to incorporate the sonnets.[6] The new edition carried an extended title indicating that all the verses were "the miscellanies of Mr. William Shakespeare which were published by himself in the year 1609, and now correctly printed from those editions." The one- and two-volume editions carried the same Advertisement in which Lintott explained that "The Writings of Mr. Shakespeare are in so great Esteem, that several Gentlemen have subscribed to a late Edition of his Dramatick Works in Six Volumes; which makes me hope, that this little Book will not be unacceptable to the Publick."[7] The publication certainly has the feel of an entrepreneurial rush job produced to capitalize on Rowe's edition. The Advertisement is the only piece of editorial apparatus and is of poor quality with errors and inconsistencies of spelling. It contains a transparent attempt to award the work a posthumous royal seal of approval. Lintott forgoes the provision of biographical information, the task having been undertaken in the "late above-mentioned Edition," but chooses to add a passage which may formerly have been "unknown, or forgotten": "That most learn'd Prince, and great Patron of Learning,

King James the First, was pleas'd with his own Hand to write an amicable
Letter to Mr. Shakespeare; which Letter, tho now lost, remain'd long in
the Hands of Sir William D'avenant, as a credible Person now living
can testify."[8]

Lintott may have been guilty of creating a greater illusion. The apparent
clarity of his title claim that the poems were correctly printed from editions of 1609 becomes obscured and could well be fraudulent, for although
the sonnets were first published in this year—and Lintott uses this edition—there were no 1609 editions of the other poems (see note 2). His
first revision was to explain that "The Passionate Pilgrime" and "Sonnets
to Sundry Notes of Musicke" came to him in a "little stitch'd Book" of
1599. "Plainly," Lintott stated, with no attempt at corroboration, "they
were published by himself." The second shift from the 1609 date was the
dismissive sleight of hand in his textual comment on "Venus and Adonis"
and "The Rape of Lucrece": "I will say nothing of [them], they being
universally allow'd to be Shakespear's, only that I have printed them
from very old Editions, which I procur'd, as the Reader will find by
my keeping close to his Spelling."[9] Any doubts about authenticity were
therefore explained by the reader's unfamiliarity with Shakespeare's
spelling rather than Lintott's possible duplicity. If Lintott was cheating,
he went to some lengths to carry it off, reprinting authentic-looking title
pages for "Venus and Adonis" and "Lucrece" stating "London: Printed
in the Year 1609," and following these with Dedications to the Right
Honourable Henry Wriothesley, Earl of Southampton, and Baron of Tich-
field. The "Venus and Adonis" Dedication is identical to the 1593 edition
except for Lintott's loss of the second "t" in "Titchfield," an omission
which he repeated in the Dedication to "Lucrece," which, apart from this
and a would/should substitution, corresponds to the 1594 edition. Unlike
the 1594 version, however, Lintott's "Lucrece" contains marginal commentary on the progress of the tale which relates, in a slightly extended
form, to the Contents list which he printed between the Argument and
the start of the poem. This would suggest that he used the 1616 edition
(which Rollins calls Q6) as his source text.[10] It would seem probable,
therefore, that Lintott conflated material from at least two sources, and
appropriated the date of the first publication of the sonnets, to create a
hitherto unknown collection and pass it off as an original text.

Lintott's fraud, if such it was, effectively deceived a number of subsequent editors. Theobald (1733), Warburton (1747), and Johnson (1765)
included tables of the editions of Shakespeare's plays in their versions of
the Collected Works.[11] Capell, in 1767–68, was the first to extend this
practice to the poems, and his list, "Editions of his Poems," begins:

I. Shakespeare's Poems. 1609. quarto. (*DES)
II. D°, no date, octavo. for Bernard Lintott.

This second item carries a footnote: "This is said, in the title page, to be an exact copy of the edition that goes before; and has the appearance of being what it professes."[12] Capell did not say that he had seen the 1609 edition and the bracketed DES may indicate that he believed it to be destroyed. Johnson and Steevens (1773) produced an almost identical list starting

> I. Shakespeare's Poems. 1609. 4to.
> II. Do, no date, 8vo. for Bernard Lintot,[13]

but amended it in their second edition of 1778 in which they divided their list into "Old Editions of Shakespeare's Poems" and "Modern Editions."[14] This device severed the connection between Lintott and 1609, the first list being headed by "Shakespeare's Poems, 1609, 4to." and the second by "Shakespeare's Poems, 8vo. for Bernard Lintot, no date." Johnson and Steevens were the first editors to include "Extracts of Entries on the Books of the Stationers' Company" as part of their prolegomena,[15] and as these extracts show little correlation with their lists of Poems it may well be that a subheading to their list of Plays—"as have hitherto been met with by his different editors"[16]—was intended to apply to the Poems too and indicates a reference taken on trust from Lintott and Capell.

Malone eventually questioned Lintott. He had clearly been vexed with questions of authenticity and had encountered problems in obtaining early editions on which to base his own editorial work: his 1780 Supplement to Johnson and Steevens contained thanks to Dr. Farmer for a copy of "Venus and Adonis" published in 1600, and his own 1790 edition expressed gratitide to Thomas Warton for a 1596 version of the same poem. The opportunity for textual comparison which this style of research afforded him enabled him to make the dismissive entry under the subheading "Modern Editions" in his "List of the Most Authentick Ancient Editions of Shakespeare's Poems": "Shakspeare's Poems, small octavo, for Bernard Lintot, no date, but printed in 1710. The Sonnets in this edition were printed from the quarto of 1609; Venus and Adonis and Lucrece from very late editions, full of errors."[17] Malone's motives—he writes off all his predecessors' work with "Spurious Editions of Shakspear's Poems have also been published by Gildon, Sewell, Evans, &c.," thus leaving himself a clear field[18]—may be questionable, but the more significant issue is Lintott's purpose.

It is likely that Lintott knew of the preparation of another collection of Shakespeare's poems, which may have prompted the expansion of his own edition from one volume to two, and which was to have equally suspect credentials. In 1710, E. Curll published *The Works of Mr. William Shakespear, Volume the Seventh, containing Venus and Adonis, Tarquin*

and Lucrece and His Miscellany Poems, With Critical Remarks on his
Plays, &c., to which is Prefix'd an Essay on the Art, Rise and Progress
of the Stage in Greece, Rome and England.[19] The size, typeface and
binding of this volume, and the blatant "Volume the Seventh" of the title
indicate that this was an attempt to capitalize on Rowe's six–volume edition of the plays published in 1709. Little wonder that Lintott, engaged
in the same opportunistic, commercial activity, should wish to give special status to his own publication through unique textual claims.

Curll's volume, generally agreed to have been edited by Charles Gildon
(who has also been proposed as a candidate for Lintott's anonymous
editor, if there was one), was a far more grandiose affair than Lintott's
and made a more sophisticated use of selling techniques. The obsequious
Dedication, to the Right Honourable Charles, Earl of Peterborow and
Monmouth, made poetry a muscular, manly, *English* activity:

> MY LORD, the publication of these Poems falling to my Lot, the Merit of the
> Poet soon determin'd me in the Choice of a Patron; the *greatest genius in*
> *Poetry* naturally flying to the *Protection of the greatest Genius in War,* for the
> MUSE has always found herself dear to the Heroes Race, who [sic] Glory and
> Praise it is her Duty and Delight to transmit to Posterity. . . . (no page number)

Having dangled this patriotic and snobbish lure, Curll then provided for
the practical needs of his readers and offered genuinely helpful companion pieces to Rowe's volumes, establishing a link which would enhance
the sales of his own volume and attract a broader audience who appreciated a commentary to make the texts accessible. He provided "An Explanation of the Old Words us'd by Shakespear in his Works," a list of
"References to the Classic Authors, &c." and, in "Remarks on the Plays
of Shakespear," gave a scheme of plots in the order of Rowe's volumes,
with some indication of sources and an identification of beautiful passages. The sections of criticism in the "Essay on the Art, Rise and Progress of the Stage," the "Remarks on the Plays" and the "Remarks on the
Poems" served the same instructional, if somewhat distorted, function.
Opinions were forcefully presented, and qualitative and quantitative judgments carefully packaged for ease of communication and consumption.
Thus, in sweeping statements that disposed of a host of sophisticated,
critical complexities, Shakespeare's poems "are genuine, more perfect in
their kind, than many, if not most, of his *Dramatic* Performances" (ii),
the work of women dramatists is dismissed—they are always "delivered
of Cripples" (442)—and it is demanded that the stage should be placed
under the jurisdiction of magistrates.

Curll and Gildon made one valuable innovation to the developing interest in Shakespeare's verse by including sections from "An Essay on Po-

etry," the narrative poem by John Sheffield, the first Duke of Buckingham and Normanby (identified as the Earl of Murlgrave [sic] in some editions of the Essay), and thus were using poetry to describe and to define poetry and were beginning to discuss Shakespeare in poetic rather than dramatic terms. Perversely they excluded Buckingham's contention that poetry was the superior art, but rehearsed his definition of poetry and its rules—true wit, a composite quality of genius, spirit and soul, and an amalgam of judgment and reason—without amendment, to conclude:

> How far Shakespear has excell'd in this way is plain from his Poems before us; but this must be allow'd him, that much of the Beauty and Sweetness of Expression, which is so much contended for is lost by the Injury of Time and the great Change in our Language since his Time; and yet there is a wonderful smoothness in many of them, that makes the Blood dance to its Numbers. (463)

This praise, perhaps because of the vigor of the final image, which is derived from both Milton and Pope, appears genuine and far removed from the unscrupulous hyperbole of most of the volume.

It seems probable that both the early eighteenth-century editions of Shakespeare's poems were tainted by the sharp practices of their publishers, compounded, in Curll's case, by a poor personal reputation and a longstanding quarrel with Pope. Edmund Curll was a known self-publicist, originating newspaper controversies to gain public attention and making false claims about the authorship of books that he published. His enmity with Pope, for example, dated from his publication of *Court Poems* by James Roberts in 1716 which contained the broad hint in the Advertisement that some lines "could have come from no other hand than the laudable translator of Homer." In the same year he received his first reprimand at the bar of the House of Lords for publishing a pirated edition of the trial of the Earl of Wintoun. His second appearance in the Lords may have some specific relevance for the reception of Shakespeare's poems. On this occasion he was charged for publishing "The Works of the Duke of Buckingham" (the author of "An Essay on Poetry"), which led to the resolution making it a breach of privilege to print, without permission, "the works, life, or last will of any lord of this house."[20] Curll was also the subject of a number of libel actions and convicted at least twice for the publication of obscene and immoral books.

The response to Curll's activities was not restricted to the courts. Swift's "Advice to the Grub-street Verse-Writers" (1726) suggested a way for "ragged and forlorn" poets to revive their "still-born Poems":

> GET all your Verses printed fair,
> Then, let them well be dry'd;
> And, *Curl* must have a special Care
> To leave the Margin wide.

> LEND these to Paper-sparing *Pope;*
>   And, when he sits to write,
> No Letter with an *Envelope*
>   Could give him more Delight.

> WHEN *Pope* has fill'd the Margins round,
>   Why, then recal your Loan;
> Sell them to *Curl* for Fifty Pound,
>   And swear they are your own.[21]

Curll was also to become the subject of much ridicule in Book 2 of *The Dunciad*. Pope alluded to his punishment in the pillory for publishing pirated texts, and the retribution exacted by the boys of Westminster School after Curll had printed an inaccurate version of the Latin oration delivered by the captain of the King's Scholars in the college hall over the body of Robert South after his death in July, 1716. Curll was enticed into Dean's Yard and tossed in a blanket. Pope conflated this incident with his own revenge on Curll—the administration of an emetic—for the publication of Roberts's *Court Poems:*

> Himself among the story'd chiefs he spies,
> As from the blanket high in air he flies,
> And oh! (he cry'd) what street, what lane but knows,
> Our purgings, pumpings, blankettings, and blows?
> In ev'ry loom our labours shall be seen,
> And the fresh vomit run for ever green! [22]

Pope also wrote of the competition between Curll and Lintott, clearly siding with the latter who was the legitimate publisher of a number of his works. He set the two in a running race which finished when Curll slid into a lake (a metaphor for a pirated text):

> Obscene with filth the miscreant lies bewray'd,
> Fal'n in the plash his wickedness had laid.
>
> (2.75–76)

A comparison between the character and reputation of Curll and Nicholas Rowe (and, indeed, subsequent editors and publishers of Shakespeare's plays) is one explanation for the lack of interest in the poems, and their prolonged status as an adjunct or a dubious additional volume rather than an incorporated part of the canon. Rowe was an institutional figure, a successful playwright with a private income and a holder of political office who was created Poet Laureate by George I in 1715. He had a number of influential relationships, including a friendship with Pope, which made him the object of criticism by Curll ("Critical Remarks on Mr.Rowe's last Play, call'd Ulysses," 1706) and Gildon ("New Rehearsal, or Bays the Younger, containing an examen of Seven of Rowe's Play," 1714). He was buried in Westminster Abbey where, like Shakespeare, he was honored with a monument that was executed by Rysbrack and adorned with verses by Pope.[23] Shakespeare's plays were associated with the establishment; the poems were the province of pirates.

This uneasy division continued. Rowe's 1714 edition, printed once again by J. Tonson, was expanded to eight volumes.[24] The plays were presented in the same order as the 1709 edition (which followed the sequence of the fourth folio of 1685), although the division between the plays and therefore the contents of the volumes differed, and the prolegomena were expanded with a "Table of the most Sublime Passages in this Author." Once more the poems were excluded and once more an unauthorized volume appeared, albeit one with a slightly closer association with the play volumes than its predecessor. The title page of the work, edited once again by Charles Gildon, made the fraudulent claim, "The Works of Mr. Shakespear, Volume the Ninth," thus suggesting a legitimate progression from the eight volumes of plays, and then continued "Printed by J. Darby in Bartholomew-Close, for E. Curll, K. Sanger, and J. Pemberton: Sold by J. Tonson in the Strand. . . ." It was not uncommon to list booksellers, but whether this was a ploy by Curll to validate his activities by using the name of Shakespeare's play publisher or whether this is evidence of Tonson making commercial use of the poems remains undetermined. It is clear, however, that the poems dwelt in a very different domain from the plays.

The next Collected Works of Shakespeare was edited by Pope and published by Tonson in 1725.[25] Pope's Preface engaged in the contemporary debates concerning Shakespeare's skills—his originality, his strength as an "Instrument of Nature," his characterization, his power over our passions, his use of dramatic rules, his want of learning and a comparison with Ben Jonson—and then he reprinted Rowe's "Some Account of the Life &c. of Mr. William Shakespear." He reproduced Jonson's "To the Memory of my Beloved, the Author" (the first eighteenth-century use of a "stand alone" commendatory verse) from the first folio, and added two items that reinforced the establishment status of the plays. The first was the Instrument of the Shakespeare Coat of Arms, thus affirming that Shakespeare was a gentleman, and the second was a list of subscribers. The list was headed "THE KING."

This presented a challenge to those who produced the unauthorized volume of Shakespeare's poems which followed Pope's edition. *The Works of Mr. William Shakespear, The Seventh Volume, Containing Venus and Adonis, Tarquin and Lucrece, and Mr. Shakespear's Miscellany Poems, to which is Prefix'd an Essay on the Art, Rise and Progress of the Stage, in Greece, Rome and England, and a Glossary of the Old Words us'd in these Works: the Whole Revis'd and Corrected, with a Preface, by Dr. Sewell* was published in 1725, printed by J. Darby for a consortium of publishers headed by A. Bettesworth. The contents of this volume are very similar to those of the Curll/Gildon version of fifteen years earlier and, as in that version, the dedication was used as a promotional device. Sewell drew a direct link between a contemporary hero and an historic one, dismissing any doubts about the quality of Shakespeare's poems with a large dollop of patriotism. The dedication, to the Right Honourable the Lord Walpole, opens:

> My Lord,
> I should not have dared to approach your Lordship with a less Poet in my Hand than SHAKESPEAR; the dead Ornament of the English Nation, being the most proper Present to its Living Glory. He, My LORD, has shared the Fate common to every great Genius, receiving very ill Returns for all his Beauties and Benefits; in amends for which, my present Endeavour is to wipe off the Dust of Age, Error and Ignorance, and Screen his valuable Remains under Your Lordship's Protection. (iii)

Sewell's sycophantic disinterring was drawing blatantly on the old boy network and, in a move that countered Pope's use of the coat of arms, came close to conferring a public school education upon the dramatist by the crafty elision of Shakespeare with Sewell and Walpole and their "common Mother, ETON" (iv).

Sewell's reputation was little better than his predecessors' (he was known, for example, to be responsible for a number of unauthorized publications which linked him to prominent writers, and to have contributed to "spurious" volumes of the *Tatler* and the *Spectator*), and he seems as prominent in the Dedication himself as those of whom he was ostensibly writing. Certainly Pope suspected him of self-aggrandizement and the pursuit of fame through association with others. In his "Epistle to Dr. Arbuthnot" (1735) Pope responded to those who he believed had attacked him, including Curll, Lintott, and Gildon, and in the first edition wrote disparagingly of "Sanguine Sew—," which he later amended to "slashing Bentley" (the editor of Milton), in a passage in which he described the injuries he had suffered at the hands of minor, unimaginative critics.[26]

In his brief, nine-page Preface to *The Works of Mr. William Shakespear, the Seventh Volume*, Sewell glanced at topical questions of authenticity and Shakespeare's learning and then redirected and resolved them with a swipe at the textual transmitters. Any original—and minor—errors, he argued, had been compounded by time and republishing:

> Whatever were the Faults of this great Poet, the Printers have been hitherto as careful to multiply them, as if they had been real Beauties; thinking perhaps with the Indians that the disfiguring a good Face with scars of artificial Brutes, had improv'd the Form and Dignity of the Person. (viii)

Enquiring "Quis tam crudeles optavit sumere Poenas?" (Who desired to inflict such cruel penalties?), he replied, "The Answer is easy, the Tribe of Editors, Correctors, and Printers, who have usually as little Pity for a Helen, as she had for her Husband." Such ebullient rhetoric swiftly disposed of the need to engage with the real issues and disguised any anxieties which may have been felt by the editor or which he may have anticipated in his readers. He went on to hope, disingenuously, that the latest edition of the plays would be error-free and wrote, with equal insincerity, "Far be it from any Hopes of mine that this Edition of his Poems should equal his [Pope's] curious Correctness: a less faulty one than the former is all the Reader is to expect" (viii). Sewell provides little original commentary on Shakespeare or his poems and there is ample evidence that Pope's estimate of him lacking "spirit, taste and sense" was both accurate and just.[27] Indeed, Pope's reaction seems a restrained response given that Sewell's only comment on Shakespeare's plays in this volume appears ridiculous in its isolation and shallowness:

> It is not my Province to speak of Shakespear's Plays; only I cannot but observe that some of them do not answer their Titles. In *Julius Caesar* for Instance, there is little of the Man or his memorable Exploits, unless what is said after his Death; and if any one were to form an Idea of him from what Shakespear makes him speak he would make but an indifferent Figure for the *Foremost of Mankind*. (xiii–xiv)

After such an incisive contribution to Shakespeare criticism, based on the gulf between his own expectation and the text, he neatly avoided the necessity of engaging in any more intellectually demanding or objective activity:

> I have already run this Preface to a great length, otherwise I should have taken notice of some beautiful Passages in the Poems; but a Reader of Taste cannot miss them. (xv)

Such a casual attitude to his task is in clear contrast with the work that was being undertaken by the editors of the plays, and is a reminder that Sewell's approach to Shakespeare was honed in the ephemeral world of the theater prologue where quite different criteria applied. There Shakespeare's presence was an unchallenged commonplace, a shorthand way of alluding to tradition, national values, and identity, and he was employed to denigrate commercial rivals, be they the competing house, the French comedians, novelty acts, or foreign singers. In his prologue to the 1721 performance of Betterton's adaptation *The Sequel of Henry the Fourth with the Humours of Sir John Falstaffe, and Justice Shallow, alter'd from Shakespear*, for example, Sewell used language remarkably similar to his Preface to manipulate Shakespeare's supposed weaknesses as well as his established strengths to engage with the new historicizing mode of the age, define a national character and affirm the security of the Hanoverian succession, while at the same time flattering his audience.[28] By adapting or adopting the rhetoric of the prologue, in which veracity and authenticity take second place to effect, to his edition of the poems, Sewell was in part responsible for consigning them to publishing oblivion for almost forty years. His comments read well and have a short-lived appeal, and his imagery is certainly vivid, but his remarks are shallow and do not stand up to critical scrutiny. His style of language is inappropriate to prompt or sustain informed interest.

While Pope's 1728 edition attracted a further "false" volume from Sewell, Pope himself, Theobald (1733), Hanmer (1744), Warburton (1747), Johnson (1765), Capell (1767–68), the posthumous second edition of Hanmer (1771), and Johnson and Steevens (1773), all ignored Shakespeare's poems. The editors were clearly concerned with differentiation and individuation and devised a number of ways of giving their editions value-added features. Theobald introduced a selection of commendatory verses, for example, Hanmer commissioned illustrations from Hayman, Warburton devised a series of classifications, Johnson opted for historicism and, while Capell chose a streamlined and simplified approach, Johnson and Steevens's edition can be seen as a summative work, representing the established state of Shakespeare scholarship sanctioned by a poet laureate, a bishop, an aristocrat, and the two most influential literary figures of the age. Yet if some of these ploys are viewed as packaging (for they were, in some instances, quite separate from any editorial process), they beg the question—why did the editors choose not to extend their product? The only publication of Shakespeare's poems between Sewell in 1728 and Bell's edition of 1773–74 was by George Steevens who included the sonnets in his *Twenty of the Plays of Shakespeare, Being the Whole Number printed in Quarto During his Life-Time, or before the Restoration, Collated where there were different Copies, and Publish'd from the Originals*, published in 1766.[29] Some of this work, principally the "Advertisement to the Reader," was reprinted in Johnson and Steevens's cumulative 1773 edition but the poems were, once again, missing from that work.

What to make of the gap? Margreta de Grazia, in her article, "The Scandal of Shakespeare's Sonnets," initially ignores it by stating, in relation to the sonnets, "that since no full edition of the 1609 Quarto was printed prior to Malone's, that belated history can be considered their only history," an argument which is factually incorrect and which would enrage those whose history is denied because it lacks detailed documentation.[30] But a gap is significant, not least because it invites the kind of conjecture that de Grazia proceeds to make. In order to support her thesis that "the scandal in the Sonnets had been misidentified. It is not Shakespeare's desire for a boy. It is Shakespeare's gynerastic longings for a black mistress" (48), she is required to lend support to a myth to validate her claim of misdirection. The myth has it that the sonnets were so shocking that they could only be presented to the public in John Benson's 1640 pronominal gender-adjusted form (the form used in the false volumes of Rowe and Pope, and later by Bell and Evans). While de Grazia exposes the very limited nature of these adjustments (in sonnets 101, 104, and 108), she underplays the fact that Lintott reprinted the 1609 edition, rather than Benson, and diminishes the significance of Steevens's 1766 republication. She makes convenient use of Rollins's very selective quotation of Steevens's footnote to Sonnet 20 which in the full version diminishes significantly his "disgust and indignation" at the phrase "master-mistress of my passion,"[31] and she confidently attributes motive and action to him:

> George Steevens . . . reprinted the 1609 Sonnets in a collection of early quartos in 1766 but *refused* to edit them for his 1793 edition of Shakespeare's complete works. While he could justify their publication as documents, he *refused* to honour them with an editorial apparatus, the trappings of a classic. [my italics] (37)

These assertions overlook his critical rivalry with Malone, the support he received from Garrick for his 1766 edition, the lack of editorial apparatus for the plays as well as the poems in that work, the fact that Steevens's "refusal" comes after rather than during the sonnets' absence, and his critical remark on the quality rather than the content of the poems: "the strongest act of Parliament that could be framed would fail to compel readers into their service."[32]

Yet even if one can identify distortion, dislodging myths remains difficult, not least because their survival is usually argued in apophatic terms. It would be helpful to find evidence of someone other than Steevens being scandalized but there is very little from the relevant period. In the first decade of the century Shakespeare was being used in theatrical prologues and epilogues to stand for England in its claim for superior wit, humor, sense, cuisine, architecture, and, not least, in matters of sex. He was both the prophylactic antidote and the approved alternative to homosexuality

(Higgons's prologue to *The Jew of Venice,* 1701), disease (an anonymous prologue to *Timon of Athens,* 1703), debauchery (an anonymous epilogue to *The Amorous Miser,* 1705), and eunuchs (Dennis's prologue to *Julius Caesar,* 1707, and Addison's prologue to *Phaedra and Hippolitus,* 1707).[33] Yet all these uses were defined in opposition to stage performances by foreigners rather than any rational regard for domestic behavior or a specific employment of Shakespeare's text, and were confined to this early period that predates any of the collected works. Which is not to say, of course, that such commercially convenient sexually orthodox applications did not have an enduring effect, and put the sonnets outside the manufactured image of Shakespeare. However, this expedient desire to conceive of Shakespeare as a sexually orthodox exemplar does not mean that any contrastingly "scandalous" aspect of the sonnets was the sole, or even the principal, cause of the long gap between eighteenth-century publications of Shakespeare poems.[34]

So what else could account for the gap? As I've tried to demonstrate, Shakespeare's poems were tainted by the reputation and unscrupulous practices of their early editors who, despite their hard-selling techniques, contributed to the outsider status of the verse. In addition, two areas warrant consideration. First, there was a great deal of verse associated with editions of Shakespeare: the practice of printing poems of praise, which culminated with Malone's inclusion of thirty-eight "Ancient and Modern Commendatory Verses on Shakspeare," developed steadily throughout the period. At the same time, verse was the medium for much of the debate generated by each succeeding edition. Theobald was attacked in verse by Pope and David Mallet, Hanmer's edition elicited a sharp retort from Pope, Warburton's plodding classifications drew verse criticism from Robertson, Thomas Edwards, and Akenside. The two models of verse—the encomium and the doggerel critical swipe—which became strongly attached to Shakespeare through the editions of his work were unsubtle and functional. Their style dulled the sensibilities of readers from such a different cultural climate, and contributed to the alienation of Shakespeare's poems.

There is a similar sense of unfittingness and disparity if one considers the staging of Shakespeare. The London theater season of 1725–26, the year of Sewell's first false volume of Pope, featured fifty-five performances of Shakespeare's plays or their adaptations, with *The Merry Wives of Windsor,* which received eight performances, as the most popular. Of the other twelve plays which were staged, six were tragedies and three were histories. Five years later the repertoire was almost identical: thirteen plays, five tragedies, four histories (with *Merry Wives* still the most popular play), *Julius Caesar* dropped, and *The Jew of Venice* added.[35] The prevailing image of Shakespeare, which both generated such performances and was reinforced by them, excluded that of the romantic poet. His verses were inappropriate for a figure who was associated with history, particularly English history, and tragedy.

It was an edition of Shakespeare which was ostensibly devoted to performance, at a time when the staged repertoire was significantly broader, which finally closed the gap. In the same year as Johnson and Steevens's work, and continuing into 1774, John Bell published the first edition which reflected theatrical practice—*Bell's Edition of Shakespeare's Plays, as they are now Performed at the Theatres Royal in London; Regulated from the Prompt Books of each House by Permission; with Notes Critical and Illustrative; by the Authors of the Dramatic Censor*—and ended the period of absence and the disassociation of plays from poems.[36] Bell saw his function as that of an obstetrician; he was concerned with the successful production of something new and vital, and had little regard for what had gone before. Not surprisingly, the prolegomena of this "living" edition had a completely different emphasis from its backward-looking predecessors and focused on Garrick who was praised as "the best illustrator of, and the best *living commentator* on, SHAKESPEARE, that ever has appeared, or possibly ever will grace the British stage" (1: reverse of iv). The sense of vitality and of the text having a contemporary life which needed careful nurturing was extended in the second Advertisement. An image from child-rearing was employed to justify the cutting of scenes and passages which were considered trifling, obscure, or indelicate: "[I]s not the corrective hand frequently proved to be the kindest? critics, like parents, should neither spare the rod, nor use it wantonly" (1:5). The advice of Gentleman, who is usually credited with the editorial work, on the use of pauses, emphasis, stops, and cadences in the "Essay on Oratory" shared the concern that the child should be presented at his best.

From volume six the edition began to print the plays which were rarely or never part of the theatrical repertoire. Each play continued to be prefaced with an engraving of a dramatic moment and an introduction but, lacking cast lists for Drury Lane and Covent Garden, the most tangible link with performance disappeared. A further change of emphasis and direction becomes apparent in the text and apparatus of volume nine, which, without prior warning and in contradiction of the title of the complete work, is headed *Poems written by Shakespear*. Were it not for the fact that this volume is clearly published by Bell one would suspect it of being a further example of entrepreneurial sharp practice as engaged in by Gildon or Sewell.

The policy change is immediately apparent from the Life of Shakespeare with which the volume opens and which, in addition to biographical information, includes a critical summary of the works of previous editors. In impugning their motives and denigrating their abilities, the tone of the passage associates the volume with the publishing and editing squabbles of the past, particularly those concerning the poems, rather than the forward-looking method which was promised in the first Advertisement. The volume then harks further back to the past by printing Jonson's "To the Memory of my Beloved, the Author," but introduces an innovative practice by making comments on the verse such as "Though the versification of this Poem is, in general, stiff, and uncouth; yet we perceive great sincerity and warmth of praise in it" (9:23). This strong editorial voice (which is not identified) is maintained throughout the Introduction that follows.

Defining poetry as the "most dignified degree of literary composition" (9: opening paragraph of Introduction) in civilized societies because of the breadth of skill required, the editor argued the relative merits of Epic Composition and Drama and concluded that the latter was the highest art because its variety called for the exercise of greater ability. This convenient conclusion enabled him to praise Shakespeare as an unequalled dramatist and excuse his failings in a lesser art. He used contemporary and historic examples to demonstrate that the best authors since Shakespeare excelled in only one branch of writing and by claiming that Dryden, Congreve, Pope, Addison, Young, Thomson, Milton, and Mason either failed at, or never attempted, the stage, he effectively elevated Shakespeare above them. Simple and flawed though this argument may be, it was an attempt at comparative criticism which was unusual in this context. It was an attempt, however, that left the editor with the difficulty of justifying the publication of what he himself had denigrated as poems in which "subjects are trifling, his versification mostly laboured and quibbling, with too great a degree of licentiousness" (9: concluding paragraph of Introduction). His first defence was straightforward: "a desire of gratifying the admirers of our Author with an *entire* edition of his works." The second defense, which excused the retention of "censurable" passages, was more subtle and distanced the editor from the decision while alluding to other authorities and playing to popular prejudices by ridiculing the behavior of the old enemy:

> We are ourselves as far from approving [some passages] as the most scrupulous of our Readers; but upon consulting the critics, we were told that to have expunged them, might appear as over-strained a piece of prudery, in Literature, as the Regent Duke of *Orleans*'s action was, in the Arts; who, toward the latter part of his life, had castigated to *imperfection* certain pieces in his fine collection of statues and painting, in order to render them more decent objects of inspection. (9: concluding sentence of Introduction)

This is an intriguing volume not least because it suggests that while the editor or publisher may have had doubts about the quality of his product there was once more a market for Shakespeare's poems.

This was confirmed in the following year, 1775, by the publication of *Poems Written by Mr. William Shakespeare,* reprinted for Thomas Evans. The Advertisement begins:

> Several editions of the Poems of Shakespear have been printed, but the eager desire to be possessed of the complete works of the noblest of poets, have rendered them scarce; it was therefore imagined, an elegant and correct edition would be very acceptable to every admirer of the author. (third unnumbered page)

Jaggard believed that this volume was intended to supplement Capell's 1767–68 edition of the Collected Works and may have been edited by him, but I can find no internal or external evidence to support this view.[37] The text is based on Sewell's work of 1728, using Benson's version of the sonnets, and there is no editorial apparatus—nothing, in fact, to suggest that Evans had done more than respond to the consumer demand, which he referred to in the Advertisement, by reprinting an old edition.

In 1780, Bathurst and his consortium published a legitimate addition, largely the work of Malone, to the "Revised and Augmented" second edition of Johnson and Steevens, which had reasserted the historical approach that Bell and Gentleman had spurned. The title promised much: *Supplement to the Edition of Shakespeare's Plays Published in 1778 by Samuel Johnson and George Steevens in Two Volumes, Containing Additional Observations by Several of the Former Commentators; To which are Subjoined the Genuine Poems of the Same Author, and Seven Plays that have been ascribed to Him, with Notes by the Editor and Others.* Yet any expectation or excitement that Shakespeare's poems were about to be incorporated into the mainstream of editorial scholarship or afforded the attentions of accredited editors is subdued by the discovery that almost four hundred pages of the first volume are taken up with the "Additional Observations" on the plays. Surprisingly little attention is given to any other preliminaries; an engraving of Shakespeare's Birthplace is reproduced opposite the title page and a brief Advertisement alludes to the editorial approach to the poems:

> Many passages in these poems being obscure, they have been illustrated with notes, in which all such parallel expressions as have been discovered in our author's dramatick performances are quoted, as furnishing a very strong proof of their authenticity. (1:iv–v)

While the footnotes by Malone and Steevens were not confined to linguistic parallels with the plays (there was some conjecture, for example, about printing errors in old copies), it is evident from the emphasis of the Advertisement that the poems were regarded as inferior to the plays and that value was accorded to them only through their congruities and not through their differences. It was their similarities rather than their intrinsic quality that vouched for their authenticity. Suspicions about their legitimacy remained, however, in the inference of guilt by association; the second volume of the Supplement is devoted to *Pericles, Locrine, Sir John Oldcastle, Lord Cromwell, The London Prodigal, The Puritan,* and *A Yorkshire Tragedy.*

In 1785 Bathurst's group published the third edition of Johnson and Steevens's work "Revised and augmented by the Editor of Dodsley's Collection of Old Plays," Isaac Reed. Steevens took no part in this edition—he claimed to have joined the ranks of "dowager editors"[38]—and while Malone contributed footnotes to some additional memorial and commendatory verse, his supplements to the second edition were dropped. Once again, therefore, Shakespeare's poems were excluded and it is not clear why. Certainly Malone's work had not lost favor—his footnotes and other contributions attest to that—and it may be that he had recalled his more substantial work as he prepared and amended material for his own edition of the collected works.

The exclusion may also indicate another swing in public demand or taste, for the next edition of Shakespeare could not have been in greater contrast to the style of Johnson and Steevens. Succinctly titled, *The Dramatic Works of Shakspeare, in Six Volumes, with Notes,* was published by the Clarendon Press from 1786 and edited by Joseph Rann, Vicar of St. Trinity in Coventry. It opened with a very brief dedication to Lord Sheffield and then embarked upon the text of the plays without any introductory comment or apparatus. Needless to say, there was no place for the poems.

If Rann's work reflected a desire for simplicity, or even an unwritten acknowledgment that the editor's task was now complete, it was a small appetite, a yearning for a quick snack perhaps, that was quickly sated. Malone's edition of 1790 was a return to the feasting of Johnson and Steevens and provided the most substantial meal to date. While his greatest editorial achievement was the quality of his textual research, his inclusion of Shakespeare's poems as a standard, rather than as a suspect, supplementary, item, was a significant and important development. Despite the critically distorting effect of his biographical approach to the sonnets, the status he accorded the verse, coupled with his diligent scholarship, made them an acceptable part of a collected works and incorporated them, at last and after almost eighty years, into the canon.

It is, however, the poems' long absence rather than their eventual inclusion that had the most significant and enduring effect. They remained outside the mainstream of critical debate and were not subjected to the same degree of scrutiny, comment, or scholarly attention. The techniques that were applied to the plays were never used with the poems; they were exempt from the classification and categorization which characterized the study of the plays and never featured in lists of beautiful or moving passages, or suffered qualitative judgment. New editions of Shakespeare's plays were regularly reviewed in a growing number of periodicals; Johnson's 1765 edition, for example, was considered in *Monthly Review, Critical Review, Gentleman's Magazine,* and the *Annual Register.* Shakespeare's poems, however, in the form of Evans's edition of 1775, were only reviewed twice. At the risk of stating the obvious, it must be noted that the absence of the poems from this important new development in eighteenth-century life increased their invisibility and compounded their questionable status. The lack of comment in both the editions of his work and in reviews also created another absence—the lack of a critical vocabulary with which to discuss or describe the poems. The practice of reproducing and commenting upon previous editors' prefaces and prolegomena gave editions of the collected plays a language which, through repetition and endorsement, became the language of Shakespeare criticism and defined the terms of the debate. The poems had no part in this process. While this lack of attention may, in the long term, have privileged the poems and left them relatively free from prejudice and received opinion, a number of important arguments—particularly those concerning authenticity, sensiblity, and aesthetic value—remained unresolved. The publishing history of the poems both raised and reinforced doubt rather than diminishing it.

NOTES

1. Nicholas Rowe, ed., *The Works of Mr. William Shakespear,* (London: Jacob Tonson, 1709), 1: xl.
2. The sonnets were first published by Thomas Thorpe in 1609 along with "A Lover's Complaint." *Venus and Adonis* was first published in 1593, and *The Rape of Lucrece* in 1594. They were both reprinted many times before the end of the century. *The Passionate Pilgrim* (which contains pieces by other authors) was published in 1599. The second publication of the Sonnets was John Benson's revision of 1640 which also included "A Lover's Complaint" and the *Passionate Pilgrim* pieces.
3. For Rowe's reference to *Venus and Adonis* and *The Rape of Lucrece,* see Rowe, 1709, 1:xxxix.
4. Edmond Malone, ed., *The Poems and Plays of William Shakspeare in Ten Volumes* (London: H. Baldwin, 1790).
5. In extolling classical tragedy Rowe wrote:

> What Shakespear durst not, this bold Age shou'd do,
> And famous Greek and Latin Beauties show.
> Shakespear, whose Genius to it self a Law,
> Could men in every Height of Nature draw,
> And copy'd all but Women that he saw.

The Ambitious Stepmother, 3d ed. (London: J. Darby, 1710), Prologue, ll. 30–34.

6. *A Collection of Poems . . . by Mr. William Shakespeare* (London: Bernard Lintott, [1709]); *A Collection of Poems in Two Volumes . . .* (London: Bernard Lintott, [1709–10]).

7. Lintott, 1709, A2.

8. Ibid.

9. Ibid.

10. Hyder Edward Rollins's *New Variorum Edition of Shakespeare: The Poems* (London and Philadelphia: J. B. Lippincott, 1938) and his *New Variorum Edition of the Sonnets*, 2 vols. (London and Philadelphia: J. B. Lippincott, 1944) provide the most authoritative details of the variants in editions of Shakespeare poems.

11. Lewis Theobald, ed., *The Works of Shakespeare*, 7 vols. (London: A Bettesworth and others, 1733); William Warburton, ed., *The Works of Shakespeare*, 8 vols. (London: J. and P. Knapton and others, 1747); Samuel Johnson, ed., *The Plays of William Shakespeare*, 8 vols. (London: J. and R. Tonson and others, 1765).

12. Edward Capell, ed., *Mr. William Shakespeare his Comedies, Histories, and Tragedies,* (London: Dryden Leach for J. and R. Tonson, [1767–68]), 1: no page number. The list precedes *The Tempest.*

13. Samuel Johnson and George Steevens, eds., *The Plays of William Shakespeare,* (London: C. Bathurst and others, 1773), 1: no page number. The list precedes *The Tempest.*

14. Samuel Johnson and George Steevens, eds., *The Plays of William Shakespeare,* 10 vols. (London: C. Bathurst and others, 1778).

15. Johnson and Steevens, 1773, 1:253–62.

16. Ibid., 1:234.

17. Malone, 1790, 1:233–34.

18. Ibid., 1:234.

19. [Charles Gildon, ed.,] *The Works of Mr. William Shakespear, Volume the Seventh* (London: E. Curll and E. Sanger, 1710).

20. *DNB*, 1937–38, 5:328.

21. Jonathan Swift, *The Poems,* ed. Harold Williams, 2d ed., (Oxford: Clarendon Press, 1966), "Advice to the Grub-street Verse-Writers," ll. 9–20.

22. Alexander Pope, *Poetical Works,* ed. Herbert Davis (Oxford: Oxford University Press, 1978, reprint 1990), *The Dunciad,* 2.151–56.

23. Shakespeare's Westminster Abbey monument was executed by Peter Scheemakers. Pope was a member of the group which commissioned it.

24. Nicholas Rowe, ed., *The Works of Mr. William Shakespeare*, 8 vols. (London: Jacob Tonson, 1714).

25. Alexander Pope, ed., *The Works of Shakespear*, 6 vols. (London: Jacob Tonson, 1725). Individual volumes are dated 1723. Pope was dilatory in providing the introductory material and the complete works was not issued until 1725.

26.

> Pains, reading, study, are their just pretence,
> And all they want is spirit, taste and sense.

Comma's and points they set exactly right,
And 'twere a sin to rob them of their mite.
Yet ne'er one sprig of laurel grac'd these ribalds,
From slashing Bentley down to pidling Tibalds:
Each wight who reads not, and but scans and spells,
Each Word-catcher that lives on syllables,
Ev'n such small Critics some regard may claim,
Preserv'd in Milton's or in Shakespear's name.
                              "Epistle to Dr. Arbuthnot," lines 159–68.

27. See "Epistle to Dr. Arbuthnot," line 160.
28. Sewell's Prologue to Betterton's *The Sequel of Henry the Fourth* (London: W. Chetwood, 1721):

> Shakespear who gave our English Stage its Birth,
> Here makes a medley Scene of War, and Mirth.
> He knew his Countrymens free Spirit best,
> We laugh in Earnest—but ne'er fight in Jest.
> Now, he in easy Scenes of Nature Charms,
> And now, your Hearts, with Martial Fury, warms:
> Proving that Rival Nations must submit,
> To English Courage—as to English Wit.
>
> . . . all Apologies for him are wrong,
> He proves his Value, by his lasting long.
> And now with Pleasure, his bright Fame surveys,
> Fresher in GEORGE's, than Eliza's Days.

29. George Steevens, ed., *Twenty of the Plays of Shakespeare* . . . , 4 vols. (London: J. and R. Tonson, 1766). I am excluding Ewing's 1771 collection printed in Dublin which I have not had an opportunity to examine.
30. Margreta de Grazia, "The Scandal of Shakespeare's Sonnets," *Shakespeare Survey* 46 (1994): 40.
31. Rollins, 1944, 1:55; Edmond Malone, *Supplement to the Edition of Shakespeare's Plays Published in 1778,* (London: C. Bathurst and others, 1780), 1:596.
32. George Steevens, ed., *The Plays of William Shakespeare,* (London: T. Longman and others, 1793), 1:vii.
33. See Pierre Danchin, ed., *The Prologues and Epilogues of the Eighteenth Century: A Complete Edition,* vol. 1 (Nancy: Presses Universitaires de Nancy, 1990). This is the most convenient source for the prologues and epilogues to *The Amorous Miser, Julius Caesar, Phaedra* and *Hippolitus* and *Timon of Athens*.
34. Specific evidence of the editions themselves is conflicting and comes from a later period that postdates the long omission. Bell, whose editorial apparatus addressed the sensibilities of women and children, included Shakespeare's poems (although he used Benson's sanitized sonnets), while in 1784 Stockdale, who was targetting what he described as "the middling and lower ranks of the inhabitants of this country" in his single-volume edition, excluded them.
35. This information is extrapolated from Emmett L. Avery, ed., *The London Stage 1660–1800* . . . , *Part 2: 1700–1729* (Carbondale: Southern Illinois University Press, 1960) and Arthur H. Scouten, ed., *The London Stage 1660–1800* . . . , *Part 3: 1729–1747* (Carbondale: Southern Illinois University Press, 1960).
36. [Francis Gentleman, ed.,] *Bell's Edition of Shakespeare's Plays* . . . , 9 vols.

(London: John Bell, 1774). Bell's edition is notoriously variable. I have cited the copies in the Shakespeare Centre Library, Stratford upon Avon.

37. William Jaggard, *Shakespeare Bibliography* (Stratford upon Avon: The Shakespeare Press, 1911).

38. *DNB,* 17:1032.

Contributors

Hardin Aasand is Associate Professor of English at Dickinson State University. Aasand earned his M.A. and Ph.D. at the University of Toronto. He has published essays on Ben Jonson and the court masques, and is currently coauthoring the source essay for and assisting with The New Variorum *Hamlet*.

Catherine Alexander has recently competed a Ph.D. dissertation, "Texts and Contexts: Shakespeare and Verse in the Eighteenth Century," at the Shakespeare Institute, University of Birmingham, which she is now turning into a book. She is Assistant to the Editor of *Shakespeare Survey*, and is working on a life of Elizabeth Montagu.

Frank Nicholas Clary is Professor of English at Saint Michael's College in Vermont. He is currently working on two main projects: the New Variorum edition of *Hamlet* and an edition of the Promptbooks related to Sir Peter Hall's RSC production of *Hamlet*, 1965–66.

A cottage industrialist, **Random Cloud**, N.F.R.S.C, is the Distinguished Dominion Compressed Gas Canada, Ltd. Professor of Textual Foreignsics at the University of Trona.

Irene G. Dash teaches at Hunter College-CUNY. She is the author of *Wooing, Wedding, and Power: Women in Shakespeare's Plays* and *Women's Worlds in Shakespeare's Plays* (University of Delaware Press, 1996). She has been awarded fellowships by the National Endowment for the Humanities, the Folger Shakespeare Library, the American Council of Learned Societies, and the Lucius N. Littauer Foundation.

Irene Fizer will be an Ahmanson-Getty Fellow at the Center for 17th- and 18th-Century Studies, University of California-Los Angeles in 1997 and has a doctorate from the University of Pennsylvania. She has previously published articles on *Evelina, La Religieuse,* and *The Coquette.*

Joanna Gondris is an Associate Lecturer at the Open University, England. She is a contributor to the forthcoming New Variorum edition of *Hamlet*, and is at work on a book about eighteenth-century editions of Shakespeare.

366

Richard F. Kennedy is Professor of English at St. Thomas University, Fredericton, New Brunswick, Canada. He is an Associate Editor of the New Variorum edition of *A Midsummer Night's Dream*.

Bernice W. Kliman is Professor of English at Nassau Community College. She is coordinator of the New Variorum *Hamlet* project, to be published by the Modern Language Association. The coeditor of *The Three-Text Hamlet: Parallel Texts of the First and Second Quartos and First Folio* (1991), she has recently published a paperback edition of *Macbeth* in performance and *The Enfolded "Hamlet,"* a diplomatic text of Q2 with material F1 variants enfolded (the inaugural issue of *Shakespeare Newsletter*'s monograph series, 1996).

Linda McJannet is Professor of English at Bentley College, Waltham, Massachusetts. She is the compiler of *Henry VIII: An Annotated Bibliography*, and the author of several articles on Shakespeare and Renaissance drama. She recently completed a book-length manuscript, "The Voice of Elizabethan Stage Directions: The Evolution of a Theatrical Code," and is now at work on a study of the uses of the East in Tudor and Stuart drama.

Margaret Maurer is Professor of English at Colgate University. She has written essays about seventeenth-century court poetry. Her recent work is on Shakespeare's comedies.

Paul Nelsen is Professor of Theatre and Drama at Marlboro College, Vermont. He is on the Editorial Board of the *Shakespeare Bulletin* and the Academic Advisory Board of the International Shakespeare Globe Centre. His publications include numerous articles on the reconstruction of the Globe Theatre, and commentaries examining issues of Shakespeare in performance.

Laurie Osborne is an Associate Professor at Colby College. Her book, *The Trick of Singularity: Twelfth Night and the Performance Editions* has recently been published. She is working currently on Renaissance female playgoers and Shakespeare on film.

Eric Rasmussen is Associate Professor of English at the University of Nevada. He is joint editor with David Bevington of *Doctor Faustus* in the Revels Plays Series and of the edition of Marlowe's works in the Oxford Drama Library. He is currently coediting the New Variorum *Hamlet* and *3 Henry VI* for the Arden Shakespeare.

Caroline Roberts has studied at Queen's University, the University of Toronto, and the University of Oxford. She is currently completing *Contexts and Controversies: Harriet Martineau and Victorian Ideology.*

Peter Seary teaches at New College, University of Toronto. He is author of *Lewis Theobald and the Editing of Shakespeare.* He is now preparing an edition of Theobald's correspondence.

Ann Thompson is Professor of English and Head of the English Department at Roehampton Institute, London. She is one of the General Editors of the Arden Shakespeare, third series, and is coeditor of *Hamlet,* forthcoming in that series. She is the author of *Shakespeare's Chaucer* and of *"King Lear": The Critics' Debate,* and coauthor of *Shakespeare, Meaning, and Metaphor.* She edited *The Taming of the Shrew* for the New Cambridge Shakespeare and is the principal author of *Which Shakespeare?: A User's Guide to Editions.* She is coeditor of *Teaching Women: Feminism and English Studies* and coeditor of a forthcoming collection, *Women Reading Shakespeare 1660–1900.* She is also General Editor of a series of books on feminist readings of Shakespeare (forthcoming).

Alan R. Young teaches at Acadia University, Wolfville, Nova Scotia. He has published many books and articles on Renaissance literature and related topics, including *Henry Peacham, Tudor And Jacobean Tournaments*, and *Emblematic Flag Devices Of The English Civil Wars.*

Index

369

dote to *Hamlet,* xvii, 164, 170, 173, 174, 179, 180; distrust of Second Folio, 157, 218–19; editing of *All's Well That Ends Well,* 15, 16–17, 43–44, 47; editing of *Cymbeline,* 83; editing of *Henry VIII,* 288–89, 290–91; editing of Shakespeare's poems, xxv, 345–46, 348, 356, 361; editorial approach of, 83, 88, 112–17; 1821 "third variorum" edition (*see* Boswell, James, the younger); on *Hamlet,* 108, 228, 232, 233, 236, 237, 239; and Hanmer (*see* Hanmer, Sir Thomas); and Johnson (*see* Johnson, Ben); knowledge of Elizabethan spelling, 133; and Pope, 108, 112; and Reed, 361; and Rowe, 112; 1790 Apparatus, xi, 115, 284, 357; Shakespeare biography by, 107, 115; Shakespeare and Shakespeare source study, xvii, 164, 179; and Steevens, 108–9, 112, 118, 132, 239, 356, 360–61; in Steevens's editions, 123, 125–26, 130, 131–32, 133; *Supplement,* 124, 345, 348, 360–61; and Theobald, xvi, 107–10, 112; on *Twelfth Night,* 211, 212–13, 215, 216, 218–20; use of First Folio, 233; use of quartos, 108, 153, 157; varias variorum editor, xi–xii, xxvi, 124, 284; and Warburton, 107, 112

Margeson, John, 291–92
Marsden, Jean, 141–42
Mason, John Monck, 81, 149, 151, 215, 221
Mason, William, 359
Massinger, Philip, 131
Maurists, 189
Maxwell, J. C., 72, 291
McGann, Jerome, xviii, 188, 193–94, 197–200
McKenzie, D. F.: anticipated by Theobald, xviii, 114; textual theory of, 113, 188, 190, 192, 198, 200, 202
McKerrow, Ronald B., 258, 319
McLeod, Randall. *See* Cloud, Random
McLuhan, Marshall, 21
Measure for Measure, 79, 215, 216–17; First Folio, 217
Melchiori, G., 33, 34–35
Memoirs of the Times, 268

Merchant of Venice, The, 125, 147, 213, 357
Merchant, Moelwyn, 331
Merry Wives of Windsor, The, 125, 135–37, 151, 216, 357
Meurice, Paul and Auguste Vacquerie, 58
Middleton, Thomas, 38, 129
Midsummer Night's Dream, A, xxiv; Johnson's 1765 editions, xxiv, 323–28
Millais, John Everett, 224
Milton, John, xviii, 106, 157, 202, 350, 353, 359
Modern Library *Shakespeare,* 17
Montaigne, 166
Monthly Review, 362
Morgan, MacNamara, xxi, 269, 273–74
Morris, Brian, 37
Mortimer, John Hamilton, 333, 337
Much Ado About Nothing, 37, 154
Munro, John, 16, 290–91

Neely, Carol Thomas, 228, 232–33
neoclassical criticism, ix, xiv, xv, 158, 268–69, 278. *See also* Aristotelian criticism
neoclassical stage conventions, 91, 95, 97
New Bibliography, 189, 190, 197
New English Dictionary, 290–91
New Historicism, 200
New Variorum *Shakespeare,* 323
Nichols, John, 105, 305, 309
North, Thomas, 110, 165, 166, 168, 170, 174, 176
Norwich, Theatre Royal, 142, 144
Nosworthy, J. M., 72
Noyes, Gertrude E., 274

old-spelling editions, 190
Orgel, Stephen, 83–84, 201–2
Othello, 160, 191, 214, 217, 237; First Folio, 158; a source of, 201, 202; variorum commentary on, 123–30
Ovid, xxi, 247, 248, 251, 262, 263
Oxford English Dictionary, xi, 291–92, 327
Oxford Shakespeare, 84, 113, 210

Palmer, D. J., 111
pantomime, 199